48-7627

A HISTORY OF THE SOUTH

VOLUMES IN THE SERIES

Volume V

THE DEVELOPMENT OF
SOUTHERN SECTIONALISM
1819–1848

A HISTORY

OF

THE SOUTH

Volume V

EDITORS

WENDELL HOLMES STEPHENSON

E. MERTON COULTER

The Development of Southern Sectionalism

1819-1848

BY CHARLES S. SYDNOR

LOUISIANA STATE UNIVERSITY PRESS

THE LITTLEFIELD FUND FOR SOUTHERN
HISTORY OF THE UNIVERSITY OF TEXAS

1948

PUBLISHERS' PREFACE

A HISTORY OF THE SOUTH is sponsored by Louisiana State University and the Trustees of the Littlefield Fund for Southern History at The University of Texas. More remotely, it is the outgrowth of the vision of Major George W. Littlefield, C.S.A., who established a fund at The University of Texas in 1914 for the collection of materials on Southern history and the publication of a "full and impartial study of the South and its part in American history." Trustees of the Littlefield Fund began preparations in 1937 for the writing of the history that Major Littlefield contemplated. Meanwhile, a plan had been conceived at Louisiana State University for a history of the South as a part of that institution's comprehensive program to promote interest, research, and writing in the field of Southern history.

As the two undertakings harmonized in essentials, the planning groups united to become joint sponsors of *A History of the South.* Wendell Holmes Stephenson, then professor of American history at Louisiana State University, and the late Charles W. Ramsdell, professor of American history at The University of Texas, were chosen to edit the series. They had been primarily interested in initiating the plans, and it was appropriate that they should be selected to edit the work. Upon the death of Professor Ramsdell in 1942, E. Merton Coulter, professor of history at the University of Georgia, was named his successor.

Volumes of the series are being published as the manuscripts are received. This is the second published volume; it follows Volume VIII. When completed, the ten-volume set will represent about twelve years of historical planning and research.

vii

AUTHOR'S PREFACE

THE treatment of the history of the South from 1819 to 1848 offered in this book falls into two broad divisions. One of them embraces developments of an internal nature; the other is concerned with the Federal relations of the South —the course of events through which this region was transformed from a position of great power in national affairs to the position of a conscious minority. The first division, the internal history, includes such physical and economic factors as Indian removal and the subsequent migration of white men and slaves from the Atlantic states into the Gulf states, the spread of the cotton kingdom into this same area, the growth of the slave trade into a business of enormous proportions, and the revolution in transportation worked by the steamboat and the railroad; changes in the mind and spirit of Southerners, signalized by the growth of the evangelical churches, the establishment of numerous colleges, new trends in literature, and a manifold humanitarian reform movement; and a democratic revolution of considerable magnitude that can be traced both in constitutional revisions in most of the Southern states and in political life generally, especially in radical innovations in the arts of securing office and of influencing public opinion.

The second broad division of this book traces a change of the first magnitude in the relationship of the South to the nation. At the beginning of the period under review Southern politicians and statesmen well-nigh dominated the Federal government; before it was ended they had seen their region decline to a subordinate political position. As their influence over national affairs waned, Southerners attempted to invent defenses against what they regarded as Northern political ruthlessness. Feelings of fear, desperation, and bitterness possessed them. Their patriotism toward the nation diminished. Their allegiance to their section increased.

The necessity for treating both the domestic history and the Federal relations of the South within a single volume has posed a difficult problem in respect to organization. Wisely or not, it was met by adopting the following general plan. The first group of chapters describes and analyzes economic, cultural, and political movements within the South during the 1820's and early 1830's. The middle chapters, retracing nearly the same years, deal with the relationship of the South to the nation. Here it was necessary to write of some subjects that are the common property of general works in American history, but at certain points in this familiar story, such as in the discussion of the Missouri controversy, in exploring the origin and significance of nullification, and in emphasizing the importance of the 1820's in the development of Southern sectionalism, the author has ventured to depart from some of the customary interpretations.

The final chapters, which cover the last years of this study, treat both the internal and external aspects of Southern history, seeking to show the effect of each upon the other, and to describe the opinions, ideas, and attitudes that emerged in the South about its own way of life and about its relationship to the nation. Thus, as the story moves on through nearly a third of a century, emphasis shifts from social and economic subjects to political events and, finally, to regional attitudes and opinions.

Limitations of space have compelled a close adherence to the main goals. The domestic history of the several states could not be recounted except at moments when some one of them was exercising extraordinary influence in the region. An extended narrative of political events during the last fifteen years of our period was shortened to an essay upon the significance of those events. By these and other curtailments space was found for dealing with topics already mentioned, for assessing the activities of county and state government, for investigating the location of political power, and, especially, for attempting to discover how men secured places of power in local, state, and national government.

The selection of topics and the apportionment of space were doubtless influenced by the author's conviction that the problem of sectionalism deserves close attention. It has a central position in the history of the South, but it is not confined to the South or even to the United States. Sectionalism is a reversal of that process briefly summarized in the familiar phrase *e pluribus unum* and illustrated by unifying movements at many times and places in history. It is an opposite flow of events from unity toward disunity. Various names have been applied to it—separatism, particularism, disunity, secession, and nationalism as well as sectionalism—but whatever the name, the movement itself is disquieting in its course and sometimes disastrous in its consequences. This movement, at least in its embryonic form, has appeared more than once in American history; but its most extreme and well-developed occurrence was in the ante-bellum South. The author has attempted to make this book something of a case study of sectionalism. It has not been his intention to defend or to condemn its emergence in the South, but rather to search for the causes and to trace the development of this remarkable instance of a movement from unity toward disunity.

This work is concluded with humility. The author wishes that he were more learned in the various fields of history—literary, constitutional, political, religious, agricultural, social, economic, and others—that he entered. He is aware that a more restricted approach would have been safer, but the subject required him to range widely. Having done so, he hopes that a benevolent law operates in behalf of those who explore more fields than they can master. To compensate for the larger risk of error there perhaps may be a greater opportunity to see new meanings and wider relationships when familiar subjects, such as McCulloch *v.* Maryland, nullification, Indian removal from Georgia, or the Southerners' legal defenses of slavery, are examined in the light of economic and political as well as of constitutional history.

This work is also ended with gratitude to many persons. To scholars whose writings have opened paths and sometimes broad highways the author is more deeply indebted than the footnotes and the critical essay on authorities may perhaps indicate. He has been met with unfailing helpfulness by the staff members of the archival collections and libraries in which he has worked. To Professors Jay B. Hubbell, B. U. Ratchford, and William B.

Hamilton, and to Mrs. Charles S. Sydnor, Mr. James S. Purcell, Jr., and the editors of the series in which this work appears he is indebted for helpful suggestions and criticisms.

C. S. S.

CONTENTS

ILLUSTRATIONS

CHAPTER I

THE UNAWAKENED SOUTH

TO discover the boundaries of the South in the year 1819, or even to learn whether there was such a thing as the South, one must examine economic and cultural, rather than political, conditions. At the beginning of that year there was no Southern political party, no slave-state bloc in Congress, and no sentiment of Southern nationalism. Only one political party, the Republican, was active in national affairs, and Southerners had much influence within this powerful organization. James Monroe of Virginia was President of the United States, and among his six cabinet members were William H. Crawford of Georgia, John C. Calhoun of South Carolina, and William Wirt of Virginia. Henry Clay of Kentucky was Speaker of the House of Representatives.

Southerners, having so large a share in the direction of national affairs, were, in general, satisfied with the way the government was being managed, and most of them were too busy with their private affairs to spend much time waving the flag and listening to speeches. At Nashville, Tennessee, for example, the Fourth of July, 1819, slipped by uncelebrated except for a patriotic sermon delivered in the Methodist Church by the Reverend John Johnson.[1] But when Southerners happened to think of it, they liked to recall the Battle of New Orleans and the events of the American Revolution; and some men could remember these things from their own experiences, for the history of the United States was then a matter of personal recollection rather than of textbooks. Five of the signers of the Declaration of Independence were "yet living to behold the fruits of their mighty effort," [2] and to be revered by the younger

[1] Nashville *Whig*, July 3, 1819.
[2] *Niles' Weekly Register* (Baltimore), XVI (1819), 400.

1

generation as living symbols of American patriotism. The General Assembly of the State of Maryland, in anticipation of the fiftieth anniversary of the signing of the Declaration of Independence, resolved that whereas "in the course of nature the surviving heroes and patriots of the revolution, will all, soon, bid the world farewell, and can never see another year of jubilee, . . . the fourth day of July next be set apart, and recommended to the people of this state, to be kept and observed as a day of thanksgiving and rejoicing, and of sending portions, one to another, and gifts to the poor, of relieving debtors from prison, and making the fiftieth Anniversary of American Independence a glad and joyful day." [3]

Though the South was at peace with the nation on political issues, it was unlike it in many phases of its economic and social life. It is therefore needful to turn to this realm to discover the dominant characteristics of the South around the year 1820 and to lay a foundation for understanding the momentous events that were soon to occur.

South of Mason and Dixon's line and the Ohio River there were ten states, exactly half the number of states in the Union. Five of of them—Maryland, Virginia, North Carolina, South Carolina, and Georgia—lay along the Atlantic coast, with their histories reaching back into the colonial period; and five were the younger inland and Gulf states of Kentucky, Tennessee, Louisiana, Mississippi, and Alabama. The last two had only recently emerged from territorial status, Mississippi having been admitted to statehood in 1817 and Alabama in 1819. For the sake of having a recognized and exact area for discussion, these ten states will be regarded as the South, because, as will presently appear, they possessed certain common traits. Along the edges of this group of states there were several border areas, but, to avoid complicating an involved story, they will be disregarded for the present. Above the Ohio River, for example, there were many people who had recently migrated from Virginia, North Carolina, and other Southern states, [4] and some

[3] Maryland *House Journal,* 1825–1826, pp. 398–99.

[4] John D. Barnhart, "Sources of Southern Migration into the Old Northwest," in *Mississippi Valley Historical Review* (Cedar Rapids), XXII (1935–1936), 49–62; "The Southern Element in the Leadership of the Old Northwest," in *Journal of Southern History* (Baton Rouge), I (1935), 186–97; and "The Southern Influence in the Formation of Ohio," *ibid.,* III (1937), 28–42.

14,000 persons had already settled in the Territory of Arkansas.[5] Florida and Texas lay outside the boundaries of the United States, but Florida was well within the limits of Southern consciousness because it was in process of being acquired and because Andrew Jackson's recent foray against the Seminole Indians had aroused a storm of newspaper controversy.

The census of 1820 revealed that the South contained a smaller part of the nation's population than formerly; 4,298,199 persons were counted in the ten Southern states, which was half a million short of being half of the population of the United States. Furthermore, there were critical differences in the character of the two peoples. A third of the Southern population, against only 2 per cent of the Northern, was black. To put the matter in more detail, there were 1,496,189 slaves in the South and practically none in the North, and there were 116,915 free Negroes in the South and approximately the same number in the North.

The white population of the Southern states was 2,685,095 persons. That of the North was nearly twice as large. There was much homogeneity within the white population of the South, where only 12,320 unnaturalized foreigners were counted in contrast to 41,335 in the rest of the nation. Furthermore, the English, Scotch, Scotch-Irish, German, French, and other colonial stocks of the seaboard South had lived together long enough to lose many of their diversities. Here and there some evidence of cultural differences remained as among the Pennsylvania Dutch of the Shenandoah Valley and in the Scotch and German settlements in North Carolina. The St. Andrew's, the Hibernian, the French Benevolent, and the German Friendly societies kept alive the traditions of some of the racial groups in Charleston.[6] Generally speaking, the melting pot had done a pretty thorough job on the colonial stocks of the South.

But, though the South differed from the North in its smaller and

[5] Throughout this chapter population figures have been taken from the United States *Census of 1820* (Washington, 1821), or *The Compendium of the Ninth Census, 1870* (Washington, 1872). The latter has been preferred because it corrects some errors in the earlier publication. However, the *Census of 1820* contains some facts that are not available elsewhere.

[6] Robert Mills, *Statistics of South Carolina, Including a View of Its Natural, Civil, and Military History, General and Particular* (Charleston, 1826), 429–30.

more homogeneous white population and in its much greater black population, there were differences within the South in respect to population density, rate of increase, and racial elements. One out of every four Southerners was a Virginian; not one in twenty-five lived in Louisiana. Maryland, Virginia, and North Carolina contained one half of all the people of the South, whereas the three Southwestern states of Louisiana, Mississippi, and Alabama contained only a tenth. But over against the smallness of the Southwest was the fact that it was growing at a great rate. Mississippi, Alabama, Louisiana, and Tennessee had increased their white population by 50 per cent or more between 1810 and 1820; neither Maryland, Virginia, North Carolina, nor South Carolina had grown as much as 12 per cent. The trend in respect to the slave population was similar.[7] Evidently, the tide was flowing to the Southwest, and the crest was yet to come, except in Kentucky which had ended its age of rapid growth and had become the third Southern state in point of population, ranking next after Virginia and North Carolina. Georgia was likewise something of an exception. Although it was one of the South Atlantic states, it was continuing to attract immigrants, and in this respect it had something of the character of the Southwest.

The Southwest, partly in consequence of its rapid growth, had a more heterogeneous population than was the case with the older South. New Orleans was the most cosmopolitan of all Southern cities, containing a fourth of all the unnaturalized foreigners in the South together with a large French element that had succeeded in maintaining a considerable measure of cultural integrity. Elsewhere in the Southwest, foreigners were not numerous, but the influx of immigrants from the South Atlantic states, from the Middle Atlantic states, and even from New England, made this region a melting pot of several American elements.

A great deterrent to growth in the Gulf states, though one that was rapidly being removed, was the fact that two vast areas were yet possessed by the Indians; and here was an ingredient that the melting pot would not assimilate. Cherokee and Creeks occupied the western half of Georgia and eastern Alabama; Choctaw and

[7] *Statistical View of the United States, . . . Being a Compendium of the Seventh Census*, 1850 (Washington, 1854), 47, 84.

Chickasaw controlled small parts of western Alabama and the northern two thirds of Mississippi. Only recently had the strip between these two areas been secured from the Creeks, but this acquisition whetted rather than satisfied the white man's land hunger. These two great islands of Indian country in the lower South were being pressed upon by a growing white population. Within, the Indians kept up tribal customs and were not subject to the laws of the states in which their lands happened to lie. Their dealings were with Federal rather than with state officials: with Indian agents, factors, and army officers. Under the influence of missionaries, officials, and other persons, Indian ways of living were becoming somewhat more like those of white men. Nevertheless, white men wanted to eject the Indians from their ancient habitations in the states of the lower South.

The most significant trait common to all parts of the South was slavery, though even in this respect there were differences among the states. At one extreme was South Carolina with a Negro population of 52.7 per cent; at the other was Tennessee where only 19.6 per cent of the population was black. Of course there were counties that reached above and below these limits. In all Southern states except Tennessee and Kentucky, Negroes constituted one third or more of the population; in five, so widely scattered as Virginia, South Carolina, Georgia, Mississippi, and Louisiana, they amounted to more than two fifths of the whole population; and in South Carolina and Louisiana they were in the majority.[8]

Furthermore, the South was more thoroughly bound to an agrarian economy than was the North. Economic life, according to the thinking of Americans of the early nineteenth century, was divided into agriculture, commerce, and manufacturing; but it was not equally divided. Of all Southerners gainfully employed, 90 per cent were engaged in agriculture as compared to 77 per cent in the rest of the nation.[9] And there was a difference in kind as well as in amount; Southern agriculture was devoted in large measure to the production of great staple crops for world markets. The North par-

[8] *Ibid.*, 85–86.

[9] This statement is based on data included in the *Census of 1820*. Perhaps it should be said that the writer is fully aware of the imperfections of the early censuses; but, being ignorant of a better source for certain kinds of information, he is using the census without interpolating warnings and cautions in connection with each statement.

ticipated practically not at all in the production of these crops, nor did it raise other crops in anything like equal measure for export abroad.

Before describing the Southern money crops it should be plainly said that they were superimposed on a background of general farming. Only rarely did Southern farmers plan to devote every effort to a single crop; even the great planters usually attempted, though with varying degrees of success, to raise such food as they and their dependents needed. Furthermore, there were a great number of farms where little if any of the staple crops were raised. As in the North, plain farmers raised nearly everything they needed on their family-sized units, and they had few economic dealings with the outside world. In large parts of the South, particularly back from the coast and away from the larger rivers, these small, self-sufficient farms predominated.

On most farms and plantations in the South, from the smallest to the greatest, sweet potatoes, cowpeas, chickens, cows, and especially corn and hogs were raised. Fruit trees, grapevines, and vegetable gardens were common though they were often neglected except when times were hard. The small grains were raised about as widely as corn, but the fields were much smaller except in the upper South. Virginia, Kentucky, and Tennessee raised enough of wheat, rye, and other cereals to supply local needs and allow a surplus for export as flour and whiskey. These states were also ahead of the lower South in quantity and quality of livestock. Horses, mules, and draft oxen as well as cattle, hogs, sheep, and poultry were to be found in all parts of the South; but in the border states they were more plentiful, and sheep were more often seen. There, likewise, greater attention was given to improving flocks and herds; notable importations of Durham, Hereford, and other breeds had been made in Kentucky in the year 1817.[10]

The distinctive character of Southern agriculture lay in its money crops: cotton, tobacco, rice, sugar, and hemp. Although methods of

[10] The chief source of information about Southern agriculture in this period is Lewis C. Gray, *History of Agriculture in the Southern United States to 1860* (Washington, 1933), and, except where otherwise noted, the following sketch of the subject in 1820 is based primarily upon Vol. II of this work. The most authoritative source for prices of the staples is Arthur H. Cole, *Wholesale Commodity Prices in the United States, 1700–1861. Statistical Supplement* (Cambridge, 1938).

cultivating and marketing all of these crops had become well established before 1820, a brief statement of the location, the peculiar traits, the relative importance, and the producing area needs to be made for each of them.

By 1820 the boundaries of the tobacco kingdom were established along lines that were to undergo little change for many years. It was not as far-flung as it once had been, for cotton and other crops had pushed it out of Georgia, South Carolina, lower North Carolina, and Mississippi.[11] Now it was contained in two great areas in the upper South. The older lay in Piedmont Virginia with extensions up into Maryland and down into the northern tier of North Carolina counties. The other, west of the mountains, centered in Kentucky. The Eastern area was the heavier producer in 1820, but the West was not far behind. In the eleven-month period ending on September 2, 1820, tobacco exports from the port of New Orleans, which was the outlet for most Western tobacco, amounted to 28,970 hogsheads,[12] and before many more years had passed, the Eastern belt had lost its primacy.[13]

But, though tobacco was not raised over as wide an area as formerly, the total crop had not declined. Nearly a hundred million pounds were shipped from the United States yearly in the early 1820's besides a considerable domestic consumption, and the value of the exported part of each crop was about $6,000,000 even at the low prices that then prevailed.[14]

Because the production of tobacco of a good quality required much painstaking care and nice judgment in performing a variety of operations, it was not profitable to raise this crop by large gangs of slave labor except under close supervision. As a natural conse-

[11] Joseph C. Robert, *The Tobacco Kingdom* (Durham, 1938), 11, 141. It had earlier been the chief crop of the interior of South Carolina (South Carolina *Reports and Resolutions of the General Assembly*, 1847, pp. 159–60), but little if any was shipped from Charleston in the year ending October 1, 1820. From Savannah, 982 hogsheads were exported within this twelve months. *Niles' Weekly Register*, XIX (1820), 192.

[12] *Niles' Weekly Register*, XIX (1820), 264.

[13] Robert, *Tobacco Kingdom*, 142–43.

[14] The average export for the five years 1821–1825 was 96,696,720 pounds. *Ibid.*, 130–32. For data on the quantity and value of exports of tobacco and other Southern staples, see the table entitled "Foreign Exports, from 1821 to 1855," in *Report of the Commissioner of Patents for the Year 1855: Agriculture* (Washington, 1856), 423 ff. This is a convenient compilation of statistics from the annual reports of the secretary of the treasury on the *Commerce and Navigation of the United States*.

quence, the tobacco kingdom was broken into smaller producing units than the other staple-crop regions. It contained some large plantations, but the typical tobacco growers were yeoman farmers, some owning a few slaves and others having none. It was said that slaves were better treated in the tobacco kingdom than in the other staple-crop regions.[15] Much Kentucky tobacco was produced entirely by white labor. No county in that state contained as many Negroes as white persons, and in only a few, chiefly in the neighborhood of Lexington, did slaves amount to more than 30 per cent of the population. The Virginia–Maryland–North Carolina tobacco belt had a larger percentage of slaves than Kentucky. Slaves constituted at least one third of the population in every tobacco-raising county in the seaboard states, and in most of them they outnumbered the whites; but in only three, Amelia, Nottoway, and Powhatan, all lying a short distance southwest of Richmond, were there twice as many black persons as white.[16] Tobacco planters usually raised most of their foodstuffs; furthermore, they often raised a second money crop, partly because tobacco was not as profitable as formerly, and partly because it left a trail of worn-out fields which would produce wheat but not tobacco.

In Kentucky, tobacco's rival was hemp. Most of the nation's hemp was grown in that state, although some was exported from Virginia and South Carolina as late as 1819, and much was raised in Middle Tennessee and, somewhat later, in Missouri. It was a Bluegrass crop, for it required rich land; and it was grown with slave labor. Its culture was less meticulous than that of tobacco, though the work was heavier, especially the task of "breaking" by which the fibers were separated from the woody parts of the plant.

Most of the Kentucky hemp crop was made into bagging and rope for baling the cotton of the lower South, but the hemp growers were not content with this arrangement. Their hopes were fixed on winning the more lucrative business of supplying cordage to American sailing vessels. The great obstacle thereto was the fact that the

[15] Robert, *Tobacco Kingdom,* 17–18; Gray, *Agriculture in the Southern United States,* I, 531–37; Ulrich B. Phillips, *Life and Labor in the Old South* (Boston 1929), 126.

[16] Maps showing the percentage of Negroes in the total population are available in Charles O. Paullin and John K. Wright, *Atlas of the Historical Geography of the United States* (Washington, 1932), plate 67E.

owners of those boats preferred Russian water-rotted hemp to the dew-rotted product of Kentucky for the simple reason that they considered it stronger and more durable. To overcome this difficulty, Kentuckians attempted both to improve their product and to raise the tariff on foreign hemp so as to drive their Russian competitor from the American market. Neither effort was successful, and the first seems to have been made with little energy.[17]

The rice country, a small strip along the South Carolina, Georgia, and lower North Carolina coasts, would have seemed to most Northerners the strangest and most bizarre part of the South; it would have seemed almost as strange to those Southerners who had never been out of the tobacco, hemp, and upland cotton regions. All would have been impressed by the cypress trees, live oaks, Spanish moss, strange birds, mosquitoes, and hordes of Negroes in this dark swampland, slashed here and there by sunlit openings where small, sluggish rivers rose and fell with the tide. It was the fresh-water tide on these rivers that set the limits of the rice country, and narrow limits they were. Near the coast, too much salt water was forced upstream by the tides to allow rice to be grown, but above salt water there was a stretch of a few miles—on no river was it more than sixteen miles—where fresh water rose and fell enough to allow proper flooding of the fields. These were laid out on the swampland that stretched back from the river channels. The South Carolina rice fields covered only some 50,000 or 60,000 acres; yet they produced three fourths of the nation's crop, with most of the remainder coming from similar swamplands in Georgia. About fifty million pounds were annually exported at a price that ranged close to three cents a pound in the 1820's and early 1830's (the price had been higher before 1820). In addition, much was sold in the United States. The planters received about $1,500,000 a year from the part of the crop that was exported.[18]

During the first half of the nineteenth century many attempts were made to harness the power of the wind, the tide, the horse, and the steam engine to the task of separating the grain from straw

17 Gray, *Agriculture in the Southern United States*, II, 821–22.

18 Rice sometimes entered the United States free of duty and sometimes under an ad valorem duty of 15 or 20 per cent which, however, seems to have conferred little benefit on the rice growers.

9

and husks. Furthermore, planters began to ship considerable parts of their crops unhusked because the import duty on paddy, as rice in this state was called, was much lower than the duty on milled rice in several European countries. Gradually the ancient flails, winnowing fans, and pestles were laid aside, and by 1822 it was remarked that the lot of rice-plantation slaves was much improved.

The close natural limits of the amount of land suitable for rice culture made each acre valuable. This fact, together with the cost of digging large canals and small ditches, of raising embankments about the fields, of building sluice gates in those embankments, of constructing husking mills, and of maintaining a large force of slaves, kept all except the wealthy from raising rice. Plantations rather than farms made up the rice kingdom. And the plantations were, of course, much larger than the rice fields. They stretched back from the swamps to include higher ground where corn, sweet potatoes, and other food crops were grown, and they contained formal gardens and plantation homes that were among the most magnificent in the United States. The rice planters, of whom there were only five or six hundred, great and small,[19] constituted one of the closest-knit and most aristocratic groups in the South.

Some of the rice planters also raised sea-island cotton, and there were, besides, many planters on Edisto, Ladies, St. Helena, and other South Carolina and Georgia islands whose only staple was this long- and silky-fibered cotton. In the aggregate they received a large income, amounting to from $2,500,000 to $3,000,000 a year. About 11,000,000 pounds, which was much the greater part of the crop, was exported annually, and the price ranged between twenty-four and one-half and thirty-three cents a pound in the early 1820's. While this was a much higher price than ordinary cotton would bring, its cost of production was estimated to be at least twice as great since the yield of sea-island per acre was smaller and its cultivation was more exacting. The income of the planters was not great, considering the large investment in land and slaves. This economic limit was perhaps as effective as natural limits (set by the

[19] This estimate was made about 1850, but there was no great change in the rice country in the previous thirty years. For information about rice, see Gray, *Agriculture in the Southern United States,* II, 721–31, 1030; James H. Easterby (ed.), *The South Carolina Rice Plantation as Revealed in the Papers of Robert F. W. Allston* (Chicago, 1945), especially pp. 6–8, 19–23, 35–49.

requirements of very fertile land and a long, hot, and humid growing season) in restricting the growth of sea-island cotton. In the
thirty years following 1820 the general trend of exports was downward.[20]

Nowhere else in all the South was the percentage of Negroes as
high as it was in the low country of rice and sea-island cotton. Small
farms and nonslaveholders were few in this hot, malarial land which
white men shunned, especially during the summer months. Even
when the planters and their families were in their country homes,
the predominance of slaves was great. In all of the South Carolina
coastal counties except Horry, the northernmost of them, Negroes
were more numerous than white people. Down the coast from
Horry there were four South Carolina counties, Georgetown,
Charleston, Colleton, and Beaufort—a strip about 150 miles long
and 50 miles wide—where 126,000 Negroes and 30,000 white
persons lived. Omitting the inhabitants of the city of Charleston,
these four South Carolina counties had six times as many slaves as
white persons in the year 1820. And down the Georgia coast through
the counties of Chatham, Bryan, Liberty, McIntosh, Glynn, and
Camden—all of the way to the Florida line—Negroes constituted
nearly three fourths of the population.

Sugar as well as rice and sea-island cotton was grown along the
Georgia coast. In 1828 there were some two hundred sugar plantations along the Savannah, Altamaha, and Oconee rivers. But Louisiana was at all times the chief sugar-producing state, for it possessed
length of growing season coupled with rich alluvial soil. By 1850
its crop amounted to more than 95 per cent of all the sugar produced
in the United States. But even in lower Louisiana the summer was
not long enough, and the planters had to make their choice between
cutting before the cane was fully ripe or running the risk of heavy
loss because of early frost. The harvest season was always too short,
and work was done under heavy pressure. Slaves were frequently
required to work every third night.

Most of the sugar plantations were in the parishes along the lower
reaches of the Mississippi River, and these constituted another part
of the South where the slaves outnumbered the whites. But this
Louisiana black belt was neither large nor populous in 1820. In

[20] Gray, *Agriculture in the Southern United States*, II, 731–39.

four parishes, Plaquemines, St. Bernard, St. Charles, and Point Coupée, slaves constituted about three fourths of the population, and there were a few others in which they constituted more than half. But in the four parishes that have been named there were less than 11,000 Negroes. Many more than this number could be found in a single county in the South Carolina low country.

The South was producing about as much sea-island cotton and rice in 1820 as it was to produce at any time in the ante-bellum period, but sugar production at that year was no more than well started. The crop increased from about 30,000 hogsheads (estimated at 1,000 pounds each) in the early 1820's to more than double that amount in the next ten years. By the middle of the century, Louisiana was producing 250,000,000 pounds a year. This great increase was due to an expansion of the sugar-producing area and to a number of improvements in sugar making. In 1817 an earlier-ripening cane, the ribbon, was introduced. Five years later steam power began to be applied to the grinding mills, and by 1830 a hundred or so of the 725 Louisiana mills had replaced oxen with steam engines. A large number of other improvements were made in rapid succession, among them the use of steam to heat the battery of kettles, and inventions for bettering the processes of grinding, heating, skimming, and filtering the syrup. Sugar making became an increasingly technical process, requiring heavy investments in elaborate machinery and skilled management as well as in land, slaves, and buildings. By 1850 a minimum sugar plantation was worth $40,000, and 75 of the 1,500 sugar estates in Louisiana were worth from $200,000 to $350,000 apiece.

There was no room in sugar growing for the small farmer, nor was there much diversification on the sugar plantations. Some foodstuffs were raised, but the sugar country was the least self-sufficient part of the South. Furthermore, sugar was unique among Southern crops in its dependence on a protective tariff. From 1816 to 1832 protection amounted to three cents a pound on brown sugar and four cents on white sugar; thereafter it was slightly less. The price range was comparatively narrow, the New Orleans wholesale price seldom dropping under five cents a pound or rising above eight cents between the years 1820 and 1850. During this period the value of the crop ranged, with few exceptions, between $3,000,000 and $12,000,000.[21]

The greatest of all the market crops of the South was short-staple, upland cotton, which was usually called simply by the name of "cotton." It was among the youngest of the Southern staples, but by 1820 its value exceeded that of all the rest. In the years 1819, 1820, and 1821 the crop averaged 353,000 bales,[22] of which three fourths was exported at an average price of well over sixteen cents a pound. Prices were lower during a large part of the next thirty years, but the size of the crop increased, just about doubling in each decade until the Civil War. The phenomenal increase in this crop was partly due to the invention in England of machines that could spin and weave enormous quantities of cotton. And within the land of cotton, economies in production were effected. Gins and presses were improved, and a few planters installed steam engines in place of gin horses. Efforts were made to cope with insect enemies and plant diseases. Improved methods of cultivation were evolved, and sometimes they were practiced. The plow came into more extensive use with cotton than with most staple crops. But perhaps the greatest boon to the cotton grower came with the introduction of better varieties of the plant, particularly one that had been brought from Mexico. By 1820 enough of this seed had been raised for it to be in wide use, and it was further improved by crossbreeding. With the planting of these newer strains, production per acre was increased, the proportion of lint to seed was enlarged, and picking was much facilitated.

A further reason for the steady increase in cotton production was the fact that this plant would grow over vast areas of the South. It was less fastidious about its environment than hemp, sugar, sea-island cotton, or rice; it liked long, hot summers; it could stand drought; and it would grow in alluvial bottom lands, in the red-clay hills of the Piedmont, in the black prairies of Alabama, or in the loess soil of southwest Mississippi. Of the money crops only

---

[21] *Ibid.*, 739–51, 1033.

[22] This and subsequent statistics are in terms of 500-pound bales. Actually, the bales varied considerably in weight, and in 1820 they were usually much lighter than 500 pounds.

tobacco would grow as widely; but tobacco was less profitable, and one suspects that it held its own in Maryland, Virginia, and Kentucky partly because the growing season in those states was not quite long enough for cotton.

The area of greatest production in 1821 was the South Carolina–Georgia Piedmont. In those two states 190,000 bales were raised—somewhat more than half of the national crop. The rest came from all the Southern states except Maryland and Kentucky. Alabama and Tennessee each produced some 40,000 bales; each of the other four states produced about 20,000 bales. In the next score of years several changes occurred in the geography of cotton. It was nearly abandoned in Virginia, and thereafter the South was rather clearly divided by an east-west line. Above it was the tobacco kingdom of Virginia, Maryland, and Kentucky. On several counts Middle and East Tennessee and the northern part of North Carolina belong with this upper or border-state segment of the South. Beneath was the somewhat larger cotton kingdom. Within it, the center of cotton production was moving westward. Between 1821 and 1839 South Carolina dropped from first to fifth place, and Mississippi rose to first. By the latter date considerably more than half of the crop was grown to the west of the South Atlantic states.

The only considerable part of the cotton country with a preponderance of slaves in 1820 was upper Georgia and South Carolina. Black counties in Alabama, Louisiana, and Mississippi were few; in Mississippi, for example, there were only four—all in the southwestern corner of the state—and only in Adams County were slaves numerous enough to form two thirds of the population. Cotton, indeed, was less closely bound to slavery and the plantation system than some of the other crops; it could be grown successfully by a plain farmer with a little land, a few simple tools, and some seed. In this respect it was like tobacco; but unlike tobacco growing, cotton culture was simple enough to be satisfactorily performed by slave labor organized in large forces. Cotton therefore offered men with small capital a chance to begin; yet it placed no limits upon those who succeeded in bettering themselves. A number of men mounted from log cabin to plantation mansion on a stairway of cotton bales, accumulating slaves as they climbed. Thus the cotton kingdom produced some things other than cotton. One was a great demand for slaves, and another was a sizeable crop of newly arrived planters.[23]

Getting the crops to market was sometimes as much work as raising them. Most of the roads were locally maintained community enterprises that converged at county seats and churches, or that led down to landings on the rivers. Of the longer roads, there were several like the Natchez Trace that were well traveled, but chiefly by flatboatmen returning home after a downstream voyage. Likewise, the great post road that paralleled the Atlantic coast some two hundred miles inland and that passed through the fall-line towns was chiefly used by travelers. Although there were some roads, like those out of the Shenandoah Valley, over which much farm produce was hauled, it was almost an axiom that the road was used for moving heavy goods only if water transportation was lacking. In the year 1818 it was said that two thirds of the market produce of South Carolina was grown within five miles and most of the balance within ten miles of a stream that was navigable or that could be made fit for navigation.[24] Naturally, land close to navigable water was worth more than land less conveniently situated, and tax assessments were fixed accordingly. In the state of Mississippi it was required that land of the best quality be valued at $12.00 an acre if it lay within eight miles of the port city of Natchez, but at only $4.00 an acre if it was more than twenty miles inland from the Mississippi River.[25]

Water transportation was easiest near the coast. The network of rivers, creeks, and sounds in the low country of South Carolina and Georgia was almost ideal for the planters of sea-island cotton and rice whose estates fringed those waters. Most of them had their own vessels that could be moved by oars, poles, or sails, and some of them, known as "pettiaugers," were fitted for sails as well as for oars. Manned by crews of plantation Negroes, they bore the low-country staples to Charleston, Savannah, or one of the lesser ports of the region. Similarly, the planters of the Maryland-Virginia Tidewater had ample natural waterways, many of which were deep enough to give anchorage to ocean vessels, thus freeing the planters

[23] Gray, *Agriculture in the Southern United States*, II, 691–720, 1026–27; *Atlas of American Agriculture*, V, *The Crops*, Sect. A. Cotton (Washington, 1918), 8–11.

[24] Columbia (S.C.) *State Gazette*, quoted in *Niles' Weekly Register*, XV (1818), 135–38.

[25] Law of June 25, 1822, in [George Poindexter], *The Revised Code of the Laws of Mississippi* (Natchez, 1824), 284–85.

from the necessity of sending their wheat and tobacco to a port town. Among the Southeastern states only North Carolina had much reason to quarrel with the natural facilities of its coast region and to advocate a program for their improvement. It had an extensive network of rivers and sounds, but nowhere did these connect with a good harbor.

Inland from the coast there was nearly equal dependence on water transportation, but the facilities were less satisfactory. The rivers that emptied into the Atlantic were relatively small and shallow. Some of those to the Southwest were large. But whether large or small, navigation on nearly all the rivers of the South was made hazardous by sand bars, mud flats, and sunken tree trunks. The upper reaches were cut off by rapids at the fall line which was virtually at tidewater in Virginia but was two or three hundred miles inland on the rivers of the lower South. Despite these difficulties, goods were brought down by boat from unbelievably far up in the headwaters of the main streams and of their tributaries.

The secret of using the smaller streams was to ride down on the crest of a winter flood which would lift boats above the normal obstructions and bear them in headlong plunges over the swollen rapids. The vessels chiefly used were great, heavy, rectangular boxes with flat bottoms and square ends, and they were about as manageable as floating freight cars. On the South Atlantic rivers, where they were usually called cotton boats, some of them were from 60 to 80 feet long and from 20 to 25 feet broad.[26] On the Mississippi River they were more commonly called flatboats. The crew was small, and its activities varied from lazy, sleepy loafing while the boat slowly floated on sluggish stretches to frantic tugging at the heavy sweeps trying to keep the fruits of a year's labor off snags, rocks, and mudbanks. The flatboat made one downstream voyage, and then it was sold for the wood that was in it or was abandoned; for the current that had floated it down kept the heavy, awkward craft from getting back.

To carry goods upstream, the keelboat was used. It was more nicely built, with pointed or rounded ends and keeled bottom, it was of extremely shallow draft, and it was narrower in proportion

[26] Ulrich B. Phillips, *A History of Transportation in the Eastern Cotton Belt to 1860* (New York, 1908), 100–101.

to its length than the flatboat. The dimensions of the *Young Eagle,* a medium-sized Mississippi River keelboat, were 90 feet 8 inches in length, 13 feet 7 inches in breadth, 2 feet 8 inches in depth, and it could carry 31½ tons burden. It was built at Pittsburgh, Pennsylvania, in 1819, and was jointly owned by residents of New Orleans and Shippingport, Kentucky.[27] On the small streams of upcountry South Carolina, the maximum limit of keelboats was six tons.[28]

While wind, oars, and rope were all used at times in moving keelboats upstream, the main reliance was on poles pushed against the bottom of the river. A crew of from twelve to twenty-four men was needed, and the work was heavy. To push a keelboat from Savannah to Augusta, a distance of some two hundred miles by the winding river, was the labor of fourteen days. A loaded wagon could cover the shorter land route in a week, but it could carry only a small fraction of a keelboat's load.[29] To get from New Orleans to the interior of Tennessee or Kentucky was the labor of months.

Since keelboats were few in comparison with flatboats, the number of boats that went upstream was small in proportion to the number that went down. The aggregate volume of the upstream cargoes of salt, iron, cloth, finery, and such things was much less than the volume of the downward flow of cotton, tobacco, flour, hemp, and whiskey. The current was taking from inland farmers a heavy toll which increased with the distance and the roughness of the river, and was greatest for those who were under the double handicap of a long upstream pull and then a considerable land haul. As the population of the interior increased, so did its dissatisfaction; and complaint was sharply accentuated when the spread of cotton culture into the upcountry in the early nineteenth century gave to its inhabitants the means to purchase foreign wares if only they could bring them home.

The steamboat, which made its appearance on the Mississippi

[27] Survey of Federal Archives, Louisiana, *Ship Registers and Enrollments of New Orleans, Louisiana* (University, La., 1941–1942), I (1804–1820), 139–40. For a general discussion of the keelboat, see Leland D. Baldwin, *The Keelboat Age on Western Waters* (Pittsburgh, 1941), especially pp. 56–84.

[28] South Carolina *Reports and Resolutions of the General Assembly,* 1847, p. 164.

[29] Balthasar H. Meyer, *History of Transportation in the United States before 1860* (Washington, 1917), 255; Baldwin, *Keelboat Age on Western Waters,* 56–84.

River in the winter of 1811–1812, was of some help. Within a decade a considerable number, mostly ranging from 200 to 300 tons, were in service on the Mississippi and were rapidly displacing the keelboat. A report of the harbor master at Natchez stated that in the twelve months ending in August, 1824, there had been 229 steamboat landings at the Natchez water front, whereas only 14 keelboats had tied up. But the flatboats, the burden bearers of downstream commerce, continued to hold their own. Within this same year 542 of them paid wharfage fees of $1.00 each at Natchez; and from other flatboats, that were charged at the rate of ten cents a day, $280.00 was collected.[30] Evidently, the new invention was proving useful to those who lived along the Mississippi and its larger tributaries; but even so, the upflow of goods continued to be less than the downflow to the disadvantage of the interior producers. Most of the rivers along the Atlantic seaboard were too small for steam navigation. The steamer *Enterprise* was put in service at Savannah in 1816 and others followed it. But ten years later cotton boats and pole boats seemed to be driving the steamboat off the shallow streams to the southeast even below the fall line.[31]

A large number of companies was formed—thirty-seven in North Carolina before the year 1815—to improve river navigation and to construct and maintain canals, bridges, and turnpikes.[32] Their chief accomplishments consisted in four canals. A South Carolina canal that was twenty-two miles long joined the Santee River with the Cooper. It was of considerable aid to upcountry producers of the Santee Valley in moving their goods to Charleston, and the merchants of that city were also benefited.[33] A shorter and far more costly canal had been built around the falls of the Potomac just above Georgetown, D.C., as part of the old plan to bring the commerce of the Ohio Valley to the Chesapeake Bay along the line of the Potomac River. Much solid rock and the considerable descent

[30] Communication of S. W. Butler, harbor master of Natchez, in Natchez *Mississippi State Gazette*, September 4, 1824. A good deal of information about flatboats and steamboat commerce on the lower Mississippi in this period is in Howard Corning (ed.), *Journal of John James Audubon Made during His Trip to New Orleans in 1820–1821* (Boston, 1929), especially pp. 50–51, 56–59, 82, 90, 98–100.

[31] Phillips, *Transportation in the Eastern Cotton Belt*, 72–77.

[32] William K. Boyd, *History of North Carolina: The Federal Period, 1783–1860* (Chicago, 1919), 92.

[33] Phillips, *Transportation in the Eastern Cotton Belt*, 36–43.

of the river at the falls made the work costly and slow. By 1819 the company had spent $7,000,000 and had accomplished little above the falls except two short canals near Harper's Ferry. Richmond had also dreamed of tapping the trade of the West. It had built a canal seven miles long around the falls of the James just above the city, and the James had been made more navigable by sluices.[34] Finally, there was the Dismal Swamp Canal, opened in 1814 after many years' work, which joined Albemarle Sound with the Chesapeake Bay. Through it, goods of part of the North Carolina low country could be taken to deep-water harborage at Norfolk; but the canal was too small for boats of sufficient size to traverse the North Carolina sounds with safety.[35]

It was perfectly clear before the year 1820 that neither county government nor private enterprise, even when incorporated by state act and granted the power to collect tolls and raise money by lotteries, was able to supply the transportation needs of the South, particularly those of the back country. In the Southwest the steamboat was promising, but in the states along the Atlantic, men were turning to state planning and state financial support with the hope of securing better transportation facilities.

According to the census of 1820 there were only seven towns in the slave states with more than 8,000 inhabitants. Baltimore, which was the largest, was the third city in the nation, and its population of 62,738 made it half the size of New York, which was the leading American city. The others were New Orleans (27,176), Charleston (24,780), Washington (13,247), Richmond (12,067), Norfolk (8,478), and Alexandria (8,218). No more than four out of every hundred Southerners lived in these larger towns. Five of these seven towns were in Maryland, the District of Columbia, and Virginia. The vast area to the south and west of Virginia, eight states in all, contained only two towns of more than 8,000 inhabitants, Charleston and New Orleans.[36]

34 Meyer, *Transportation in the United States*, 265–66, 269–70.

35 Phillips, *Transportation in the Eastern Cotton Belt*, 15–16.

36 These statements are based on the table entitled "Comparative Population of the Largest Cities in the United States," in *Statistical View of the United States*, 1850, pp. 192–93; *Census of 1820*; and *Twelfth Census of the United States, 1900, Statistical Atlas* (Washington, 1903), 40 and plate 22. It should be noted these are not in complete agreement.

All seven of the larger towns, as well as a number of lesser ones, like Savannah, New Bern, and Mobile, were seaports where vessels engaged in the foreign and coasting trade picked up the goods that had been brought from neighboring islands or from upriver farms and plantations. The busiest part of most of the towns was the water front. Wharves and docks, warehouses and streets were cluttered, especially in the winter and spring, with hogsheads of tobacco, bags and bales of cotton, barrels of rice, tar, and turpentine, piles of lumber, staves, and shingles, and with all manner of imported goods. The quantity and price of these, especially of the articles of export, determined in large measure the prosperity of the towns.

The merchants and factors who managed this import-export trade were important persons; and they and their numerous employees and dependents—clerks, roustabouts, warehouse laborers, and others—sometimes made up the major part of a town's business population. Such was the case in Charleston.[37] Planters were permanent or part-time residents of most of the towns, and lawyers, ministers, and physicians were often counted among the leaders in urban affairs; but manufacturers were seldom numerous or influential except in Baltimore, Richmond, and Petersburg. Furthermore, most of the towns had a considerable floating population: sailors from distant lands, river boatmen ("alligator-horses" they called themselves in the West), immigrants from the Old World, New England peddlers, farmers and planters from the interior, and travelers from far and near.

Each port city was likely to have one or more subsidiary upriver towns. Savannah had its Augusta, Richmond its Lynchburg, Mobile its Montgomery and Demopolis, and New Orleans had Baton Rouge, Bayou Sara, Natchez, and others far upstream. Many of these, like Weldon, Augusta, Tuscaloosa, and Louisville, had grown up where river travel was interrupted by rapids. Others, especially in the lower Mississippi Valley, were built on land high enough to be safe from overflow in flood time. But all were located where land-borne commerce converged at a river, and all of them served as distributing points for goods that had been brought up by boat. They were like the seaports in their close relationship to

[37] *Census of 1820.*

water transportation, and the names of some of them, like North Port in Alabama and Port Gibson, East Port, and Cotton Gin Port in Mississippi, indicate their main economic function. Roughly speaking, the towns of the South were strung along two concentric rings, the major towns along the coast and the lesser ones along the fall line. Nowhere was there a town of more than 2,500 inhabitants that was not on navigable water.

Some of the interior dry-land towns, and some of the coastal towns that for one reason or another failed to get much commerce, were pleasant, unhurried places. Such were Williamsburg, Annapolis, Hillsboro, Pineville, Walterboro, and the little Washingtons of North Carolina, Georgia, and Mississippi. Some of them were or had been colonial or state capitals, some contained academies or colleges, some were county seats, and some were summer resorts for low-country planters. They were related to agriculture rather than to commerce and manufacturing, and they were focal points in the social, cultural, religious, and political life of the surrounding countryside. Their importance should be measured not by the number of their inhabitants but by the number of persons who attended their churches, county courts, and social functions, and by the political, social, and economic power of these persons.

Each of the seaport towns, with its trade area of lesser towns, farms, and plantations, amounted to a semi-independent city-state. The river was the bond of union within its domain, the port was the door, and the ocean was the corridor to the outside world. But there were no lines of trade and commerce going from these lesser capitals to one great regional economic capital. By the divergence of the Southern rivers out to an extensive seacoast, nature had ruled against the establishment of a single clearinghouse and control center for the South. The two largest cities, Baltimore and New Orleans, were, in their interests and activities, partly in and partly out of the South. They were situated on its outer edges, and both of them had close contacts with the North: Baltimore through its proximity thereto and New Orleans through its trade connections with the upper Mississippi Valley. Both of them were more cosmopolitan and less Southern than Charleston and some of the smaller towns.

Carrying the staples from seaport to distant market was far less of a problem to Southerners than the prior task of getting them from farm to port. There were freight, insurance, commission, and other charges to be paid, of course; but the complicated commercial and transportation problems of foreign and coastal trade did not weigh heavily on the shoulders of Southerners. They sailed comparatively few ships and built almost none. In 1821, when the registered tonnage of the United States amounted to 619,000 tons, the tonnage registered at New Orleans was 16,000, at Charleston 16,000, at Savannah 7,000, and at Mobile 1,000, making a total of 40,000 for all the cotton ports. At Chesapeake Bay ports, somewhat more was registered, Baltimore leading with 45,000 tons.[38]

With a vast export and few ships of their own, Southerners were obviously depending on others to carry their goods. The share taken in English and Continental bottoms is indicated by the fact that foreign tonnage entering and clearing the cotton ports in 1821 was more than four times as great as the tonnage locally owned.[39] Northern ships also took away great quantities of Southern staples. New York came into the lead after the peace of 1815 by developing a triangular trade which carried cotton from the South to England, manufactured goods from England to New York, and Northern and foreign goods from New York to the cotton ports. In much of the trade the triangle was modified into a two-sided shuttle: cotton was taken from the South to New York and thence to England, and goods were brought back to the South over the same route. By 1822 about one sixth of Southern export cotton was clearing from the port of New York, where it constituted two fifths of that city's exports and was a major factor in establishing its primacy among American ports. Besides cotton, a good deal of tobacco, naval stores, and rice was shipped abroad from New York—enough to constitute a seventh of that city's exports. Its merchants also secured most of the business of handling the goods that went south in exchange for

[38] *American State Papers* (Washington, 1832–1861), *Commerce and Navigation*, II, 752–53.

[39] Compare the figures above with those in Robert G. Albion, *The Rise of New York Port* (New York, 1939), 392–93. This study and another by the same author, *Square-Riggers on Schedule* (Princeton, 1938), especially Chap. III, "Enslaving the Cotton Ports," contain much information about the foreign trade of the South in the 1820's and 1830's.

Southern staples. New York was becoming in some measure the imperial city of the South.[40]

Although New York was outstripping other Northern ports in capturing Southern trade, it had by no means all of it; for Southern exports were, for that time, enormous. Cotton was the most important single item on the list of British imports,[41] and it amounted to nearly half the total of all exports from the United States. During the three-year period beginning October 1, 1820, the average annual value of exported American products was $43,653,714; and of this amount cotton, rice, and tobacco constituted more than two thirds. Besides, the pine forests of the Carolinas produced most of the $400,000 worth of tar, pitch, and turpentine that was annually shipped from the United States.[42] Flour, lumber, linseed oil, and other articles were also shipped from the South, but in what quantities it is impossible to discover.[43]

South Carolina led all the states of the Union in the export of domestic products in the year ending on September 30, 1820,[44] and 96 per cent of its export was from the port of Charleston in the form of cotton and rice. New York was a close second, and then came Louisiana, Georgia, Maryland, and Virginia. Five of these six states were in the South, and the value of their domestic exports ranged from $8,690,539 for South Carolina down to $4,549,137 for Virginia.[45]

New Orleans was chief of the Southern ports because it handled great quantities of flour, tobacco, and other upriver goods as well as the sugar of Louisiana and the cotton of the lower valley. In the eleven-month period ending September 2, 1820, it shipped 67,017 bales of cotton to Great Britain, 29,765 to France, 3,946 to the "North of Europe," and 19,116 to the East coast of the United States. Of tobacco, 13,886 hogsheads were sent to the Eastern sea-

[40] Albion, *Rise of New York Port,* 95–101.

[41] *Ibid.,* 99.

[42] *American State Papers, Commerce and Navigation,* II, 470–71, 601, 731.

[43] See, for example, Richmond *Enquirer,* August 4, 1820.

[44] If foreign as well as domestic products be counted, New York and Massachusetts were ahead.

[45] *American State Papers, Commerce and Navigation,* II, 470; *Niles' Weekly Register,* XIX (1820), 192.

board, 4,132 to the Hanse Towns, and about 10,000 to "sundry places." More than three fourths of its 23,607 hogsheads of sugar were shipped to the Atlantic states, and the rest was sent up the river. The West Indies and ports on the Gulf of Mexico received about half of the flour that left the city. Of its total export, nearly two thirds was to foreign ports, the rest was coastwise.[46]

The ships that shuttled up and down the coast and back and forth across the Atlantic, like the transverse threads in a loom, bound the South into a far-flung, complex economic system. Speaking in general terms, England supplied manufactured goods, the North provided commercial services, and the South furnished agricultural staples. The South was part of an international economic system, and its inhabitants regarded free trade as the cornerstone of their prosperity.

The South's part in this international trade has frequently been called colonial, with the implication that its status was inferior. It was, indeed, not much different from what it had been before American political independence was accomplished, but this fact does not prove that the planters of cotton, rice, and tobacco had less bargaining power or smaller profits than English manufacturers or Northern shippers. True enough, agriculture was sometimes imposed upon: manufactured goods were sometimes shoddy, and commercial dealings were occasionally sharp. But farmers and planters administered irritations as well as suffered them: tobacco hogsheads and cotton bales are known to have reached England with cores of wood and stone, and indebted planters did not always pay their debts. It would seem to be more correct to view Southern agriculture as one of the three elements in a world economic system in which each member contributed to the well-being of the others and for which each was reasonably well paid.

Whichever way the advantage lay, Southerners were not dis-

---

[46] *Niles' Weekly Register*, XIX (1820), 264. The difficulty of securing data about the coasting trade was explained in the Richmond *Enquirer*, August 4, 1820. It remarked that the provisions of the existing law allowed three fourths of the coasting vessels that touched at Richmond to avoid reporting at the customhouse. The one fourth clearing from this port during the first six months of 1820 consisted of 6 ships, 29 brigs, and 147 sloops and schooners; and they bore away 406 hogsheads and 1,686 kegs of tobacco, 10,739 barrels of flour, and unknown quantities of coal, wheat, hemp, and other products.

satisfied with their part of the business. Each year in the early 1820's their staples were sold abroad for more than $30,000,000, and with this credit they purchased large quantities of foreign goods and services. For example, Greenwood Leflore, a Choctaw chieftain, spent some $10,000 in France for the furnishings for one room of his Mississippi plantation home. The floor was covered with a seamless, handwoven Aubusson carpet; the chairs, sofas, and ottoman were of Louis XIV period, covered with gold leaf and upholstered in crimson, silk-brocaded damask; the table and cabinet were ornamented with tortoise-shell and brass buhlwork; and the clock and candelabra with brass and ebony. The furnishings included great mirrors, paintings, and other objects.[47] The Duchess of Orleans, according to family tradition, happened to see Leflore's furniture before it was shipped and expressed much surprise that an old Indian should want such things. If an explanation had been attempted, the Duchess should have been told that the Indian's four hundred slaves raised much cotton which was sold abroad and that he was thus able to demand the best that foreign markets had to offer.

Leflore's purchases, incongruous as they may seem, nevertheless illustrate the tendency of planters to rely on the distant markets where their staples were sold for many of their finer material possessions. By so doing they gave an urbane and cosmopolitan character to the interior of many a remote plantation home; but at the same time they were depriving Southern artisans and craftsmen of the more lucrative and challenging kinds of work. Furthermore, Southern artisans were handicapped by having to compete with the skilled slaves of the plantation; and while the workmanship of those slaves was sometimes of a high order, they could not swell the numbers and increase the strength of a free artisan class.[48]

Most of the white artisans of the South fabricated iron, wood, and hides to the simple needs of an agricultural society or ground its grain into meal, grits, and flour; and in smaller numbers they made a living at printing presses, at potteries, and in establishments

[47] Florence R. Ray, *Chieftain Greenwood Leflore and the Choctaw Indians of the Mississippi Valley* (Memphis, 1936), 62–64.

[48] Thomas J. Wertenbaker, *The Old South: The Founding of American Civilization* (New York, 1942), Chap. VI, makes a number of thoughtful observations about the plight of artisans in the Old South.

for producing linseed oil, lumber, paper, spinning wheels, cotton gins, rifles, pistols, Windsor chairs, and twine for making seines. They were widely scattered over the face of the country, and they were to be found in areas of yeoman farms as well as of large plantations. Franklin County, Georgia, located near the head of the Savannah River, was a land of small farmers in 1820. Four out of every five of its inhabitants were white. In this county there were four makers of "cabinet furniture, 14 shoemakers, 30 smiths, 9 wheelwrights, 11 hatters, 13 tanners, 6 wagon makers, and 3 saddlers." [49] Cumberland County, in the Virginia Piedmont, had been settled much longer, and only a third of its 11,000 inhabitants were white. Yet it contained much the same assortment of artisans. There were "in this county 13 mills which grind for the toll, 19 blacksmith's shops, 12 boot and shoe shops, 6 wheelwright's shops, 5 cotton gins running 176 saws, 4 cabinet maker's shops, 4 saddler's shops, 3 tailor's shops, 3 tan yards, 1 coach maker's shop, 1 watch maker and silver smith, 2 hatter's shops, and 1 distillery." Furthermore, since much wheat was grown in Cumberland County, there were, besides the thirteen toll mills, six flour mills that were presumably selling to more distant markets. They employed 36 men and ground 92,000 bushels of wheat, worth $101,414, into flour, thereby adding some $21,000 in value.

Towns and cities naturally attracted a larger and more varied group of artisans. New Orleans, with a population some two and one-half times as large as that of Cumberland County, Virginia, contained "105 shoemakers, employing 753 persons; 13 tinmen, 63 persons; 31 watchmakers, 155 men; 16 druggists, 24 men; 20 bakers, 103 men; 77 segar makers; 17 coopers, 189 men; 32 milliners, 131 girls; 32 blacksmiths, 113 men; 17 armorers, 70 men; 11 saddlers, 43 men; 4 cart factories; 1 fringemaker; 5 tanners; 10 cutlers; 11 joiners; and 43 carpenters." And in the surrounding parish of Orleans there were "31 sugar mills, 11 saw mills, 3 soap factories, 1 spirits turpentine [distillery], 1 grist mill, 1 brewery, 41 shoe-

[49] This and the following material on artisans and manufacturing are taken (except where otherwise noted) from *Digest of Accounts of Manufacturing Establishments in the United States and of Their Manufactures* (Washington, 1823), compiled as part of the census of 1820. Hereafter cited as *Digest of Accounts of Manufacturing Establishments*, 1820. The pages of this volume are not numbered, but the material is arranged by states and counties. A few changes in punctuation have been made.

makers, 6 tanners, 1 hatter, 15 silversmiths, 9 blacksmiths, 11 distilleries, 3 rope walks, and 11 brick yards."

Throughout most of the South the artisans were too few in numbers and too dependent on agriculturalists to constitute a self-conscious and influential group. But in some of the towns it was otherwise. At Norfolk they took a prominent place in processions through the streets, after the fashion of the medieval guilds of England, the tailors carrying a banner depicting Adam and Eve, with the words, "Naked and ye clothed me," and some of the other crafts displaying their skills on platforms mounted on wheels.[50] In various towns, mechanics' institutes and library societies were formed, and artisans occasionally banded together for political purposes. It was said during an election in Baltimore in 1829 that "The mechanicks have their cabals to perpetuate their power." [51]

Most of the artisans worked alone or with two or three helpers; rarely did as many as ten men work in a single shop. Obviously, most of these small establishments were serving the local countryside. Those that supplied more distant markets were of two kinds: large numbers of small producers of a single commodity concentrated in several areas, and a few large industrial establishments. Whiskey seems to have been made chiefly under the first of these arrangements. Stills were scattered widely over the South, but in some areas there was an unusually large number of small producing units. In Knox County, Tennessee, there were 65 small distilleries in which 81 men operating 102 stills made 99,115 gallons of whiskey in a single year. In Rowan County, North Carolina, 160 establishments containing 269 stills operated by 221 men made corn and rye whiskey worth $42,000. In western Maryland and in several other areas, mostly remote from the seaboard and its transportation facilities, large quantities of whiskey were made. Likewise, a considerable number of saltmaking establishments were concentrated in parts of western Virginia. In Kanawha County, 23 saltworks, worth nearly $700,000, employed 401 persons, most of whom were men. And the same conditions prevailed in the milling industry. In

50 This was on July 4, 1831. Wertenbaker, *Old South,* 235.
51 So wrote John P. Kennedy in his Journal, 1829–1840 (microfilm copy in the Duke University Library; original manuscript in the Peabody Library, Baltimore), October 8, 1829. He added: "I wish we could . . . leave individuals in society dependant on their own respectability."

Frederick County, Virginia, toward the northern end of the Shenandoah Valley, 84 men operating 50 mills produced in a year flour worth $300,000. And in several other Virginia counties milling was an industry of considerable importance.

In contrast to the production of whiskey, salt, and flour in groups of small establishments, tobacco and iron were sometimes worked in units of considerable size. In various parts of Virginia and Maryland there were rather large ironworks turning out pig iron and castings, bar iron, nails, firearms, plow irons, and a variety of other articles. Extensive coal mines were being exploited, especially in the neighborhood of Richmond. In fact, Virginia was the leading coal-producing state in the Union in 1820. Shenandoah County was one of the chief centers of the state's iron industry, for its five establishments were worth $305,000 and gave employment to 250 men, 112 women, and 62 children.[52] Across the mountains in Kentucky and Tennessee the iron industry had gained a foothold. One establishment in Bath County, Kentucky, was large enough to employ 160 persons. Kentucky also contained a number of hemp factories and ropewalks for producing cordage, rope, yarn, twine, and cotton bagging. The center of the industry was in Fayette County, where there were more than a dozen establishments, though some had been closed by hard times in 1820. There were more woolen and cotton mills in Kentucky and Maryland than elsewhere in the South.

Although there were some tobacco factories in Kentucky, there were more in Virginia, especially at Richmond and near-by Petersburg. In 1819 eleven tobacco manufacturers employed 655 hands in Richmond, and the Petersburg factories employed 105. These and other factories converted about one sixth of the Virginia crop into plug and twist for chewing and produced small amounts of snuff, pipe tobacco, and cigars, mostly for the American market. This was only a beginning; in the 1830's the Virginia factories had grown to the point where they were processing half of the state's crop.[53]

Virginia, Maryland, and Kentucky were more like their North-

[52] In addition to the sources previously cited, see Kathleen Bruce, *Virginia Iron Manufacture in the Slave Era* (New York, 1931), especially pp. 87–148.

[53] Robert, *Tobacco Kingdom*, 162–64, 185, 188, 223–24; *Report of the Commissioner of Patents for the Year 1855: Agriculture*, 424.

ern than their Southern neighbors in the number and size of their manufacturing establishments; they contained nearly two thirds of all Southerners engaged in manufacturing in 1820. There were, of course, sugar mills in Louisiana, rice mills in South Carolina, and cotton gins and presses over much of the lower South, but these were usually part of the equipment of plantations. In the cotton South, large-scaled industry was seldom found separate from planting. In South Carolina, for example, the existing records—which are very imperfect—suggest that the largest manufactories in the state were 6 tanyards employing 91 men in St. Philip's Parish and 2 cotton mills at Spartanburg. The latter, with 744 spindles, turned out cotton yarn. They employed 10 men, 13 women, and 15 children.[54]

But, though manufacturing was further advanced in the border states than in the lower South, every Southern state was mainly agricultural in character. In all the South only about 100,000 persons were reported to be engaged in manufacturing, which was a tenth of the number engaged in agriculture; and the number engaged in manufacturing included blacksmiths, wheelwrights, shoemakers, and other "persons of the mechanical profession or handicrafts."[55] There were probably more field hands in single counties of the South Carolina low country than there were factory laborers in all the South; and a considerable number of the factory laborers, especially those who worked with tobacco, iron, and hemp, were slaves. There were planters whose laboring force was larger than that of any factory in the South.

In the North, and especially in Pennsylvania and the Ohio Valley, manufacturing was making more progress. Factory workers and artisans constituted twice as large a part of the population in the North as they did in the South. Furthermore, Northern industry was more diversified, some of its branches were less dependent on agriculture than was generally the case in the South, many of the producing units were larger, and there were hope and planning for future development.

The South of 1819 can be regarded either as an area with com-

[54] For information on cotton manufacturing in the early South, see Broadus Mitchell, *The Rise of Cotton Mills in the South,* in Johns Hopkins University *Studies in Historical and Political Science,* XXXIX, No. 2 (Baltimore, 1921), 17 ff.
[55] Besides the *Digest of Accounts of Manufacturing Establishments,* 1820, *passim,* see Instructions Nos. 5 and 6 in *Census of 1820.*

mon traits that set it off from the rest of the nation or as a patch-work of subregions and internal tensions. It was indeed both, be-cause elements of unity and of diversity were present. There were dissimilarity and in some instances conflict between small farmers and larger planters, between merchants, farmers, and manufac-turers, between the major staple kingdoms and between towns and valleys in a single kingdom, between country and town, between border states and Gulf states, between producers for American markets and producers of export goods, between Atlantic seaboard and Mississippi Valley, and between religious bodies, social groups, and the two races.

Two of the contrasts, and each was really a bundle of contrasts, formed the background of important political events. One was be-tween low country and upcountry. The low country was older and better provided with those social institutions and material posses-sions that come with age; it had more slaves, better transportation, larger towns, and more Episcopalians; it produced a large share of the staple crops, and it consumed a large part of the comforts and luxuries. The upcountry was different on nearly every count except in South Carolina and the part of Georgia near Washington and Augusta where cotton planting was creating similarity to the low country. Furthermore, it seemed unlikely that most of the up-country could escape from the handicaps caused by poorer soil and inadequate transportation facilities.

This conflict was apparent to some degree in all the states, and it was usually a major force in politics. In those states that bordered the Atlantic the conflict was between west and east; in the other states the compass directions were different. East Tennessee, a land of small farmers in mountain valleys, was much like western North Carolina, whereas West Tennessee had much in common with east-ern North Carolina. In Mississippi, the older, wealthier planting region was in the neighborhood of Natchez in the southwestern corner of the state, while the poorer frontier region was to its east and northeast.

Naturally, the policies of a state government would depend in large measure on whether the upcountry or the low was in control; and the unity of the South—or at least its apparent unity—would depend largely on whether all of the states were controlled by similar divisions. In short, government might do much to emphasize the unity or the diversity within the South.

A second major contrast was between the upper South and the cotton states. Agriculture in the border states of Maryland, Virginia, and Kentucky was sufficiently diversified to include tobacco, wheat, and hemp as money crops; and agriculture was supplemented in some measure by manufacturing and commerce. Over most of the lower South, cotton was the predominant money crop—rice and sugar were raised only at its eastern and western edges—and there was scarcely any manufacturing to diversify its economic life. Just as these states had only one main crop, so they had only one main market, and it was abroad; whereas much of the wheat and tobacco and most of the hemp of the border states were sold within the United States. Finally, the areas of heaviest slave concentration were in the lower South; in the border states slavery was less profitable and free Negroes were more numerous. In short, the characteristics of Maryland, Virginia, Kentucky, and perhaps Tennessee, as well as their geographical location, made them a border area between the cotton states and the North.

But if the border had much in common with the North, parts of the cotton states had preoccupations and characteristics that were distinctly Western. Immigrants were moving in, and they were confronted with many of the usual frontier problems, especially the problem of getting the Indians out of large parts of Georgia, Alabama, and Mississippi. On many questions the people of these states could be expected to act and vote as Westerners rather than as Southerners. Of all the Southern states, South Carolina had least in common with either the North or the West. In view of this rainbow of variations it would obviously make considerable difference whether regional leadership was in the hands of Virginia or of South Carolina or of one of the Southwestern states like Tennessee or Mississippi.

But divergencies within the South, great as some of them were, should not overshadow the fact that all ten of the states below Mason and Dixon's line and the Ohio River had certain things in common. All were predominantly agricultural, and in many areas the producing unit was the plantation—a social, governmental, and economic world in itself. There was a widespread interest in the export of staples to distant markets. There was the problem of two dissimilar races living in the same land. Slavery as a system of labor and of social control was of concern to every state. And there were traditions and attitudes and institutions that were the result of these regional traits. Of course, none of these characteristics had the same force in every small part of the South, but there were no Southern states that did not feel their force.

No one of these Southern characteristics was new in 1819, and on the eve of that year hardly any person seemed to regard them as disturbing. A few men with deep insight regarded the social and economic differences between South and North with foreboding just as a few men in the previous generation had done. But their fears seemed groundless. Regional differences had not borne the evil fruit of sectional bitterness. It is easy to find clear and distinctive differences between the South and the North, but contemporary Southerners seemed to be comparatively unaware of and almost totally undisturbed by that fact. Perhaps it is anachronistic to speak of Southerners at the beginning of the year 1819. The sense of oppression and the sectional patriotism that were soon to appear had not yet become visible.

CHAPTER II

LOCATION OF POLITICAL POWER

IN one sense, the Southerner, like all other Americans, was a much-governed individual, because he lived under a complex political system that included local, state, and national forms of government. In another sense he was comparatively free from political authority. Taxes were light, and neither state nor national government touched him at many points or controlled many areas of his life. But in 1820 changes were being made. In the next score of years, government made increasing demands upon the individual, and one and another of the various levels of government were encroaching upon the domains of the others. A large number, perhaps the majority, of the chief events in Southern history during these years consisted in attempts to add to or subtract from the powers of local, state, or national government or in attempts to shift control from one set of hands to another. It was natural, then, for thoughtful inhabitants of the region to become increasingly preoccupied with political questions. Particularly, they were questioning whether each of the three kinds of government was doing the things it ought to do, and whether each was under the control of those who ought to control it.

Leaving questions about national government until later, the present chapter, in pages that are too few for the purpose, deals with local and state government about the year 1820.

The great majority of Southerners were countrymen who looked to their counties or, in Louisiana and the low country of South Carolina, to their parishes as the proper units of local government.[1]

[1] The county existed in Louisiana, but by 1820 it was hardly more than an electoral district. Robert D. Calhoun, "The Origin and Early Development of County-Parish Government in Louisiana," in *Louisiana Historical Quarterly* (New Orleans), XVIII (1935), 124, 136-37.

There were 447 counties and parishes in the year 1820 in the states and territories south of Mason and Dixon's line and the Ohio River. Mississippi with 17 counties and Maryland with 19 had the smallest numbers of any of the Southern states; Virginia, with 103, had the largest. While there were several counties with scarcely 1,000 inhabitants and, at the other extreme, some that included populous towns or cities, three out of every four counties contained between 3,000 and 15,000 inhabitants, and most of them were between 600 and 1,000 square miles in extent. Those of small size were generally near the coast; most of the larger ones were in the sparsely settled mountain regions or near the frontiers where the process of dividing larger counties into smaller ones was not yet finished.[2]

Most Southerners, by making an early start, could ride horseback to the courthouse, transact business, gossip with friends, and return home all in a day's time. Usually they timed their visits for the Mondays when the county court was in session, for on those days the county seat was transformed from a sleepy village into a confusion of men, horses, and carriages. Aside from the business of the court, men bargained for livestock and provisions, auctioneers sold land and slaves, vendors of panaceas plied their trade, and grogshops were busy. Farmers and planters assembled to carry on private as well as public business, to lay political plans, to catch up on the news, and to enjoy the society of their friends. Though the court was the excuse for the day, the day was a social institution in itself— one of the most important in the ante-bellum South. A friend of the old order once remarked: "I like the old fashioned mode of the Virginia people in coming together, and sitting down and having a good dinner, and drinking a glass of toddy . . . and sitting side by side on the court green . . . and exchanging opinions." [3]

The governing body of the counties was commonly called the county court. However, there was some diversity on this score. In Georgia it was called the inferior court, in Louisiana the police jury

[2] These statements are based on data contained in *Compendium of the Ninth Census, 1870.*

[3] Historical Records Survey, *Inventory of the County Archives of Virginia, No. 21. Chesterfield County* (Charlottesville, 1938), 27, n. 22, quoting *Virginia Constitutional Convention. 1850–51. Debates and Proceedings . . .* , I, suppl. No. 60. See also, J. Winston Coleman, Jr., *Slavery Times in Kentucky* (Chapel Hill, 1940), 115–18; Edward Ingle, *Local Institutions in Virginia,* in Johns Hopkins University *Studies in Historical and Political Science,* III, Nos. 2–3 (Baltimore, 1885), 90–91.

exercised parish authority, and elsewhere other names were used. But in respect to the activities of local government there was much similarity throughout the South.[4] The Louisiana police jury, for example, had the power to levy taxes, to establish a schedule of fines for infractions of its regulations, to appoint certain parish officials, to police slaves, to regulate taverns and grogshops, to make and repair roads, establish ferries, and remove obstructions from navigable streams, to regulate the form and height of fences, and to make rules governing cattle ranging.[5]

The Virginia county court had authority to levy taxes, to provide for the upkeep of county buildings, and to build new roads and repair old ones, using the compulsory road work required of all male citizens. It registered wills and deeds and supervised fiduciary relationships, and it had authority over every county officer except overseers of the poor. Besides, it possessed large judicial power, both in civil and criminal cases, in this respect exceeding the authority of the Louisiana police jury.[6]

Some insight into the functioning of county government can be gained from an examination of the income and expenditures of some of the counties. In the year 1830 the nineteen counties of Maryland spent $180,000. This sum was raised by tax levies that varied among the counties from a maximum rate of $1.60 to a minimum rate of fifty-seven cents on each $100.00 of property valuation. It cost approximately $20,000 to levy and collect the tax, and

[4] Throughout this chapter statements about county and state government are based on provisions in the state constitutions unless other citation is given. For the text of the state constitutions, see Francis N. Thorpe (comp.), *The Federal and State Constitutions, Colonial Charters, and Other Organic Laws* (Washington, 1909).

[5] Henry A. Bullard and Thomas Curry (comps.), *A New Digest of the Statute Laws of the State of Louisiana* (New Orleans, 1842), 640–41.

[6] Historical Records Survey, *Inventory of the County Archives of Virginia, No. 21. Chesterfield County*, 24–25, 77–78, 145–46. This is among the most valuable of the numerous inventories of county records because it contains an article on "The Evolution of County Government in Virginia," prepared by Lester J. Cappon. Further support for the generalizations made above can be found in Order Books of the various counties, many of which can be consulted in photostat or microfilm (Division of Archives, Virginia State Library, Richmond).

A brief description of the powers of the North Carolina county courts is in Paul W. Wager, *County Government and Administration in North Carolina* (Chapel Hill, 1928), 17; and the exercise of these powers is amply illustrated in the County Court Minutes, 1823–1831, of Pasquotank County, N.C. (North Carolina Department of Archives and History, Raleigh).

"insolvent taxes" amounted to nearly $3,000. This left some $157,000 to be spent for the following purposes: about $42,000 was allocated to the administration of justice, of which more than $7,000 was for the orphans court, $24,000 for securing jurors, and lesser amounts for state's witnesses, state's attorneys, coroners and jurors on inquests, jail and jail physicians, and the costs of prosecuting criminals. Another $20,000 was allocated to various county officers: to clerks of courts, who received nearly half that amount, to sheriffs, who received $6,647, to criers and bailiffs of county courts, to constables, and to keepers of the courthouses. Roads, bridges, and ferries cost the counties $35,000. A larger amount, nearly $40,000, was spent for public relief: $27,000 for almshouses, nearly $12,000 for pensioners, and over $1,000 for the care of lunatic paupers and the burial of paupers. Of the lesser expenses of county government, $2,000 was paid to judges and clerks of elections, $430 to inspectors of weights and measures, $1,586 for crow heads and wolf and panther scalps, and nearly $14,000 for various "miscellaneous" expenses.[7]

The Kentucky counties operated on much smaller budgets, spending an average of less than $1,000 in the year ending October 10, 1832, and securing their funds from taxes on property, taverns, studhorses, and law processes.[8] However, county government accomplished much more than the amount of its expenditures would seem to indicate; for much was done, such as the maintenance of roads, without the expenditure of money, and some county officers were paid by fees rather than by salaries from the public treasury.

Besides the governing body of the county, there were other officials whose various duties indicate the range of local government. The sheriff was the most important of them, and particularly so in Virginia, where he possessed powers that were divided in some other states among two or more officials. The duties of the Virginia sheriff, which were performed in large measure by deputies, were threefold; he was the chief administrative officer of the county, executing the orders of the county court, enforcing the laws, and managing

[7] Data for the above paragraph were taken from an itemized statement of the cost of government in each county in Maryland in the year 1830 which was published in Maryland *House Journal*, 1830–1831, pp. 165–71.

[8] Kentucky *Senate Journal*, 1832–1833, table following p. 36.

the jail; he was tax collector and treasurer of the county; and he conducted elections, holding the poll and certifying results.

In the exercise of his great powers the Virginia sheriff was closely bound to the court by sentiment as well as by law, for custom required that the office be given to one of the members of the court as a reward for long service on the bench.[9] In Kentucky this practice was required by the constitution, which further enjoined that due regard be paid to seniority and rotation. Although there was an occasional deviation from these customs and requirements, the relations between the sheriff and the county court were usually cordial.

In addition to the sheriff, the county officers of Virginia were a coroner, who held inquests in cases of violent or unnatural death, and who acted as sheriff in case of a vacancy in that office; a clerk, who recorded the actions of the county court, and, in general, was the chief keeper of county records; two commissioners of revenue, who listed property and persons for purposes of taxation; school commissioners, who supervised the education of indigent children; [10] militia officers who, in addition to their military duties, sometimes exercised police functions, especially in the management of slaves; and a considerable number of justices of the peace and constables. The justice of the peace, who was also called squire or magistrate, was a minor judicial officer who could settle cases of debt involving small sums, institute lunacy proceedings, order the arrest of criminals, and perform some other acts. The constable was the police officer of the magistrate's court, summoning witnesses, whipping slaves, and serving warrants and attachments. Other Virginia county officers were road surveyors and viewers, later known as road commissioners, whose duty it was to make recommendations to the county court concerning the roads and to supervise the work done thereon, and overseers of the poor who were empowered to apprentice poor orphans, put vagrants to work, and provide food,

[9] *Report of the Revisors of the Code of Virginia,* 5 reports (Richmond, 1847–1849), I, 266. The descent of the shrievalty among the senior justices can be traced in the several MS. volumes entitled "Register of Justices and County Officers" (Division of Archives, Virginia State Library).

[10] In 1818 each county was authorized but not required to appoint from five to fifteen school commissioners.

shelter, and medical care for the needy—duties that had been performed before the Revolution by parish vestries.[11]

Counties all over the South employed nearly the same officials as did Virginia. There were some variations in terminology, and in some states the financial powers of the sheriff were vested in a county treasurer or trustee. But even in the Louisiana parishes there were clerks of the courts, justices of the peace, constables, sheriffs, coroners, and tax assessors.[12]

It was with these local officers rather than with officers of the state at large or of the nation that the citizen carried on most of his business with government; and from this experience as well as from the importance of the actions and decisions of the county governing bodies, he naturally came to regard the county as having much and perhaps paramount importance among the governments to which he was subject.

Although the county touched the citizen frequently and forcibly, the citizen seldom had any control over it, for local government was thoroughly undemocratic in most of the counties of the South. It was only in the three lightly populated states of Georgia, Alabama, and Louisiana that the people could elect their local rulers in the 1820's, and in them democracy was a recent innovation. In Georgia, which was the most democratic of the three, county government was vested in a body known as the inferior court whose powers were about the same as those of the Virginia county court. The five justices who constituted this court, as well as the sheriff, clerk, coroner, surveyor, justices of the peace, and constables, were popularly elected. In no case was their term of office for more than four years.[13] As for Alabama, the county court after 1821 was merely a judicial tribunal presided over by a single justice who had been chosen by the legislature for a six-year term. Administrative and legislative functions of county government were vested in a board of five men, one of whom was the judge of the county court and the

11 Historical Records Survey, *Inventory of the County Archives of Virginia, No. 21. Chesterfield County,* 48–67, 82, 89–90, 94, 98–101, 124, 134, 145–46, 149–50, 154.

12 Historical Records Survey, *Inventory of the Parish Archives of Louisiana, No. 35. Natchitoches Parish* (University, La., 1938).

13 Oliver H. Prince (comp.), *A Digest of the Laws of the State of Georgia* (Athens, 1837), 180–81, and references under "County Officers" and "Inferior Courts" in the Index.

other four, who were popularly elected for three-year terms, were known as commissioners of revenue and roads. The sheriff, the clerk of the county court, justices of the peace, and constables were also popularly elected for terms that ran in most cases for three years.[14]

The Louisiana parish police jury was likewise a mixed body with appointed and elected members; but after 1824, when justices of the peace ceased to be ex-officio members, all of the members were popularly elected, one from each ward of the parish, except the president of the police jury. This office was held by the parish judge, who was appointed by the governor for a four-year term. Most of the other parish officials were appointed.[15]

While this outcropping of democracy in three states of the lower South was important, it was less important than the number of states would indicate, for they contained only a fifth of the counties of the South and less than a fifth of the people. By growth and by additions to their ranks they were to have much influence in the future, but in 1820 the seven states whose local government was undemocratic deserve more attention.

In the four states of Virginia, Kentucky, North Carolina, and Tennessee control over county affairs was vested in that ancient institution, the county court. Its powers were legislative, executive, and judicial. All were exercised by the same body of men, for there were no checks and balances under this form of local government. To the Virginia county courts, according to Thomas Jefferson, were entrusted "the justice, the executive administration, the taxation, police, the military appointments of the county, and nearly all our daily concerns." [16] Furthermore, the Virginia courts selected virtually every other local officer except the overseers of the poor who were popularly elected.[17]

Perhaps the greatest of the court's powers was the right to choose

14 John G. Aikin (comp.), *A Digest of the Laws of the State of Alabama* (Philadelphia, 1833), 82, 86–87, 100, 245, 299, 387.

15 Bullard and Curry (comps.), *New Digest of the Statute Laws of the State of Louisiana*, 639–47; Calhoun, "Origin and Early Development of County-Parish Government in Louisiana," *loc. cit.*, 56–160, especially pp. 85–88, 118–19, 125, 135, 140.

16 Thomas Jefferson to John Taylor, May 28, 1816, in Andrew A. Lipscomb (ed.), *The Writings of Thomas Jefferson* (Washington, 1903–1904), XV, 20.

17 Historical Records Survey, *Inventory of the County Archives of Virginia, No. 21. Chesterfield County*, 24–25, 134.

its own new members. Each court was composed of all the justices of the peace in the county, and they held office for life. In case of a vacancy or of the necessity for enlarging the number of justices, the Virginia court made a nomination to the governor who thereupon commissioned the nominee. The Kentucky courts were required to make plural nominations of magistrates, and for some other officers plural nominations were required in both states.[18] But in actual practice the courts managed to whittle down this gubernatorial power. The court of Lincoln County, Kentucky, plainly told the governor "that it is the wish of this court that Richard Singleton [one of its two nominees for a justiceship of the peace] be commissioned." [19]

On occasion, the court could use more vigorous measures. Thomas Elley, Esquire, appeared before the court of Oldham County, Kentucky, with a commission signed by Governor Joseph Desha, appointing him to the office of sheriff. The court, not wanting Elley in that office, set the amount of his bond at $40,000. When it seemed likely that he would find securities for that large sum, it increased the required amount to $60,000, which Elley, though a man of considerable property, could not meet. Thereupon the court informed the governor that he had failed to qualify and requested the appointment of Abram B. Morton.[20] In short, as Jefferson said of Virginia, and his statement is equally true of Kentucky, the members of the county governing bodies were "self-appointed, self-continued, holding their authorities for life, and with an impossibility of breaking in on the perpetual succession of any faction once possessed of the bench." [21]

Because Virginia and Kentucky county courts had the right to perpetuate themselves and to choose most of the other local officers,

18 A Kentucky county court was required to nominate two men to the governor when either a sheriff, coroner, surveyor, or justice of the peace was to be appointed. Constitution of 1799, in Thorpe (comp.), *Federal and State Constitutions*, III, 1282–85. A Virginia county court had to nominate two men for coroner, or three men for the office of sheriff. Historical Records Survey, *Inventory of the County Archives of Virginia, No. 21. Chesterfield County*, 25, 99.

19 Governor Joseph Desha Papers (Kentucky State Historical Society, Frankfort), 1828, Sec. 1, Box 42, Jacket 296.

20 *Ibid.*, 1824, Sec. 1, Box 32, Jacket 231.

21 Jefferson to Taylor, May 28, 1816, in Lipscomb (ed.), *Writings of Thomas Jefferson*, XV, 20–21.

because these and some other of the courts' powers derived from the written constitution and were therefore beyond legislative control, and because yet other of their powers derived from what amounted to an unwritten constitution that was already old when state and Federal constitutions were written, one is tempted to say that in both Virginia and Kentucky the relationship between county and state was quasi-federal.

The same system of local government prevailed in North Carolina and Tennessee to the extent that justices of the peace composed the county courts, held office for life, and chose practically all other county officers.[22] But the methods of choosing magistrates were different. In Tennessee, vacancies were filled by the legislature; in North Carolina, by the representatives in the General Assembly. In these two states the courts were thus deprived of the self-perpetuating independence they enjoyed in Virginia and Kentucky. However, there is no reason to think that the power of the magistracy was much reduced by this arrangement. The legislature could hardly effect a sudden revolution in county government when the justices, once appointed, held office for life. Nor would it be likely to desire such a revolution because the legislature itself was under the control of the magistrates.[23]

At the sessions of the county courts there were seldom many justices on the bench when only routine matters were to be considered. In North Carolina, where three justices were a quorum, the court sometimes had to adjourn from day to day pending the assembling of that small number; and sometimes the members agreed to hold court in rotation in the hope that business would not be delayed by lack of a quorum. But when the tax rate was to be set or when a sheriff or county solicitor was to be elected, there was no scarcity of magistrates, for the law required the presence of a majority of them

[22] For North Carolina see, in addition to the constitution, Henry Potter et al. (revisors), Laws of the State of North-Carolina (Raleigh, 1821), especially I, 302–303; II, 1344; and Bartholomew F. Moore and Asa Briggs, Revised Code of North Carolina (Boston, 1855), especially pp. 151, 154, 155. For Tennessee see, in addition to the constitution of 1796, John Haywood and Robert L. Cobbs, The Statute Laws of the State of Tennessee (Knoxville, 1831), I, 195–209.

[23] See below, p. 50. Dealings between the two houses of the Tennessee legislature over appointments of justices of the peace can be followed in their journals. For example, see Tennessee Senate Journal, 1820, pp. 145–48, 171; Tennessee House Journal, 1820, pp. 180, 200.

on such occasions and the importance of these decisions usually attracted more than a majority.[24]

Perhaps it was well that most of the justices stayed away from most of the meetings of court, for they were too numerous to do the judicial and administrative work with efficiency. The smallest number of magistrates in any Tennessee county was fifteen in Morgan County. The average for this state was thirty-eight, and in Bedford County there were ninety-seven.[25] The number in the Kentucky counties ranged between nine and twenty-four.[26] The Virginia and North Carolina counties had an average of about thirty-five.[27]

All told, there were about 8,000 justices in the four states of Virginia, Kentucky, North Carolina, and Tennessee. They had almost complete control over the local government of some 2,700,000 people—nearly two thirds of the inhabitants of the South. Sometimes they governed well, for behind the courts there was an ancient and honorable tradition which tended to impart a sense of *noblesse oblige*. But when they governed poorly, as of course they did at times, the people of the county had no redress on election day.

County government was also undemocratic in the three remaining Southern states, South Carolina, Mississippi, and Maryland. The county court with its usual extensive powers existed in Mississippi, but after 1822 it was composed of only three persons, a presiding justice and two associate justices chosen by the state legislature to serve during good behavior.[28] The affairs of Maryland counties were conducted by several bodies—the levy court whose chief functions were to levy taxes and provide for the upkeep of roads, the

[24] Examples of fluctuations in attendance can be found in the County Court Minutes, 1823–1831, of Pasquotank County, N.C. (North Carolina Department of Archives and History).

[25] There were 2,364 justices in the 62 counties of Tennessee. Tennessee *House Journal*, 1831, p. 381. The constitution limited the number of justices of the peace to two in each captain's district and three in each county seat.

[26] Lists of justices of the peace holding commissions in March, 1830, for most of the counties of Kentucky can be found in Sec. 1, File Box 44, Jacket 310 (Kentucky State Historical Society).

[27] "Register of Justices and County Officers, 1780–1822" (Division of Archives, Virginia State Library). For the names of the North Carolina justices, see Colin McIver, *The North-Carolina Register, and United States Calendar, for the Year of Our Lord 1823* (Raleigh, 1822).

[28] [Poindexter], *Revised Code of the Laws of Mississippi*, 27, 71, 294. See references in Index for appointment of county officers.

county court which was a judicial body, the orphans court, and the commissioners of the tax. From three to seven persons served on each of these bodies, and all of them were appointed by the governor and council who, in turn, were chosen by the state legislature. Some held office for limited terms and others for life. The sheriff was the only county officer who was popularly elected.[29]

A somewhat similar system prevailed in South Carolina. Here the conduct of local affairs was divided among a number of boards, chief of which were commissioners of free schools, commissioners of courthouses and jails, commissioners of the poor, and commissioners of roads. The last were the most important of the local administrative bodies. Besides being charged with maintenance of roads, bridges, and ferries, they were empowered to levy taxes, and they licensed tavern keepers, retailers of spirituous liquors, and billiard-table keepers. Except for commissioners of the poor and sheriffs, who were popularly elected, the members of the other boards as well as justices of the quorum and of the peace, and election managers for each precinct in the state, were chosen by the legislature. In nearly every case they were chosen for limited terms of office. Some of the boards, for instance the commissioners of free schools, could, in the absence of legislative action, choose their successors; but the legislature possessed ultimate authority, and its frequent use thereof is attested by the large volume of legislation on local matters, much of it of a minute character.[30]

In South Carolina, therefore, and to a less extent in Maryland and Mississippi, power was focused at one point in the state rather than at small points all over it; and the great power of the legislature was not counterbalanced by local institutions responsible either to the few or the many in the parish or county. Hence, the legislature could in some measure impose unity upon the state,

[29] In addition to the Maryland constitution, see William Kilty et al., The Laws of Maryland (Annapolis, 1799–1820), Sess. 1794, Chap. 53; Sess. 1798, Chap. 34; and references under levy courts, county courts, orphans court, and commissioners of tax in the Index.

[30] The numerous laws relating to the personnel and work of the various boards may be consulted in the Statutes at Large of South Carolina, 1682–1866 (Columbia, 1836–1875). Of special importance is an act of December, 1825, "to Reduce all the Acts and Clauses of Acts of the General Assembly of this State, Relating to the Powers and Duties of the Commissioners of Roads, into One Act." See also Columbus Andrews, Administrative County Government in South Carolina (Chapel Hill, 1933), 14–20.

using its power to break down local opposition groups. Control over the legislature was therefore extremely important to the South Carolina politician, and an understanding of the character and composition of the South Carolina legislature is proportionately important to the student of this period of South Carolina history.

In the eastern South, the legislature was almost as important in state government as the county court was in Virginia local government. Besides making the laws, it chose nearly all other state officials. For example, the Maryland legislature in two consecutive days in December, 1819, elected a governor, five members of the council, and two United States Senators. The senate, acting separately, elected a successor to one of its members who had resigned.[31] The governor and councilors, chosen by the legislature for one-year terms, and therefore presumably in thorough accord with legislative opinion, were empowered by the constitution to appoint judges, militia officers, registers of the land office, surveyors, an attorney general, and some other state officials. The legislatures of Virginia, North Carolina, South Carolina, and Georgia possessed at least as great electoral powers, and perhaps more, for they chose virtually all state officials directly.

Under this system there was little chance for the chief executive to develop policies contrary to the legislative program, because his term was short and he had no veto power except in Georgia. This subordination of the executive branch to the legislative, together with the fact that the electorate could reach the executive only through the legislature, created a strong resemblance to the British system of cabinet responsibility to the parliamentary majority.

Away from the Atlantic seaboard, in the states of Kentucky, Tennessee, Louisiana, Mississippi, and Alabama, there was somewhat more of popular voting, and legislative and executive branches were co-ordinate to the extent that each received its mandate directly from the people. The governor, and sometimes a lieutenant governor, were popularly elected. Even so, the legislature was generally regarded as the most powerful branch of government. Governor Thomas B. Robertson of Louisiana publicly announced that "The Legislature is here, under the constitution, the paramount

[31] Maryland *Senate Journal,* 1819–1820, pp. 4, 7, 8.

authority." Although he was governor, he approved this arrangement.[32]

Besides its power within the state, the legislature frequently determined the state's position on national issues. It adopted resolutions on important Federal questions, it elected United States Senators and sometimes instructed them how to vote, and it often decided the state's vote in Presidential elections either by electing Presidential electors or by nominating an electoral slate which met with no effective opposition. Even the Representatives in the lower House of Congress, popularly elected though they had been, were closely tied to the legislature. Fifty of the sixty men who represented Virginia in the House of Representatives and five of the six Senators in the decade beginning in 1831 had been members of the state legislature.[33]

The legislature, then, was the controlling element in state affairs and it strongly influenced the state's position in national affairs. It was the most representative branch of government, and in the South Atlantic states its members were the only state officeholders elected by the people. It is therefore important to discover how legislatures were chosen if one would know the extent to which state government reflected the opinions of all classes of people and of all sections of the state.

In North Carolina, Virginia, and Maryland each county had the same number of representatives in the lower house; four for each county in Maryland, and two for each county in Virginia and North Carolina. The significance of this arrangement lies in the fact that by 1820 the eastern counties had, on the average, smaller white populations than the western counties. Georgia tipped the scales in favor of the older and wealthier East by apportioning seats in the lower house on the basis of "federal population"; namely, the whole white population and three fifths of the Negroes. South Carolina accomplished the same end by giving equal weight to white inhabitants and to the amount of taxes paid to the state.

[32] Louisiana *Senate Journal*, 1820–1821, p. 21.

[33] Compare lists of Virginia Senators and Representatives in the Twenty-second through Twenty-sixth Congresses, in *Biographical Directory of the American Congress, 1774–1927* (Washington, 1928), with the legislative rolls in *Thirteenth Annual Report of the Library Board of the Virginia State Library, 1915–1916* (Richmond, 1917).

The seaboard senates were also under Eastern dominance. In North Carolina and Georgia each county had one senator; in South Carolina and Virginia, contiguous counties were grouped into senatorial districts. Maryland weighted the scales for the East by allocating six senators to the sparsely populated Eastern Shore and nine to all the rest of the state, each group being chosen by an electoral college consisting of two electors from each county. None of these senates could be reapportioned except by constitutional amendment, and only in the states of Georgia and South Carolina was there provision for periodic reapportionment of seats in the lower house.[34]

The seaboard rule of treating counties as political equals resulted in glaring inequalities. Jefferson once exclaimed: "Upon what principle of right or reason can any one justify the giving to every citizen of Warwick as much weight in the government as to 22 equal citizens in Loudoun?"[35] It was asserted in Maryland in 1819 that a reapportionment on the basis of white population would give Baltimore County six representatives instead of four and Baltimore City seventeen instead of two, and that many other counties would be greatly reduced in legislative strength.[36] Admittedly, these were extreme cases. The general situation may be illustrated by considering Virginia. Its average Tidewater county had less than two thirds as many white inhabitants as the average county in the rest of the state and less than half as many as the average county in the Shenandoah Valley.[37] In Virginia and in some other states separate representation was given to certain designated towns, and nearly all of these were on tidewater.

Away from the seaboard—in Kentucky, Tennessee, Louisiana, Mississippi, and Alabama—seats in both houses, except the Louisiana senate, were allocated to counties or groups of counties in

[34] The formation of new Western counties afforded a constitutional means of lessening Eastern strength in the senates, but the Easterners guarded this point closely. See below, Chap. XII.

[35] Jefferson to John H. Pleasants, April 19, 1824, in Richmond *Enquirer*, April 27, 1824. He was comparing the number of voters in the two counties. According to the *Census of 1820* there were 26 white persons in Loudoun County to every one in Warwick.

[36] Annapolis *Maryland Gazette and Political Intelligencer*, September 9, 1819.

[37] For a list of the counties in each of the four great divisions of the state, Tidewater, Piedmont, Valley, and Tramontane, see the constitution of 1830.

approximate ratio to white population.[38] In order that representation might reflect increases or decreases in the population of the counties, there was provision, once more with the exception of the Louisiana senate, for reapportionment of both houses at frequent intervals, in no case longer than seven years.

Under these Western rules of government the center of political power should have been at all times very close to the center of white population in each state. But in the five seaboard states the Eastern areas had undue power from which they could be dislodged only by constitutional amendment, and these were the Southern states that had most political weight in the nation. Over half of all the Southern Representatives in Congress in 1820 had come from Virginia, North Carolina, and South Carolina.

This concentration of power in the East gave an upward lift to the center of power, for the East was the home of most of the planters. But this was not the only foundation for aristocratic control over state government. A number of other devices written into constitutions and laws enhanced the power of the rich and diminished the power of the poor.

In the first place, the ballot was not given to all men in the South in 1820. The single fact that slaves could not vote removed from political influence about a third of the population. Even within the white population there were many who had no political power, and there were others whose power was small. The people, in a political sense, were less numerous than the people in a biological sense; and among the political people there were both pygmies and giants.

In Virginia, which restricted the suffrage more sharply than other states, a man could vote only if he owned at least fifty acres of unimproved land or twenty-five acres with a house on it. Jefferson estimated "that the nonfreeholders compose the majority of our free, adult male citizens." [39] In South Carolina and Tennessee a landowner could vote under certain circumstances when a landless man could not, and in Louisiana and to some extent in Georgia and Mississippi the ballot was restricted to taxpayers. North Carolina

[38] White population was the basis in Mississippi and Alabama; the number of qualified voters in Kentucky (where all white men could vote) and Louisiana (where taxpayers could vote); and the number of taxable inhabitants in Tennessee.

[39] Jefferson to Pleasants, April 19, 1824, in Richmond *Enquirer*, April 27, 1824. This letter is also printed in Lipscomb (ed.), *Writings of Thomas Jefferson*, XVI, 28.

followed the plan of having two classes of voters: taxpayers could vote for members of the lower house, but the ownership of fifty acres of land was essential to voting for state senators. In all other Southern states the man who could vote for members of the lower house of the state legislature was qualified to vote in other state elections. There were only three states, Maryland, Kentucky, and Alabama, where voting was totally unrelated to possessions or to tax payment, and in Alabama and Maryland this was a recent innovation.

Property qualifications for officeholding reinforced property qualifications for voting in every state except in the three which permitted all white men to vote. While the requirements differed from state to state, property requirements as a general rule were higher for officeholding than for voting, and they advanced according to the prominence of the office. In Louisiana, for example, a member of the lower house had to own land worth $500; a member of the senate, $1,000; and the governor, $5,000. South Carolina differed from the other Southern states in establishing two categories of property qualifications, depending on whether the officeholder was resident or nonresident of the district he represented. Under either condition he had to own property in the district; but if nonresident he had to own more than three times as much as a resident to be eligible for either the house or the senate.

Plural voting and viva-voce voting were practiced in several states. In Virginia, South Carolina, to a limited degree in Kentucky, and perhaps elsewhere a man could vote in each constituency in which he owned the requisite amount of property.[40] In Virginia and Kentucky voting was oral and public through the ante-bellum period. At a long table, placed on the courthouse green or inside the courthouse, sat the election judges and their clerks, flanked by the candidates or their representatives. Each voter announced his preference before this official table and the assembled crowd. When the election was close and whiskey plentiful, there was ample reason for the timid to vote with the crowd rather than according to convictions, and where elections were conducted in this manner it is altogether likely that lesser folk sometimes voted like their more

[40] Plural voting was ended in South Carolina in 1819. South Carolina *Acts*, 1819, p. 102.

powerful neighbors, especially if they were obligated to them.[41]

Elections were conducted in a good many states by agents of the legislature or of the county courts. The South Carolina legislature selected all the voting places in the state, named the managers for each precinct, and determined in each instance whether voting should continue for one day or for two.[42] In Virginia, Kentucky, North Carolina, and Tennessee elections were held by sheriffs, sometimes assisted by other persons who had been appointed by the court;[43] and in the first three of these states if the election included several counties—as in choosing Congressmen and state senators— the sheriffs of the district would assemble to compile the returns, certify the results, and perhaps talk about future elections.[44]

In these county-court states, the magistracy was likely to have some control over popular elections of legislators, Congressmen, and Presidential electors through its management of the election machinery. Besides, the justices themselves could vote, and presumably they could influence the dozens of officers subordinate to the county court; and all of these men—subordinates and superiors —were likely to have kinsmen and friends. Even those who were outside the court circle might hesitate to let it be known that they were voting against the court's ticket. That body had too much power to be antagonized with impunity.

An examination of the personnel of some of the state legislatures indicates that the courts had considerable success in controlling popular elections. By constitutional prescription justices of the

[41] The best account is in Albert J. Beveridge, *The Life of John Marshall* (Boston, 1916–1919), II, 413–16. Though an election in 1799 is here described, there was no important change by 1855. See John S. Wise, *The End of an Era* (Boston, 1899), 55–56; Raleigh *Semi-Weekly Standard*, February 28, 1855.

Some Virginia election officials reported the names of all voters in the county who had participated and how each had voted. See, for example, the returns for the Presidential election of 1832 (Division of Archives, Virginia State Library).

[42] South Carolina *Acts*, 1819, pp. 94–102.

[43] Joseph Tate, *A Digest of the Laws of Virginia* (Richmond, 1823), 185–89; Charles S. Morehead and Mason Brown, *A Digest of the Statute Laws of Kentucky* (Frankfort, 1834), I, 590–91; Potter *et al.* (revisors), *Laws of the State of North-Carolina*, I, 318–22; Haywood and Cobbs, *Statute Laws of the State of Tennessee*, I, 80–85.

[44] Virginia constitution of 1776; Potter *et al.* (revisors), *Laws of the State of North-Carolina*, II, 1226. Samples of the official reports of these meetings of sheriffs can be seen in "Election Returns," 1833, Sec. 1, Box 48, Jacket 341, in John H. Breathitt Papers (Kentucky State Historical Society).

peace were allowed to retain their commissions even though they were elected to the state legislature; thus it was possible for one man to be a member of the chief governing body of the state as well as of the county court. In the early 1830's, 37 per cent of the Kentucky state senators and 20 per cent of the representatives were magistrates. While there is no way of knowing how many more of the legislators were bound to the court cliques by ties of friendship, kinship, and political alliance, it is significant that another 11 per cent of the representatives bore family names of justices in their respective counties.[45]

In the North Carolina legislature of 1822, 55 per cent of the senators and 43 per cent of the representatives were magistrates, and an additional 7 per cent of the senators and 12 per cent of the representatives bore the surnames of justices in their counties.[46] The same condition existed in Virginia. In the three sessions of 1819–1820, 1831–1832, and 1844–1845, which were chosen as samples, the justices constituted between 42 per cent and 56 per cent of the membership of each house and senate. Besides, there were other delegates and senators who bore the surnames of justices in their counties, the percentages ranging between 9 and 29 in these six bodies. Those who were either justices or who bore the surnames of justices amounted to more than 58 per cent of the membership of every house and senate, and in four of them they constituted more than 70 per cent of the members.[47]

[45] These and the following statements must be taken as approximately rather than as absolutely correct since there are a number of chances of error. The Kentucky statements are based on a comparison of lists of justices of the peace in March, 1830, Sec. 1, File Box 44, Jacket 310 (Kentucky State Historical Society), which are complete for over two thirds of the counties, with the names of representatives and senators from those counties as they are given in the *Senate Journals* and *House Journals*. The senate was checked for three consecutive annual sessions, beginning with the one which assembled in December, 1830; the house for two sessions, beginning at the same date.

[46] Membership lists of the county courts and of the two houses of the legislature can be found in McIver, *North-Carolina Register . . . 1823*, pp. 19–21, 23–41.

[47] Virginia General Assembly, session of	1819–20	1831–32	1844–45
Percentage of delegates who were justices	53.7	55.0	45.2
Other delegates with surnames of justices	9.4	15.3	13.3
Total	63.1	70.3	58.5
Percentage of senators who were justices	42.0	50.0	56.2
Other senators with surnames of justices	29.2	28.1	22.0
Total	71.2	78.1	78.2

Whatever the legislatures did in these states was done in large measure by the county squires. Furthermore, their power extended beyond county courts and legislative halls. A large proportion of the militia officers were justices,[48] and the justices were powerful in party organization in the era of the nominating caucus. In the Presidential election of 1820 the Virginia state caucus set up a state-wide machine with committees of five or six members in each county and borough in the state. More than half of these six hundred or so men were magistrates.[49]

It is sometimes said that within the United States, sovereignty rests with the people. But Jefferson once remarked, when his thoughts were running in political rather than geographical channels: "the sum of the counties makes the State." [50] He was saying, in effect, that the county oligarchies dominated the state government. So they did; but it would be a mistake to regard the magistrates as an unbroken, disciplined phalanx. Magistrates were not the sort of men to accept discipline and regimentation. Among themselves they differed on many grounds, and often their rival claims to legislative or Congressional seats were carried before the people in bitterly fought elections. Nor were the magistrates drawn up in hostile array against their neighbors. As men of local substance and prominence, they were usually respected, their leadership was seldom challenged, and it was generally recognized that they were bearing the burden of government with little or no re-

---

For the legislative rolls, see *Thirteenth Annual Report of the Library Board of the Virginia State Library, 1915–1916,* and for lists of justices in each county, the "Register of Justices and County Officers, 1780–1822," and *ibid.,* "1786–1845" (Division of Archives, Virginia State Library). The earlier Register was used in checking the 1819–1820 session, the latter in checking the 1844–1845 session, and both were consulted for the 1831–1832 session. Let it be repeated that the percentages given above are only approximations. In a few instances legislators are counted as justices who were not so at the moment but were to be commissioned a year or two later. On the other hand, some men not counted as justices may have been such, for the lists of justices are lacking for a few counties.

[48] Compare, for instance, the list of North Carolina militia officers with the list of justices, in McIver, *North-Carolina Register . . . 1823,* pp. 22–42, 89–91.

[49] The list of committeemen published in the Richmond *Enquirer,* February 22, 1820, was compared with the "Register of Justices and County Officers, 1780–1822" (Division of Archives, Virginia State Library).

[50] Jefferson to Taylor, May 28, 1816, in Lipscomb (ed.), *Writings of Thomas Jefferson,* XV, 21.

muneration. About as close as one can come to describing this complex situation is to say that democracy in the upper South was tempered and held in partial check by the influence of the squirearchy, and that the upper South in 1820 was the more populous and influential part of the region.

Under this system, government was notably conservative and stable, and it was fitted close to the social and economic order of things. Since business was mostly agricultural, government was not disturbed by tensions between representatives of commerce, agriculture, and industry. Nor was there much conflict, except in Maryland, between the political order and the economic, for the leaders of one were the leaders of the other. Of course there were many who were dissatisfied, but those who were disgruntled with social and economic conditions had little chance of getting enough political power to enable them to revolutionize society and business. Political conservatism was further strengthened by the fact that power was in experienced hands. The life tenure of the magisterial office was a guarantee in Virginia and Kentucky and to a less extent in North Carolina and Tennessee that affairs of state would not be suddenly entrusted to inexperienced hands.

The character of political leadership and the rules under which one sought political preferment in the powerful county-court states were profoundly influenced by the system of government. To attain high power, one had to begin his career within the county oligarchies or with their blessing. Family connections were extremely important. It was best to be born into an influential family, but misfortune in this regard might be repaired by a proper marriage or by the establishment of professional or social ties with the ruling families. Yet, whatever the means employed, it was more important to win the favor of the few who already had power than it was to court the multitude with demagogic arts. The virtues, vices, and political techniques of the successful politicians were those of the leaders of an oligarchy.

Much that has been said can be summed up in three statements. In the first place, throughout most of the South the power to govern reposed far up in the economic pyramid of an agricultural society, resting chiefly in the substantial farmers and planters. Secondly, equalitarian, universal manhood suffrage was approximated only in some of the younger, smaller states of the Southwest, especially in Alabama. Thirdly, the center of political power was east of the South's geographical and population centers.

The consequences of these facts were profound, both in state and national affairs. In determining state policy on such vital questions as taxation, banking, and transportation, the slaveholding Easterner had more power than the small farmers of the upcountry in all the South Atlantic states, and the poor man had little power wherever he lived. Furthermore, expressions of Southern opinion on national questions—whether registered in debates and votes in Congress, in resolutions of state legislatures, or in Presidential elections—reflected in large measure the views of the Eastern, planting, slaveholding parts of the South. The poor man and the Westerner were insufficiently consulted.

It was well known at the time that the political mirror did not perfectly reflect the opinions of all. Upcountry farmers, poor men of all sections, and ambitious men who were outside the court circles were the chief advocates of change. The Eastern planter, whose power was great in the existing arrangement of government, was the champion of the existing order; and he knew that the state constitution which gave him power must be defended. Thus he occupied in state politics the same position that he, as the representative of the South, was to occupy in the critical national struggles of the 1820's; state politics, then, afforded an excellent training camp for the national arena, and this fact may account in part for the political experience and the acumen in constitutional debate which permitted Southern politicians to wield more power in the nation than the population of their region would seem to warrant.

CHAPTER III

ENLIGHTENMENT OF PUBLIC OPINION

AMONG the places and institutions through which Southerners could give and receive ideas and opinions were the family, the plantation, the crossroads blacksmith shop, the village tavern, the market place of the city, sales days and county-court days, meetings of the state legislature, newspapers, churches, schools, and colleges. Some of these operated only in the neighborhood; others extended over wider areas and, as it were, federated local opinions into regional opinions. Some exercised a transitory influence; others made their influence felt more slowly but perhaps more abidingly. Among the chief of these were the churches and the colleges. Compared with what they have since become, they were few in number and small in size in the early nineteenth century; but in the next thirty years they were to experience much growth. Through these years they were to help shape the opinions of Southerners upon a number of questions; and in a more general but perhaps a more important way, they had a share in determining the character, the attitudes, and the degree of education among the more influential members of Southern society.

Not one Southerner in ten was a church member in the 1820's according to the fragmentary statistics that are available. The four states of Virginia, North Carolina, South Carolina, and Georgia, with a total population of more than 3,000,000 at the end of that decade, then contained only 99,000 Baptists, 94,000 Methodists, 23,000 Presbyterians, and even fewer Episcopalians, Roman Catholics, Lutherans, and Moravians.[1] In Kentucky only one person in

[1] An "ecclesiastical register" showing the number of communicants and ministers of the churches in each state can be found in the *American Almanac and Repository of Useful Knowledge for the Year 1832* (Boston, 1831), and on p. 170 there is a note

twelve was a church member in the year 1820. The great majority of these were Methodists and Baptists, each numbering about 21,000 as compared with 2,700 Presbyterians, 1,000 Cumberland Presbyterians, and 500 of all other church members.[2] Ten years earlier the Catholic Church had six priests and an estimated membership of 16,000 in the Diocese of Kentucky, which covered a much larger area than the state of Kentucky.[3]

The numerical weakness of the churches was not offset by strength of leadership. In the largest of them, the Baptist and Methodist, there were no educational requirements for entering the ministry; and most preachers were distinguished for zeal rather than for learning. Furthermore, few of them could give undivided attention to their spiritual duties because they had to supplement their scanty pay by farming or some other occupation. Catholics, Episcopalians, and Presbyterians required an educated ministry and attempted to give reasonably adequate financial support to their clergymen. But the Catholics had little strength except in New Orleans and Baltimore, and the small number of Episcopal and Presbyterian clergymen may be gauged by the state of affairs in North Carolina. Only eight Episcopal clergymen were in that state in the year 1822, and only forty-six Presbyterian ministers together with five "Licentiates, or unordained Preachers." [4] There were not more than ten Presbyterian ministers in both Mississippi and Louisiana.[5]

But, though church members were only a small fraction of the total population and though most of the preachers were ill-fitted for positions of leadership, religion in the South was experiencing

---

about the sources of these data. See also, Henry S. Stroupe, "The Religious Press in the South Atlantic States, 1802–1865" (Ph.D. dissertation, Duke University, 1942), 71–72.

[2] William W. Sweet, *The Story of Religions in America* (New York, 1930), 311–12. In another work this author increases his estimate of Kentucky Baptists in 1820 by some ten thousand. *Religion on the American Frontier: The Baptists, 1783–1830* (New York, 1931), 26.

[3] *Mémoire présenté à Son Éminence le cardinal Fransoni préfet de la propagande par les ordres du souverain pontife, dans lequel j'expose l'état de mon diocèse en 1810, et celui où il est en 1836* (n. p., n. d.), 12.

[4] McIver, *North-Carolina Register . . . 1823*, pp. 92–99.

[5] William W. Sweet, *Religion on the American Frontier: The Presbyterians, 1783–1840* (New York, 1936), 52.

significant changes. In the first place, the cool hand of deism was being lifted from the religious thought of the region. True enough, deists and skeptics could be found in the 1820's, but those who professed to be such were fewer and less prominent than they had been a generation earlier. In 1836 President Thomas Roderick Dew of William and Mary College, an institution where the brighter students at the beginning of the century had regarded religion as base superstition, reported that "Avowed infidelity is now considered by the enlightened portion of the world as a reflection both on the head and heart . . . and he who now obtrudes on the social circle his infidel notions, manifests the arrogance of a literary coxcomb, or that want of refinement which distinguishes the polished gentleman." [6]

Perhaps the Unitarian churches that were being established in the larger Southern towns in the 1820's and 1830's were attracting some of those who might earlier have been regarded as deists: it is significant that Jefferson in 1822 expressed the hope that all the young men of his day would become Unitarians. But Unitarianism was not to attain the popularity in fashionable and intellectual circles that deism and skepticism had earlier possessed.[7] Furthermore, the strength of the Unitarians and of the surviving deists was small in the 1820's as compared with the growing popularity and influence of the fervent, emotional Methodists and Baptists. The philosophical, liberal strain was fading out of religion in the South; but the trend was not so much from liberalism to conservatism as it was from intellectualism to emotionalism.

A second trend that was in progress in 1820 was an emphasis upon a religion of works. Besides trying to be good, Christians were increasingly striving to do good, and out of their labors there was born an impressive array of agencies and organizations. One major accomplishment was the establishment of a religious press. Seventeen religious periodicals were founded within the states of Virginia, North Carolina, South Carolina, and Georgia during the 1820's

[6] *Southern Literary Messenger* (Richmond), II (1836), 768; Clement Eaton, *Freedom of Thought in the Old South* (Durham, 1940), 15–16, 280–85.

[7] Clarence Gohdes, "Some Notes on the Unitarian Church in the Ante-Bellum South: A Contribution to the History of Southern Liberalism," in David K. Jackson (ed.), *American Studies in Honor of William Kenneth Boyd, by Members of the Americana Club of Duke University* (Durham, 1940), 327–66.

besides ten that had earlier been established, all since the year 1802.[8] Although many of these journals died in early infancy, enough of them survived to become influential in shaping the opinions of church members about foreign affairs, political and social domestic questions, agricultural reform, and, of course, moral and religious issues.

Christian activity expressed itself chiefly in the creation of societies to support domestic and foreign missions, to encourage the distribution and reading of the Scriptures, to establish Sunday schools, to foster education in general, and to strive to bring about temperance, peace, and other desirable conditions. In the language of the times, the work of these organizations constituted the "benevolent movement," which aimed "at nothing more or less than the greatest good of our country. . . . [And it constituted] not the benevolence which exhausts itself in sighs and tears, and sentiments. . . . But . . . the benevolence of action." [9] The religious periodicals vigorously championed the benevolent movement. "In proportion as they increase in circulation," said a writer of the times, "the pulse of spiritual life begins to beat, and those who were before motionless, now become active in the cause of Christ." [10]

Local benevolent societies were ordinarily affiliated with the appropriate national organization. For example, the Mississippi Conference Missionary Society, which supported a missionary at Pensacola and another among the Choctaw Indians during the year 1824, was an affiliate of the national Missionary Society of the Methodist Episcopal Church.[11] In view of later developments, it is significant that Southern Christians were willing to co-operate with Northern Christians in denominational and charitable enterprises.

Any attempt to describe Southern education in the 1820's must begin with a recognition of the fact that there was no systematic

8 Stroupe, "Religious Press in the South Atlantic States," 61.

9 Fayetteville *North Carolina Telegraph*, May 26, 1826, quoted *ibid.*, 85.

10 *The Christian Almanac for . . . 1825* (Charleston, n. d.), 14, quoted *ibid.*, 86.

11 Natchez *Mississippi State Gazette*, November 13, 1824; Stroupe, "Religious Press in the South Atlantic States," Chap. IV. The numerous annual reports and other publications of the local societies throw much light on their relationships to national organizations. These reports can best be sought through the lists of early printed materials prepared by Douglas C. McMurtrie. For a guide to these lists, see Charles F. Heartman, *McMurtrie Imprints, A Bibliography of Separately Printed Writings by Douglas C. McMurtrie . . .* (Hattiesburg, Miss., 1942).

hierarchy of schools. The lack of standardization is indicated by the bewildering variety of names: grammar schools, private schools, public schools, common schools, primary schools, free schools, old-field schools, institutes, academies, seminaries, collegiate institutes, colleges, universities, and some others. Furthermore, the name of an institution frequently indicated what it had once been or what the teacher or trustees hoped it would become rather than what it then was. Speaking of the two Maryland colleges, St. John's and Washington, a legislative committee in 1820 reported that they had sunk to the level of "respectable academies, or schools of the second grade." [12] Jefferson College in Mississippi fluctuated between academy and college status, and sometimes taught the most elementary subjects.[13] Many Georgia academies, so it was charged in 1837, "are misnamed; for an academy supposes instruction in the higher branches of education; but some are no better than 'old field schools.' " [14]

Generally speaking, there were three stages in education. In the first, reading, writing, and arithmetic "through the rule of three" were taught by parents, tutors, governesses, spinster aunts, or in schools variously known as primary, common, or old-field schools. If the teacher was competent and willing, more advanced subjects might be taught to a few of the older pupils. The school building was frequently a log cabin, and the staff was usually a single teacher who was paid by the parents of the pupils.[15]

At the second level, emphasis was placed on Latin, Greek, and mathematics, and the schools that taught at this level were usually called academies. They were ordinarily incorporated by a legislative act which vested control in a board of trustees. Like the more elementary schools, academies were chiefly supported by tuition fees, but a few of them had some endowment. Among the best was David

---

[12] Maryland *Senate Journal*, 1819–1820, p. 45.

[13] Charles S. Sydnor, *A Gentleman of the Old Natchez Region: Benjamin L. C. Wailes* (Durham, 1938), 48–51, 204–206.

[14] Adiel Sherwood, *A Gazeteer of the State of Georgia* (2d ed.; Philadelphia, 1829), 241.

[15] For a contemporary outline of the three levels of education, see Maryland *Senate Journal*, 1819–1820, pp. 45–47; for descriptions of one-teacher schools, see [Augustus B. Longstreet], *Georgia Scenes, Characters, Incidents, etc. in the First Half Century of the Republic* (Augusta, 1835), 76–85; Philip H. Gosse, *Letters from Alabama, (U.S.) Chiefly Relating to Natural History* (London, 1859), 43–45.

Caldwell's school in Guilford County, North Carolina, and one conducted at Willington in upcountry South Carolina by Moses Waddel. Both of these men were Presbyterian ministers. At times Waddel had more than two hundred students, some of whom, such as William H. Crawford, Hugh S. Legaré, George McDuffie, James L. Petigru, and John C. Calhoun, did great credit to their teacher.[16] But these two schools were far ahead of most academies in size, influence, and length of life. Many academies had only a single teacher, and he was likely to be a minister. Hardly ever did the teacher have more than one or two assistants. As for numbers, thirty-one academies were chartered in Georgia before the year 1820,[17] and fifty-two were reported in North Carolina in the year 1822.[18] It must be remembered, however, that a good many academies did not merit their names.

A major indictment of this regime in which parents were expected to make all arrangements for the education of their children was the cloud of ignorance that lay heavy over much of the South. During the 1830's various persons estimated that about a third of the adult white people of Alabama, Louisiana, Virginia, and North Carolina were illiterate,[19] and there is no reason to think that conditions were better in other slave states.

Many Southerners were much disturbed by this state of affairs,

16 John D. Wade, *Augustus Baldwin Longstreet* (New York, 1924), 23–24; sketch of Moses Waddel, in Allen Johnson, Dumas Malone, and Harris E. Starr (eds.), *Dictionary of American Biography* (New York, 1928–1944), XIX, 300.

17 Edgar W. Knight, *Public Education in the South* (Boston, 1922), 89.

18 McIver, *North-Carolina Register . . . 1823*, pp. 61–64.

19 George W. Pierson, *Tocqueville and Beaumont in America* (New York, 1938), 641; Eaton, *Freedom of Thought in the Old South*, 64–67; and several documents quoted in Charles L. Coon (ed.), *The Beginnings of Public Education in North Carolina: A Documentary History, 1790–1840* (Raleigh, 1908), I, 454; II, 550–52, 600–602.
Governor David Campbell of Virginia sought information from the county clerks as to the number of applicants for marriage licenses who could not sign their names. A tabulation of the clerks' replies showed:

Year	Number of licenses granted	Number who could not write
1817	4,682	1,127
1827	5,048	1,166
1837	4,614	1,047

Campbell pointed out that there was no significant improvement in this twenty-year period, and, secondly, that "the education of females it is to be feared is in a condition of much greater neglect" than that of men. Only males were required to sign applications. Virginia *House Journal*, 1839, Doc. No. 1, pp. 3, 9–10.

and hardly any proposition was more widely supported in pulpit, press, and legislative halls than that the educational situation was bad and that it ought to be improved. There were some who believed that better schools would bring about an improvement in morality and religion. Others stressed the usefulness of knowledge to the individual. Governor Thomas Mann Randolph of Virginia quaintly observed: "Man is every day taught, by the accidents and sufferings of life, to rely upon the knowledge he can acquire of those laws [of nature] for his safety, health and comfort, for the extension of his limited power over nature, and the means of diminishing his humiliating imbecility." [20]

But the good of the democratic state rather than of the man was usually emphasized. As was said before the North Carolina legislature: "the education of youth [is] the only durable basis of every thing valuable in a government of the people, . . . It is the boast of a republican government that all men are born equal; but . . . let the few monopolize the science of the country and they at once monopolize its sovereignty." [21] Pointing to the Old World in warning, Governor Thomas Bennett of South Carolina asserted that "The despotisms of continental Europe have borrowed their energies from the ignorance of those they govern: but in our own free and happy country, all moral and physical stability is proportioned to the cultivation of the mind. This is at once the safeguard of the liberties we now enjoy, and the prolific source of future greatness." [22]

A few men were so bold as to propose that government ought to provide schools for all children. Shortly before and during the 1820's a dwarfed and crippled form of this dream was enacted into law in most of the Southern states. South Carolina under the terms of an act passed in 1811 created local officials known as commissioners of free schools whose duty it was to establish separate schools for poor children or, as an alternative, to make arrangements for entering them in existing private schools. South Carolina was more

20 Message of December 4, 1820, in Virginia *Senate Journal*, 1820, p. 7.

21 North Carolina *House Journal*, 1819, pp. 7–8.

22 Quoted in South Carolina *Reports and Resolutions of the General Assembly*, 1847, p. 232. Pages 195–245 contain an important collection of documents about the early history of education in South Carolina. For sentiments similar to Governor Thomas Bennett's, see Georgia *House Journal*, 1820, p. 5.

generous toward education than most of the Southern states in that it appropriated nearly $40,000 a year for this purpose during the 1820's and 1830's. Furthermore, it allowed nonpaupers to be educated at public expense provided not all the appropriation was needed for educating paupers. But this was an unpopular arrangement. One of the governors warned in 1822 that "The bounty of the state should not be permitted to paralyze individual exertion." [23]

Virginia, by an act of 1810 that was radically revised in 1818, created an endowment called the literary fund. So did a number of other states in the years ahead. Literary funds were variously accumulated from escheats, fines, forfeitures, bank and internal-improvement stock, taxes, state-owned land, and refunds and land grants from the Federal government. On October 1, 1819, the Virginia literary fund amounted to $977,000 of invested capital and $208,000 of "disposable funds." During the previous twelve months the fund had produced an income of $63,000, and out of this sum $42,000 had been disbursed to school commissioners for the education of indigent children.[24]

By laws passed in 1822 and 1823 Georgia created a poor-school fund, spending $20,000 for the education of paupers in existing elementary schools and academies; and Tennessee established a literary fund in 1823. At one time its prospects were good, for Tennessee had much public land; but most of this property was squandered through mismanagement.[25] The young state of Mississippi started a literary fund in 1821 with the proviso that neither principal nor interest was to be used until it amounted to $50,000. That point was reached in 1833, and the legislature then ordered it to be invested in stock of the Planters' Bank of Mississippi. A literary fund was created in Kentucky in 1821 and in North Carolina in 1825, and the states of Alabama, Louisiana, and Maryland were attempting in various ways to provide elementary education for poor children in the 1820's. The Maryland budget for the year 1819 in-

[23] South Carolina *Reports and Resolutions,* 1847, pp. 232-33, *passim; Acts and Resolutions,* 1819, pp. 9, 60, and folded sheet following p. 60.

[24] A detailed report of the "President and Directors of the Literary Fund" is in Virginia *House Journal,* 1819, pp. 183-84.

[25] Besides Knight, *Public Education in the South,* 135-38, see Nashville *Whig,* October 17, 1821; Tennessee *House Journal,* 1831, pp. 311-13, 410.

cluded an item of $11,900 described as "donations to colleges, academies and schools." [26] Louisiana, under a system operative since 1811, appropriated $600 a year, later increased to $800, to each parish for the support of grammar schools. Appropriations in 1824 for education amounted to $27,670.[27]

The following condensation of a routine report made by "The Administrators of Public Schools in the Parish of East Baton Rouge," Louisiana, shows in some detail how state funds were used to educate poor children; and it further shows that considerably more than half of the children in this parish were not attending school.[28]

Wards	Teachers	Pupils who pay	Pupils for whom the state pays	Amount paid by state	Total taught	Children of proper age to be taught
1	2	41	4	$ 32	45	94
2	2	19	26	209	45	124
3	—	—	no school	—	—	—
4	1	12	3	30	15	60
5	1	9	6	72	15	35

In one way or another the system of public education was defective in nearly every Southern state. In South Carolina the wealth of a district, measured by its payment of taxes into the state treasury, was as important as its population in determining its share of free-school funds. Thus, the District of Spartanburg received only $1,500 whereas the wealthier parishes of St. Philip's and St. Michael's received $5,100; yet Spartanburg contained more voters and presumably contained more needy children.[29] Discrimination against the poor was charged in other states. The plain farmers of Tennessee wanted common schools, and they alleged that colleges existed for the rich. In the course of a controversy over education it

26 Annapolis *Maryland Gazette and Political Intelligencer*, February 1, 1819. For data on subsidies to education a few years later, see Maryland *House Journal*, 1825–1826, pp. 35–36.

27 Louisiana *Senate Journal*, 1820–1821, pp. 11–13; Louisiana *House Journal*, 1824–1825, p. 95.

28 Summarized from the full report for twelve wards, dated December 31, 1827, in Baton Rouge *Gazette*, January 5, 1828.

29 South Carolina *Reports and Resolutions*, 1847, p. 206.

was said that "We are . . . a divided people, and distinguished in our rules of policy by sectional feelings and principles." [30] In Virginia a citizen of the West wrote: "We blame not the aristocracy of the East nor the memory of Mr. Jefferson for erecting and liberally endowing one great Eastern university . . . we only blame them for not granting similar favors to the West and good common schools to the whole country." [31]

There were other criticisms. It was alleged that the poor-relief system of education humiliated the children whom it sought to aid and thereby kept most of them from attending school. Another evil in the system was remarked by two of the governors of South Carolina, one of whom observed that it had become "a reproach to be a teacher of a Free School, as it is regarded [as] *prima facie* evidence of a want of qualification," [32] while the other asserted that the free-school fund had "in fact, been perverted, in many instances, into the support of indigent and incompetent school-masters." [33]

The sorry state of public education was due to the inherent difficulty of providing education for a thinly scattered population, to an insufficient number of competent teachers, to the unwillingness of the taxpayers to support a full-fledged public-school system, to competition for state funds among advocates of schools, roads, canals, and banks, and to an inadequate administrative system. Ordinarily, state administration was left to the governor or to a legislative committee, and therefore for all practical purposes the state school system lacked "a superintending head, a director, a centre of communication, of accountability, of responsibility." [34] The local school

[30] Nashville *Whig*, June 20, 1821; Thomas P. Abernethy, "Andrew Jackson and Southwestern Democracy," in *American Historical Review* (New York), XXXIII (1927–1928), 70.

[31] Quoted in William A. Maddox, *The Free School Idea in Virginia before the Civil War*, in Teachers College, Columbia University, *Contributions to Education*, No. 93 (New York, 1918), 96.

[32] Governor B. K. Henagan, November 24, 1840, in South Carolina *Reports and Resolutions*, 1847, p. 242.

[33] Governor George McDuffie, November 24, 1835, *ibid.*, 1847, p. 237. For the strictures of Governor Bennett, see *ibid.*, 1847, pp. 232–33. The weaknesses of the elementary educational program in Virginia were analyzed by Governor Thomas M. Randolph, December 4, 1820, in Virginia *Senate Journal*, 1820, p. 8; and numerous criticisms of the North Carolina system are in Coon (ed.), *Beginnings of Public Education in North Carolina*, II, 559–64, and elsewhere.

[34] South Carolina *Reports and Resolutions*, 1847, p. 216.

commissioners, acting without much guidance except the text of the law and serving usually without compensation, were expected to decide which children needed aid, to arrange for their education, to handle funds made available by the state, and to make periodic reports. Though the commissioners were often notoriously lax in performing their duties, only one penalty was imposed upon a school commissioner in South Carolina within a twelve-year period. In that instance, a commissioner was fined for failure to attend a meeting, and he instantly resigned his office.[35]

For college education, a good many Southern youth went to the North or to England. In 1820 there were fifty at Harvard, which was popular in South Carolina; forty-seven at Yale, which attracted students chiefly from South Carolina and Georgia; and forty-two at Princeton, mostly from Virginia and North Carolina. Maryland students were enrolled in all three of these institutions. Southern students also attended the University of Pennsylvania, Columbia, Brown, the United States Military Academy, as well as some of the medical schools and academies in the North.[36] In 1822 a Virginia magazine estimated that "during the last twenty years about $300,-000 a year has been carried from Virginia for purposes of education." [37]

Within the Southern states there were not many more than a dozen colleges and universities in 1820, and several of them were having a struggle to keep open. William and Mary, the oldest, had only 11 students in 1824; [38] Hampden-Sydney was turning out no more than 4 or 5 graduates a year; [39] and Transylvania, which was perhaps the most flourishing, had 140 students in the year 1819.[40] Unless the boys in the preparatory departments of the colleges be counted, the total number of students in Southern colleges in 1820 was probably less than 1,000.

An amazingly large share of this small annual crop of college

[35] *Ibid.*, 215.

[36] Charles F. Thwing, *History of Higher Education in America* (New York, 1906), 254–55.

[37] *Evangelical and Literary Magazine* (Richmond), V (1822), 89.

[38] Alma P. Foerster, "The State University in the Old South" (Ph.D. dissertation, Duke University, 1939), 134, n. 12.

[39] Hampden-Sydney, *General Catalogue of Officers and Students, 1776–1906* (Hampden-Sydney, Va. [1908]), 4, 46–57.

[40] Foerster, "State University in the Old South," 169–70.

students became leaders in education, law, politics, the ministry, and other fields in the 1830's, 1840's, and 1850's.[41] Furthermore, a large per cent of the political leadership of the year 1820 had attended college even though there had been only one college in the South when some of the older public men had been of college age. Forty per cent of the 111 Representatives and Senators from the Southern states in the Sixteenth Congress (1819–1821) were college men, and nearly 30 per cent had graduated. Most of them were alumni of Episcopal and Presbyterian institutions, especially William and Mary and Princeton; only a few had attended a state university, and four of these had studied at the University of North Carolina when it was under strong Presbyterian influence. They had attended Northern and Southern institutions in almost equal numbers.[42]

All of the Southern colleges were allied either with church or state in the year 1820; and the church colleges, with the single exception of the College of Georgetown, founded by the Catholics in 1815, were under Presbyterian or Episcopal influence. The Episcopalians continued to have some influence over William and Mary in Virginia, Washington and St. John's colleges in Maryland, and the College of Charleston in South Carolina. All four of these institutions were in coastal towns, and all were in tidewater areas that had been settled early; but none of them was in a flourishing condition. Presbyterians had established Hampden-Sydney and Washington College (now Washington and Lee University) in Virginia and Transylvania in Kentucky. After losing control over Transylvania, the Kentucky Presbyterians established Centre College. Members of this denomination founded three colleges in Tennessee: Greeneville (now Tusculum), Cumberland, and East Tennessee (earlier known as Blount and subsequently evolving into the University of Tennessee). All of these, in contrast to the Episcopal colleges, were far in the interior, most of them were in sight of the mountains, and some were remote from any town. Their lot was cast with the Scotch-Irish upcountry rather than with the lowlands.

41 The alumni catalogues and histories of the institutions strongly support this statement. Some data are presented in Albea Godbold, *The Church College of the Old South* (Durham, 1944), 196–97.

42 These statements are derived from material in the *Biographical Directory of the American Congress, 1774–1927.*

65

Except for Centre College and the eighteenth-century College of William and Mary, all of the colleges, Episcopal and Presbyterian alike, had been founded about the time of the American Revolution, and they were no older in 1820 than some of the men who were teaching in them.[43]

Younger by half than the church colleges were the institutions of higher education that had been established by the states, namely, the University of North Carolina, the University of Georgia, the College of South Carolina, the College of Orleans, and the University of Maryland. Instead of founding new institutions, Kentucky had in a measure taken over Transylvania, and Tennessee had adopted Cumberland and East Tennessee. Jefferson College in Mississippi received some assistance from the state and from the Federal government.[44] Besides these chartered institutions, there were a few others, like Salem and Guilford in North Carolina, which, though yet unauthorized to grant degrees, were making substantial contributions to higher education.

Of the institutions that were related to the state, only Transylvania and the University of Maryland with their strong medical schools and South Carolina College with its fixed income and secular, rationalistic spirit differed in any important respect from the church colleges. For all practical purposes, the Tennessee colleges, the University of North Carolina, and the University of Georgia were Presbyterian colleges. Neither they nor the church colleges received much support from either church or state, and the institutions of both kinds were usually controlled by self-perpetuating boards of trustees and were mainly staffed by ministers. The burden of higher education was being carried by individual Christians

[43] Unless otherwise noted, this discussion of Southern colleges and universities is based on Foerster, "State University in the Old South"; Godbold, *Church College of the Old South;* and Donald G. Tewksbury, *The Founding of American Colleges and Universities before the Civil War,* in Teachers College, Columbia University, *Contributions to Education,* No. 543 (New York, 1932), 32–54, *passim.*

[44] Tewksbury, *Founding of American Colleges and Universities,* 32–37, gives charter dates and some other information about all of these institutions except Cumberland and Jefferson. For the former, see Foerster, "State University in the Old South," 39–42; and for the latter, Sydnor, *Benjamin L. C. Wailes,* 48–51, 204. In comparing charter dates it should be noted that the church colleges were usually in operation before their charters were granted; the state universities usually did not open until some years after they had been chartered.

rather than by organizations, and the load rested chiefly upon the presidents, professors, and trustees.

The curriculums of the church colleges and of most of the state universities were essentially the same. Latin, Greek, and mathematics were the core; however, students were expected to have laid a good foundation in these subjects in the academy so that their college study of the classics could rise above the level of grammar and of stumbling translation and at least border on the study of literature, philosophy, and religion. The college curriculum included, especially in the upper classes, philosophy, science, and other studies. The usual courses in philosophy were mental philosophy, moral philosophy, and logic. Those in science were ordinarily known as natural philosophy, which included physics and chemistry, and natural history, which dealt with zoology, botany, mineralogy, and geology. Astronomy and geography were sometimes taught. Naturally, the work in the sciences reflected the immaturity of the times in respect to scientific knowledge. The colleges also offered, though with less uniformity, courses in "the law of nature and nations," political philosophy, general history, chronology, English grammar and composition, rhetoric, belles-lettres, agriculture, surveying, and navigation. The institutions differed somewhat from one another, but the church colleges as well as the state institutions included within their curriculums much more than the classical trilogy of Latin, Greek, and mathematics.[45]

Each of the institutions regarded its schedule of studies as a fixed program that students ought to follow; for faculties and trustees thought they knew better than students what courses young men ought to study. Nevertheless, irregular students were tolerated, but pains were taken to point out that "by *irregular students* are meant such as do not pursue systematic courses of study. It is by no means intended that any student shall be *irregular* as to moral conduct." [46]

In physical plant, most of the colleges consisted of one or two

[45] For samples of curriculums, see Alfred J. Morrison, *The College of Hampden-Sidney: Calendar of Board Minutes, 1776–1876* (Richmond, 1912), especially pp. 73–74, 93–95; Jefferson College, *Laws of Jefferson College, Located in the Town of Washington, State of Mississippi* (Natchez, 1820); and McIver, *North-Carolina Register . . . 1823*, pp. 59–61, which gives the University of North Carolina curriculum. For curriculums of the 1840's, see Godbold, *Church College of the Old South*, 191–94.

[46] Jefferson College, *Laws*, 1820, p. 8.

rather plain, rectangular brick buildings which contained class-
rooms and sleeping quarters of the students. Near at hand were
several faculty homes and the steward's house where most of the
students boarded. To judge from their letters home, the steward's
table was at best plain and monotonous. The cost of "Board, etc."
at the University of North Carolina was from $13 to $15 a month.
Tuition was $30 a year.[47]

The daily schedule began with prayers at sunrise, which were
sometimes followed by one recitation before breakfast. Classes
ordinarily met from nine to twelve in the morning and from two
to four in the afternoon. Evening prayers were at five, and by eight
o'clock all students were expected to be in their rooms studying.[48]
Instead, however, they sometimes amused themselves "throwing
logs of wood from the upper stories to the great injury of the house,
and evidently endangering the life of individuals; taking the bell
out of the teachers room, secreting it, and ringing it at an unseason-
able hour of the night." [49]

In literary societies with mouth-filling names like Demosthenian,
Philanthropic, Eutraphelian, and Philomathesian, students learned
parliamentary procedure, practiced public speaking, and debated
current questions as well as timeworn topics that perennially intrigue youthful minds. Some of the societies founded libraries, and
most of them enlivened the college community with their public
debates and their social occasions. The fact that the highest and
almost the only extracurricular honors attainable by college students lay in the field of oratory and debating helps to explain certain of the characteristics of Southern leadership in the years ahead.

The faculty usually consisted of a president who carried a heavy
teaching load along with his other duties, two or three professors,
and a tutor to conduct the preparatory department. Inasmuch as
the large majority of faculty members had been educated in the
North and were natives of the North as well, they tended to make
the Southern colleges approximate their alma maters. Therein was
one of the reasons why the state university was so much like the

[47] McIver, *North-Carolina Register* . . . *1823*, pp. 59, 61.

[48] Foerster, "State University in the Old South." 119–20.

[49] Morrison, *College of Hampden-Sidney: Calendar of Board Minutes, 1776–1876*,
p. 68.

denominational college: both were patterned after such Northern colleges as Princeton, Yale, and Harvard.

Among the Northern colleges, Princeton was by far the most influential over Southern education. It was the alma mater of most of the teachers and presidents of the Southern colleges in the early 1820's, and it was, in a sense, the grandparent of other faculty members who had studied at a Southern college where the Princeton tradition was strong. Most of these Princeton teachers in the South had studied mental and moral philosophy—the college subjects that bore most directly on questions of personal conduct and social behavior—with Princeton's great president, John Witherspoon; and the foundation of many a course on these subjects in Southern colleges was a manuscript or later a printed copy of Witherspoon's lectures.[50] Through Witherspoon, one of the main roots in the family tree of Southern education went back to the common-sense philosophy and Calvinistic theology of Scotland. This Scotch Presbyterian influence was reinforced in the generation that came after Witherspoon. Robert Henry, professor of logic and ethics at South Carolina College, of whom it was said that he taught South Carolinians to think, had studied for some years at Edinburgh. And James Henley Thornwell, a leading Presbyterian theologian and a president of this same college in the 1830's, was a close student and exponent of Scottish common-sense philosophy and of conservative Calvinism.[51] If there be such a thing as a Presbyterian type of mind, Southern college boys were brought into close contact with it in the early nineteenth century.

Scarcely any new colleges were opened in the South during the 1820's except the University of Virginia in the year 1825. However, several that had been dormant were revived near the beginning of the decade and some others experienced considerable growth. Transylvania reached an enrollment of four hundred students in the year 1825 and became for a short time one of the largest colleges in the nation. The same zeal for educational improvement that led the states to arrange for the common-school education of paupers was

[50] Donald R. Come, "The Influence of Princeton on Higher Education in the South before 1825," in *William and Mary Quarterly* (Williamsburg), third series, II (1945), 359–96.

[51] Paul L. Garber, "The Religious Thought of James Henley Thornwell" (Ph.D. dissertation, Duke University, 1939).

partly responsible for this revivifying and expansion of state institutions of higher learning. Higher education was fortunate in not being fitted into a poor-relief program. Instead, government showed its interest in its colleges near the beginning of the 1820's by replacing some of the self-perpetuating boards of trustees with boards chosen by the legislatures. In some states the governor was made an ex-officio member of the board. The states also provided modest amounts of money for buildings, books, scientific equipment, and, in some instances, for ordinary running expenses. In 1819 the University of Georgia began to receive an annual income of $8,000 as interest on funds received from the sale of its lands, and the state appropriated $25,000 for buildings. For several years Kentucky made annual grants to Transylvania ranging from $3,000 to $10,000 for books and equipment. Small appropriations were made to the two Tennessee institutions for the purchase of scientific apparatus. South Carolina College was granted $14,000 a year. The wealthiest of them all was the University of Virginia with an annual income from the state of $15,000 besides initial loans of $200,000 for buildings and equipment.[52]

Furthermore, some of the state colleges were cutting loose from Northern leadership and from ecclesiastical influences. The trustees of the University of Georgia chose for president Moses Waddel, the master of Willington Academy, who had graduated from Hampden-Sydney rather than from one of the Northern colleges. True enough, Waddel was a Presbyterian minister who intended to use his new office "to communicate to public education the spirit of Christianity"; [53] but some of his contemporaries in the other colleges were not closely tied to any of the denominations or to the colleges of the North. Thomas Cooper at South Carolina College was anticlerical, and he was a transplanted Englishman. The first faculty of the University of Virginia consisted of five Englishmen, a German, and two Americans. A few years later the University of North Carolina departed widely from the usual pattern when it chose former Governor David L. Swain as its president. Swain was neither a minister nor a graduate of a Northern college. Indeed, he had had

[52] Foerster, "State University in the Old South," 133–38, 155, 169–70, 182–86, 202–207; South Carolina *Acts and Resolutions*, 1819, folded sheet following p. 60; Louisiana *Senate Journal*, 1820–1821, pp. 11–13.
[53] Quoted in Foerster, "State University in the Old South," 162.

little connection with any academic hall, for he was a self-taught man whose life had been spent chiefly in political activities.

There was some broadening of the curriculum. An increasing interest in science was illustrated by the election to the faculty of the University of North Carolina of Denison Olmsted and Elisha Mitchell both of whom had studied at Yale with Benjamin Silliman; and there was a growing interest in modern languages, particularly at Virginia and Transylvania. While some of these developments are to be accounted for by educational trends in the North and abroad, one must not overlook the educational philosophy and the activities of several men who were laboring in the South, especially Philip Lindsley at Cumberland College, Thomas Cooper at South Carolina College, Horace Holley at Transylvania, and Thomas Jefferson in Virginia.

Lindsley was obviously looking to the future rather than to the present when he refused the presidency of Princeton to come to Cumberland in the year 1824, for Cumberland then had only thirty students. He firmly believed that a university ought to change and expand so as to keep pace with social and economic changes; and he was constantly preaching this philosophy on the platform and on the printed page. He wanted physical education to be given a place in the colleges; he made plans for lifting the teaching profession from its lowly state and making it into "an honorable calling and profession"; and he thought that a university should provide education in agriculture, horticulture, civil and military engineering as well as in the liberal and mechanical arts. He saw no reason why the West should not build a university that would exceed any in the East. But though he changed the name of his institution from Cumberland College to the University of Nashville, brought it some reputation throughout the South and West, and accomplished some improvements, few of his great dreams were realized.[54]

While Lindsley aimed at expansion and multiplication of courses, Cooper was chiefly concerned with establishing in South Carolina a spirit of experimental, untrammeled, scientific inquiry. His open hostility to ministers and to the church subjected him to much criticism before his retirement in 1834. But before this came to pass, he had exerted great influence. His lectures in political economy and

[54] *Ibid.*, 165-66, 176, 178, 187, 199-200, 206-208.

history dealt with South Carolina problems, and his bold approach to public questions paved the way for much of the subsequent political thought of the state. South Carolina College became the center of political as well as of educational thought in its state to a degree unequaled by any other state institution in the South. Thornwell, who succeeded Cooper, asserted that South Carolina College had made the state and its people what they were.[55]

Holley, who was made president of Transylvania in 1819, shortly after the Presbyterians had lost control, was a Boston Unitarian. More tactful than Cooper and less of a dreamer and speechmaker than Lindsley, Holley was somewhat more successful in making his institution into a university. During his presidency Transylvania consisted of a department of moral philosophy, a school of law, and a school of medicine as well as of a grammar school. The medical school, with such faculty members as Doctors Samuel Brown, Charles Caldwell, Benjamin Dudley, and Daniel Drake, became one of the best and largest medical schools in the United States, attracting 281 students in the year 1826. According to its advertisements, special attention was given to diseases that were most frequent in the Southwest.[56]

Overshadowing Holley, Cooper, and Lindsley was Thomas Jefferson, whose influence on the movement to bind state and education together is to be measured both in the creation of the University of Virginia and in his conversations and writings over a good part of the previous half century. He exchanged ideas with Holley and Cooper, especially the latter; Lindsley's program expressed many Jeffersonian thoughts; and Archibald De Bow Murphey proposed for North Carolina, though in vain, an educational system similar to that which Jefferson had advocated in Virginia.[57]

The only part of Jefferson's educational plan which was given a reasonable trial in Virginia in his day was the University of Virginia. Its distinction, aside from its physical appearance and its early and rapid growth, consisted in the nature and organization of

[55] Dumas Malone, *The Public Life of Thomas Cooper, 1783–1839* (New Haven, 1926), 253, 260–74, 290–305.

[56] Foerster, "State University in the Old South," 163–65, 169–70, 187–93, 203–204, 209.

[57] *Ibid.*, 166–67, 208–209. Murphey's proposals can be conveniently found in Coon (ed.), *Beginnings of Public Education in North Carolina*, I, 105–11, 123–46.

its curriculum, the quality of its faculty, its faith in the honor and judgment of the students, and the attempt to make education serve practical purposes as well as nurture a genteel culture.

With the hope of securing teachers of international distinction who could construct a university that would differ in kind as well as in quality from the prevailing type of American college, Jefferson commissioned his young friend Francis Walker Gilmer to go abroad in search of a faculty.[58] Each of the eight professors was placed in charge of one of the schools into which the university was divided: ancient languages, modern languages, mathematics, natural philosophy, natural history, anatomy and medicine, moral philosophy, and law. Among these fields of study the students, who were expected to be of reasonable maturity, were free to select their work, usually attending the lectures of at least three professors each year. But all who sought a diploma from the university were required to study the ancient languages, for as Jefferson explained, "these languages . . . constitute a basis of good education and are indispensable to fill up the character of a 'well-educated man.' " [59] Among the noteworthy features of this curriculum were the range of subjects, the fact that modern languages were given an independent status, and the fact that half of the schools were devoted to the sciences and mathematics.

In contrast to the medical school at Transylvania, that at Virginia first taught medicine as a cultural rather than as a professional study. Nevertheless, its work included anatomical dissection and was in some respects superior to the work done in some of the professional medical schools. Likewise, the law school, although it offered work leading to the professional degree of "Barrister of Law," was not designed for the primary purpose of turning out practicing attorneys. Despite its name, the school of law was in large measure a school of government, designed to turn out political leaders and, if the fates were kind, a few statesmen.

In planning the buildings of the University of Virginia, Jefferson made his greatest contribution to the classical revival in Amer-

[58] Philip A. Bruce, *History of the University of Virginia, 1819–1919* (New York, 1920–1922), I, 334–76.
[59] Foerster, "State University in the Old South," 146; Bruce, *University of Virginia,* I, 322–34.

ican architecture. It was by no means his first, for his decision in the 1780's that the new capitol of Virginia should be patterned after a Roman temple was responsible for the creation of the first monument of the classical revival in America.[60] Through his subsequent work and through the architectural efforts of Benjamin H. Latrobe, Charles Bulfinch, William Thornton, and others, examples of classical architecture appeared in various parts of the nation, notably upon Capitol Hill in Washington. Jefferson was especially active in giving classical form to the Virginia plantation mansion, lavishing many years upon the development of his beloved Monticello and assisting his neighbors who were planning to build or who wished to transform their Georgian homes into the new style that was also very old.

Jefferson's originality in designing the campus of the University of Virginia consisted in combining the architectural patterns of the ancients with an educational philosophy which was modern and which was in large measure his own creation. Envisioning a university of distinct and semi-independent schools, he did not want to combine them after the prevailing custom of America and England into one or several monumental buildings. Instead, he planned a modest two-story building for each of his schools, with a hall below for classes and living quarters above for the professor and his family. These lodges, as he called them, he placed in two rows facing each other across a green lawn. Furthermore, to bring students and professors together in the close relationship that had proved so valuable to him as a student at William and Mary, he placed one-story dormitories in the spaces between the lodges. Down the entire length of each Lawn, as the two rows of lodges and dormitories were called, was a colonnaded way "to give a dry communication between all the parts." Two similar rows, known as Ranges, were built outside and parallel to the Lawns. The Lawns were joined at their higher end by a dominant Rotunda which served as a library. In arranging the units in his "academical village" Jefferson began with an educational idea rather than with a book of architectural plans; but in using Palladio's drawings to give classical façades to each of the lodges and in fronting each Lawn with white columns he was

[60] Fiske Kimball, *Thomas Jefferson and the First Monument of the Classical Revival in America* [Harrisburg, Washington, 1915], 5.

indulging his preference for classical architecture. Furthermore, he was helping to fix the classical revival upon academic architecture just as the Virginia and the national capitols had fixed it upon the monumental buildings of government.[61]

The classical revival reached South Carolina chiefly during the decade in which the University of Virginia was established. It was introduced by Robert Mills, a talented Carolinian who had studied with Jefferson and Latrobe. Mills converted the congregation of the First Baptist Church of Charleston and a number of other South Carolina congregations to the construction of church edifices after the style that was originally designed for worship by the Greeks and the Romans. Among the more notable of his secular buildings in South Carolina is the Record Building which is said to have been the first building of fireproof construction in America.[62]

As the classical revival moved inland from the coast, it became less Roman and more Greek. Furthermore, it seemed to gain popularity, especially in domestic architecture. The older towns along the coast had ended the period of their greatest growth at an earlier time, but the height of the classical revival coincided with the expansion of the cotton kingdom into the Southwest. The results of this coincidence are evident in the homes and public buildings of such towns as Athens, Macon, and Milledgeville, Georgia; Tuscaloosa, Huntsville, and Montgomery, Alabama; and Natchez, Columbus, and Holly Springs, Mississippi. Furthermore, the influence of the University of Virginia in establishing the classical form as the favorite type of academic architecture was reflected on the campuses of the universities of Georgia, Alabama, and Mississippi, at Davidson College, at what has come to be known as Washington and Lee University, and at other colleges and universities.[63]

Generalizations about Greek-revival architecture in the South must be made cautiously, for there is much to be learned about

[61] Bruce, *University of Virginia*, I, 179; Lewis Mumford, *The South in Architecture* (New York, 1941), Chap. II, "The Universalism of Thomas Jefferson."

[62] Helen M. Pierce Gallagher, *Robert Mills: Architect of the Washington Monument, 1781–1855* (New York, 1935), 51–52, 80–84.

[63] Talbot F. Hamlin, *Greek Revival Architecture in America* (New York, 1944), especially Chap. VIII, "The Provincial Greek Revival: in the Old South"; J. Frazer Smith, *White Pillars: Early Life and Architecture of the Lower Mississippi Valley Country* (New York, 1941).

American architectural history, and over this phase of Southern history the romanticists have placed a thick layer of extravagant sentiment.[64] Nevertheless, enough of the white-columned great houses can be found on the plantations and in the towns of the cotton South to set it off architecturally from Tidewater Virginia with its Georgian emphasis and from low-country South Carolina with its architectural diversity and uniqueness. Even though the Greek revival affected much of America, it may be that in the South the buildings of Greece and Rome, more often than elsewhere in America, found proper and harmonious settings.

[64] James C. Bonner, "Plantation Architecture of the Lower South on the Eve of the Civil War," in *Journal of Southern History* (Baton Rouge), XI (1945), 370–88, is a reminder that only a small share of the planters lived in Greek mansions.

CHAPTER IV

TOWARD A MORE PERFECT SOCIETY

STATE government in the early nineteenth century was chiefly concerned with protecting persons and property and maintaining a system in which individual conflicts could be settled in an orderly manner. It was little more than a protective shield behind which men could work out their own salvation; or could fail to do so. Not much attention was given to schemes for improving the economic and intellectual lot of the citizens, and scarcely any state funds were spent for such purposes.

Most state laws embodied minor amendments to the governmental structure of the state, the counties, and the towns. A few of them modified the body of civil and criminal law. There were many semiprivate acts incorporating religious, educational, and charitable societies or empowering individuals or companies to build roads, bridges, and ferries. Very rarely did the state appropriate funds for any of these purposes, though it sometimes authorized private individuals or corporations to hold lotteries or to charge fees for services rendered. In short, the state practically never initiated, planned, or supervised schools, roads, religious institutions, charity, or other such services for the people, though it permitted and in a measure encouraged private individuals to undertake these tasks. If a man wanted such things he had to rely upon his own or his neighbors' efforts, or upon his county or town, or upon incorporated private effort.[1]

To provide financial support for this relatively simple kind of

[1] For the character of state legislation the main source, of course, is the published laws of the several Southern states. An analysis of the legislation of one of them is in Fred N. Cleaveland, "Service Legislation of the North Carolina General Assembly from 1777 to 1835" (M.A. thesis, Duke University, 1942).

government the Southern states relied mostly upon taxes on land and slaves. The state tax rate in South Carolina was thirty-seven and one-half cents on each $100.00 of assessed valuation of land and urban buildings, and twice as much on all stock in trade. There was a poll tax of seventy-five cents on each slave, and of $2.00 on each free Negro between the ages of fifteen and fifty, unless he were a pauper. This schedule, which was known as the general taxes, produced $262,000 in the year ending on October 1, 1819, an amount which was considerably more than half of the state's income. The remainder was interest on stock of the United States, profits from the Bank of the State of South Carolina, and small sums, no one of which amounted to more than a few thousand dollars, derived from taxes on peddlers, plays, and shows, from fines and forfeitures collected by the county courts, and from other minor sources.[2]

Virginia's income was of similar origins. Most of it was produced by the general tax on land, slaves, horses, and carriages. A considerable amount came from bank stock and Federal securities that were owned by the state of Virginia. Besides, $66,000 was produced by a tax on merchants and peddlers and by license fees collected from keepers of ordinaries and houses of private entertainment; and something over $30,000 was derived from court fees.

The other Southern states likewise relied heavily on taxation on land and slaves. In addition, Kentucky enjoyed considerable revenue from land sales and from dividends on bank stock, Louisiana derived a sixth of its income from taxes on gambling houses and on lotteries, Maryland secured most of its income from investments and from a tax on lotteries, and Georgia received $55,000, which was about one fourth of its annual income, from bank-stock dividends.[3]

[2] South Carolina *Acts and Resolutions*, 1819, pp. 3–7, and the folded sheet following p. 60.

[3] Except as otherwise noted, this discussion of state finances is based on the fol lowing tabulations, reports, and estimates by state treasurers, comptrollers, governors, and legislative committees:

Maryland: statements for 1818 and estimates for 1819 in Annapolis *Maryland Gazette and Political Intelligencer*, February 1, 1819.

Virginia: report of joint committee of house and senate to examine the treasurer's accounts for the year ending September 30, 1819, in *House Journal*, 1819–1820, p. 119, and estimates for the following year, *ibid.*, 172–73.

South Carolina: comptroller general's statements for the year ending October 1, 1819, in *Acts and Resolutions*, 1819, table following p. 60.

Taxes were obviously designed to produce revenue rather than to regulate. Among the chief exceptions were license fees upon keepers of ordinaries and houses of private entertainment, upon retailers of spirituous liquors,[4] and upon hawkers and peddlers.

As for expenditures, a large share in all states was for salaries and contingent expenses of the legislative, executive, and judicial branches of government. Some of the states were putting considerable sums into debt liquidation or into investments that were expected to produce income. The total of other kinds of expenditures was small, sometimes amounting to hardly one tenth of the budget, and only in South Carolina, Georgia, and Virginia did it approach the halfway mark.

With expenditures restricted to little more than maintenance of the minimum activities of government, state budgets were small. In Maryland, North Carolina, Georgia, Kentucky, and Louisiana, annual expenditures were between $150,000 and $200,000. Mississippi spent only $40,000 while, at the other extreme, South Carolina spent $445,000 and Virginia $630,000 in the twelve months ending in the autumn of the year 1819. But in South Carolina and Virginia a large share of the amount was invested. South Carolina placed $171,000 in capital of the Bank of the State of South Carolina, and Virginia converted two thirds of an accumulated treasury balance of $390,000 into permanent investments. The following year the state of Georgia took a similar step.

Kentucky: report of the joint committee to examine the treasurer's accounts for the year ending November 10, 1819, in *House Journal*, 1819–1820, pp. 204–205, and "A Statement of Receipts and Expenditures at the Treasury of the State of Kentucky, from 1819 to 1829, inclusive," *ibid.*, 1829–1830, facing p. 166.

Louisiana: sketchy and uninformative abstracts from the treasurer's report for the year 1820 appear in *Journal de la Chambre des Representans*, 1820–1821, pp. 12, 62–63, and a detailed committee report on the accounts for 1824 in *House Journal*, 1824–1825, pp. 95–96.

Mississippi: some information about Mississippi finances for the year 1819 is in a message of Governor David Holmes, in *House Journal*, 1820, p. 12. A treasurer's report for the fourteen months ending on December 31, 1823, is in the Natchez *Mississippi State Gazette*, January 10, 1824.

North Carolina: information on the state of the North Carolina treasury for the year ending October 31, 1819, is in the *House Journal*, 1819, pp. 21–23.

Georgia: "An Abstract of the Treasury of the State of Georgia on the 31st October, 1820," a folded sheet following the title page of *Senate Journal*, 1820.

4 Annapolis *Maryland Gazette and Political Intelligencer*, February 1, 1819.

79

It is hardly necessary to say that the financial condition of the Southern states was excellent. Most of them were entirely free from debt, and none of the others was deeply involved. A number of them owned bank stock, Federal bonds, or other productive securities. Most of them were showing annual treasury balances ranging from $20,000 to $60,000.

But this condition was not to last much longer. State government was on the point of expanding its scope to embrace new and expensive activities, and this expansion was to raise problems of administration and finance as well as to challenge existing concepts of the proper bounds of state activity.

Some of the states muddled their way into expanded programs with little understanding of what they were doing, but here and there the merits of various proposals were discussed. Two questions were frequently raised: one was whether the undertaking was actually needed by the people, the other was whether the state treasury would receive returns from the expenditure.

To particularize, schools were generally regarded as urgent needs, but at the same time it was a known fact that they would cost much money and that they would not pay annual dividends. In contrast, banks, although they were regarded as less desirable, were producing considerable sums for the treasuries of most of the states; hence, it seemed reasonable to suppose that a state might invest its surpluses from year to year and eventually have an income from interest and dividends which would, in the words of a Maryland legislative committee, be "competent to all the purposes of government, without the imposition of any description of taxes whatever." [5] But while it was pleasing to contemplate a tax-free state, banks were not, according to the thinking of the day, nearly so needful as schools, and many persons regarded banks as positively injurious to society.

A third proposal, to use state funds for the construction of roads and canals, seemed to combine the good points of the two previous schemes. There was certainly a great need for better ways of getting cotton and tobacco to market and of bringing manufactured goods back to the farms. At the same time it seemed reasonable to expect a considerable return in the form of tolls. A Virginia governor ad-

[5] *Ibid.,* February 1, 1819.

vocated converting the state's holdings of bank stock into road, river, and canal stock in order, as he explained, for the people as well as the treasury to profit.[6]

Such reasoning helps to explain why transportation projects were generally supported while education received only small sums in the 1820's. The great need for state aid to education was not denied, but there was an implicit decision in the South Atlantic states to build roads first and then to support education more adequately. In the Southwest, where credit facilities were lacking and where natural waterways were fairly adequate, banks rather than internal improvements were usually given first place. Thus it was that some of the states invested part or all of their literary funds in bank stock or in internal improvement projects with the object, of course, of increasing the literary fund by dividend earnings and in the meantime of putting their capital to use in providing roads, canals, or banks.[7] The internal improvement program in the seaboard states and banks in the Southwest were thereby given priority in the expanding program of state activities, and they were made the foundation of the investment phase of state finance.

Although no two of the Southern states followed the same plan in respect to internal improvements, North Carolina's course contained many features that were common to the others. In the year 1815, the legislature first began to apply state funds to internal improvements by purchasing stock in a number of transportation companies, some new and some old. Most of these companies were endeavoring to make the Roanoke, the Tar, the Neuse, the Cape Fear, the Catawba, and the Yadkin rivers more navigable. Meanwhile, steps were taken to develop an integrated program for the state to follow. Hamilton Fulton was employed as state surveyor, and from

[6] Message of Governor Thomas M. Randolph, December 11, 1819, in Virginia *Senate Journal,* 1819–1820, p. 31. Nearly all the Southern governors were vigorous advocates of internal improvements at state expense. See their messages in the senate and house journals of the various states.

[7] The interrelation of the special funds with each other and with the general treasury accounts can be seen in most of the material cited previously in n. 3, and can be followed in similar materials for subsequent years. See, for example, the statements of Governor Gerard C. Brandon of November 16, 1830, concerning the investment of Mississippi state funds in bank stock which was then placed in the Literary Fund, Mississippi *House Journal,* November-December, 1830, pp. 9–10, and the report of the state treasurer on the condition of the Bank of Mississippi, *ibid.,* 44–51, 163.

time to time he made reports to the legislature. In 1819, Archibald De Bow Murphey, acting president of the North Carolina Board of Internal Improvements, published a thoughtful essay setting forth the transportation needs of various parts of the state and discussing the relationship between transportation, commerce, and the general economic well-being of North Carolina.[8]

Following suggestions in these documents, the legislature in 1819 established an internal-improvement fund to consist of income from state-owned stock in the banks of New Bern and Cape Fear and of proceeds from the sale of land recently acquired in the western part of the state from the Cherokee Indians. This fund was placed under the administration of a Board of Internal Improvements consisting of the governor and six commissioners elected by the legislature. The board purchased stock in public-works companies and made loans to some of them. Besides, it made outright appropriations for projects undertaken by special commissioners and by county courts. Most of the money was spent on attempts to improve natural waterways. Slightly more than half of all expenditures were in the eastern part of the state where there was less need than in the western. However, westerners on their way to market were helped by some of the improvements in the east. But none of them was of lasting benefit. By 1829 more than a quarter of a million dollars had been spent, and the fund was virtually exhausted due to declining income from bank stocks, difficulty in collecting from the purchasers of Cherokee lands, defalcations of the state treasurer, and failure of most of the internal-improvement companies to pay dividends to the state.[9]

South Carolina's experience was similar except that it plunged more deeply, spending $1,000,000 in the four years ending in 1822 and nearly $500,000 more in the next six years. At one time more than a thousand workmen who had been brought down from the North were employed by the Board of Public Works. The work consisted chiefly in constructing canals, dams, locks, and sluices at and above the fall line on the Wateree, Congaree, Saluda, and other

[8] Archibald De Bow Murphey, *Memoir on the Internal Improvements Contemplated by the Legislature of North-Carolina; and on the Resources and Finances of That State* (Raleigh, 1819); Meyer, *Transportation in the United States,* 273.

[9] Boyd, *North Carolina: The Federal Period,* 91–99; Cleaveland, "Service Legislation of the North Carolina General Assembly," *passim.*

rivers. By the year 1825 it was possible for a boat loaded with forty bales of cotton to descend from near Abbeville "all the way to Charleston, passing 3 canals and ten locks on the Saluda, 1 canal and 5 locks on the Congaree, and the 13 locks of the Santee Canal, making a total descent of 207 feet." [10] In addition, a major highway, known as the State Road, was built from Charleston to Columbia and somewhat farther westward.

In 1828 the ten-year period of heavy expenditures for canals and roads in South Carolina came to a close. Soon afterward the State Road fell into complete neglect; it had never been in first-rate condition and toll fees had been too high for most people to pay. For example, it cost $9.00 to take a four-horse wagon over this road from Charleston to Columbia and back again. A scant twenty years later Governor David Johnson asserted that all the canals constructed around the rapids "at an immense expense" had, with a single exception, "proved entirely useless." [11] The state of Georgia engaged in a similar attempt to provide water transportation for its citizens, but, being warned by the experiences of South Carolina, it proceeded cautiously and did not spend nearly so much money.

Maryland and Virginia were likewise striving to provide waterways for their back-country farmers, but in these two states there was a second and greater object in view: to push transportation lines far enough westward to tap the Ohio and Mississippi Valley and to secure at least a share of its great commerce. The Eastern cities were the chief promoters of such plans. Baltimore, Georgetown, and Richmond each dreamed of becoming the entrepôt of the West, and each understood that it was in competition with the others and with the cities of Pennsylvania and New York.

Virginia's main hope for establishing an all-water route from Richmond to the Ohio lay in improving navigation on the James and Kanawha rivers and in joining them by a canal. The scheme had the further advantage of promising to benefit residents of the James and Shenandoah valleys and of parts of western Virginia. A

10 Meyer, *Transportation in the United States*, 257.

11 Message to the legislature, November 29, 1847, in South Carolina *Reports and Resolutions*, 1847, p. 163. The documents on this phase of South Carolina history can be consulted in David Kohn (comp. and ed.), *Internal Improvement in South Carolina, 1817–1828* (Washington, 1938), and a brief history of the movement can be found in Phillips, *Transportation in the Eastern Cotton Belt*, 83–94.

beginning had already been made in the canal and locks that had been built around the falls of the James at Richmond. Taking up the task in nearly the same year that the two Carolinas and Georgia began their internal-improvement programs, Virginia in 1816 created a fund for internal improvements and established a Board of Public Works to carry on the major project as well as some lesser developments in other parts of the state.[12] Within the next ten years $1,230,000 of borrowed money was spent on the James and Kanawha rivers. The state thereby incurred annual interest charges of $72,000, much more than the completed parts of the work were earning. Then for some years the work stood still, although the state continued to spend money on other projects under something of a pork-barrel system.[13]

Virginia also collaborated with Maryland in reviving an earlier attempt to build a canal along the north bank of the Potomac River. In the late eighteenth and early nineteenth centuries, a private organization known as the Potomac Company had performed the difficult and expensive feat of building canals and locks around the Little and the Great Falls above Georgetown, but in 1819 it had become bankrupt, having spent $7,000,000 for these and some minor accomplishments. To resume this undertaking, the states of Virginia and Maryland chartered the Chesapeake and Ohio Canal Company in the years 1823 to 1825. Its purpose was to extend the canal westward along the Potomac River until it reached the coal banks on the eastern base of the Allegheny Mountains, some twenty-five miles west of Cumberland, Maryland. In addition to transporting coal, the proposed canal was expected to aid farmers on both banks of the river, and it was hoped that goods from the Ohio Valley would be brought to the head of the canal and thence to the beginning of deepwater navigation at Georgetown. Virginia, Maryland, and the Federal government all supported this work for a time, but Virginia and the Federal government soon withdrew, and by 1830 only twenty miles of the canal were open to navigation.[14]

[12] Benjamin W. Leigh, *Revised Code of the Laws of Virginia* (Richmond, 1819), II, 201–205.

[13] Wayland F. Dunaway, *History of the James River and Kanawha Company*, in Columbia University *Studies in History, Economics and Public Law*, No. 236 (New York, 1922), 74, 86.

[14] Meyer, *Transportation in the United States*, 265–69.

The people of the Southwest were likewise keenly interested in getting their goods to market, but for a variety of reasons they did not tax themselves to that end. They could rely on the efforts of the Easterners to meet some of the transportation needs of the West; their younger and more thinly populated region had less money to spend; they were comparatively well supplied with natural waterways; and Federal aid in the form of 3 per cent of the proceeds from public-land sales was available to the newer Western states. Being less sensitive than Virginians and Carolinians about state rights, they did not hesitate to accept this money and sometimes to ask for more, arguing that an "equitable portion of the national revenue" ought to be spent in the West on navigable streams and for the establishment of armories and arsenals to match Federal expenditures for lighthouses and fortifications along the Atlantic coast.[15]

The most useful canal in the western South, opened in the year 1828, was around the falls of the Ohio at Louisville, Kentucky. Although it was only two and one-half miles long it was a well-built and extremely useful work, for it gave passage around the major obstruction to traffic on the greatest artery of Western and Southwestern commerce. Much of the cost, which amounted to some three quarters of a million dollars, was met by the Federal government. Navigation on extended reaches of the rivers of Kentucky was improved at a cost of nearly $5,000,000.[16]

The most pretentious single canal in the Southwest was a complete failure. Congress granted 400,000 acres of land to the state of Alabama in the year 1828, with the object of getting a canal constructed around Muscle Shoals on the Tennessee River. The land was sold for $1,400,000, and a canal 14¼ miles long, 60 feet wide, and 6 feet deep was finished in the year 1836. But after a year it fell into disuse and in time into ruins because it had been so constructed that boats could enter it only at certain stages of the river.[17]

[15] Louisville *Public Advertiser*, September 9, 1820, quoted in New Orleans *Louisiana Gazette*, September 28, 1820.

[16] Meyer, *Transportation in the United States*, 280–81; Edmund Flagg, *The Far West*, in Reuben G. Thwaites (ed.), *Early Western Travels, 1748–1846*, XXVI (Cleveland, 1906), 49–51 n.

[17] William E. Martin, *Internal Improvements in Alabama*, in Johns Hopkins University *Studies in Historical and Political Science*, XX, No. 4 (Baltimore, 1902), 43–44.

Scarcely one of the Southern waterway improvements earned enough to pay interest on the investment. Some of the capital had been borrowed from funds designed for the eventual support of schools and colleges, and by its loss the cause of education was dealt a heavy blow. Furthermore, the general failure of the program left the upcountry embittered against the low-country rulers of the state; and there was a tendency for towns like Charleston and Richmond to be envious of their successful Northern rivals in the race for Western trade.

Nature was largely responsible for the failure of the South to develop satisfactory waterways. It ruled against the establishment of a water connection between South Atlantic ports and the West, enforcing its edict with a formidable mountain barrier. Maryland alone among the slave states overcame this obstacle, and it could do so only because it was able to strike around the northern flank of the mountains. Nature also made it difficult to develop small-scale, domestic waterways to serve the Southern upcountry. This was a hilly region, containing many small streams. The improvement of each of these could consume large funds, and none of the valleys produced enough goods to support expensive improvements.

But nature was not solely responsible. Sectional rivalry within the states dissipated funds in too many directions, and lack of technical knowledge contributed to the failure. As the North Carolina Board of Internal Improvements explained in 1833: "The Science of engineering was . . . little understood and no individual could be obtained competent to direct our operations." [18] Political knowledge was also insufficient for the task in hand. State government was attempting to play the role of entrepreneur, but it had no experience to guide it in planning and administering an extensive economic program.

The internal-improvement program was but a part, although a very large part, of a general movement carried on by individuals, societies, and state governments to improve economic conditions in the South during the 1820's and 1830's. A handful of scientists, like Denison Olmsted and Elisha Mitchell of the University of North Carolina and Thomas Cooper and Lardner Vanuxem of South

[18] Quoted in Boyd, *North Carolina: The Federal Period,* 98.

Carolina College, showed commendable zeal in the early 1820's for discovering information about the natural resources of the region.[19] Agricultural reformers like John Taylor and Edmund Ruffin, both of Virginia, were suggesting better ways of farming, and periodicals for the dissemination of agricultural knowledge were founded. In 1819, John S. Skinner established at Baltimore the *American Farmer*, which proved to be the first agricultural periodical in the United States to be published for a considerable span of years. Nine years later the *Southern Agriculturist and Register of Rural Affairs* began its comparatively long life at Charleston, South Carolina.[20]

While Taylor's pleas for deep plowing, crop rotation, and the proper use of manure had been published somewhat earlier, his writings, particularly the *Arator*,[21] had great influence upon Southern agriculture for many years. Ruffin, who succeeded Taylor as the principal leader in the field of Southern agricultural reform, declared that "Almost every intelligent land-holder became a reader of Arator, and which book also constituted generally his earliest and sole agricultural study." [22]

Ruffin's principal contribution to agricultural improvement was to counsel the application of marl as a restorative of certain types of exhausted soil. His idea was conceived while reading Sir Humphry Davy's *Elements of Agricultural Chemistry*,[23] and his early experiments were conducted on his own worn-out land in eastern Virginia. In 1818 he expounded his theories and described his favorable results before the Prince George Agricultural Society. Three years later he published them in Skinner's *American Farmer* [24] and in 1832 in a volume entitled *An Essay on Calcareous Manures*,

19 Charles S. Sydnor, "State Geological Surveys in the Old South," in Jackson (ed.), *American Studies in Honor of William Kenneth Boyd*, 86–108.

20 Albert L. Demaree, *The American Agricultural Press, 1819–1860*, in Columbia University *Studies in the History of American Agriculture*, VIII (New York, 1941), 13, 15, 23–38.

21 [John Taylor], *Arator; Being a Series of Agricultural Essays, Practical & Political. By a Citizen of Virginia* (Georgetown, D.C., 1813). Biographies of Taylor are listed in the bibliography.

22 Quoted in Gray, *Agriculture in the Southern United States*, II, 780.

23 Sir Humphry Davy, *Elements of Agricultural Chemistry* (London, 1813).

24 *American Farmer* (Baltimore, Washington), III (1821), 313–20.

which went through several editions. The following year he in-augurated the *Farmer's Register,* a monthly magazine which he edited for ten years.[25]

Another characteristic of this movement for agricultural reform was the creation of agricultural societies. They were not a new phe-nomenon, for a number of them had been formed during the pre-vious century. Nevertheless, there was a significant renewal of in-terest in agricultural organizations after the War of 1812. Among those that were formed between 1815 and 1819 and that escaped the high mortality rate common to organizations of this kind were the Albemarle County and the Fredericksburg societies in Virginia, and the Pendleton, South Carolina, society of which John C. Cal-houn was an active member. Within the same period, state agricul-tural societies were founded in Kentucky, Virginia, North Carolina, and South Carolina,[26] and in 1822 six county societies were reported in North Carolina.[27]

Some state governments were persuaded to give aid to this agri-cultural movement. In North Carolina, for example, the legislature created a State Board of Agriculture in 1822 and authorized it to spend as much as $5,000 a year to support local agricultural so-cieties, to purchase and distribute seeds, and to publish the reports and proceedings of county societies. Furthermore, the legislature directed the Board of Agriculture to supervise a geological survey of the state which Denison Olmsted proposed to make, and it ap-propriated $250 a year for five years toward his expenses. Before the end of the decade several brief reports on the geology of North Car-olina had been published.

In several other Southern states agriculture was joined with geology for the benefit of the farmers. By 1835, six states had ini-tiated state geological surveys which were usually carried on under the supervision of the board of agriculture, the board of public

[25] Avery O. Craven, *Edmund Ruffin, Southerner: A Study in Secession* (New York, 1932), 49–72. For the general background, see Avery O. Craven, *Soil Exhaustion as a Factor in the Agricultural History of Virginia and Maryland, 1606–1860,* in University of Illinois *Studies in the Social Sciences,* XIII, No. 1 (Urbana, 1926), especially pp. 72–121.

[26] Gray, *Agriculture in the Southern United States,* II, 784–85.

[27] McIver, *North-Carolina Register . . . 1823,* p. 100, lists six. Twice as many were chartered by the legislature from 1818 to 1822.

works, the literary board, or a state-affiliated college. The reports of these surveys made available a good deal of more or less useful information about transportation routes, soil, marl, agricultural chemistry, water supply, iron, coal, building stone, gold, and a number of other natural resources.[28] In such ways as these the state was beginning to assume the burden of supplying information that would lead to the economic improvement of its citizens; but the task of exploiting that knowledge, except as it related to transportation, was left to the individual.

Along with these attempts to improve economic conditions, a social reform movement of moderate proportions was under way in the South in the 1820's and 1830's. It was influenced at a number of points by contemporary reform movements in the North and abroad,[29] but some of its roots went deep into Southern history. In part it was a second growth of an earlier reform movement. During the Revolutionary period men had set out to establish a more perfect democracy, end slavery, ameliorate prison conditions, establish schools and colleges, enlarge economic advantages, and provide complete religious freedom. But although much had been accomplished, particularly in Virginia, this movement had lost momentum before all its goals were reached: enthusiasm for the perfect society had diminished with the passage of the years, familiarity with evils had calloused sensitive feelings, and prosperity had alleviated some of the ills.

The "benevolent movement" and moral crusade of the churches helped to urge humanity out of the complacent halfway house in which it had settled, and the Panic of 1819 revealed some of the imperfections in the old way of doing things. Thoroughly respectable, hard-working men and women were being cast into prison for debt. Widows, orphans, cripples, and poor immigrants and travelers were suffering, and their hard lot aroused the pity of those

[28] Sydnor, "State Geological Surveys in the Old South," *loc. cit.;* Fletcher M. Green, "Gold Mining: A Forgotten Industry of Ante-Bellum North Carolina," in *North Carolina Historical Review* (Raleigh), XIV (1937), 1–19, 135–55; Boyd, *North Carolina: The Federal Period,* 100–101.

[29] For sketches of this movement, with emphasis on developments in the North, see John B. McMaster, *A History of the People of the United States, from the Revolution to the Civil War* (New York, 1883–1913), IV, 522–69; John A. Krout and Dixon R. Fox, *The Completion of Independence, 1790–1830* (New York, 1944), *passim.*

who were more fortunate. As if economic chaos were not enough, yellow fever struck in New Orleans, Natchez, and elsewhere in the summer of 1819, and in the following January, fire destroyed a large part of the city of Savannah.[30]

In the face of these and other hardships the old custom of praising all that was American and of affecting condescension toward unfortunate Europeans oppressed by a tyrannous "coalition of monarchs"[31] seemed unrealistic and even silly. Anyone proposing to speak on current conditions could not avoid at least a glance at the dark side of the picture. Consequently, when the governors of the Southern states faced their legislatures in the winter of 1819 and 1820, most of them spoke after the fashion of the governor of North Carolina when he said: "To pourtray [sic] the civil, religious and political advantages of our highly favoured country, would not only be more fashionable, but would assuredly be a more grateful task to the patriot and philanthropist, than a survey of the dark and portentous side of the picture; but while my bosom swells with gratitude to the All Wise and beneficent Disposer of Events for the benefits bestowed on us, I feel too much respect for your intelligence and discernment to believe you have assembled for the purpose of being congratulated and congratulating each other on the residuum of political happiness which we enjoy, while so much remains to be done to improve and ameliorate the condition of society."[32]

Although most of the governors regarded schools and colleges, canals and roads, and better credit facilities as being among the chief needs of society, they likewise advocated, though with less unanimity, improvement of public health, particularly by stronger quarantine regulations, correction of the state militia systems, better facilities for caring for poor and sick transients, establishment of libraries, reform of criminal codes, creation of state penitentiaries or the betterment of those already in existence, and more humane treatment of debtors.

[30] Mississippi *House Journal*, 1820, pp. 8–9; Louisiana *Senate Journal,* January–March, 1820, p. 5; E. Merton Coulter, "The Great Savannah Fire of 1820," in *Georgia Historical Quarterly* (Savannah), XXIII (1939), 1–27.

[31] Message of Governor Jacques P. Villeré, January 5, 1820, in Louisiana *Senate Journal,* January–March, 1820, p. 4.

[32] North Carolina *House Journal*, 1819, p. 7.

To sketch in any systematic way the accomplishments in all of these directions for all of the states of the South is impossible, but a few generalizations can be ventured about the character and scope of this complex movement, and a few illustrations can be offered. There was, in the first place, a growing awareness that port towns such as New Orleans, Savannah, Charleston, Natchez, and Louisville had reasonable grounds for asking aid in caring for sick and starving sailors and immigrants. Records of the Louisville Hospital for the year 1829 indicate that the need was not of local origin. Within the year the hospital received 144 sick and disabled boatmen and mariners—"that active but useful portion of our fellow beings, who are necessarily exposed, by their occupation, to the vicissitudes of heat and cold, and the pestilential atmosphere of a southern climate." Inasmuch as they hailed from ten or so foreign countries and from nearly every state in the Union, it seemed proper for the city to receive help in caring for them; and the state of Kentucky contributed $3,604 to this hospital during this year.[33]

At New Orleans, where the problem of sick and homeless transients was particularly great, the famous old Charity Hospital began to receive state aid in 1813,[34] and at the end of the decade a new building was erected with state funds after some discussion of whether to move the institution out of the center of the city or to leave it where accidents "daily occur to sailors, bricklayers, and other workmen, who are liable to falls, as also to persons who may chance to receive wounds in affrays." [35] In the year 1824 the state contributed more than $20,000 to Charity Hospital.[36] As the burden increased, a wider basis of support was sought, though in vain. Louisiana asked all of the states bordering the Mississippi and Ohio rivers to contribute to the establishment of three additional hospitals to be strategically located along the lower Mississippi River for the care of sick and disabled boatmen.[37] Other states likewise

[33] Report of managers of the Louisville Hospital, December 12, 1829, in Kentucky Senate Journal, 1829–1830, pp. 88–92.

[34] Helen E. Marshall, Dorothea Dix, Forgotten Samaritan (Chapel Hill, 1937), 76.

[35] Louisiana Senate Journal, January–March, 1820, pp. 30–31; ibid., 1820–1821, pp. 50–51.

[36] Louisiana House Journal, 1824–1825, p. 95.

[37] Louisiana Senate Journal, 1820–1821, pp. 42–43; Kentucky House Journal, 1820, pp. 296–300.

aided existing hospitals or created new ones. Georgia appropriated $5,000 for the Savannah Poor House and Hospital for the year ending October 31, 1820,[38] and South Carolina appropriated funds for a state hospital two years later.[39] In 1836, Mississippi authorized the Natchez Hospital to receive indigent boatmen and paupers, and three years later it began appropriating $5,000 a year to this institution.[40]

There was a growing feeling that towns ought to be helped in their attempts to ward off epidemics such as yellow fever. Self-interest as well as humanitarianism dictated such action because the port town was the gate through which epidemics usually entered the state, but controversy over whether yellow fever was imported or locally generated created confusion as to the best means of avoiding it. In 1819 Louisiana passed a quarantine law. Under its operation a quarantine officer was stationed at the mouth of the river at Balize, and a director of the quarantine was stationed at the lazaretto. But the following year a committee of the senate expressed the belief that this arrangement had proved ineffective, and it recommended the establishment of a board of health. The committee evidently believed in the local-origin theory because its report declared that "the filth of the streets, gutters, levees, backyards, privies, etc. [of New Orleans] is and has been for many years eminently calculated to give origin to disease or favour its spreading." [41] South Carolina granted $1,000 to Charleston in the year 1819 to aid in maintaining a quarantine.[42] A number of the states had regulations, most of which were of long standing, to limit the spread of smallpox. In 1824 Louisiana paid $1,500 "for vaccine matter." [43]

There was some improvement during these years in the care of insane persons. They had often been placed in the same institutions with the physically ill, but there was a growing tendency to separate them. State government was also assuming a larger share of responsibility in caring for mental cases. At Charity Hospital in

[38] Georgia *Acts,* 1819, p. 99.

[39] Marshall, *Dorothea Dix,* 79.

[40] Mississippi *Acts,* 1836, p. 261; *ibid.,* 1839, pp. 292–93.

[41] Louisiana *Senate Journal,* January–March, 1820, pp. 40–41, 46–47.

[42] South Carolina *Acts and Resolutions,* 1819, table following p. 60.

[43] Louisiana *House Journal,* 1824–1825, p. 95.

New Orleans, one wing containing twenty-four apartments was set aside for mental patients in 1820, and twenty years later the state appropriated $25,000 for a separate building for "lunatics." [44] Virginia, which was the first state in the Union to establish an institution devoted exclusively to the care of mental cases, spent $12,409.59 in the year ending September 30, 1819, for "the lunatic hospital," and in 1828 it opened a second institution, the Western Lunatic Asylum, at Staunton.[45] In 1819 Kentucky spent $10,853.05 for "Lunatics," and the Lunatic Asylum at Lexington was opened in January, 1824.[46] Maryland opened its state hospital in 1816, South Carolina in 1828, Tennessee in 1840, and Georgia in 1841.[47]

Some insight into the operation of these institutions is afforded by a report of the commissioners of the Kentucky Lunatic Asylum for the year 1829. The institution had received 240 patients in the six years since it had been opened, and of these, 78 had been discharged, 56 had died, 12 had "eloped," and 94 remained at the end of the period. Forty-eight of the last group were men and 46 were women. The state appropriation for the year 1829 was $10,900, of which nearly half was spent for erecting a new wing. Besides, the institution received $1,113.04 for the care of nine inmates who were listed as "pay patients." [48]

Paupers who were neither physically nor mentally ill continued to be helped principally by kindly individuals and by local government, though the state occasionally gave aid under unusual circumstances. In 1819 the South Carolina legislature appropriated $8,000 to aid the city of Charleston in caring for transient poor, and $500 was given to Georgetown and the same amount to Beaufort. These funds were to be administered by the governing body in each town.[49] The governor of Georgia advanced $10,000 from his contingent fund to the city authorities of Savannah for alleviating the distress "of the poorer class of citizens" occasioned by the fire of 1820.[50]

Orphans, likewise, were ordinarily cared for in privately sup-

[44] Marshall, *Dorothea Dix,* 70, 76, 77.

[45] *Ibid.,* 79; Virginia *House Journal,* 1819, pp. 119, 172.

[46] Kentucky *House Journal,* 1819–1820, pp. 204–205; *ibid.,* 1829–1830, pp. 182–86.

[47] Marshall, *Dorothea Dix,* 77, 79–80.

[48] Kentucky *House Journal,* 1829–1830, pp. 182–86.

[49] South Carolina *Laws,* 1819, pp. 8–9.

[50] Georgia *Senate Journal,* 1820, p. 5; Coulter, "Great Savannah Fire of 1820 " *loc. cit.,* 8.

ported institutions or in private homes under the supervision of the county courts. However, the Louisiana legislature, after hearing a report on the Poydras Female Orphan Asylum, began to grant aid which amounted to $3,000 in the year 1824. The report explained that this institution, where "necessitous orphans . . . find a secure shelter and solace in their misfortunes," was so managed that "their education is suitable to their condition, their acquirements are more solid than brilliant: habits of industry, order oeconemy [*sic*] and cleanliness." [51]

There was a growing conviction that specialized training ought to be made available to the deaf and dumb, but there seemed to be hardly enough of them in any one state to warrant the establishment of a deaf and dumb school. Half a dozen years after Kentucky had created such an institution at Danville in 1823, only twenty pupils were enrolled, six of whom were "pay charges" and the others state-supported.[52] Virginia established a school for the deaf and dumb in 1839. Maryland followed the sensible plan of arranging with a Pennsylvania institution to receive Maryland cases. In 1829, two years after this plan went into effect, Maryland paid $700 for this service.[53] The following year Mississippi disbursed $200 "on account of the Deaf and Dumb children of the State." [54] Soon afterward, the state of Georgia, under the urging of its eccentric deaf citizen, John Jacobus Flournoy, discovered that there were 145 deaf and dumb persons, of all ages, in the state, and appropriated $3,000 to provide for the education of some of them in the American Asylum at Hartford, Connecticut.[55] In 1844 Tennessee appropriated $1,000 to establish a school for the deaf and dumb at Knoxville. The following year it was observed that no state south of Tennessee had such an institution.[56]

51 Louisiana *Senate Journal,* January–March. 1820, pp. 39–40; Louisiana *House Journal,* 1824–1825, p. 95.

52 Kentucky *House Journal,* 1829–1830, pp. 215–18.

53 *Niles' Weekly Register,* LVII (1839), 136, 153; Maryland *Senate Journal* 1829–1830, p. 9.

54 Mississippi *House Journal,* November–December, 1830, p. 45.

55 E. Merton Coulter. *John Jacobus Flournoy, Champion of the Common Man in the Antebellum South* (Savannah, 1942), 40–42.

56 Tennessee *Laws,* 1843–1844, pp. 213–14; Tennessee *Senate Journal,* 1843–1844, pp. 409, 417–19; Tennessee *House Journal,* 1845, Appendix, 237; *History of Tennessee* (Nashville, 1886), 287–88.

State aid for the blind was less extensive. Virginia arranged for their care by attaching a school for the blind to its institution for the deaf and dumb. James Champlin, a young blind preacher, is said to have established a private school for the blind in Nashville before 1843, and in the following year the Tennessee legislature appropriated $1,500 to establish a state school for the blind in that city.[57]

Slavery continued to be recognized within the South as a grave social problem. Perhaps Southerners were less concerned about it than they had been in the Revolutionary period, but during the course of the Missouri debate, responsible Southern spokesmen openly admitted that slavery was evil; and ten years later there occurred the greatest and most searching discussion of the nature and problem of slavery that was ever held in the South, the debate in the Virginia legislature in 1832. Several antislavery journals appeared in the slave states: *The Emancipator,* founded in East Tennessee in 1820; *The Genius of Universal Emancipation,* which was moved to Tennessee from Ohio in 1821 and was later moved to Baltimore; and *The Abolition Intelligencer,* founded in Kentucky in 1822.[58] Benjamin Lundy, editor of *The Genius of Universal Emancipation,* estimated in 1827 that there were 106 antislavery societies with 5,150 members in the slave states whereas there were only 24 such societies with 1,475 members in the free states, not counting 10 or 12 in Illinois about which he could get no information.[59]

But these facts by no means indicate that Southerners generally were conscience-stricken over slavery. A large part of Southern hostility to slavery was localized in East Tennessee and among the Quakers in central North Carolina. Furthermore, the hostility of some Southerners to slavery was founded on something very different from sympathy for the oppressed. When Governor David

[57] Tennessee *Laws,* 1843–1844, pp. 213–14; Tennessee *Senate Journal,* 1843–1844, pp. 417–19; James Champlin, *Early Biography, Travels and Adventures of Rev. James Champlin, Who Was Born Blind* (Columbus, Ohio, 1842); *History of Tennessee,* 289.

[58] Arthur Y. Lloyd, *The Slavery Controversy, 1831–1860* (Chapel Hill, 1939), 20, n. 69.

[59] *The Life, Travels and Opinions of Benjamin Lundy . . .* (Philadelphia, 1847), 218. See also, Stephen B. Weeks, "Anti-Slavery Sentiment in the South," in Southern History Association *Publications* (Washington), II (1898), 87–130.

Holmes of Mississippi warned that "The evils arising from this odious practice [the slave trade] are constantly . . . increasing," and that there would be serious results "unless the traffic is wholly prohibited," his concern was for the welfare of the Mississippi white man.[60] Governor Randolph of Virginia put the matter very bluntly. He deplored the "error of our ancestors in copying a civil institution from savage Africa," because, as he reasoned, "The want of moral motives and defect of intelligence, the too common absence of settled character, that marks the race degrated [*sic*] by slavery, if not by nature," was injurious to the state of Virginia. In short, his dislike for slavery was based on aversion to the Negro rather than on pity, and he therefore did not regard emancipation as an acceptable solution. Alleging that free Negroes were already causing great annual loss by their "secret pillage," he suggested that the legislature arrange for their deportation, and that it use certain funds of the state to purchase slaves "just arrived at the age of puberty" and remove them from the United States. To diminish the Negro population more rapidly under this scheme, he favored sending a double portion of females.[61]

There was much support throughout the South in the 1820's for plans to deport Negroes, and some of those who favored these plans did so for nobler motives than Governor Randolph professed. Haiti, Africa, and unsettled parts of the Western territories of the United States were suggested as possible places to which Negroes could be sent, but the only serious effort that came out of the discussion was the organization in Washington in 1817, of the American Colonization Society. It was a national society, but in its genesis and life it was strongly supported in the slave states. Indeed, its incorporation followed close on the heels of a petition from the Virginia legislature to the Federal government that it "obtain an asylum, beyond the limits of the United States, for such persons of colour, as had been, or might be emancipated under the laws of this commonwealth." [62] This organization was quickly endorsed by the legislatures of Georgia, Maryland, and Tennessee, and in the year 1826,

---

[60] Message of January 4, 1820, in Mississippi *House Journal*, 1820, pp. 10–11.

[61] Message of December 4, 1820, in Virginia *Senate Journal*, 1820–1821, pp. 13–15.

[62] Herman V. Ames, *State Documents on Federal Relations* (Philadelphia, 1906), 195–96.

forty-four of the fifty-seven auxiliary local societies in the United States were in the slave states.[63]

During the first ten years or so of its life, the American Colonization Society was careful to disclaim any desire to interfere with slavery, and it set as its main purpose the return to Africa of such free Negroes as were willing to emigrate. However, some church members, slaveowners, and other Southerners with strong humanitarian feelings saw in this movement a means of granting to slaves freedom and a better chance in life. A considerable number of them were sent to Liberia, and large contributions were made to the society from the slave states.[64]

The multiplication of debtors during the depression years that began in 1819 made many persons—relatives and friends as well as victims—aware of the harshness of their treatment. Imprisonment was their usual lot. In Virginia the debtor was "sometimes indiscriminately thrown into [the county jail along] with the common felon." [65] In Louisiana, debtors, assassins, thieves, and other criminals were "all heaped up together in a common yard," whites and blacks together.[66] But public opinion was becoming aroused. The governor of North Carolina declared that imprisonment for debt "seems to be a remnant of that gothic policy which prevailed during the ruder ages of society; a policy as barbarous as it is useless." He added the shrewd observation that abolition of this penalty "may have the effect of curtailing the extended system of credit that exists at present." [67]

In one way and another the lot of debtors was improved in several states, especially in the Southwest. The Mississippi constitution of 1817 and the Alabama constitution of 1819 provided that no citizen should be imprisoned for debt unless he refused to give up his estate. Women were exempted from imprisonment for debt

---

[63] McMaster, *History of the People of the United States*, V, 213.

[64] Charles S. Sydnor, *Slavery in Mississippi* (New York, 1933), 204–206; Early L. Fox, *The American Colonization Society, 1817–1840*, in Johns Hopkins University *Studies in Historical and Political Science*, XXXVII, No. 3 (Baltimore, 1919), 212–15; and, for an example of the emigration to Africa of slaves manumitted for that purpose, *African Repository* (Washington), VII (1831), 217–18.

[65] Message of Governor James P. Preston, December 6, 1819, in Virginia *House Journal*, 1819–1820, p. 7.

[66] Louisiana *Senate Journal*, January–March, 1820, p. 28; *ibid.*, 1820–1821, p. 23.

[67] Message of November, 1819, in North Carolina *House Journal*, 1819, p. 9.

in Kentucky in 1820,[68] in Mississippi in 1824, and in Tennessee in 1827.[69] After 1842 men were no longer imprisoned for debt in Tennessee, and the humane Mississippi laws in respect to debtors were further liberalized in 1839 and 1840.[70]

North Carolina's efforts to cope with this problem illustrate the uncertain, faltering course sometimes taken on the path of progress. Following the governor's recommendations, and under the influence of Murphey, imprisonment for debt was abolished in 1820, but it was reinstituted in 1821. Two years later women were exempted, and men were given a slight chance to escape imprisonment under special circumstances. In 1829, Murphey was compelled to spend twenty days in prison as part of the legal procedure of settling his debts, but for part of the time "old Jimmy Doak," the sheriff, left the door open because the jail was poorly lighted and ventilated. Finally, in 1844 imprisonment for debt was ended in North Carolina except when the creditor made oath that the debtor had property which could not be reached by a *facias faciendum*.[71]

The exemption of women from imprisonment for debt was but one of several steps taken to improve their condition. Under the law, the married woman's lot "was always hazardous, frequently humiliating, and often tragic," because she lacked property rights. However, her real condition was usually determined less by the letter of the law than by "her character, that of the man she married, . . . and . . . public opinion." Furthermore, there is evidence in occasional legislative acts and in several enlightened court decisions that public opinion about women's rights was improving.[72] North Carolina in 1819 granted to divorced women the right to possess property and money acquired after the divorce, and twenty-five years later it granted to the married woman the right to act as

<hr/>

[68] Kentucky *Acts*, 1819, p. 976.

[69] Haywood and Cobbs, *Statute Laws of the State of Tennessee*, I, 144.

[70] Abernethy, "Andrew Jackson and Southwestern Democracy," *loc. cit.*, 69; Tennessee *Acts*, 1842, p. 15; E. Bruce Thompson, "Reforms in the Penal System of Mississippi, 1820–1850," in *Journal of Mississippi History* (Jackson), VII (1945), 66–70.

[71] Boyd, *North Carolina: The Federal Period*, 257–58; sketch of Archibald De Bow Murphey, in *Dictionary of American Biography*, XIII, 345–46.

[72] For the quotations above, see Eleanor M. Boatwright, "The Political and Civil Status of Women in Georgia, 1783–1860," in *Georgia Historical Quarterly*, XXV (1941), 324; and for an account of the changing status of women before the law, see the entire article.

executor without bond being given by her husband. Four years later the husband was denied the right to dispose of his wife's real estate without her consent.[73] A Mississippi act of February 15, 1839, gave to the married woman the right to possess property in her own name and free from liability for her husband's debts provided the property had not been acquired from her husband after marriage.[74] Georgia provided in 1829 that a widow should inherit the entire estate of her intestate husband provided he left no lineal descendants. Previously she had been entitled to only half.[75] In some of the states there was a tendency to facilitate divorce by transferring the power to grant divorces from the legislature to the courts.

There was a good deal of feeling that the administration of justice ought to be improved, but there was not much agreement as to the cause of the evil or as to the proper remedy. In Kentucky it was complained that there was too rapid a turnover "in the appellate tribunal,"[76] in Maryland that too many laws had been passed and that "a multiplicity of laws is an incalculable mischief,"[77] in Virginia that jury service was evaded by substantial citizens,[78] and in Louisiana that access to the courts was difficult and was so expensive as to be nearly prohibitive for the poor.[79] Recodification of state law was widely urged, and digests or codes were published in most of the states in the early 1820's.[80]

Two objects were in view in this reworking of the law. One, of course, was to facilitate finding the law. The other, and perhaps the more important one, was to soften some of its harsher provisions,

[73] Boyd, *North Carolina: The Federal Period*, 259.

[74] Mississippi *Acts*, 1839, pp. 72–73. The community-property system of Louisiana gave the wife a more favorable position in respect to property than she had in the common-law states.

[75] Boatwright, "Status of Women in Georgia," *loc. cit.*, 312.

[76] Kentucky *House Journal*, 1819–1820, p. 19.

[77] Message of Governor David Martin, December 30, 1829, in Maryland *Senate Journal*, 1829–1830, p. 18.

[78] Message of Governor Randolph, December 4, 1820, in Virginia *Senate Journal*, 1820–1821, p. 9.

[79] Message of Governor Villeré, January 5, 1820, in Louisiana *Senate Journal*, January–March, 1820, pp. 4–8.

[80] Pleas for codification can be found in the governors' messages of most of the states. A code or digest was published in Virginia in 1819; North Carolina and Tennessee, 1821; Kentucky, Georgia, and South Carolina, 1822; Alabama, 1823; Mississippi, 1824; and Louisiana, 1825.

particularly in respect to the severity of penalties for crime. Penalties were indeed harsh in some states, and public opinion was aware of the fact. A Georgia newspaper announced with regret that "Whilst other states are striving to keep up with the march of moral sentiment . . . citizens [of Georgia] can now be hung, and whipped, and cropped, and branded, put in the stocks, placed in pillories." [81] Governor Jacques P. Villeré of Louisiana said that it was "the opinion entertained by our most enlightened jurists . . . [that] the common law that governs us, exists here as it did in England, before it had been amended and modified, or in other words, in its most imperfect state." [82]

Furthermore, it was said that society should abandon the ancient idea of retribution in dealing with criminals and should adopt practices designed to reform them.[83] But to do this, the state needed a penitentiary to which criminals could be committed for extended sentences, instead of being sent to the pillory, whipping post, and scaffold of the jailyard; and the penitentiary cost more to build and maintain than the instruments of quick and ofttimes mutilating punishment.

Some of the states, notably Virginia, Maryland, Georgia, and Kentucky, operated penitentiaries, but by the year 1820 they were fearfully overcrowded. The Virginia building was so inadequate that 12 of its 209 inmates had to be locked each night in a room 12 by 14 feet.[84] In Kentucky 71 convicts were crowded into 17 cells, each measuring 6 by 8 feet. With only one small grated window in each cell, it was "inconceivably distressing in hot weather." Besides the inhumanity of such conditions, there was not enough space for the convicts to be employed to best advantage in such occupations as stonecutting, shoemaking, and the making of chairs.[85]

[81] *Daily Savannah Republican*, November 6, 1832. In 1820 the state of Georgia was making appropriations to a penitentiary. See the treasurer's report for 1820, a folded sheet in Georgia *Senate Journal*, 1820.

[82] Message of January 5, 1820, in Louisiana *Senate Journal*, January–March, 1820, p. 7.

[83] Message of Governor Thomas B. Robertson, December 18, 1820, in Louisiana *Senate Journal*, 1820–1821, pp. 20–24; message of Governor Randolph, December 4, 1820, in Virginia *Senate Journal*, 1820–1821, pp. 11–13.

[84] Virginia *House Journal*, 1819–1820, pp. 130–32.

[85] Kentucky *House Journal*, 1819–1820, pp. 185–86. The chief occupations in the Maryland penitentiary were weaving and dying, cordwaining, hatmaking, and sawing of marble. For other occupations and the annual value of the products of the

In 1825 the state of Kentucky rid itself of a troublesome problem by leasing the labor of its convicts to an enterprising merchant for $1,000 a year, a larger building was constructed, and four years later it was reported that prisoners were placed in separate cells at night and that the cost of the institution was being met by the labor of the inmates.[86] The governor urged further reforms, citing Auburn, Sing Sing, and Wethersfield as examples of enlightened management, and he recommended the segregation of juvenile offenders into a proposed "house of refuge." [87] The Maryland legislature was likewise contemplating the establishment of an institution for youthful offenders and was urged to "follow the laudable example set before us by the States of Massachusetts, New York, and Pennsylvania, in their liberal encouragement of institutions of this kind." [88]

Some of the other Southern states, among them Louisiana, Mississippi, and Tennessee, were giving thought in the year 1820 to the need of a state penitentiary and of a reformation of the penal code.[89] In the panic year 1819, when suffering was widespread, Felix Grundy introduced a bill in the Tennessee house of representatives to provide for a penitentiary and a revision of the criminal laws of the state. It was defeated, and the penitentiary was not established nor the criminal laws revised until ten years later, though hardly a session of the legislature passed without a discussion of the subject.[90]

Maryland institution, see *Digest of Accounts of Manufacturing Establishments*, 1820.

[86] Kentucky *House Journal*, 1829–1830, pp. 52–57; Blake McKelvey, *American Prisons: A Study in American Social History prior to 1915* (Chicago, 1936), 31.

[87] Message of Governor Thomas Metcalfe, December 8, 1829, in Kentucky *House Journal*, 1829–1830, pp. 14–17. He stated that 630 persons had been committed to the penitentiary during the past thirty years, and that no women had been prisoners during the past few years.

[88] Message of Governor Thomas K. Carroll, December 29, 1830, in Maryland *House Journal*, 1830–1831, p. 19.

[89] Message of Governor David Holmes, January 4, 1820, in Mississippi *House Journal*, 1820, p. 10; message of Governor Villeré, January 5, 1820, in Louisiana *Senate Journal*, January–March, 1820, p. 6.

[90] E. Bruce Thompson, "Reforms in the Penal System of Tennessee, 1820–1850," in *Tennessee Historical Quarterly* (Nashville), I (1942), 291–308. James Campbell, who was instrumental in securing the passage of the 1829 legislation, wrote on January 5, 1830, an excellent account of how the passage of the laws was accomplished and of the sources of the ideas for the establishment of the Tennessee penitentiary, for its government, and for the reformation of the criminal code. This four-page MS. memorandum is in the David Campbell Papers (Duke University Library, Durham).

Despite much agitation through many years, Mississippi did not authorize the erection of a penitentiary until 1836. It was put into use in 1840, one year after the adoption of an enlightened penal code.[91] A new building with 150 cells was constructed in Georgia in the late 1830's, and in that decade and the next Louisiana, Alabama, and Texas built penitentiaries.[92] Although Louisiana adopted revised codes of civil law and of practice in 1825, it failed to adopt one of the most enlightened penal codes of its generation, the work of Edward Livingston.[93] South Carolina, for all of its leadership in the defense of Southern interests, lagged behind most of the states of the South in respect to reformation of its criminal code and judicial system and in the creation of a state penitentiary.[94]

The Southern states were not alone during these years in their attempts to accomplish humanitarian reforms and secure economic improvements. Progress was afoot in other parts of the United States and across the Atlantic. In some matters, the South was near the head of the procession, as in its zeal for state support for higher education; and in others it lagged. The only considerable difference grew out of slavery; but slavery, almost paradoxically, lessened the impact of some other problems in the South because responsibility for caring for physically or mentally incapacitated slaves rested on their owners rather than upon government or private charity.

The participation of the South in this widespread reform movement is more significant than any peculiarities in the character of the movement in the South. By attempting social reforms, Southerners were admitting that there was much in their society that needed to be reformed, a fact which many of them were soon to deny. Furthermore, they showed a willingness to borrow ideas from Massachusetts, New York, and Pennsylvania,[95] thus showing an absence of the sensitive insularity that was increasingly to characterize

[91] Thompson, "Penal System of Mississippi," *loc. cit.,* 64–67.

[92] McKelvy, *American Prisons,* 32–33.

[93] William B. Hatcher, *Edward Livingston, Jeffersonian Republican and Jacksonian Democrat* (University, La., 1940), 253, 259, 262–88.

[94] Lillian A. Kibler, *Benjamin F. Perry, South Carolina Unionist* (Durham, 1946), Chap. XIII.

[95] Besides the Maryland and Kentucky material immediately above, see the Campbell memorandum cited in a previous note, and message of Governor William Carroll, in Tennessee *House Journal,* 1831, pp. 8–16.

their thought. Finally, they seemed as willing as other parts of the Union for state government to assume responsibilities that had previously rested on the individual or on local government. The states were beginning to be transformed into something more powerful and more expensive than they had hitherto been; to their ancient function of protecting persons and property they were adding the planning, support, and execution of various economic and social services, most of which had previously been performed by local government. It is significant that there was far less protest within the South against this expansion of state activity than there was against the contemporary expansion of activities by the Federal government.

CHAPTER V

CRISES IN BUSINESS AND POLITICS

PROSPERITY blossomed in the United States for several years following the Peace of 1815; then, beginning in the year 1819, a succession of evil years, like the ill-favored kine in Pharaoh's dream, devoured the substance of Europe and America.[1] The course of the depression in the southern part of the United States can be traced in the declining prices on the Richmond market. Cotton, which sold for thirty-three cents a pound at the beginning of the year 1819, was down to twenty cents by June, and by fall it brought no more than from fourteen to eighteen cents. Through these same months the prices of bacon, whiskey, flour, and many other commodities slumped from 10 to 30 per cent. The decline of tobacco prices had begun earlier and descended to even lower depths, dropping from a range of $20.00 to $40.00 a hundred pounds in 1815 and 1816 to a range of $4.00 to $8.00 in June, 1819. Bank stocks dropped along with commodity prices. In the first nine months of the Panic year, shares in the Bank of the United States slid from 110 to 92.5; in the Virginia Bank from 115 to 75; and in the Farmers' Bank of Virginia from 112 to 75. Thereafter these stocks began to creep upward, but commodity prices were no better in the fall of 1820 than they had been a year earlier, nor was there much improvement before the end of 1822.[2]

The beginning of the War of 1812 set the stage for a depression,

[1] Except where otherwise noted, this account of the Panic has been drawn from the following sources: Ralph C. H. Catterall, *The Second Bank of the United States* (Chicago, 1903), Chaps. I–IV, XVI; Samuel Rezneck, "The Depression of 1819–1822, A Social History," in *American Historical Review*, XXXIX (1933–1934), 28–47; Joseph H. Parks, "Felix Grundy and the Depression of 1819 in Tennessee," in East Tennessee Historical Society *Publications* (Knoxville), No. 10 (1938), 19–43.

[2] See prices current in the Richmond *Compiler* through the years 1819–1820 and, for tobacco prices, Robert, *Tobacco Kingdom*, 137–40.

but events across the Atlantic gave the signal for the tragic drama to begin. The South, because of its great export trade, was peculiarly sensitive to these events. Immediately after the Napoleonic Wars there was a strong European demand for Southern staples. Under the incentive of high prices, planters of cotton and tobacco enlarged their fields, and by the year 1819 their crops were about one third above normal. But by this date the flurry of postwar buying had ended in Europe, and the prices of Southern export crops were at once depressed. So great was the fall in prices that the planters found their income decreasing despite the increase in production. To stay in business, they needed to cut expenses in proportion to their reduced income, but this operation was impossible in many instances because a large part of agricultural expense consisted in an irreducible load of carrying charges for mortgages. Land and slaves had been bought and improvements had been made with borrowed money, and the amount of the loans had been determined by the high prices and bright prospects of farming when times were good. The costs of carrying the large debts remained constant while farm income declined.

The chief creditors of the farmers at this time were the Federal government and the banks. To the government, $22,000,000 was due on September 30, 1819, owed by those throughout the United States who had purchased public land on credit. More than half of this amount was owed by purchasers of land in Alabama and Mississippi.[3] Some of the purchasers were large-scale speculators, some were hard-working small farmers who had bought on margin, as it were, with the expectation of paying for their land with high-priced cotton, tobacco, and other staples. With diminished money income, payments could not be kept up, and debtors faced the prospect, under existing Federal law, of losing their equity. However, there was a possible avenue of escape: debtors were also voters, and in proportion to their numbers they shared in managing the concern to which they were obligated. Nor were they slow to exercise this power; they soon forced Congress to place the public-land question upon its list of active political questions, and, as will be discussed in a later chapter, the debtors gained a measure of relief from the creditor government.

[3] *American State Papers, Public Lands*, III, 460.

The farmers were more deeply in debt to the banks than they were to the government. Some of the debt was direct, and some was indirect through the medium of merchants and factors who were creditors of farmers and debtors to the banks. But the nature and exact amount of bank loans cannot be known, nor can precise statements be made about any detail of state banking at the time of the Panic because essential data are lacking. In 1833 one who had been collecting bank statements for seven years decided that his material was not worth publishing and contented himself with presenting statistics collected by Albert Gallatin even though he knew them to be incomplete in many respects.[4] Gallatin's tables, although they are the best that are available, give but few figures about each bank, and none whatever about many of them.[5] Furthermore, he published statements as of January 1, 1820, after the Panic had been in operation a number of months. But perhaps the situation did not change profoundly in that time, for a distressed bank did not then quickly break. Facing a run, it refused to pay out specie but it did not necessarily close its doors.

According to Gallatin's tables, 101 of the nation's 307 state banks were south of Pennsylvania and the Ohio River. There were others that he did not discover; and this was in the day, though it was nearly at its close, when individuals and business houses issued paper money, especially fractional currency.[6] The number of incorporated state banks in the slave states ranged from one in Mississippi to forty-two in Kentucky; in most of these states there were from three to five. They were subject to very little inspection and regulation, and a large capital stock could be created on paper with contributions by the stockholders of only small amounts of specie or of anything else that had real value. In many cases, but by no means all, a considerable part of the stock was owned by the state, and its share of the profits eased the tax burden and blinded the eyes of critics.

[4] William M. Gouge, *A Short History of Paper Money and Banking in the United States* (Philadelphia, 1833), Pt. II, 223. On pp. 127–50 of this work there is a useful account of state banking.

[5] Albert Gallatin, *Considerations on the Currency and Banking System of the United States* (Philadelphia, 1831), 97–106; Davis R. Dewey, *Financial History of the United States* (12th ed.; New York, 1934), 153–54.

[6] Davis R. Dewey, *State Banking before the Civil War* (Washington, 1910), 143–51.

As far as can be judged from the incomplete returns, state banks in all parts of the Union had extended credit too far, and there are several reasons for thinking that those in some parts of the South were in an especially precarious position. The very fact that Gallatin experienced extraordinary difficulty in securing their statements renders their operations suspect. Furthermore, such statements as he could secure indicate that Southern banks kept smaller amounts of specie on hand to meet demands of depositors and holders of notes than did the banks of the North, the ratios being about 1 to 4.7 in the South and 1 to 4.0 in the North.[7]

Judged by specie holdings and by strength displayed in weathering the financial storm, banks in Virginia and Louisiana, and perhaps those in South Carolina and Mississippi, were on a sounder footing than those in other Southern states. At the opposite extreme were the banks in Kentucky, Tennessee, and Alabama. The Mobile Bank illustrates the extreme insecurity of some of the smaller institutions. Its charter, which was granted in November, 1818, limited its capital to $500,000 and required that half of this

[7] If the banks of the South Atlantic states be compared with those of the Southwest the fact emerges that the latter, despite their bad reputation, reported more specie in proportion to note circulation and deposits than did those in the older Southern states. In fact, their ratio was better than that in the North. But perhaps these comparisons mean little or nothing because of the high proportion of nonreporting banks in the Southwest.

The following comparison of conditions of state banks on January 1, 1820, is based on statistics printed in Gallatin, *Considerations on the Currency and Banking,* 102–103.

	South Atlantic states (Md., D. C., Va., N.C., S.C., Ga.)	Gulf and Mississippi Valley states (Ala., Miss., La., Tenn., Ky.)	Total Southern states (col. 1 plus col. 2)	Total of all states outside of the South
Number of banks whose statements were available to Gallatin	28	26	54	158
Capital	$19,665,198	$7,998,410	$27,663,608	$35,072,234
Circulation	$12,009,074	$2,615,548	$14,624,622	$12,016,982
Deposits	$ 5,084,159	$2,826,277	$ 7,910,436	$11,534,523
Specie	$ 3,195,060	$1,600,122	$ 4,795,182	$ 5,876,981
Ratio of specie to total circulation and deposits	1 to 5.4	1 to 3.4	1 to 4.7	1 to 4.0
Number of banks for which Gallatin could not secure statements	15	32	47	48

be paid in specie. But by 1820 "only $70,000 had been subscribed to its capital, and only about $8,000 of this sum had been paid in specie. While an agent was sent North with a part of this modicum of specie to purchase plates [for printing notes] and materials for putting the bank into operation, robbers seized the balance." Nevertheless, the directors issued notes, exchanged some of them for notes of another small Alabama bank which they then presented for specie, and thus acquired enough gold and silver "to set their tottering infant upon its feet." [8]

It was commonly asserted, without much proof beyond the strong probabilities in the case, that Southern banks froze too large a share of their funds into long-time loans. They could hardly have done otherwise in a region so predominantly agricultural. Comparatively little short-time commercial paper could have been offered to them in comparison with the large demand for extended loans to finance purchases of land and slaves.

To explain why Western and Southern bankers were doing business on a somewhat more reckless scale than the national norm, it is unnecessary to assume that they possessed more than their share of cupidity and ignorance. These traits were all too prevalent throughout banking circles the nation over, and nowhere could they have been worse than in Philadelphia. A more probable explanation of the overexpansion of Southern banking lies in certain characteristics of the economic order of the region. In the South the demand for money, even the legitimate demand, far outran the supply. Under the system of slavery, agriculture was conducted under an expanded capital investment, for money was needed to purchase labor as well as land, and banks and other sources of credit were asked to supply more capital than would have been needed for farming operations with free labor. The situation was especially acute in the newer states of the South—Georgia, Alabama, Mississippi, Tennessee, and Kentucky—where settlements were young or were yet being made. Gallatin's exposition of the money shortage of a new economic society was applicable to these younger states:

"Amongst the first emigrants, there are but few possessed of much capital; and these, generally employing it in the purchase of

[8] Albert B. Moore, *History of Alabama* (University, Ala., 1934), 211.

land, are soon left without any active resources. The great mass bring nothing with them, but their industry, and a small stock of cattle and horses. A considerable portion of the annual labor is employed in clearing, inclosing, and preparing the land for cultivation. . . . Within a very short time, our numerous new settlements, which in a few years have extended . . . from the Alleghany to the Mississippi and beyond it, afford the spectacle of a large population, with the knowledge, the intelligence and the habits which belong to civilized life, amply supplied with the means of subsistence, but without any other active capital, but agricultural products, for which, in many instances, they have no market." [9]

Although state banks, especially in the newer areas, overexerted themselves in puffing up small specie holdings so as to satisfy the insatiable appetite for currency and credit, they seldom succeeded. Hence, a demand existed for the new source of credit which came to the South with the establishment in 1817 of the second Bank of the United States. Although welcomed by many would-be borrowers, this bank was feared by the state banks because it was a rival and because one of its major duties was to restrict their note-issuing activities; and it was disliked by old-school Southerners who believed that Congress had no constitutional power to create such an institution.

Being welcomed and repelled at the same moment, the management of the Bank of the United States considered it expedient to win favor by a conciliatory and generous policy, especially in its dealings with the state banks. Of the first nineteen branches established, ten were located south of Pennsylvania and the Ohio River, and they quickly began doing business on a large scale, particularly those at Charleston, New Orleans, Nashville, and Louisville. They discounted generously, they issued notes freely, and they made little attempt to collect balances that developed in the course of their dealings with state banks. In effect, they were placing a good share of their capital at the disposal of the state banks. Also, they were draining most of the capital of the Bank of the United States into the South and West, a process which was brought about in the following manner. Branches in these regions issued bank notes which

[9] Gallatin, *Considerations on the Currency and Banking*, 67–68.

in the normal course of trade made their way to the North and East where they were presented for redemption. Thus, the bank's Northern and Eastern branches paid out specie for the notes of the Southern and Western branches. The latter, finding their specie holdings unreduced by the first issue of notes, proceeded to issue more. By May of 1819 nearly half the capital of the bank, which amounted to $35,000,000 in all, was controlled by branches in the slave states. If Philadelphia, the headquarters of the bank, be omitted, these ten branches held three quarters of the capital. The total amount controlled by the five branches in New York and the New England states was less than the amount controlled by each of the branches at Baltimore, Richmond, Charleston, Savannah, New Orleans, Lexington, or Louisville.

By 1819 the Bank of the United States, like the state banks in the South and West, had expanded its credit to the limit; neither was in a position to extend further credit to the farmers who were being squeezed between the iron pincers of falling prices and fixed, heavy debts. To make matters worse, the banks chose this moment to call for the repayment of loans that would normally have been carried longer. The initiative in this policy of curtailment was taken by the Bank of the United States with a series of measures beginning in July, 1818. Due to speculation and fraud at its offices in Philadelphia and Baltimore, as well as to the activities of the Southern and Western branches, the bank reached a point where its specie fund was only $2,357,000 and its immediate liabilities were $22,372,000. Collapse seemed imminent. Since much of the trouble could be laid at the doors of the Southern and Western branches, upon them was placed most of the burden of making retrenchments. On July 20, 1818, the bank decided to curtail $5,000,000 in discounts at Philadelphia, Baltimore, Richmond, and Norfolk. A month later and again on October 30, additional restrictions were placed upon discounts, and Southern and Western branches were ordered to send $700,000 in specie to Philadelphia.[10] Furthermore,

10 Catterall, *Second Bank of the United States*, 51–52, gives the amounts of specie required as follows:

Charleston	$150,000	Fayetteville	$100,000
Lexington	100,000	Richmond	50,000
Louisville	100,000	Cincinnati	50,000
Chillicothe	100,000	Pittsburgh	50,000

they were directed to begin collecting at a rapid rate the balances that were owed them by the state banks. Although these accounts were overdue, a worse day for payment could scarcely have been chosen. The state banks, not having much specie in their vaults, could pay their debts only by collecting a part of what was owed to them, and collection at this moment of depressed prices proved to be extremely difficult. Most of the banks, being unable to gather in enough specie to meet the demands of the Bank of the United States and to redeem such of their own notes as were presented, suspended specie payments.

By November 20, 1818, the Bank of the State of Kentucky had suspended, and by January all the other banks in that state had adopted the same policy. Their notes dropped to a discount of from 20 to 30 per cent. At Nashville, the Farmers' and Mechanics' Bank suspended specie payment on June 18, 1819. Four days later the Nashville Bank did likewise, and by the following month no bank in Middle Tennessee would pay specie. On September 11 the Nashville *Whig* published a list of fourteen Western banks that had adopted this policy. The highly speculative Planters' and Merchants' Bank at Huntsville, Alabama, suspended specie payments in 1820, and, by act of the legislature, state treasury notes were placed on a par with the depreciated currency of this bank.[11]

In the older states along the Atlantic, where there had been less speculation, the banks weathered the storm somewhat better. Yet, even here they were severely shaken. In South Carolina the Charleston banks were ordered to pay $130,535.50, which amounted to about one fifth of their accounts, to the Bank of the United States. In North Carolina, the Fayetteville branch of the Bank of the United States virtually refused to accept anything but specie in payment of accounts from the state bank although various kinds of currency had previously been acceptable.

As specie payments were suspended, the notes of the banks that had adopted this course declined in value, a decline which was accelerated by the fact that many banks continued to issue paper money after their tills were closed upon gold and silver. With bank notes variously discounted, currency transactions became confused

11 Thomas P. Abernethy, *The Formative Period in Alabama, 1815–1828* (Montgomery, 1922), 94–95.

and sometimes costly. For example, the retail merchants of Richmond found that at least half of the paper money received in the course of business had been issued by North Carolina and other out-of-state banks and was unacceptable to Richmond banks in payment of notes due by the merchants. The merchants were therefore under the necessity of going to the brokers who charged a 5 per cent fee for exchanging the North Carolina notes for money that the banks would accept.[12]

The policy of contraction begun by the Bank of the United States had tremendous effects at each of the levels down which it worked. The chain of pressures was first exerted upon the branches of the bank; the branches passed on the demands to the state banks; the last sought to collect from independent banks, merchants, planters, and others whose accounts were due. Before the depression was over, all who stood in this sequence of pressures had taken losses. By August 30, 1822, the Bank of the United States had lost over $3,000,000. Over half of that amount was lost at Baltimore; nearly $900,000 was lost in the branch offices south and west of that city. In this area where the Bank of the United States suffered heavily, the various state banks likewise incurred undetermined but heavy losses. Even less calculable was the enormous volume of losses suffered by those who stood at the end of the chain of bank pressures; the farmers, merchants, and businessmen of all sorts who were pressed for payment by the banks and by each other.

But, though the aggregate of their losses cannot be known, the impact of the depression upon them can be illustrated. At one term of the court of Davidson County, in which Nashville is situated, between 500 and 600 suits for debt were entered.[13] From Lexington, Kentucky, came reports that factories representing a capital of half a million dollars were idle, and that "a deeper gloom hangs over us than was ever witnessed by the oldest man. The last war was sunshine, compared with these times." [14] At Baltimore, rents de-

[12] Richmond *Compiler*, June 9, 1819. A similar situation in Georgia is described in Thomas P. Govan, "Banking and the Credit System in Georgia, 1810–1860," in *Journal of Southern History*, IV (1938), 177–78.

[13] Abernethy, "Andrew Jackson and the Rise of Southwestern Democracy," *loc. cit.*, 67.

[14] Rezneck, "Depression of 1819–1822," *loc. cit.*, 31. A number of complaints about hard times in Kentucky can be found in *Digest of Accounts of Manufacturing Establishments*, 1820.

clined from 40 to 50 per cent, long lists of insolvents were published in the newspapers each week, and it was estimated that the population of the city declined by 10,000 between the years 1815 and 1820.[15] A wharf and several storehouses in Alexandria, Virginia, that had once cost $17,000 brought only $1,250 at auction in 1820. The value of property depreciated from one half to three fourths in Richmond; half of it was mortgaged to the banks; [16] and between 1817 and 1820 the population of this city dropped from 14,352 to 12,046.[17] Rural real estate likewise depreciated as is evidenced by valuations through these years in a number of North Carolina counties.[18] Senator Thomas Hart Benton of Missouri summed up the situation west of the Appalachians in his assertion that "All the flourishing cities of the West are mortgaged to this money power. They may be devoured by it at any moment. They are in the jaws of the monster! A lump of butter in the mouth of a dog! one gulp, one swallow, and all is gone!" [19]

In a land of free speech it was but natural for the Panic to unloose the floodgates of popular diagnosis and prescription. Conservatives as well as radicals told their fellow men how to escape from their ills. To the wing of opinion which has been dubbed the "Time and Patience" school there were many adherents, among them several governors of the Southern states who, while thinking it their duty to inform the legislatures that there was a panic in the land, were either devoid of ideas as to its cause and cure or else thought it unwise to fan the smouldering embers of popular discontent. These state executives were like President Monroe, who professed himself unable to "regard these pressures . . . as otherwise than in the light of mild and instructive admonitions, warning us of dangers to be shunned in the future; teaching us lessons of economy." [20] Likewise, there were some unofficial spokesmen who declared that conditions would right themselves in due season provided men would practice economy and exercise patience.[21] In similar vein

[15] *Niles' Weekly Register,* XIX (1820), 40.

[16] Rezneck, "Depression of 1819–1822," *loc. cit.,* 31–32.

[17] Richmond *Compiler,* November 9, 1820.

[18] Albert R. Newsome, *The Presidential Election of 1824 in North Carolina* (Chapel Hill, 1939), 24–25, n. 68.

[19] Quoted in Catterall, *Second Bank of the United States,* 67.

[20] Quoted in Rezneck, "Depression of 1819–1822." *loc. cit.,* 39.

[21] Nashville *Whig,* June 26, July 3, 10, 17, 24, 1819.

the conservative *Maryland Gazette and Political Intelligencer* advised its readers to cease railing at banks and imploring Congress for relief legislation. Instead, so it counseled, "Let us turn from the wickedness of our ways, [and] humble ourselves before the throne of Almighty God." [22]

But patience, humility, and frugality, commendable virtues though they be, were uncomfortable in practice and constituted too passive a program for debt-ridden men who were facing the loss of all they possessed. Therefore, under a leadership that was neither humble nor patient, several states undertook radical programs of debtor relief. The Tennessee legislature passed a stay law in 1819 which granted a two-year delay in the payment of debts unless the creditor was willing to accept notes of the state bank or notes that were equally depreciated. To end the "taking of excessive usury," the legal rate of interest was set at 6 per cent. By a more radical measure the legislature sought to compensate for the "diminution of the circulating medium" by creating the Bank of the State of Tennessee with power to issue $1,000,000 in paper money and to make loans to the maximum amount of $1,000 to any one borrower. The notes of this loan office were guaranteed by income from the sales of certain public lands belonging to the state and by ordinary revenues that were not otherwise appropriated. As October 15, 1820, approached, the day for the opening of the institution, there was much anxiety in the state over whether the new money could be manufactured in Philadelphia and brought to Tennessee in time for the land sales that were scheduled to begin on November 1. The progress of the bank's agent was reported in the newspapers as he hurried to Philadelphia where the notes were printed, back to Nashville where they were signed, and thence to Knoxville. There the bank was opened on time, and the notes were distributed to individuals in the form of loans. The cycle was completed almost at once when the borrowers returned the notes to the state as payment for the public land which they were buying.[23]

This chapter in the history of fiat money was closely paralleled in several other Southern states. In Kentucky a stay law was enacted

[22] Annapolis *Maryland Gazette and Political Intelligencer*, June 3, 1819.

[23] Parks, "Felix Grundy and the Depression of 1819," *loc. cit.*, 22–34; Nashville *Whig*, July 26–October 17, 1820.

and a Bank of the Commonwealth was created with neither capital, specie, nor stockholders. Its only asset was an appropriation of $7,000 to cover the cost of engraving and printing notes to the amount of $3,000,000.[24] In Alabama a slightly more substantial state bank was organized in 1824,[25] and four years later the state of Georgia established a similar institution.[26] These two states, like Tennessee, were careful to guard against the engrossment of the newly created credit by a few persons by requiring that loans be widely distributed in small amounts.

Relief measures such as these, though they might alleviate economic distress for the moment, carried no promise of a return of prosperity nor guarantee against a repetition of present evils. Hence, even while dosing the financial system with palliatives, men tried to find and eradicate the roots of the trouble. From the wreckage of shattered plans, deferred hopes, and property losses they looked about for the forces that had brought disaster and, whether wisely or foolishly, they concluded that their troubles could be charged to the banks, especially the Bank of the United States; to the Supreme Court, especially its doctrine of broad constitutional construction; and to the financial power and commercial shrewdness of the northeastern part of the United States. The processes by which the multitude of individual, small-scale, personal grievances were bundled up into a few broad, regional hostilities deserves examination, for herein the Panic helped to shape the regional mind into a complex of likes and dislikes that in time formed one of the bases of a Southern program and Southern action.

Among all the imaginable causes of the Panic, the one to which the Southern mind most frequently turned was the banks. According to a Kentuckian, "of all evils which can be inflicted upon a free state, banking establishments are the most alarming. They are the vultures that prey upon the vitals of the constitution, and rob the body politic of its life blood." [27] With no great change of metaphor, a Tennessean described them as the "horse-leeches" of the country which "drained every drop of blood they could suck from a suffer-

24 Rezneck, "Depression of 1819–1822," *loc. cit.,* 45.
25 Abernethy, *Formative Period in Alabama,* 99–100; Moore, *History of Alabama,* 214–17; Gouge, *Paper Money and Banking,* Pt. II, 136.
26 Govan, "Banking and the Credit System in Georgia," *loc. cit.,* 173.
27 *Niles' Weekly Register,* XVII (1819), 19.

ing community." [28] John Clark, Governor of Georgia, asserted that "the opinion . . . now almost universally prevails, that the pecuniary embarrassments of the citizens is [*sic*] greater in proportion as you approach the vicinity of a bank." [29] Governor Randolph of Virginia, son-in-law of Thomas Jefferson, declared that banks helped capitalists rather than ordinary men and issued paper money whereas specie was a better circulating medium.[30]

Among the many who blamed the banks, there were some who attempted to discriminate between their good and bad characteristics. It was asserted in a letter published in the *Louisiana Gazette* [31] that "the great causes of the commercial embarrassments now felt through the United States are to be traced, to the number of banks established throughout it, and the false system of business pursued by their directors." According to the Richmond *Enquirer*,[32] bad banking consisted in the overissue of notes with a consequent inability to pay specie in time of pressure. One of the wisest analyses of the defects of banking was from the pen of "Economicus" who, writing in the *Carolina Centinel,* asserted that banks should lend only for short terms and only to men of capital who sought to supplement their own funds with money borrowed from the bank. But, continued "Economicus," instead of following this cautious policy "our numerous banks have sometimes stretched their loans to the utmost . . . to enable one man to buy real estate; another to build houses and to buy furniture; a third to buy whole crops of tobacco and flour . . . a fourth to purchase the fixed capital of large manufactories. . . . We wanted to take short cuts to fortune." [33]

Many persons came to regard the Bank of the United States as the chief cause of their plight; they would have agreed that the history of the Panic could be summarized in the sentence: "The Bank was saved and the people were ruined." [34] There was a measure of

[28] Quoted in Parks, "Felix Grundy and the Depression of 1819," *loc. cit.,* 27.

[29] Quoted in Govan, "Banking and the Credit System in Georgia," *loc. cit.,* 165.

[30] Message to the legislature, December 4, 1820, in Virginia *Senate Journal,* 1820, pp. 16–18.

[31] New Orleans *Louisiana Gazette,* February 5, 1819.

[32] Richmond *Enquirer,* June 1, 8, 1819.

[33] Quoted in Rezneck, "Depression of 1819–1822," *loc. cit.,* 34–35.

[34] Quoted in Catterall, *Second Bank of the United States,* 61.

truth in this statement because the bank's contraction of credit had indeed occasioned untold hardship; and some of the state banks, faced with the necessity of compelling their clients to pay their obligations, made the most of this opportunity to shift the blame to the Bank of the United States. It was but a short step from hostility to the bank to hostility to the Middle and Eastern states where the bank was said to be owned. The way in which individual distress could be transmuted into sectional antagonism was illustrated by the statement that a "wild son of Tennessee who has been with Jackson, can ill brook that his bit of land, perhaps his rifle, should be torn from him by a neighbouring shopkeeper, that the proceeds may travel eastward, where the 'sceptre' of money has fixed itself." [35]

Western and Southern hostility toward the East was further heightened by a commotion over shawls and peddlers. Following a custom that began with Adam, men blamed their troubles upon their helpmates; in this instance they complained that women had been extravagant in purchasing such luxuries as shawls, leghorn hats, and cakes for teas. Hezekiah Niles asserted that Baltimoreans had been buying shawls from abroad at $500 apiece.[36] Out in the poorer West, Tennesseans were accused of having purchased them in such quantities, even though at small prices, that $40,000 in specie had been drained out of a single bank within the first six months of the year 1819.

While no one ascribed the Panic solely to shawls, it was asserted that the excessive purchase of unnecessary goods had drained money from the South to the North, and from the nation to England. Responsibility for this hurtful operation was placed partly upon those who had spent their money so foolishly and partly upon the artful, shrewd salesmen who had brought in the goods and taken out the money. To keep money from leaving the United States, it was suggested, to the subsequent distress of the South, that a tariff barrier be created; but to restrict its flow from the South to the North could not be accomplished so simply. Tennesseans were urged to develop "Domestic Manufactures" so that money could be kept at home, and they were advised to establish something of a

[35] Quoted in Rezneck, "Depression of 1819–1822," *loc. cit.*, 38.
[36] *Niles' Weekly Register*, XIX (1820), 39–40.

boycott lest they continue to be the "prey of the mercenary, sharp, keen cleverness of the importer of *cheap goods*." [37]

The peddlers who brought in the goods and took out the money were objects of especial dislike. Niles considered them much less respectable than scavengers, and he described them as "a worthless set of beings and generally rogues, too lazy to get their living honestly. I never see one of them prowling near my house without thinking where I can put my *cane*." [38] Three months later he reported that "Some of the southern states are jealous of the designs of the 'northern travelling pedlars'—they are said to have increased of late to an 'alarming degree.' " [39] North Carolina doubled its tax upon those who peddled goods grown or manufactured outside the state,[40] and the Kentucky legislature debated a similar proposal. In the course of the debate a member of the lower house declared with considerable warmth: "I hope fifty dollars will be retained in the bill—for why? because pedlars are generally Yankees, who are capable of imposing upon, and swindling our plain, homespun Kentuckians. When they come here as preachers, they inculcate principles diabolical and unscriptural—and when they come in the character of pedlars, what will they do?" [41]

By contrasting the supposed simplicity and honesty of the farmer with the crafty shrewdness of the Yankee salesman, by calling attention to the debtorship of the West and South to the wealthier Northeast, and by intensifying hatred for the Bank of the United States, which was looked upon as an Eastern institution, the Panic tended both to bind the South and the West together and to consolidate public opinion within these areas upon a platform of common likes and hatreds. Roughly speaking, the Panic had divided the nation by a diagonal line running from northwest to southeast. Unless the dissatisfaction below this line was assuaged, so a Kentuckian wrote, it would lead "with a steady and certain pace, to civil war and a dissolution of the union." [42]

---

[37] *Ibid.;* Nashville *Whig*, December 6, 1820.
[38] *Niles' Weekly Register*, XIX (1820), 40.   [39] *Ibid.*, 243.
[40] North Carolina *Acts*, 1817, p. 7; *ibid.*, 1821, p. 3.
[41] Kentucky *House Journal*, 1819–1820, pp. 228, 233–34, 307–308. To correct the distortion of these strictures, one should read Lewis E. Atherton, "Itinerant Merchandising in the Ante-Bellum South," in *Bulletin of the Business Historical Society* (Boston), XIX (1945), 35–59.   [42] *Niles' Weekly Register*, XVII (1819), 11.

But this prophecy was much too gloomy. It failed to take account of the fact that the debate over slavery in Missouri was separating the Northwest from its alliance with the slave states, and it overlooked the further fact that the Panic created disunity and local hostilities in a number of the Southern and Western states. In Tennessee, for instance, the program of debtor relief drew its support from the newly settled Cumberland basin of which Nashville was the center; it was strongly opposed by the small farmers of the valleys of East Tennessee. In North Carolina an unsuccessful but vigorous movement toward debtor relief and bank regulation drew most of its strength from the western and northeastern parts of the state. In Georgia the more violent attacks upon the banks were made by members of the Clark party which found its principal strength among the small farmers in the newer and poorer parts of the state. In Maryland the rising democracy, which was strongest in the large urban center of Baltimore, controlled the lower house of the state legislature. The federalistic conservatives of the older planting counties and of the ancient town of Annapolis were in a majority in the state senate, and they could therefore block radical measures proposed by the house of representatives. Assuming a superior air, the senate on one occasion returned a relief measure to the lower house with the notation that it "contains so many interlineations, erasures and blots, that the meaning of several parts thereof is rendered doubtful and uncertain. We presume it has been sent us in this condition by mistake." [43]

Thus the Panic, an economic occurrence, had important political consequences. Within the several states it raised new issues relating to banking, currency, debt moratoria, and interest rates, and the consideration of these questions usually intensified sectional feeling between the debtor upcountry and the creditor urban centers. But while the depression served to accentuate petty divergencies throughout the South, it likewise operated to unify the South and the West in hostility against the Bank of the United States and against the creditor East; and it brought to the attention of Congress such questions as tariff, Federal land policy, and the need of a national bankruptcy law. In considering these national questions the Southern Congressmen usually voted as a unit. The economic

[43] Maryland *Senate Journal*, 1819–1820, p. 24.

upheaval thus had a share in giving to the South a political platform.

By placing these important questions upon the agenda of Congress and of state legislatures, the depression increased the tempo of political activity and brought a renewed zest for greater democracy. Most of the solutions proposed for the problems would have the effect of diminishing the area of free enterprise and of increasing government's control over economic life. Inasmuch as the fortunes of the individual would therefore depend in greater measure than heretofore upon his political power and skill, it behooved the franchised to use the ballot and the unfranchised to win it. The importance of possessing political power was clearly taught by the varying fortunes of the rival forces in the several states: in those where the democratic movement had made most progress the debtors were successful in passing laws that limited the power of the rich in their dealings with the poor. In states where debtors failed to pass such measures they turned with renewed determination to the task of destroying the political barriers that stood in their way. The Panic was thus the forerunner of attempts at political revolution and constitutional reform.

The far-reaching social and political repercussions of the Panic were closely matched by a contemporary controversy over slavery. The stage was set nearly a year in advance when a petition from the Missouri Territory was presented to the House of Representatives on March 16, 1818, praying that statehood be granted. Final action not having been reached before adjournment, a similar memorial was introduced on December 18, 1818, in the next session of Congress. In due course a bill to enable Missouri to proceed to the drawing up of a state constitution came before the House on February 13, 1819. Thereupon, James Tallmadge, Jr., a Representative from New York, introduced an amendment to prohibit the further introduction of slaves into Missouri and to provide for the gradual emancipation of those already there; in brief, Missouri would be granted statehood only if it presented an antislavery constitution. With the introduction of this amendment the Missouri question was transformed from routine business into the most exciting issue that had been before Congress in years.[44]

[44] In this discussion of the debate over the admission of Missouri the essential

After several days of sharp debate, the House accepted the first part of Tallmadge's amendment by the vote of 87 to 76. With one exception, every Representative from the slave states opposed the measure; and all but ten of the free-state Representatives favored it. The second clause of the amendment passed by nearly the same vote. The enabling act, thus amended, was sent to the Senate on February 17. There, after another debate, the two clauses of the Tallmadge amendment were struck out by votes of 22 to 16 and of 31 to 7. Again the division was sectional, but not so sharply as in the House. Neither body would recede from its position before the termination of the Fifteenth Congress.

The debate which had begun in Congress was continued with much vehemence in newspapers, state legislatures, public meetings, and pamphlets. Though it ranged far and wide, most of it was confined to a few arguments. Part of the debate grew out of the fact that Missouri was within the territory purchased from France in 1803. Advocates of the amendment asserted that the whole question was without precedent so far as Missouri was concerned, because west of the Mississippi, slavery had been neither prohibited, as it had been in the old Northwest Territory, nor allowed, as in the Southwest Territory. Opponents of the amendment claimed that the admission of Louisiana in 1812 as a slave state—and Louisiana was the only state yet carved from the Louisiana Purchase—constituted a favorable precedent, and they further sought to find a sanction for slavery in Missouri in that part of the treaty of 1803 which guaranteed to the inhabitants of the Louisiana Territory all the rights of person and property which they were enjoying at the moment of transfer. The arguments on both sides appear unconvincing, and this part of the debate is chiefly important because it indicated a belief that all subsequent trans-Mississippi states would follow in the path of Missouri.

A more important point was the assertion by Representatives of the free states that slavery was wrong, whether viewed under the laws of morality, the dictates of humanity, the teachings of the Scripture, or the principles of democracy, and that it should therefore be prohibited in Missouri. They declared that "The *slavery of*

source is, of course, the *Annals of Congress*. It seems unnecessary to give page citations thereto except in the case of quotations.

121

man is abhorrent to every noble and honorable feeling." [45] "Slavery is contrary to the spirit of our republican institutions—in its effects subversive of the prosperity and best interests of society . . . and . . . it is the duty of every good citizen to use all constitutional and proper means to procure its melioration, and to prevent its extension." [46] While this attack far exceeded in volume and intensity of feeling any previous discussion of slavery in the United States, it should be noted that with few exceptions the attack was upon the institution rather than upon the character of the slaveholders.

In answering this attack, Southern spokesmen expressed surprise that it had been made, and they complained of the intemperate zeal of those who made it. For instance, Thomas Ritchie, editor of the Richmond *Enquirer,* published a contribution entitled "Scriptural Researches . . . in demonstration that slaveholding never was prohibited by the Word of God" in the hope that "It may too have the good effect . . . of softening down some of those fiery enthusiasts to the East, who cite the bible, without reservation, as an authority on all occasions for charging the southern people with inhumanity." At the same time, he admitted that slavery was evil. "We protest," he declared, "in our own name, and that of so many others, that we do not vindicate servitude; we wish no slave had touched our soil; we wish it could be terminated. As republicans, we frankly declare before our God and our country, that we abhor its institution." But, he added, "does not every man, unless he be a fanatic, conceive how difficult it is for us to be rid of it, in a manner consistent with our future peace and tranquillity?" [47] Ritchie was in nowise exceptional in his condemnation of slavery. Robert R. Reid of Georgia declared in Congress: "For my own part, surrounded by slavery from my cradle to the present moment, I yet

> *'Hate the touch of servile hands;*
> *'I loathe the slaves who cringe around:'*

[45] [Philadelphia?] *Aurora,* quoted in Richmond *Enquirer,* December 11, 1819.

[46] Philadelphia *American Daily Advertiser,* quoted *ibid.,* January 25, 1820. The *Enquirer* published many other Northern antislavery resolutions. Numerous indictments of slavery were made in Congress and in resolutions by public meetings and legislatures of the Northern states.

[47] Richmond *Enquirer,* February 10, 1820.

and I would hail that day as the most glorious . . . which should behold . . . the black population of the United States placed upon the high eminence of equal rights." [48] Governor Randolph of Virginia, in a message to the legislature, stated that "The deplorable error of our ancestors in copying a civil institution from savage Africa, has fixed upon their posterity a depressing burden." [49] Tagged on to such statements was the opinion, frequently expressed, that slavery would be no worse by its extension to the West. Spreading it thin over a wider area "would tend to soften the evil and to accelerate its abolition." [50]

The Southern answer to the attack upon slavery was, in the language of the court, a demurrer; Southerners took the position that a debate upon the alleged evils of slavery was beside the issue because, in their opinion, Congress lacked power under the Constitution to exclude slavery from Missouri. "Why . . . talk of the evils of slavery?" they asked. "Prove you have the *right* to act before you indulge your feelings." "The East and the South stand on very different grounds. The former says, 'We believe it to be *expedient* to restrict slavery;' the latter, 'We believe a restriction to be a breach of the constitution which we have sworn to support.' " [51] Because of the refusal of Congressmen from the slave states to debate the ethics of slavery, the major battle in the Missouri debate was joined on the question of whether Congress possessed the power to impose binding restrictions upon a state as it entered the Union. Lacking clear and certain precedents, the debaters drew their arguments chiefly from constitutional theory and from opposing interpretations of the words of the Constitution: "New States may be admitted by the Congress into this Union"; and "The Congress shall have power to . . . make all needful rules and regulations respecting the territory or other property belonging to the United States."

Rufus King, who was the ablest of the antislavery speakers, asserted that inasmuch as the Constitution imposed no limitation upon Congress in the exercise of this power, Congress had full right

---

[48] *Annals of Congress,* 16 Cong., 1 Sess., 1025.
[49] Virginia *Senate Journal,* 1820, p. 13.
[50] Richmond *Enquirer,* February 10, 1820.
[51] *Ibid.,* December 11, 1819; January 11, 1820.

to prescribe conditions which a state must meet before being admitted. Furthermore, he insisted that a state, after it was in the Union, could not annul the articles that had been imposed upon it by Congress. King defended his thesis with learning and skill.[52]

On the other side, William Pinkney of Maryland, in attempting to prove that new states should be admitted as absolute equals of the original states, and no less sovereign than they, argued that "if you have this power of [imposing restrictions], you may squeeze down a new-born sovereign State to the size of a pigmy, and then taking it between finger and thumb, stick it into a nitch [sic] of the Union, and still continue, by way of mockery, to call it a State in the sense of the Constitution." [53] The lower house of the Kentucky legislature, while deliberately avoiding the expression of any opinion for or against slavery, likewise reasoned that if Congress could "trammel or control the powers of a territory in the formation of a state government; that body may, on the same principles, reduce its powers to little more than those possessed by the people of the district of Columbia; and whilst professing to make it a sovereign state, may bind it in perpetual vassalage, and reduce it to the condition of a province." [54]

In Virginia it was "Resolved, That the General Assembly of Virginia will support the good people of Missouri in their just rights to admission into the Union; and will co-operate with them in resisting with manly fortitude, any attempt which Congress may make to impose restraints, or restrictions, as the price of admission, not authorized by the great principles of the constitution." [55]

[52] Rufus King's views are best stated in "The Substance of Two Speeches," in Charles R. King (ed.), *The Life and Correspondence of Rufus King* (New York, 1894–1900), VI, 690 ff. He also asserted that Congress had earlier imposed restrictions upon states admitted to the Union; but this part of the debate was inconclusive and complex. Southern spokesmen denied that Congress had ever forced into any state constitution provisions contrary to the will of the people of that state. For discussion of the constitutional questions raised in this debate, see Andrew C. McLaughlin, *A Constitutional History of the United States* (New York, 1935), 372–82; Homer C. Hockett, *The Constitutional History of the United States, 1826–1876* (New York, 1939), 148–68.

[53] *Annals of Congress,* 16 Cong., 1 Sess., 395. William Pinkney's able speech covers pp. 389–417.

[54] Kentucky *House Journal,* 1819–1820, pp. 159–60. Similar resolutions can be found in Maryland *Senate Journal,* 1819–1820, p. 31.

[55] Virginia *House Journal,* 1819–1820, p. 109; Virginia *Senate Journal,* 1819–1820. pp. 31–32, 71, 73–87, 100.

Advocates of the Tallmadge amendment were by implication defending loose construction of the Constitution and the extension of national power; their opponents, in contrast, were advocating strict construction and state rights. This alignment was at variance with previous trends. For nearly twenty years New England Federalists had been drifting in the direction of state rights, localism, and perhaps secession; during those same years the dominant Republican South and West had been developing the powers of the national government despite the objections of a few Old Republicans like John Randolph. The sudden reversal of these trends when the Tallmadge amendment was offered, the quick shift to nationalism in New England and to state rights in the South, indicates that most men on both sides were ready to barter constitutional consistency for political profit. A few Northern votes, however, seem to have been turned against the amendment by constitutional considerations.

Similarly, Northern concern over the plight of the slave could not be explained by previous trends. Before the controversy began there had been little difference between North and South in respect to the volume and vigor of antislavery expressions. Doubtless the South, without being quite aware of the fact, had become more firmly attached to slavery since the invention of the cotton gin; and doubtless some Northern antislavery men, having set slavery on the road to extinction in their own states, gained confidence in their cause and looked forward to its further restriction. But the great outburst of Northern antislavery sentiment over the Missouri question cannot be regarded as the fruition of widespread Northern compassion for the slave, for there is no evidence that such sentiment was general throughout the North before the Tallmadge amendment was offered.

Inasmuch as there was nothing in the recent history of humanitarian or constitutional thought to explain the Northern crusade against slavery, Southerners began to suspect that there was more to the attack than appeared on the surface. The Richmond *Enquirer*, December 16, 1819, charged that there was "some sinister design, something inimical to the interests of the southern states, behind the specious mask of humanity." Similar suspicions were ironically expressed by Governor Thomas B. Robertson of Louisiana when he declared to the legislature of his state that "on the subject of slavery, all we have to ask is this, that our Eastern and Northern brethren would forgive us the vice, or immorality, or misfortune (as they indifferently term it) of holding slaves, as we forgive them the disengenuousness [sic] that would convert the circumstance into purpose of unholy ambition." [56]

What was the "unholy ambition" that slaveholders thought they glimpsed behind the veil of compassion for the slave? Some professed to see signs of an attempt to rebuild the Federalist party, and occasionally it was hinted that King was making a bid for the presidency. [57] Others, remembering the Hartford convention, alleged that the controversy had been aroused by "the management of those men who are a second time attempting to sever the Union," so as to create a separate New England confederation. [58] Again, it was asserted that the purpose behind the antislavery restrictions was to "exclude a very great majority of the citizens of the Southern States from a participation of the benefits and advantages ever to be derived from the fertile western regions, and confine them and their posterity, with their slaves and their posterity, to the narrow limits which they now possess." [59]

Some of these charges were exaggerations, others were unprovable. However, the assertion that the Missouri controversy was a stratagem of the East for capturing political power deserves the most careful examination. Hitherto, political lines had seldom been drawn between slave and free states. Instead, the alignment for many years had been between New England on the one hand and a South-West alliance on the other; and against this agrarian alliance, which included free as well as slave states, the commercial East had fought a long and losing battle. In probing for the cause of its political degradation, New England had early put its finger on the three-fifths clause of the Constitution and had inveighed against it in season and out for more than thirty years before Missouri applied for statehood. To escape from the adverse operation of the slave ratio, some Easterners had even professed a willingness to

[56] Louisiana *Senate Journal*, 1820–1821, p. 22. Also quoted in Nashville *Whig*, January 31, 1821.

[57] Richmond *Enquirer*, February 17, 1820.

[58] New Orleans *Louisiana Gazette*, March 14, 1820.

[59] Richmond *Enquirer*, December 16, 1819.

disrupt the Union. Many of them had spoken against it with bitterness and anger and had made it the scapegoat of a host of New England troubles.[60]

Making the kind of calculation that Congressmen from the free states had been making since the year 1791, King, while speaking for the Tallmadge amendment, estimated that if the three-fifths clause were abrogated, the slave states would lose twenty Representatives and twenty Presidential electors, and that Virginia would be shorn of seven of its twenty-three Representatives. The effect of the clause, he added, "has been obvious to the preponderance it has given to the slave holding states over the other states. . . . But the extension of this disproportionate power to the new states would be unjust and odious." [61] In short, the Northeast, having convinced itself that slavery was a cause of its political plight, objected to the creation of another slave state. Support for the Tallmadge amendment amounted to a blow at political thralldom as well as against Negro slavery.

How much Tallmadge planned and foresaw when he offered his proposal is unknown. It is possible that he was moved solely by humanitarian considerations, and Ritchie readily admitted on January 22, 1820, that "Many of the eastern men are very sincere in the course they take." But whatever Tallmadge's motive, no sooner was debate started on the amendment than it became apparent that here at last was the magic wedge that would pry the free states above the Ohio River away from their customary political alliance with the slave states. The eight Representatives from the Northwest all voted with the East.[62] At once the East began to hope and the South began to fear that this new alignment would become permanent. John Quincy Adams believed that the importance of the amendment was not foreseen "even by those who brought it forward," but that its discussion "disclosed a secret: it revealed the basis for a new organization of parties. . . . Here was a new party ready formed, . . . terrible to the whole Union, but portentously terrible to the South—threatening in its progress the emancipation

[60] Albert F. Simpson, "The Political Significance of Slave Representation, 1787–1821," in *Journal of Southern History*, VII (1941), 315–42, is of fundamental importance in understanding the attitude of New England.

[61] *Niles' Weekly Register*, XVII (1819), 219.

[62] Frederick J. Turner, *Rise of the New West, 1819–1829* (New York, 1906), 165.

of all their slaves, threatening in its immediate effect that Southern domination which has swayed the Union for the last twenty years, and threatening that political ascendency of Virginia, upon which Clay and Crawford both had fastened their principal hopes of personal aggrandizement." [63]

King's analysis of the political implications of the controversy was expressed in a letter to his son: "I feel much concern for the issue, which, if decided against us, settles forever the Dominion of the Union. Not only the Presidency, but the Supreme Judiciary, at least a majority of its members, will forever hereafter come from the slave Region. . . . So that the decision of Missouri, will also determine whether the Citizens of the free States are to hold even their actual political Rights, or to be hereafter debarred of some of the most important of them. Old Mr. Adams, as he is the first, will on this hypothesis be the last President from a free state." [64] The St. Louis *Enquirer* asserted on November 10, 1819, that "No people ever understood a political question better than the people of Missouri understand this. They know that . . . it is a question of *political power* between the Northern and Southern interests." [65]

Although Adams was confiding his thoughts to his diary, and King was writing to his son, Southerners did not need their help to decipher the political situation. The leading Virginia newspaper declared that if the East succeeded, then " 'the sceptre will depart from Judah:' and Virginia influence . . . will be heard of no more." [66] Charles Pinckney of South Carolina asserted that Northern opposition to slavery in the new states was unrelated to "the love of liberty, humanity, or religion," but sprang rather from "the love of power, and the never-ceasing wish to regain the honors and offices of the Government, which they know can never be done but by increasing the number of the non-slave holding States." [67]

When the Sixteenth Congress convened on December 6, 1819, there was a fresh eruption of Eastern declamation against the evils

[63] Charles Francis Adams (ed.), *Memoirs of John Quincy Adams* (Philadelphia, 1874–1877), IV, 529.

[64] King (ed.), *Life and Correspondence of Rufus King,* VI, 267.

[65] Quoted in Frank H. Hodder, "Side Lights on the Missouri Compromises," in American Historical Association, *Annual Report,* 1909 (Washington, 1911), 154.

[66] Richmond *Enquirer,* December 16, 23, 1819; February 3, March 7, 1820.

[67] *Annals of Congress,* 16 Cong., 2 Sess., 1144.

of slavery, and a renewed attempt by Southern Congressmen to prove that new states ought to be admitted with as full self-determination as the older states possessed. For some weeks there was a deadlock. The advocates of the amendment had a majority in the House; the South, with the assistance of several Northern Senators, controlled the Senate. A compromise was finally reached under which Maine, which had recently applied for statehood, was to be paired off with Missouri: one to be admitted as a slave state, the other as a free state. To speak more accurately, each was to be admitted without restriction, but it was well understood that Maine opposed slavery whereas Missouri desired it. After all the great controversy, Congress was back where it started; it did not vote slavery in or out of Missouri but left the decision to its people.

As a further part of the compromise, Congress decided that slavery should be prohibited in the rest of the Louisiana Territory above the line of 36 degrees and 30 minutes. The status of slavery in the territories was not discussed until near the end of the protracted controversy, and it was debated in Congress for only a few hours.[68] The division created by this line was extremely unequal. Only one state, Arkansas, was expected to be formed below the line, but a considerable number could be created in the free part of the Louisiana Purchase. Thus, to get Missouri into the Union as a slave state, the South bartered away the prospect of slavery being much extended, and because of this fact many Congressmen from the South refused to vote for the compromise. Eighteen of the twenty-three Virginia Representatives were in the opposition. It should be remarked that Southern opposition was not based on the opinion that Congress lacked power to control slavery in the territories, for there were few at this time who held to such a view. It was based, rather, on the calculation that the slave states were trading the long future for the short present, and that by rights it ought not to be necessary to purchase Missouri's entrance.

Although Missouri's desires had little or no influence in the struggle, it is worth noting that its inhabitants became exceedingly restive over the long delay, that they professed opposition to any

[68] James A. Woodburn, "The Historical Significance of the Missouri Compromise," in American Historical Association, *Annual Report*, 1893 (Washington, 1894), 256–57, 290.

restriction upon their freedom of choice in the writing of a constitution, and that they wished a proslavery constitution. When at last the enabling act was passed, Missouri acted quickly. A convention, meeting at St. Louis, adopted a proslavery constitution on July 19, 1820. Popular sentiment cannot be accurately determined because the constitution was not submitted to the people. Thirty-eight of the thirty-nine delegates favored slavery, but the elections of members to the convention indicate that public opinion was divided somewhat more equally, perhaps two to one in favor of slavery.

Missouri stirred up another controversy by including a clause in the constitution which it submitted to Congress on November 16, 1820, directing the legislature to prohibit free Negroes from entering the state. Once more Congress set to quarreling, perhaps with more bitterness and suspicion and with more threats of violence than in the earlier debates. But this second phase of the controversy was soon ended by a rather meaningless compromise. This disturbance in Congress did not last long enough to cause much excitement throughout the nation.[69]

To what extent the great controversy over Missouri stirred Americans is not easily determined. In December, 1819, the Richmond *Enquirer* stated that the question had raised much more excitement in the North than in the South; but two months later it reprinted the opinion of the Georgetown *National Messenger* that "The agitation of the public mind in Virginia, respecting the proposed restriction on Missouri, is represented as being more violent, and more extensive than on any occasion in recent history."[70] A month later the *Enquirer* observed: "The integrity of the Union was rudely assailed. It became the topic of ordinary conversation."[71] Other Southern papers showed less concern over the fate of Missouri. The Annapolis *Maryland Gazette*, the Nashville *Whig*, and the Natchez *Mississippi State Gazette* gave little or no space to the controversy; far less in some instances than to the current controversy over Andrew Jackson's conduct of the Seminole War. The

[69] Hodder, "Side Lights on the Missouri Compromises," *loc. cit.*, 153–61; Woodburn, "Historical Significance of the Missouri Compromise," *loc. cit.*, 265–81.

[70] Richmond *Enquirer*, December 3, 1819; Georgetown *National Messenger*, February 14, 1820, quoted *ibid.*, February 17, 1820.

[71] Richmond *Enquirer*, March 10, 1820.

Mississippi State Gazette, under the heading "Time is Money," argued that Congress was wasting money that ought to be devoted to more important matters, and it calculated the number of hours and minutes that each Congressman had consumed in talking about Missouri.[72]

Congressmen, editors, and other leaders were more disturbed than the common people. Near the height of the excitement the Baltimore *Patriot* observed that "The people do not yet participate in the unhappy heat of zeal and controversy, which has inflamed their Senators and Representatives." [73] But if the rank and file were not greatly disturbed, some of the keenest political observers of the time were apprehensive and in some cases frightened. Thomas Jefferson, in oft-quoted words, wrote: "This momentous question, like a fire bell in the night, awakened and filled me with terror. I considered it at once as the knell of the Union. It is hushed, indeed, for the moment. But this is a reprieve only, not a final sentence." [74] Henry Clay expressed the belief that within five years "the Union would be divided into three distinct confederacies." [75] Thomas W. Cobb of Georgia declared in Congress: "We have kindled a fire which all the waters of the ocean cannot put out, which seas of blood can only extinguish." [76] Joseph Brevard, editor of the Columbia, South Carolina, *Telescope,* wrote: "I deprecate still more [than the present discord] the infinite train of evils and miseries to which it may lead." [77] And John C. Calhoun thought that the question might lead to a dissolution of the Union, and that should this come to pass the South would be compelled to ally itself with England.[78]

Why did these men take so tragic a view of the Missouri controversy? The clearest explanation came from the pen of the aged Jefferson. "A geographical line," he wrote, "coinciding with a

[72] Natchez *Mississippi State Gazette,* April 1, 1820; also, Nashville *Whig,* March 8, 1820.

[73] Baltimore *Patriot & Mercantile Advertiser,* February 17, 1820; reprinted in Nashville *Whig,* March 8, 1820.

[74] Paul L. Ford (ed.), *The Writings of Thomas Jefferson* (New York, 1892–1899), X, 157.

[75] Reported by John Quincy Adams, in Adams (ed.), *Memoirs of John Quincy Adams,* IV, 525–26.

[76] *Annals of Congress,* 15 Cong., 2 Sess., I, 1204.

[77] Quoted in New Orleans *Louisiana Gazette,* March 14, 1820.

[78] So Adams reported in Adams (ed.), *Memoirs of John Quincy Adams,* IV, 530–31.

marked principle, moral and political, once conceived and held up to the angry passions of men, will never be obliterated; and every new irritation will mark it deeper and deeper." [79] The debate over the admission of Missouri had drawn this sort of line. To questions of an essentially political nature that had divided the agrarian South from the commercial East, a new issue was now added: the question of restricting slavery because it was morally wrong. The economic and political grievances of the East were, by being merged with a hatred for slavery, raised from the low level of self-interest to the higher plane where feelings of righteousness and self-sacrifice could stir the souls of men.

John Quincy Adams confided to his diary thoughts that well illustrate the remarks of Jefferson. Forty years before the Civil War, he wrote that it would be noble to die that men might be set free from slavery. Meditating on the possibility that the slavery question might sever the Union, he was yet willing to contemplate its dissolution on this question, and on no other, believing that "the Union might then be reorganized on the fundamental principle of emancipation. This object," he wrote, "is vast in its compass, awful in its prospects, sublime and beautiful in its issue. A life devoted to it would be nobly spent or sacrificed." Thinking of civil war and of an insurrection by the slaves, he declared: "So glorious would be its final issue, that, as God shall judge me, I dare not say that it is not to be desired." [80]

This episode of American history revealed two facts of great significance for the Southern states. The first of them was that New England's political opposition to the three-fifths clause was now entwined with the humanitarian movement against slavery. The second disclosure was that the Northwest had withdrawn from its long-standing alliance with the South. For twenty years this alliance had ruled the nation. It was now ended, at least for the moment, and replaced by a political union of the free states of the East and of the West. Common prudence required the South to regain its Western ally if possible and, on the chance of failure, to take stock of its separate political resources. Alone, the slave states would be outnumbered in the House of Representatives and in the electoral

[79] Ford (ed.), *Writings of Thomas Jefferson,* X, 157.
[80] Adams (ed.), *Memoirs of John Quincy Adams,* IV, 531; V, 210.

college. They would be on the defensive, and it was obvious that the Senate offered them their only check on hostile legislation. Slave-state insistence on equality in the Senate was not, as has often been asserted, a cause of the Missouri controversy, but it was made during the course of that controversy into a cardinal principle of Southern political policy.

CHAPTER VI

FROM ECONOMIC NATIONALISM
TO POLITICAL SECTIONALISM

THE Sixteenth Congress (1819–1821) of the United States faced an unusual number of critical domestic problems. Besides the Missouri controversy, consideration had to be given to the tariff, internal improvements, a Presidential election, the national bank, a bankruptcy bill, and public-land policy. This difficult set of problems was created by the interplay of three forces. The effort of New England to throw off the yoke of its political subordination brought on a realignment of the sections and, in discussions of slavery, a union of political self-interest with the older current of humanitarian liberalism. Secondly, the Panic of 1819 caused distressed citizens to turn to Congress for protective duties and relief measures in the fields of banking, bankruptcy, and public lands. Thirdly, the War of 1812 and the prior struggle of the United States to remain at peace in a war-torn world convinced many Americans that their government should take steps to avoid a repetition of recent difficulties.

To assure the development and security of the nation, a program was evolved calling for the creation of a strong navy to protect the nation and prevent the destruction of its coasting trade, a protective tariff to encourage the development of essential industries, a system of roads and canals to facilitate the exchange of goods between the parts of the nation, and a national bank to stabilize and supply currency for business transactions. Obviously, this program proposed that the Federal government enlarge the scope of its activities and increase its expenditures; and it marked a departure from laissez-faire philosophy. The government was now to assume the power to force certain areas of economic life out of their accustomed patterns into new ones.

Most of the advocates of this new program were in the rising generation of public men who had shouldered the responsibility for bringing the United States into and through the War of 1812. They had been known as War Hawks; they were now coming to be called Young Republicans. Besides Calhoun, the group included Langdon Cheves, who was also a South Carolinian, Henry Clay and Richard M. Johnson of Kentucky, and Felix Grundy of Tennessee. In the South, the Young Republicans were strongest in South Carolina and the Southwest, and their activities constituted something of a revolt against the established power of Virginia in national affairs.

Of the older statesmen there were some, like James Madison, who had reluctantly and tentatively modified their earlier beliefs to the extent of accepting economic self-sufficiency as a necessity, at least for a time.[1] There were others who viewed the new program with unmitigated hostility. Such men were called Old Republicans, and they were especially numerous in Virginia where John Randolph of Roanoke, John Taylor of Caroline, Justice Spencer Roane, John Tyler, and in some measure Presidents Madison and Monroe sought to block the new trend. With them were Nathaniel Macon of North Carolina, William H. Crawford of Georgia, and Charles Tait and Bolling Hall of Alabama. These and other Old Republicans were less of a party, or even a faction in a party, than a group of individuals who thought much alike. Most of them were old in years and political experience, few of them had much ambition for personal advancement in politics, several lived in frugal simplicity, and they were singularly incorruptible and unchangeable. To the Young Republicans they seemed "too unyielding, too uncompromising, too impracticable," as Calhoun said of Randolph.[2]

Nearly all the Old Republicans believed that the Constitution meant exactly what it said, and that the government ought to take no step beyond constitutional boundaries even though the goal were good or were widely desired. Therefore, they objected to entering upon several parts of the program of economic nationalism unless the Constitution should first be amended. Some of the Old

---

[1] Joseph J. Spengler, "The Political Economy of Jefferson, Madison, and Adams," in Jackson (ed.), *American Studies in Honor of William Kenneth Boyd,* 16–17.
[2] *Cong. Globe,* 25 Cong., 2 Sess., Appendix, 70.

Republicans went further; they objected to the idea that the government ought to expand its activities even by the process of constitutional amendment. They loved individual liberty, they feared government, and they feared the Federal government more than state and local government.

The interplay of forces and of viewpoints is illustrated by the case of the second national bank. It had been chartered in 1816 as an important part of the program of the Young Republicans. Naturally, there was some hostility to it, and this hostility was greatly increased, especially in the South and Southwest, during the Panic of 1819. Heavy taxes were imposed upon the bank by the states of Maryland, Tennessee, Georgia, North Carolina, Kentucky, and three states north of the Ohio River, and similar measures were considered but not enacted in Virginia and South Carolina.[3] Had these laws remained in force the bank would have been crippled if not killed; and multitudes of Southerners and Westerners believed that its destruction would improve their personal fortunes. It was at this moment when public opinion and state laws were arrayed against the bank that the Supreme Court came to its rescue in the case of McCulloch v. Maryland.[4] Not unnaturally, much of the popular animus toward the bank was then directed against the Court and against its broad and nationalistic constitutional doctrines.

An earnest and persistent critic of the Court's pronouncement was Ritchie, editor of the Richmond *Enquirer*. With the assistance of an able corps of contributors, he sought to expose "the alarming errors of the Supreme Court of the United States in their interpretation of the Constitution," and to warn that "Whenever states rights are threatened or invaded, Virginia will not be the last to sound the tocsin." [5] Ritchie attacked with great force, but with dignity; and toward Chief Justice John Marshall he was courteous. A major attack was prefaced by these words: "The Supreme Court of the United States is a tribunal of great and commanding authority; whose decisions, if not received as 'the law and the prophets,' are always entitled to the deepest attention. To the presiding Justice of that court, we are always ready to pay that tribute, which his

[3] Catterall, *Second Bank of the United States,* 64–65.
[4] 4 Wheaton 316 (1819).
[5] Richmond *Enquirer*. March 30, 1819.

great abilities deserve—but no tribunal, however high; no abilities, however splendid, ought to canonize the opinions which are advanced. We solemnly believe the opinion of the supreme court in the case of the bank to be fraught with alarming consequences; the federal constitution misinterpreted, and the rights of the states and the people to be threatened with danger." [6]

During this discussion, the *Enquirer* denied the right of the Court to ultimate authority in "controversies to which a State and the United States may become parties" and proposed other means of settling issues involving the rights of states.[7] Elsewhere through the South, newspapers joined the hue and cry against the Court. The Nashville *Whig* printed with editorial approval a recent letter by Jefferson objecting to the doctrine that the judiciary was the ultimate arbiter of all constitutional questions.[8] From Kentucky came the proposal that the Constitution be amended so as to give to the Senate appellate jurisdiction in all cases affecting a state or a state law.[9] Obviously, the states were attempting, but thus far without success, to discover a way of protecting their interests from adverse decisions by the Supreme Court.

The main contention of a contributor to the Richmond *Enquirer* [10] was that the bank, as bad as it was, was less dangerous than the doctrine of broad constitutional construction. He asserted that "the doctrines advanced by the court are so erroneous, and . . . allow a latitude of construction so boundless, that they will, inevitably, be applied by the advocates of the seductive system of internal improvements, and national grandeur, to cases which do not lie, and I pray to God never may be brought within the pale of federal legislation." In listing the prospective dangers of broad construction, he was necessarily indefinite; five years later he could have been more precise.

Perhaps the chief effect of all the discussion of McCulloch *v.* Maryland—and it scarcely died down before it was revived by the

[6] *Ibid.*, June 11, 1819. Most issues of the *Enquirer* from March 30 through July, 1819, gave space to questions that were suggested by the case of McCulloch *v.* Maryland.

[7] *Ibid.*, June 11, 15, 18, 22, 1819; January 30, February 1, 1821.

[8] Nashville *Whig*, December 12, 1821.

[9] Rezneck, "The Depression of 1819–1822," *loc. cit.*, 46.

[10] Richmond *Enquirer*, July 23, 1819.

decision in the case of Osborn *v.* The Bank of the United States [11] —was to teach the uncertain and the uninformed that constitutional questions are not altogether academic and unimportant. The hardships of the Panic they knew from bitter experience. They had come to believe that these hardships were due in large measure to the Bank of the United States, and now they were being taught that this evil thing existed because of loose constitutional construction. Thus the abstract question of strict construction, so dear to the hearts of a few Virginians, was beginning to become tangible and understandable to common men all over the South and West.

The advocates of national economic independence were far less successful in establishing a national system of roads and canals than they had been in establishing a national bank; yet their efforts in that direction aroused much sectional hostility. Prior to 1820 the Federal government had spent less than $2,000,000 for the improvement of communications within the United States. Most of this was for a single project, the Cumberland Road, which was designed to be the great artery of trade and commerce between the seaboard and the Ohio Valley. Much of the rest had been used in driblets to open roads between remote settlements in the Western territories. Some of these, like the Natchez Trace, were hundreds of miles long, but hardly any one of them had cost the government more than $10,000.[12]

In 1819 Calhoun, who was now Secretary of War, presented to Congress a broad plan of internal improvements which included an inland waterway through the rivers, bays, and sounds of the Eastern coast from Boston to Savannah; a highway, roughly parallel to the waterway, extending from Maine to Louisiana; and a canal to connect the Potomac with the Ohio.[13] Finally, in 1824, Congress passed a measure known as the general-survey bill authorizing the President to have surveys made for such roads and canals as he regarded as of national importance for commercial, military, or postal purposes. While the bill did not bind the government to build

[11] 9 Wheaton 738 (1824).

[12] *Reports of Committees of the House of Representatives,* 21 Cong., 2 Sess., No. 77, "Internal Improvements." See especially pp. 35 and 65.

[13] Report on Roads and Canals, communicated to the House of Representatives, January 14, 1819, in Richard K. Crallé (ed.), *Works of John C. Calhoun* (New York, 1851–1856), V, 40–54.

roads or canals, it was obviously a first step in that direction.

The vote and the debate on the survey bill are significant. Clay eloquently presented the needs of the West, whose Congressmen were unanimously in favor of the bill. The measure was also supported by the Middle states, Pennsylvania, Maryland, New Jersey, and Delaware, toward which the tide of Western commerce would flow in greater volume with improvements in transportation. By the union of Western and Middle Atlantic interests, the bill gained 115 supporters in the House. The 86 opposition votes came from New York and New England and from the Atlantic states below Maryland, the two flanks of the Middle-states outlet for the West.

In Virginia, North Carolina, South Carolina, and Georgia there were friends as well as enemies of the survey bill. In the western parts of Virginia and North Carolina, where there was great need for better transportation facilities, the bill met with some favor; and in South Carolina, where the Young Republicans were strong, there was considerable support for this part of the new economic nationalism. The slave states were not of one mind about internal improvements. The chief conflict was between the Southwestern states, which approved, and Virginia and North Carolina, which strongly opposed.[14]

It is perfectly obvious that the votes on the general-survey bill were determined largely by the varying interests of the different parts of the nation. Yet John Randolph placed his own opposition on a different basis. He professed to be less concerned over the immediate issue, internal improvements, than over the dangers of loose construction. "If Congress possesses the power to do what is proposed by this bill," he said, "they may emancipate every slave in the United States. . . . And where will they find the power? They may . . . hook the power upon the first loop they find in the Constitution; they might take the preamble—perhaps the war making power—or they might take a greater sweep, and say, with some gentlemen, that it is not to be found in this or that of the granted powers, but results from all of them—which is not only a dangerous but *the most* dangerous doctrine." [15]

[14] For map showing the House vote on the Survey Bill, February 10, 1824, see Turner, *Rise of the New West*, ff. 232.

[15] *Annals of Congress*, 18 Cong., 1 Sess., 1308.

But in spite of warnings from the Old Republicans that it was dangerous to sell the birthright of strong local government for the mess of pottage of national money for roads, the bill was passed. Thus, by 1824 the national government was beginning to assume responsibility for building highways and canals. The advocates of the program prophesied that a good system of communications would bind the parts of the nation closer together; but the debate over the program was serving exactly the opposite purpose. Furthermore, in those parts of the nation where there was opposition to internal improvements at Federal expense, adherents were won to the doctrine of strict constitutional construction.

A third measure proposed by the advocates of the new economic order was tariff protection for American industry, particularly for the new manufacturing concerns that had been started during the War of 1812. From considerations of national policy, moderate protection was granted in the tariff of 1816. The Panic of 1819 brought a demand for its continuance and for greater protection, and the demand at this later date sprang chiefly from interested manufacturers. Although they had been damaged less than the farmers during the depression, they wanted a return of previous prosperity. The tariff seemed to afford a means of attaining it.[16] So, they began to frame memorials, petitions, resolutions, and remonstrances which were published in newspapers and pamphlets and were sent in large quantities to Congress. The centers of the agitation were Pennsylvania, New Jersey, New York, Ohio, and Kentucky, an area that corresponded roughly with the region that was giving chief support to the proposed scheme of internal improvements.[17] Opposition to protection was likewise related to self-interest, being strongest in the exporting South Atlantic states and in the parts of New England where shipping and commerce yet overshadowed manufacturing.[18]

The Sixteenth Congress showed an early disposition to favor protection by electing Henry Clay to the speakership. Clay had come

[16] Frank W. Taussig, *The Tariff History of the United States* (8th ed.; New York, 1931), 19–24.

[17] Many of these petitions can be found in *American State Papers, Finance*, III, *passim*, and in *Annals of Congress*, 16 Cong., 1 Sess., Appendix, 2307–48.

[18] Edward Stanwood, *American Tariff Controversies in the Nineteenth Century* (Boston, 1903), I, 180.

to Congress from the hemp-growing region of Kentucky, and he himself was a grower of that crop which was one of the few agricultural products of the nation that could profit by protection. Furthermore, the House divided its former Committee of Commerce and Manufactures into two distinct committees, and Clay appointed no man to the Committee on Manufactures unless he was a friend of protection. Through its chairman, Henry Baldwin of Pennsylvania, this committee introduced a bill which provided for a complete revision of the tariff.

Baldwin's frankness in presenting the measure pitched the debate on a dignified and restrained level, which is notable in view of the fact that the bill came up for consideration on April 21, 1820, immediately on the heels of the exciting debate over the admission of Missouri. Baldwin frankly stated that the bill was designed to give greater protection as well as to increase revenue. There was little discussion of the revenue features of the bill, for the government was facing an annual deficit. Its protective features consisted in increases of from 20 to 100 per cent in the duties on cotton and woolen textiles, forged iron bars, glass, hemp, and other less important articles.[19]

Naturally, Baldwin was the chief defender of the measure, but he was assisted by Clay and others; and Clay was particularly helpful in parliamentary strategy. In their statements and in the great body of petitions, the following arguments were advanced. Manufacturing, which was in a distressed condition, would be benefited by protection, and the improvement of manufacturing would react favorably upon agriculture and commerce. While somewhat vague as to how commerce would be helped, the benefit to agriculture was explained in the "home market" argument, namely, that prosperity in the manufacturing population would give the farmer a better market for his corn, wheat, and meat. The larger demand and better prices ought to more than recompense him for the higher prices that he might have to pay for clothing and other articles of American manufacture. Obviously, this argument was directed to the Western and Northern farmers who were raising corn, wheat, and

[19] The debate in the House over the tariff is reported in *Annals of Congress*, 16 Cong., 1 Sess., 1914–2140, 2145–56. A brief summary of the arguments is in Stanwood, *American Tariff Controversies*, I, 179–91.

meat rather than to cotton and tobacco planters who could not expect to sell much of their crops to the factory population of the nation.

In addition to asking protection because of its primary value to manufacturers and its secondary value to farmers, Baldwin repeated the arguments used in support of the tariff of 1816 to the effect that protection would help the entire nation to be flourishing and independent by supplying its own food, clothing, and means of defense. And he tried to carry the arguments of economic nationalism further by arguing, somewhat unconvincingly, that a new source of government income, which seemed to be needed in view of the present deficits, might be found in prospective taxes on goods whose manufacture would be stimulated by the protective tariff.

The opponents of protection, chief of whom were John Tyler, Philip P. Barbour, and William S. Archer, of Virginia, Ezekiel Whitman of Massachusetts, and William Lowndes of South Carolina, insisted that times would improve without recourse to protection; and they denied that manufacturing was entitled to special aid. There was talk, too much it seems, of the increase in smuggling that higher duties would entail; and Archer asserted that "an extended manufacturing system" would bring into being "a population distorted and decrepid [sic], as respects both bodily and mental endowments, especially marked by imbecility and abasement. How unlike our ancestors achieving the Revolution!" [20]

Tyler, with less imagination and more logic, insisted that protection would create an endless spiral. Temporary prosperity induced by protection would attract fresh capital to manufacturing, thereby increasing competition and diminishing the prices of the products. Meanwhile, wages would have been raised by the industrial expansion, and costs of production would once more exceed those abroad. At that point "the foreign competitor again enters your market, and again will our ears be deafened with cries for relief," which, if granted, would only start a new cycle.[21]

Having thus argued that protection could serve only as a temporary palliative to the ills of the manufacturers, the opponents of the measure considered its effects upon agriculture and commerce.

20 *Annals of Congress*, 16 Cong., 1 Sess., 2032.
21 *Ibid.*, 1954.

They claimed that it would seriously curtail the business of New England importers, and would increase the costs of hemp cordage, flax sails, iron, and other commodities needed by the shippers. They failed to meet clearly the "home market" argument, but they argued with much force that farmers, as well as all other consumers of manufactured articles, would be compelled by the tariff to pay tribute to the manufacturers.[22] They prophesied that this evil would tend to increase, for, as Whitman of Massachusetts said, "Avarice is never satisfied." [23]

Answering the assertion that the development of factories would safeguard the nation in time of war, Tyler asked whether America with her farms could not survive a blockade longer than could England with her factories. He further argued that differences in climate, resources, and age made nations dependent upon one another and that any interference with "the ordinances of Heaven itself" must result in a decline in those arts which improve and embellish human life. These laissez-faire, free-trade arguments were echoed in Southern newspapers. If manufactures do not flourish, is it not a proof, asked the Richmond *Compiler*, "that we are not yet ripe for them? Most of our countrymen would rather plough than weave. Why? because they find it more to their interest to do so. They make more by it." [24] The New Orleans *Louisiana Gazette* echoed the opposition of the Richmond *Compiler* to the tariff in the words: *"Let us alone."* [25]

The debate ranged over nearly every argument that was later used for or against protection with a single notable exception: the constitutionality of a protective tariff was not challenged at this time. But one may well question whether logic and arguments changed many votes, since nearly every Congressman voted according to the local interests of his constituency.

[22] See, for example, the "Memorial of the Virginia Society for promoting Agriculture to the Congress of the United States, in opposition to the several Memorials and Petitions praying for additional duties upon Foreign Imports," in Richmond *Enquirer*, February 19, 1820. The files of this paper through the year 1820 contain protests against the tariff from Fredericksburg, Norfolk, and Portsmouth as well as from Richmond.

[23] Quoted in Stanwood, *American Tariff Controversies*, I, 189.

[24] Richmond *Compiler*, October 18, 1820.

[25] New Orleans *Louisiana Gazette*, August 10, 1820.

The measure passed the House in a series of votes which found 91 members in favor of protection and 83 opposed. Representatives of the great middle belt of the nation—Pennsylvania, Delaware, New Jersey, and New York along the seaboard, and Ohio, Illinois, and Indiana in the West—were almost unanimous in approving protection, casting 63 votes for the measure and only one against. The "home market" argument seems to have convinced the farmers of these states that they would at least not suffer as factories expanded. The votes of New England, where there was rivalry between commerce and manufacturing, were nearly evenly divided, being 19 in favor of the bill and 18 opposed to it. Daniel Webster publicly spoke against it although he was not in Congress at this time.[26]

The South was almost as solid in its opposition to the measure as the Middle states were in its favor. South of Pennsylvania and the Ohio River there were 63 votes against and only 8 votes for the tariff, and most of those 8 votes came from the border states of Kentucky and Maryland.[27] But though the Southwest and the South Atlantic states united in opposing protection, the brunt of the defense was carried by representatives from the older South, and especially by Virginians. There was a tendency in the Southwest to think, as the Nashville *Whig* expressed it, "that it is more important that the tariff of duties shall now be settled and hereafter stable, than that it should be either of a greater or less amount." [28]

In the Senate the measure was rejected on May 4, after scarcely any debate, by a vote of 22 to 21. The vote reflected the same geographical division as was evident in the House. Thus, the tariff of 1820 failed to pass.

In the Congressional reapportionment of 1823 the antitariff South Atlantic states gained no new seats in Congress; the Southwestern states, where tariff sentiments were less fixed, gained nine seats; and the Middle Atlantic and Ohio Valley states—the centers of protariff sentiment—gained nineteen new seats. Under this pro-

[26] Stanwood, *American Tariff Controversies*, I, 196–97.

[27] There were 4 votes for protection and 3 against by the Kentucky Congressmen, Speaker Clay not voting. The writer has followed Stanwood, *American Tariff Controversies*, I, 192–93, whose analysis covers the series of related votes on this measure. An analysis of the final House vote is in Turner, *Rise of the New West*, 145–47.

[28] Nashville *Whig*, May 10, 1820.

pitious circumstance the Committee on Manufactures reported a tariff bill to the Eighteenth Congress on January 9, 1824. From February 10 until its passage on April 16 the measure was almost constantly before the House. It was passed by the Senate on May 13. Both of the Senators from the new state of Missouri voted for the measure.

The debate was focused on the question of protection even more exclusively than in 1820, for no one could assert that the government needed more revenue. The Treasury was now reporting substantial surpluses each year. The participants in the debate showed that they were familiar with the terms of the bill, with economic conditions in America, and with Britain's recent experience with protection. Among the points which were elaborated more thoroughly than before was the question of the relation between protection and wages. Curiously, each side presented views that were the opposite of those that later prevailed. Further, there was much argument about the balance of trade, but definitions varied so widely that this part of the debate was inconclusive.

One of the ablest passages in the debate was Clay's lucid and cogent exposition of the home-market argument. It was not met with much ability by opponents of protection, but Southerners attempted to show that the agriculture of their region would suffer despite Clay's theories. Christopher Rankin of Mississippi estimated that the American market took only 40,000 bales of cotton annually whereas England consumed ten times as much, and he asserted that protection in America might cause England to turn elsewhere for its cotton. He argued that if the South were stripped of a market for its most important product, it could no longer purchase Northern grain and manufactured goods.[29] Randolph, assuming that Northerners were more interested in the well-being of the slave than of his master, explained that "the profits of slave labor had been, for a long time, on the decrease, and that, on a fair average, it scarcely reimbursed [the master for] the expense of the slave." He concluded that a further reduction in the master's income, such as would be accomplished by protection, must inevitably bear heavily upon the slave.[30]

29 *Annals of Congress,* 18 Cong., 1 Sess., 2009–25.
30 *Ibid.,* 2256.

It was during this debate that the constitutionality of a protective tariff was for the first time seriously attacked. Barbour of Virginia asserted that inasmuch as the Constitution granted to Congress the power to lay and collect taxes, duties, imposts, and excises, the tariff was perhaps not a violation of the letter of the Constitution. But, he added, "this bill does violate the spirit of the Constitution. The power to impose taxes, duties, etc., . . . was given to us for the purpose of raising revenue, which revenue is to be applied to the ends pointed out in the Constitution. Now, . . . by this bill, . . . we shall be using this power . . . for another and different one." [31]

Clay, in answer, declared that while "no doubt revenue was a principal object [of the power to tax] with the framers of the Constitution . . . may not the duties and imposts be so laid as to secure domestic interests?" He added: "The gentleman from Virginia has, however, entirely mistaken the clause of the Constitution on which we rely. It is that which gives to Congress the power to regulate commerce with foreign nations. The grant is plenary, without any limitations whatever, and includes the whole power of regulation." [32] Thus, in 1824 the tariff question began to be debated from the standpoint of constitutional interpretation just as the issues of a national bank and of Federal internal improvements had earlier been drawn to that vortex to which all phases of the program of economic nationalism seemed to drift.

In addition to the debate on protection in general, there was some discussion of industries which this tariff was expected to benefit: cotton and woolen goods, New England rum, and Kentucky whiskey, hemp, and iron. The opponents of protection attempted to play off the interests of some of these groups against each other. Webster, who was yet unconverted to the cause of protection, reminded the soapmakers that they would be injured by the tallow duty which was being imposed to aid the whalers of New Bedford. Amendments added in one or the other of the Houses reduced nearly all of the duties proposed by the Committee on

[31] *Ibid.*, 1918. In February, 1823, one year before Philip P. Barbour's speech, Thomas R. Mitchell of South Carolina had asserted without elaboration that there were "constitutional difficulties" in a protective tariff. *Ibid.*, 17 Cong., 2 Sess., 1002.

[32] *Ibid.*, 18 Cong., 1 Sess., 1994.

Manufactures. The bill in its final form granted slight increases over the existing duties on woolen goods and considerable increases on raw wool, thus helping the sheep growers but not the manufacturers of wool cloth. An increase in the duty on hemp helped Kentuckians but hurt New England shipowners.[33] Led by this hope and by the presence of some manufactures in the state, the Kentucky Representatives and Senators voted unanimously for the measure.

Those who wanted protection were not content in 1824 to send up petitions and to trust to their elected representatives, and American legislative history entered upon a new phase with the appearance in Washington of an active, vigorous lobby. James Hamilton, Jr., of South Carolina charged that there was "more outdoor than indoor legislation in regard to the bill." [34] Robert Y. Hayne, also of South Carolina, gave solemn warning to the interests that were seeking special favors "that we will not hold ourselves bound to maintain the system; and if capitalists will, in the face of our protests and in defiance of our solemn warnings, invest their fortunes in pursuits made profitable at our expense, on their own heads be the consequences of their folly." [35]

The geographical division upon this bill both in the House and in the Senate was very similar to what it had been in 1820. The Middle region, both east and west, was almost unanimously for protection. Kentucky in 1824 threw its lot wholly with the states north of the Ohio River, giving 11 votes in the House for the bill and none against, and the new state of Missouri gave its lone vote for protection. New England continued to be divided, 15 of its Representatives voting for protection and 23 against; but more than two thirds of the New England Senators favored this tariff. The South Atlantic states cast 56 votes against the bill and 4 for it, of which one was from western Virginia and the other 3 were from Maryland. Fourteen of the Representatives from the Southwestern states were against the tariff and only 2, both from Tennessee, were for it. The 4 Senators from Tennessee and Kentucky voted for protection. Thus, the slave states, with the exception of Kentucky and Tennessee, were almost unanimous in their opposition to the tariff.

---

[33] Stanwood, *American Tariff Controversies*, I, 226–35.
[34] Quoted *ibid.*, 237.   [35] *Annals of Congress*, 18 Cong., 1 Sess., 649.

In both Houses of Congress the votes were close, being 107 to 102 in the House, and 25 to 21 in the Senate.[36]

With the passage of this bill, protection entered a new phase. Granted in 1816 as a temporary expedient and on the philosophy of national economic interest, eight years later it was put on a more permanent basis, and the argument of national interest was reinforced by the pleas of manufacturers who were seeking favors for their industries. Increasingly, the tariff had come to be viewed from the standpoint of sectional interest rather than of national policy.

The Panic was largely responsible for the introduction into Congress of bills to provide for Federal regulation of bankruptcy and to abolish Federal imprisonment for debt. Both failed to pass, though the bankruptcy bill was considered three times, first in 1820. It was killed chiefly by the votes of the Southern and Western states.[37]

A greater and a more persistent question, which was brought to a crisis by the Panic, had to do with the system under which men bought land from the government. Since the early part of the century, public lands could be purchased in tracts of 160 acres or larger. The minimum price was $2.00 an acre, but some land brought much higher prices because sales were made at public auction. Furthermore, land could be bought on credit with payments spread over a period of four years. Under this system about $44,000,000 worth of land had passed into private hands by the end of 1819, but only half of the purchase price had been paid. After the Panic struck, there was little likelihood that remaining payments could be made as they came due.

This great debt could be viewed from the standpoint of the Federal Treasury which was the creditor, or of the citizens who were the debtors. Under the existing law thousands of men, settlers and speculators alike, would lose not only their land, but the payments they had already made to the government and such improvements as they had made on their holdings. They wanted relief, even at the

[36] For a map of the House vote on this measure, see Turner, *Rise of the New West*, ff. 242. For analyses of the vote, see *ibid.*, 242–43; Stanwood, *American Tariff Controversies*, I, 239.

[37] Rezneck, "The Depression of 1819–1822," *loc. cit.*, 44; F. Regis Noel, *A History of the Bankruptcy Clause of the Constitution of the United States of America* (Gettysburg [1918]), 134–36.

cost of reducing the prosperity of the Federal Treasury; and they were joined in their demands for a revision of the land laws by prospective purchasers who wanted the price of land to be reduced. The clamor for relief was greatest in the West, and especially in the Southwest. In Alabama alone more than three quarters of a million acres had been sold between 1815 and 1820 at an average price of well over three times the minimum of $2.00 an acre, and much uncleared land had brought as much as $30.00 an acre.[38]

Thus the issue was drawn between Westerners who wanted relief from debt and low prices in future purchases and Easterners who wanted income from public land to carry as much as possible of the cost of government. But the issue was confused by several circumstances. Income from land sales was needed to support the program of internal improvements that the West wanted. And there were some Easterners, especially in the South Atlantic states and in parts of New England, who favored low-priced lands for the very reason that they opposed a government program of internal improvements. Furthermore, men on both sides of the fence knew, because of the economic depression, that some sort of remedial legislation was needed.

In the spring of 1820 a compromise measure was enacted which ended the credit system. To compensate the Westerner, who liked the credit system, the price was lowered to $1.25 an acre and the minimum amount of land that might be purchased was reduced to 80 acres.[39] Thus, for as little as $100.00 a man could purchase a farm. Theoretically, it might not be of the best grade of land, for the auction system was retained; but in actual practice the price averaged only three cents an acre above the minimum during the next twenty-two years.[40]

The land act of 1820 left the existing debt untouched, but almost yearly from 1821 to 1832 Congress granted extensions of time, offered discounts for early payments, and allowed purchasers to relinquish part of their holdings, retaining only as much as they

[38] Payson J. Treat, *The National Land System, 1785–1820* (New York, 1910), 142, 157, 408–11.

[39] *Statutes at Large of the United States,* 16 Cong., 1 Sess., Chap. LI. Some 80-acre tracts had been on sale since 1817, but this minimum was not applied to all public-land sales until 1820. Benjamin H. Hibbard, *A History of the Public Land Policies* (New York, 1939), 75.   [40] Hibbard, *Public Land Policies,* 102.

had paid for. Under this series of acts the debt rapidly decreased to $12,000,000 by September 30, 1821, and to half that amount by June 30, 1825. By 1832 it was almost extinguished.[41]

With questions of credit and debt out of the way, other aspects of the land question, growing out of the increase of Western population and political influence, began to receive greater attention. For a long time Westerners had advocated a policy, known as pre-emption, which would allow men who had settled on public land before it was opened to sale to purchase at the minimum price without competitive bidding. Persons of this sort had no legal rights, for unauthorized settlement on public lands had been illegal since 1807; nevertheless, many arguments were advanced in their behalf by Western Congressmen, especially by Senator Benton.

In addition to pre-emption privileges, Westerners advocated a further reduction in the price of public lands, and they argued that the government could forgo part of its income from land sales because of the steady decline in the national debt. Such issues kept alive the conflict between East and West, and retarded collaboration between the South Atlantic states and the Southwest. On the public-land question, the ties of the Southwest were with the Northwest rather than with the Southeast.

Those who opposed a Federal program of internal improvements were much disturbed at the growing tendency of the government to finance roads and canals by direct grants of land. When Indiana, Mississippi, Alabama, and Missouri were admitted as states, Congress provided that 3 per cent of the income from the sale of land in each state should revert to the state to be spent on roads and canals and that an additional 2 per cent should be spent under the direction of Congress to provide better transportation facilities to that state. In 1823 and 1824, Congress began the practice of making special grants of land to subsidize the construction of designated roads and canals.[42] If this policy were allowed to go unchecked it was useless to argue that Congress lacked the constitutional power to appropriate money for internal improvements; therefore, Old Republicans opposed appropriations of land as well as of money for internal improvements by the Federal government.

[41] Treat, *National Land System,* 152, 154, 161.
[42] Hibbard, *Public Land Policies,* 85, 234–37.

The wave of apprehension sweeping over the South because of the increase of Northern power in the Federal government and because of the directions to which this power seemed to be turning is indicated by two controversies over slavery that arose early in the 1820's. One of these began with a resolution adopted by the Ohio legislature on January 17, 1824, which invited Congress and the legislatures of the several states to consider a plan of gradual emancipation of the slaves in the United States, the Negroes to be colonized abroad as they became free, and the costs of the scheme to be borne by the Federal government "upon the principle that the evil of slavery is a national one, and that the people and the states of this Union ought mutually to participate in the duties and burthens of removing it." [43] Except in the generous offer that the North share with the South the costs, this plan differed hardly at all from proposals earlier made by some of the most responsible statesmen of Virginia. Within eighteen months, eight Northern states, including every Northwestern and Middle Atlantic state, had endorsed the proposal, and on February 18, 1825, King, of New York, introduced a bill in the Senate proposing the creation of a fund from the sale of public lands to carry out the purposes of the Ohio resolution.

The harshness of the Southern rejoinder to these proposals can hardly be explained. The South Carolina senate characterized the Ohio resolution as "a very strange and ill-advised communication," and the lower house declared "that the people of this state will adhere to a system, descended to them from their ancestors, and now inseparably connected with their social and political existence." Governor George M. Troup of Georgia, whose feelings were already stirred to a high pitch of irritability by a controversy with the national government about the Indians, told his legislature on May 23, 1825, that "our feelings have been again outraged by officious and impertinent intermeddlings with our domestic concerns." He asserted that if the power of the national government over slavery were once allowed, emancipation could be accomplished even though Federal funds for slaveholders were withdrawn. Therefore, he urged Georgians to be wary, for very soon, he prophesied, "the United States' Government, discarding the mask, will openly lend itself to a combination of fanatics for the destruction of every

[43] Ames, *State Documents on Federal Relations*, 204.

151

thing valuable in the Southern country; one movement of the Congress unresisted by you, and all is lost. . . . I entreat you, therefore, most earnestly, now that it is not too late, to step forth, and, having exhausted the argument, to stand by your arms." [44]

Tension over slavery had been increased by the discovery at Charleston in 1822 of a plot for a slave insurrection. The city, and the South generally, was deeply stirred, and inasmuch as the leader of the movement was a free Negro by the name of Denmark Vesey there was strong sentiment in favor of isolating slaves from free Negroes. As an outgrowth of this feeling, the South Carolina legislature passed a law on December 21, 1822, requiring free Negro seamen on any vessel entering a South Carolina port to be imprisoned until the vessel was ready to depart. Objections to the law were raised both by Northern and British masters of vessels. In a test case brought before the Federal courts, Judge William Johnson, a citizen of South Carolina, held the law unconstitutional; and in consequence of protests lodged with the State Department by the British government, William Wirt, attorney general of the United States, ruled likewise that the law was unconstitutional. But despite these opinions, South Carolina continued to enforce the law, and in subsequent years Georgia, Alabama, North Carolina, Florida, and Louisiana passed similar measures.

The controversies between the Southern states on the one side and the United States and Great Britain on the other covered more than twenty years, but within a year or two of the passage of the South Carolina Negro Seamen Act a significant fact had been revealed, namely, that when a state disagreed with the nation over the constitutionality of a measure, it was possible, at least under some circumstances, for the state to defy the nation. And there was another revelation in the course of this controversy: a party to a controversy over the constitutionality of a law might appeal to a higher law than the Constitution of the United States. The South Carolina senate, by a vote of 36 to 6, asserted that "the duty of the state to guard against insubordination or insurrection among our colored population, . . . is paramount to all *laws,* all *treaties,* all *constitutions.* It arises from the supreme and permanent law of nature, the law of self-preservation; and will never, by this state, be renounced,

[44] *Ibid.,* 203–209.

compromised, controlled or participated with any power whatever." [45] The assertion that there was an imperative superior to the Constitution was contrary to the current trend of Southern thought, for at this time the South was building constitutional defenses for itself. The lower branch of the South Carolina legislature refused to concur in the revolutionary philosophy of the senate.

By the middle of the 1820's notable progress had been made toward realizing the program which the Young Republicans had laid down in 1816 for solving some of the critical problems of the nation. The bank and a tariff that gave moderate protection had been attained in 1816. Eight years later the bank was still in existence after weathering severe attacks at the time of the Panic; the tariff had been raised after the second of two vigorous fights; a beginning had been made in the use of public lands to subsidize internal improvements; the general-survey bill, which looked toward greater Federal aid to transportation, had been passed; and it had been proposed that the extinction of slavery and the removal of the Negro from the United States be made a Federal responsibility.

This chapter in American history is of particular importance in Southern history. Paradoxical as it may seem, the postwar nationalism of 1816 was leading not to unity but to disunity, because most men could not help looking at each part of the program from the standpoint of local interest rather than of national welfare. Furthermore, they discovered that certain measures, like the tariff, could be carried beyond their original purpose of national advantage to a point which permitted the sacrifice of one section of the nation to another.

The novelty in this situation lay not in a sudden increase of human selfishness but in the increased volume of Federal legislation of an economic character. Measures affecting banking, transportation, foreign trade, domestic manufactures, agriculture, bankruptcy, slavery, and public-land policy came before Congress in rapid succession. The vote upon each of these measures followed a sectional

[45] *Ibid.*, 204–209, for the essential documents. For an account of the extended controversy, see Philip M. Hamer, "Great Britain, the United States, and the Negro Seamen Acts, 1822–1848," in *Journal of Southern History*, I (1935), 3–28. A sketch of the Denmark Vesey plot is in Herbert Aptheker, *American Negro Slave Revolts* (New York, 1943), 268–76.

pattern, with the South Atlantic, the Southwestern, the Ohio Valley, the Middle Atlantic, and the New England states each voting pretty much as a unit. While the alignment was not the same on successive questions, there was, nevertheless, a tendency, seen and feared by many, for the South and the North to be arrayed against each other on the major issues.

A politician in Philadelphia wrote to a friend in Richmond in 1820 that "Three measures now agitate the Union; one, the Missouri, has been decided in favour of the Southern states, the 2nd the Tariff, has been and will be rejected through the influence of the Southern and Eastern states, against the Middle and Western states. Would not policy and a spirit of conciliation suggest that the Southern states should concede the 3rd, I mean the bankrupt system?" [46] An editorial in the Richmond *Enquirer* asserted that the general effect of certain of these issues was to create "a contention between northern and southern feeling—a sort of contention, which is at all times the most unpleasant, and which is most solemnly deprecated by the illustrious Washington in his farewell address to his countrymen." [47]

To say that the South was of one mind on the issues of the early 1820's is an oversimplification. Nevertheless, Congressmen from the slave states were almost unanimous in opposing a protective tariff, the Tallmadge amendment, and a Federal bankruptcy law; and most of the South disliked the national bank, though with less unanimity. On these important questions the powerful South Atlantic states and the Southwest were in essential agreement. However, on another group of issues, notably internal improvements, public-land policy, and to some extent constitutional construction, the Southwest differed from the seaboard. In short, the allegiance of the Southwest was divided between the Southeast and the upper West, and this fact was to be a potent influence in Southern history for some years to come.

In the year 1820 the South Atlantic states were the more powerful part of the slave states, and the opinion of this dominant part of the South needs close analysis. A significant fact about the position of the South Atlantic states is that they were on the negative side of practically every current national issue. Innate conservatism does

[46] Richmond *Enquirer*, November 10, 1820. [47] *Ibid.*, May 19, 1820.

not explain this fact; for Southern thinking had not previously been distinguished for its conservatism. The explanation lies rather in two other circumstances. In the first place, the cotton and tobacco states, being more deeply involved in foreign trade than other parts of the United States, were naturally the stanchest adherents to the old laissez-faire system and the chief opponents of a program which was designed in some measure to shut off the nation from the rest of the world. In the second place, the census of 1820 showed that population was growing less rapidly in the South Atlantic states than in the rest of the nation. The consequence would be a decline in political power. With this prospect ahead, representatives of this region objected to an enlargement of Federal powers, particularly those powers by which one part of the nation might enrich itself at the expense of another part of the nation.

The growing realization within the slave states that they were being injured by the new trends in national policy is extremely significant, for thus it was that political self-consciousness was implanted in the South. The germ of this awareness of danger was in the small number of men who insisted, even in the burst of expansive national feeling following the War of 1812, that the national government ought to be restricted to narrow limits by a rigid adherence to the words of the Constitution. They viewed each phase of the new nationalistic program with alarm. As that program began to work some injury to the slave states and to threaten greater harm, a number of Southerners began to listen with more attention to the dire warnings of the Old Republicans. But it is doubtful whether this turn of events brought much cheer to the elder prophets. Their ranks were thinning, and those who were left believed that the return to strict construction was too late to save their country from serious injury. The nationalistic movement had gone too far to be stopped, and the Constitution had been mutilated beyond repair. John Randolph, speaking against the tariff of 1824, said it was a waste of breath "to argue about the constitutionality of this bill; I consider the Constitution a dead letter." [48] He and his fellows had

48 *Annals of Congress*, 18 Cong., 1 Sess., 2360–61. John Taylor of Caroline lacked Randolph's gift for finding the right phrase, but Taylor more than any other one person hammered out the Southern line of constitutional defense. His *Construction Construed, and Constitutions Vindicated* (Richmond, 1820), was directed chiefly against the Bank of the United States and the opinion of the Supreme Court in McCulloch

suffered the curse imposed on some men of extraordinary foresight: they saw where the course was leading, but they could not open the eyes of those at the helm.

But the Old Republicans were not without influence in the history of the South. They lived long enough to teach the younger generation of Southern statesmen the almost forgotten language of strict construction. Once, before Jefferson became President, the Republicans had professed a belief in strict construction. Most of them abandoned that faith after their party came to power. There were a few, however, who guarded the arsenal of constitutional arguments and passed out weapons to the younger generation of Southerners in the 1820's. Thus it was that Southern opposition to the various phases of the new economic nationalism, an opposition that was chiefly economic, was quickly joined at nearly every point with the doctrines of strict construction and state rights.

Within a very few years the South had come a long way on the road to sectionalism. Always it had differed in some measure from other parts of the nation in its economic and social life, and these differences had occasionally determined political action and constitutional thinking; but there was no such thing as a separate and distinct Southern Congressional bloc or Southern political platform before the year 1820. About this time, however, the South Atlantic states began to take a common stand on a number of vital national issues and on some of these issues the Southwest agreed with the South Atlantic states. In nearly every respect the South Atlantic platform was negative, and around this platform, which was essentially dictated by self-interest, a wall of constitutional arguments was being erected, thus investing it with the righteous garb of legality and high principle.

An extreme sectionalism throughout all the slave states was, however, still far off. The Southwest was much less discontented than the South Atlantic states; a strong potential of distrust and anger had not yet been built up; and constitutional justification of violent action had not been perfected.

---

v. Maryland; his *Tyranny Unmasked* (Washington, 1822), attacked the expansion of the powers of the national government especially in respect to the protective tariff.

CHAPTER VII

END OF THE VIRGINIA DYNASTY

THE TENSIONS and cross-purposes that were developing around the year 1820 were reflected hardly at all by political parties: it was thus possible for the administration of Monroe to be called an Era of Good Feeling because it was devoid of party warfare when, as a matter of fact, his years in office were notable for the rise of many bitterly contested issues. This lack of correspondence between party structure and political realities was an unstable and transitory condition that was to be terminated by the destruction of the existing party organization. Then, after several years of political chaos, new political organizations were created that more nearly reflected fundamental political realities. These changes greatly reduced the influence of the South in national politics. The present chapter will trace this story from the period of a well-organized but unrealistic party situation into the period of political chaos.

From the War of 1812 until the election of 1824 the Republican party was, for all practical purposes, the only party in the nation. The moribund Federalist party ceased making nominations for the presidency. This being the case, election day had no importance in Presidential elections, for the Republican nomination was a sure guarantee of office.

The election of 1820 will illustrate the operation of this one-party situation. James Monroe, who was nearing the end of his first term as President, was generally accepted by his party as their candidate for a second term. So unanimous was this agreement that when a heavy rain interfered with the scheduled meeting of the Congressional caucus, the party leaders did not trouble to hold another meeting. The Federalists made no nomination, and in nearly every state all of the Presidential electoral candidates were pledged to vote for Monroe as President and for Daniel D. Tompkins of New York as Vice-President.

The voters, being left with no function except to approve the will of the party leaders, did not trouble to vote. In Richmond, Virginia, only 17 votes were cast, and in the whole state only 4,321. In 53 of the 62 counties of North Carolina the vote was 3,567; in Kentucky it was less than 8,000; and in Mississippi it was only 751.[1] The popular vote in these states did not amount to more than one per cent of the total population, although in some contemporary gubernatorial elections nearly 10 per cent of the population voted for the contending candidates.

Since the Republican nomination rather than the election was the critical point in the choice of a President, the system of making nominations needs to be explored in some detail. The ultimate choice between rival Republican candidates lay with the Republican members of Congress meeting in a party caucus. Naturally, this meeting was preceded by private discussions and arrangements, but the meeting itself was not a secret, clandestine affair. The time and place were previously announced in the papers; the galleries were open to spectators; and the press reported its proceedings. It was possible for the ordinary citizen to know whether the members of the caucus reflected public opinion. The participants, being active politicians, were likely to be well informed about public opinion in their constituencies; and being subject to periodic elections, they were likely to respect that opinion. Furthermore, they knew the names of candidates who had been placed in nomination by the legislative caucuses of the states.

The caucus system thus served to bring together at one place the opinions of the various parts of the nation, and it afforded a way of reaching a final decision among the various candidates for the nomination. It served the further function of making proper arrangements for getting the nominees elected. Some of the state legislative caucuses made up slates of electoral-college candidates

---

[1] For citations to support these figures, and for a more detailed and annotated discussion of the subjects treated in the early part of this chapter, see Charles S. Sydnor, "The One-Party Period of American History," in *American Historical Review*, LI (1945–1946), 439–51, especially p. 442.

pledged to vote for the party ticket; Congressional and state caucuses appointed corresponding committees to work for the success of the party nominees; and the Virginia caucus of 1820, following the customary practice in that state, appointed Republican committees of about six members in each county and borough in the state. About half of these committeemen were members of the powerful county courts. The caucus system, by its tie-up with the legislatures, and in Virginia with the county courts, gave to the politicians of the conservative eastern, planting counties of the South Atlantic states great power in President making.

Among the South Atlantic states—indeed, in all the nation—no state had more power within the Republican party than Virginia. In every Presidential campaign through that of 1820 the Republicans always turned to Virginia for their Presidential candidate, and none but Virginians had ever attained the presidency except John Adams for a single term. Obviously, it was to the interest of the South Atlantic states, and especially to the interest of Virginia, to retain the existing party organization; and within these states, the eastern squirearchy had most to gain by maintaining the supremacy of the Republican party and its organization for making nominations.

Just as obviously, there were many Americans who would welcome the end of the existing political organization. Upcountry Southerners as well as residents of the Mississippi Valley were restive under a system that was controlled in the East. Some of the Northern states, especially New York and Massachusetts, were envious of Virginia's long-continued success in sending its citizens to the presidency. Voters in many parts of the country wanted some way of expressing their opinion for or against issues that seemed to them to be vital. But perhaps the chief threat to the old order in politics came from several relatively young Republican politicians who had rapidly risen to prominence during the War of 1812. Some of them had great ability, and all of them had too much ambition to wait patiently while the elder statesmen of the party gave the presidency first to one and then to another of their own conservative group. In the campaign of 1824 several of the younger Republicans raised the standard of rebellion against the old leaders of the party, and they sought recruits in the areas of discontent. Generally speaking, they first tried to gain control over the existing party organization; when that plan failed, they then sought to destroy that organization. Among the more prominent of the political rebels were William Lowndes and John C. Calhoun of South Carolina, Henry Clay of Kentucky, Andrew Jackson of Tennessee, and John Quincy Adams of Massachusetts.

The person against whom these party leaders were aligned was William H. Crawford. Throughout the long campaign it was generally agreed that he had the backing of the caucus organization. He had missed being nominated in the Congressional caucus of 1816 by only a narrow margin, and as 1824 approached, his favored position became increasingly clear. In that year Crawford was fifty-two years old, and there was much to commend him for the highest office in the nation. He was, to use the phrase, a Virginia colonial. He had been born in that state, and he enjoyed the friendship of some of the leading Virginia politicians; nevertheless, by his early removal to Georgia he avoided the outcry that would have been raised against any Virginia candidate. In his upward path, he had attained prominence in the conservative faction in Georgia politics, had served in the United States Senate and as minister to France, and had entered Madison's cabinet as secretary of war. He was soon transferred to the Treasury Department, and he retained that post through both of Monroe's administrations.

Tall, ruddy, and hearty in appearance, Crawford looked like a country squire, and his views on public questions suited the eastern squirearchy of the South Atlantic states. He held the rights of the states in great respect, and he favored economy, simplicity, and retrenchment in national government, even to the extent of reducing the armed forces of the nation. He opposed the use of Federal funds for internal improvements, and he opposed a high protective tariff, though he was not in this respect an extremist. Although he favored the maintenance of a national bank, most of his views were in general accord with those of such Old Republicans as Madison, Macon, and Randolph; and such powerful newspapers as the Richmond *Enquirer* and the Raleigh *Register* were his champions during the campaign.

From the nature of the case, Crawford did not need to appeal to the people in an active and vigorous campaign. If the organization of the only existing party was for him, there was little that he needed to do except to retain the support of the leaders of Congress, state legislatures, and county courts.

The earliest clear challenge in the South to Crawford was issued by Calhoun. He had been born in upcountry South Carolina, near Abbeville, but by marriage and other ties he had established important connections with the low country. His education was excellent. Like Crawford, he had studied with Moses Waddel. Later he had been graduated from Yale College. He had then studied law at Tapping Reeve's school at Litchfield, Connecticut, and in a Charleston law office. From the South Carolina legislature he was advanced to Congress in 1810, and within two years he had, by good fortune, won wide recognition as chairman of the Committee on Foreign Affairs. His efforts in behalf of American success during the War of 1812 were so energetic that he was referred to as "the young Hercules who carried the war on his shoulders." [2] Joined with his diligence were other qualities that made him seem almost too perfect. He was considered "the most elegant speaker that sits in the House. . . . His gestures are easy and graceful, his manner forcible, and language elegant; but above all, he confines himself closely to the subject, which he always understands, and enlightens every one within hearing." [3]

After a Congressional career of distinction he advanced to the cabinet, where he served for seven and one-half years as secretary of war under President Monroe. In this office he showed marked talent for administration, and he earned the respect of John Quincy Adams who served with him in the cabinet. Adams appraised him as "a man of fair and candid mind, of honorable principles, of clear and quick understanding, of cool self-possession, of enlarged philosophical views, and of ardent patriotism."

In his views on public questions Calhoun was considered an advocate of the national bank, a protective tariff, a firm foreign policy, a strong army and navy, and a large scheme of internal improvements at Federal expense. Perhaps he was best known for his interest

---

[2] Opinion of Alexander J. Dallas, quoted in Ulrich B. Phillips, "John Caldwell Calhoun," in *Dictionary of American Biography*, III, 412.

[3] James C. Jewett to General H. A. S. Dearborn, Washington, February 5, 1817, in *William and Mary Quarterly*, XVII (1908), 143.

in internal improvements. In Adams' opinion he was "above all sectional and factious prejudices more than any other statesman of this Union with whom I have ever acted." [4] Whereas Crawford's chief supporters were elderly men, Calhoun, who was ten years the younger, had been associated with the Young Republicans. He and Crawford had usually disagreed in cabinet councils; now their opposing views on nearly every important question were aired before the people.

Before tracing the course of Calhoun's campaign, a word must be said about his nationalism. His opinions in the campaign of 1824 must be surmised chiefly from his activities before he entered the cabinet, and it may be that he had begun to have doubts about his nationalistic views before he entered upon this campaign. But if so, it would have been inexpedient for him to announce them, since his hopes for the presidency hinged largely on winning Pennsylvania and its neighbors. Compared with Crawford's conservatism, Calhoun's progressive platform made him appear as the champion of change and progress—like Jefferson in the previous generation. But there were differences. Speaking broadly, Jefferson had been chiefly concerned with freedom of the mind and spirit and with social reforms, and his program for accomplishing his goals had consisted mostly in abolishing laws that hampered and restricted the individual; Calhoun's objectives lay largely in the economic realm, and he sought to accomplish his ends by passing laws rather than by repealing them—by more rather than by less governmental regulation and activity. From this viewpoint, the Calhoun of the early 1820's seems to have been more of a Hamiltonian than a Jeffersonian.

Calhoun's campaign was in two stages. First, he tried to capture the caucus machine from Crawford and turn it to his own advantage. When this attempt failed, his campaign changed into an attack upon the party organization as well as upon Crawford.

Having won the support of the legislature of his own state, Calhoun planned the next stage of his campaign with an eye to the political situation in other states. It was obviously useless for him to try to capture Georgia or Virginia from Crawford, Kentucky from Clay, Tennessee from Jackson, or New England from Adams.

[4] Adams (ed.), *Memoirs of John Quincy Adams*, V, 361.

He must concentrate upon the states that had no favorite sons, particularly upon the larger states—New York, Pennsylvania, North Carolina, and Maryland.

North Carolina was the critical slave state. Its fifteen electoral votes were surpassed in the South only by Virginia, and they were more than the combined votes of Alabama, Mississippi, and Louisiana. Maryland with eleven electoral votes was next in importance in the South. But Maryland used the district system of choosing electors, whereas North Carolina chose them on a state-wide ticket. Hence, a candidate could win a majority of the popular votes in Maryland and lose some of the electoral votes; in North Carolina, he would receive them all.

Calhoun's campaign in North Carolina began in the western part of the state. This was the logical point of attack, for in the West there already existed much hostility against the Eastern politicians who were supporting Crawford; Calhoun's platform, especially his program of internal improvements, was acceptable to western Carolinians; and commercial ties connected western North Carolina with Calhoun's state.

With the Salisbury *Western Carolinian* as his chief organ, and with Charles Fisher, its editor, as his chief supporter, Calhoun first concentrated upon the legislative elections of August, 1823. These elections would determine the political complexion of the legislature that would, in caucus, nominate a slate of electors. Calhoun, fully aware of what was at stake, wrote: "Your election of members of the Legislature will doubtless be attended to also. It is of great, I may say almost of decisive importance." [5] In these elections, Calhoun failed to win a majority in the legislature, partly because of the underrepresentation of the western counties where most of his strength lay. The legislature was pro-Crawford, and in time it put in nomination a Crawford electoral ticket. Crawford's supporters likewise won in most of the North Carolina Congressional races of that summer. [6]

In Virginia and Maryland, contests occurred over the legislative

[5] Albert R. Newsome (ed.), "Correspondence of John C. Calhoun, George McDuffie and Charles Fisher, Relating to the Presidential Campaign of 1824," in *North Carolina Historical Review*, VII (1930), 479.

[6] Newsome, *Presidential Election of 1824 in North Carolina*, 54–58.

elections, though in the former they were not of much significance, for Crawford was clearly the Virginia favorite. But in Maryland there was considerable opposition to the caucus system, especially to the nomination of legislative candidates by county committees of local politicians. This opposition was expressed in conservative Anne Arundel County by the following resolution that was adopted at a popular meeting: "Resolved, That as freemen and republicans, we will not be bound to support any measures that a caucus may adopt." [7] The town of Annapolis sent caucus men to the legislature, but the anticaucus men won the election in the county, and they published the following gloating communication in the local newspaper: "The whole anti-caucus ticket has succeeded. The chosen few who have heretofore dictated to the yeomanry of Anne-Arundel, may now prostrate themselves in the dust; their reign is over; the people in their might decreed its end. Exult my friend, as every Republican should do, at the right of choosing representatives for this populous county being again claimed and exercised by its only legitimate owners—an intelligent and determined people." [8]

The Maryland farmers and planters who controlled the caucus organization in their state were challenged by a Baltimore-sponsored proposal that electors be chosen on a general ticket rather than by the existing district-ticket system. The attempt came to naught due to the overrepresentation of the rural counties in the legislature. [9]

By the end of the summer of 1823 it was clear that Calhoun had failed to gain enough strength in the North Carolina and other legislatures to hope for control over the caucus machine. His supporters therefore made a radical change in strategy: they sought to stir the people up to the point of revolting against the organization which Calhoun had failed to capture. This new stage of the fight, which did not reach its full development until well in the year 1824, was a turning point in the campaign and was of profound significance in American political history. Assemblies of men, wherever they collected, whether on court days, at militia musters, as grand juries, and on special call, were requested to express their preferences among the various candidates. In the early days of this appeal

---

[7] Annapolis *Maryland Gazette and Political Intelligencer*, September 4, 1823.

[8] *Ibid.*, October 9, 1823. See also, *ibid.*, October 7, 1824.

[9] *Ibid.*, December 18, 1823; January 29, February 5, 1824.

to the people, Calhoun's friends were active in initiating these un-official polls. But they quickly sensed a danger in this new technique. As one of them wrote: "I am afraid if the thing is started in earnest, that Jackson & Crawford too, would be recommended in too many places; so I think it best to be silent." [10]

In short, the people would not be managed; they, whose voices had long been silenced in Presidential elections, now refused to echo the cries of the leaders who arranged the meetings. The people did not hesitate to vote as they pleased, and usually they preferred Jackson. As soon as this phenomenon was apparent, Calhoun's friends drew back from what they had precipitated, and Crawford's supporters dared not instigate many straw ballots, perhaps no more than five in North Carolina. But Jackson's managers, quickly sens-ing the importance of the new development, made the public meet-ing their chief campaign technique. In more than a hundred meet-ings in North Carolina, Jackson was shown to be the popular favorite.[11]

In other states, Jackson's supporters made use of straw ballots and direct appeals to assembled voters. In Virginia, where Jackson met with but little favor in the newspapers,[12] public meetings at Freder-icksburg and Winchester were among the earliest indications of activity in his behalf.[13] The Ninth Mississippi regiment of militia was requested by "a number of respectable citizens" to express its preference for President. The result was 454 for Jackson, 18 for Adams, and 3 for Crawford.[14]

The full force of the popular revolution in favor of Jackson be-came apparent in the spring of 1824. Hitherto, Jackson's and Adams' supporters had followed much the same course as Calhoun had followed in the early part of his campaign. They had fought Crawford rather than the Republican party organization, and the adherents of all three candidates had sometimes worked together. In North Carolina they had organized the People's party. In the

10 Newsome (ed.), "Correspondence of John C. Calhoun, George McDuffie and Charles Fisher," *loc. cit.*, 500.

11 Newsome, *Presidential Election of 1824 in North Carolina*, 84–85, 119–21, 138–39, 150.

12 Horace L. Bachelder, "Presidential Election of 1824 in Virginia" (M.A. thesis, Duke University, 1942), Chap. V, "The Jackson-Calhoun Ticket."

13 *Norfolk and Portsmouth Herald*, March 24, 1824; cf. *Niles' Weekly Register*, XXVI (1824), 53; Alexandria (Va.) *Herald*, April 21, 1824.

14 Natchez *Mississippi Republican and Literary Register*, October 13, 1824.

early stages of the campaign, this party was under the dominance of Calhoun men; but when the campaign changed into an attack upon the caucus and an appeal to the people, Calhoun rapidly lost strength, and the People's party came under the control of the supporters of the popular Jackson.

A similar trend was evident in some other states; it reached a crisis on March 4, 1824, in Pennsylvania when a convention at Harrisburg nominated Jackson for President and Calhoun for Vice-President. In the face of this development, Calhoun withdrew from the race for the first office and centered his hopes on the vice-presidency, which he won by an overwhelming majority in the fall election. He had done as much as Jackson, and perhaps more in its early stages, to destroy the caucus system and to inaugurate, by direct appeal to the people, a new day in democracy. But his part was to be forgotten; the movement became known as Jacksonian democracy.

A second upset in this race, one that was about as disconcerting as Calhoun's withdrawal, came in September, 1823: Crawford suffered a severe stroke of paralysis which forced him into seclusion for the rest of the campaign, nearly blind and completely incapacitated. His friends remained faithful, or perhaps unduly optimistic about his recovery; and the Congressional caucus nominated him on February 14, 1824. However, such a nomination carried little weight because only 68 Congressmen voted in this caucus whereas 193 did not. Obviously, the party organization was disintegrating.

Neither Crawford nor Calhoun had many adherents in the Mississippi Valley. Westerners did not like Crawford's platform; they had little influence in the caucus and no respect for it; and some of them had been shocked by Crawford's heretical suggestion that the white man might solve the Indian question by domestication or even by intermarriage. As for Calhoun, the West liked much of his platform, but it never took the man to its heart. In the spring and early summer of 1819, President Monroe had made a leisurely swing around the circle in the South. As he went down through the Southeastern states, his young secretary of war, Calhoun, was given much honor at receptions, dinners, and balls. But when the party turned west and began to move up through Tennessee and Kentucky, Calhoun was forgotten and Jackson was the favorite. At a great dinner in Kentucky the toast to "General Jackson" came next after the toast to "The President of the United States." [15]

Perhaps the best explanation of the failure of Crawford and Calhoun to gain a following across the mountains is to be found in a statement that appeared in the Louisville *Public Advertiser:* "We have been almost unanimously in favor of the election of a western President—not because our favorite happened to be a *western man,* but because we felt attached to certain principles which would be most effectually sustained by the election of one of the western candidates." [16]

Another of the Western candidates was Henry Clay. Though his youth had been passed in Virginia, he had become thoroughly identified with the West, particularly with the hemp-growing region of Kentucky. Clay's national reputation was made in Congress, where, for some years, he was Speaker of the House. First known as the leader of the War Hawks, he later became the champion of a program, somewhat unctuously called the American System, which included a protective tariff, internal improvements, and the sale of public lands. While his plan was essentially the same as Calhoun's, it differed somewhat in emphasis; and Clay went further in fitting its parts into an integrated program. It is possible that his personal reputation injured him. He was thought to be too fond of liquor, cards, and horse racing, and there were some who wondered whether his vigorous, slashing criticisms of Jackson, Adams, and other leaders were founded on principle or were dictated by political ambitions and egocentric cocksureness. In 1824 he was not much more successful in winning Eastern adherents than Calhoun and Crawford were in gaining Western adherents.

With Calhoun out of the race and neither Clay nor Crawford able to get a following except in his own section, the contest was narrowed to Adams and Jackson. Though they differed widely in most respects, even in appearance—for Jackson was thin of body and long of face while Adams was inclined to rotundity—they were alike in that they were the only candidates who could get votes in both the East and the West. A partial explanation of this fact may

[15] Richmond *Enquirer*, July 20, 1819, and April through July, *passim;* Nashville *Whig, and Tennessee Advertiser,* June 5, 1819.
[16] Louisville *Public Advertiser*, November 13, 1824.

be that little was known about the views of either man on domestic issues.

Adams, the son of President John Adams and a graduate of Harvard College, was distinctly a New Englander; yet, the ties that bound him to his section were somewhat loose. He had never been an orthodox party man nor active as a politician, not even in his own behalf in this campaign. Although he was considered a moderate nationalist, his views on foreign policy were more thoroughly formulated and better known than his opinions on domestic issues; for his public life had been spent almost entirely in representing the United States at various courts abroad and in managing the State Department under President Monroe.

The Adams campaign in the South was neither noisy nor aggressive, and this moderation permitted him to win the votes of some who had first planned to vote for Crawford or Calhoun. He appealed chiefly to the conservative wing of society which feared the unpredictable and wanted government to be in the hands of experienced statesmen. His North Carolina supporters "based their preference on his superior abilities as a statesman, his thorough knowledge of domestic and foreign affairs, his long public service under Jefferson, Madison, and Monroe, his republican simplicity of manners, and his sterling integrity." [17] A Virginia newspaper observed that inasmuch as a vote for Crawford would be thrown away, Virginia ought "by designating her next of choice, John Q. Adams, [to] gratify the oldest and most populous section of the United States—one that prejudices apart, has a community of interests with her." [18] The main argument of Adams' supporters was that their candidate was an experienced statesman; his enemies responded: "To us his merits appear to be merely those of an excellent clerk." [19]

The Jackson men emblazoned their banner with the military renown of their hero. Although a plain man of North Carolina observed that "Every good general ant fite for a presidance," [20] most of the common people thought otherwise. A discouraged opponent noted that "the people are fascinated & influenced by the splendor

[17] Thus summarized in Newsome, *Presidential Election of 1824 in North Carolina,* 143–44.

[18] Richmond *Constitutional Whig,* February 24, 1824.

[19] Natchez *Mississippi Republican and Literary Register,* January 14, 1824.

[20] Quoted in Newsome, *Presidential Election of 1824 in North Carolina,* 135.

of his military fame *alone*. It is not that they think or care about his being an able statesman that they will vote for him. . . . [He] has slain the Indians & flogged the British & spilled his blood in defence of his country's rights—therefore he is the bravest, wisest, & greatest man in the nation—even the memory of Washington is lost in the blaze of the Genl's Glory & in the glare of his bloody laurels." [21] Another anti-Jackson man wrote: "It is very difficult to electioneer successfully against Genl. Jackson—his character and his services are of that kind which *alone* the people can appreciate and feel—one cup of *generous whiskey* produces more military ardor, than can be allayed by a month of reflection and sober reason." [22] No wonder Jackson's friends had found militia musters good occasions for pushing his candidacy!

It was fortunate for Jackson's supporters that they did not have to say much about his civil career, for it was brief and undistinguished. Because attention was focused so closely on his military career, his opponents were forced to seek weak spots in that armor. As far back as 1819, when it was asserted that he had high political aspirations, the Richmond *Enquirer* had fulminated against "his taking of the lives of prisoners, his capture of neutral posts contrary to orders," and had declared that it ought to be proved "that in a land of laws no man could violate his orders with impunity; and that in a land of liberty, the military was kept strictly subordinate to the civil power." [23]

Various statements during the election show that men considered this contest as something of a class struggle. The New Orleans *Louisiana Gazette* [24] suggested that wealth was opposed to Jackson when it declared that "the market has been rumaged, and the wine-cellers culled, presses have been bought, and writers hired" to com-

21 P. H. Mangum to Willie P. Mangum, Orange County, April 15, 1824, in Willie P. Mangum Papers (North Carolina Department of Archives and History).

22 John Owen to Bartlett Yancy, Bladenboro, N.C., July 21, 1824, Miscellaneous Papers, Series One, II, 105, quoted in Newsome, *Presidential Election of 1824 in North Carolina*, 137.

23 Richmond *Enquirer*, May 11, 1819. The *Enquirer*'s criticism of Jackson's management of the Florida war began late in 1818 and lasted until the late spring of 1819. It drew forth a strong rebuttal from the Nashville *Whig, and Tennessee Advertiser*, January 9, 1819. See also, Richard R. Stenberg, "Jackson's 'Rhea Letter' Hoax," in *Journal of Southern History*, II (1936), 480–96.

24 New Orleans *Louisiana Gazette*, November 23, 1824, and the previous issues.

pass his defeat. A Mississippi newspaper plainly said that the Adams party was aristocratic; the Jackson party democratic.[25]

Although the popularity of Jackson with the plain people was a noteworthy feature of the campaign, it should be made clear that he was neither poor nor previously allied with champions of democracy. As a matter of fact, he was a well-to-do planter; he had been a large-scale, bold land speculator; and in Tennessee politics he was allied with the conservatives on the current issues of money and banking.[26]

Furthermore, neither he nor his friends were offering the people in the 1824 campaign a program of democratic reform. This is not to say that Jackson was engaging in subterfuge or that the people were incorrect in their belief that he was at heart a plain man; but neither can it be said that he consciously unfurled the banner of democracy. Without much help from Jackson, the plain people were stirred into political rebellion against their customary rulers during the campaign of 1824; and they espoused Jackson primarily because of his military reputation. In short, it is more accurate to say that democracy made Jackson than to say that Jackson made democracy. He profited by the release of pre-existing political-economic tensions: the desire of the tramontane Westerner for power in national government and the demands of South Atlantic Westerners for more equitable distribution of power in state government.

The increase in the number of popular votes indicates that democracy was on the march. In the nation, nearly five people voted in 1824 for every two who had voted in 1820.[27] The increase was especially pronounced in the Southern states. In North Carolina, where the contest was close, ten times more votes were cast in 1824 than four years earlier. In those states where electors had hitherto been chosen by the legislatures, the demand for popular elections became strong. Before another Presidential election, the choice of electors was given to the people in Georgia and Louisiana; only in

[25] Natchez *Mississippi Republican, and Literary Register,* June 30, 1824, and *passim* throughout the year 1824. Note also the references to "the people" in statements, quoted above, by North Carolina opponents of Jackson.

[26] Abernethy, "Andrew Jackson and the Rise of Southwestern Democracy," *loc. cit.,* 64–77.

[27] Sydnor, "The One-Party Period of American History," *loc. cit.,* 442, 449.

South Carolina was the old system retained, and here it was not abandoned before the Civil War.

A second revelation of much significance was the popularity of Jackson. He received 55 of the 108 electoral votes of the South: the votes of North Carolina, South Carolina, Tennessee, Alabama, and Mississippi, together with 3 of the 5 Louisiana electoral votes and 7 of the 11 Maryland votes. In the seven Southern states in which electors were popularly chosen, his popular vote was as large as the combined vote of his three opponents. Nor was his popularity restricted to any one part of the South. In every Southern state except Virginia and perhaps Georgia, he was second choice if he was not first, and in two thirds of the states he was first.[28]

He was strongest west of the mountains and in the western parts of certain Eastern states, particularly in Maryland and North Carolina.[29] The generalization might be ventured that the younger the region and the fewer its slaves, the greater was Jackson's popularity; he was weakest in the areas where slaves were numerous and in the Eastern Tidewater and Piedmont where political power had long been held. South Carolina was the only exception to this rule.

Next to Jackson in point of popular votes was Crawford. Nearly all of his 30,000 votes were in two areas of the Atlantic states; one was his own state, Georgia, together with several adjacent counties in North Carolina and Alabama, and the other was the old tobacco kingdom in Piedmont Virginia, northern North Carolina, and Tidewater Maryland. There was scarcely a county in the South Atlantic states, except in South Carolina, with more than 50 per cent of its population slave, that did not vote for Crawford.[30] Georgia gave all of its 9 electoral votes to him, Virginia its 24, and Maryland one; a total of 34.

[28] Jackson was first choice in every Southern state except Georgia, Virginia, Kentucky, and perhaps Maryland. In Maryland he won fewer popular votes than Adams, but he got most of the state's electoral votes. In Kentucky he was second; in Virginia he was third; Georgia opinion about candidates other than Crawford is not measurable. For the popular vote in this election, see material accompanying the 1824 map in the Appendix.

[29] In North Carolina the Jackson and Adams votes were merged in the People's party. But it is evident that Adams' strength lay near the coast. Newsome, *Presidential Election of 1824 in North Carolina*, 148–50.

[30] Compare map of the 1824 election in Appendix with Paullin and Wright, *Atlas of the Historical Geography of the United States*, plate 67, E and F.

Adams received over 22,000 popular votes in the South; over half of these were cast in Maryland. He won only 5 electoral votes, 3 in Maryland and 2 in Louisiana. But over against this poor showing stand several facts. First, he had many followers in North Carolina who joined with the Jackson men in the People's party and who, though losing their political identity for the time being, were numerous and influential. Second, Adams was the only candidate besides Jackson who could win votes both in the seaboard—Maryland, Virginia, and North Carolina—and in the Southwest—Louisiana, Mississippi, and Alabama. Third, he appealed to the more substantial elements of society. He carried the planting counties of the Southwest just as Crawford carried such counties along the seaboard; Quakers and perhaps some other men with religious convictions preferred him to the martial hero; and he had the backing of the urban commercial interests. The general pattern of his vote showed that most of his followers lived in or near the coastal towns or in plantation regions; and it is significant that his Southern electoral votes came altogether from Maryland and Louisiana, where the two largest Southern cities were located.

The vote in Baltimore may serve to illustrate the urban reaction to this election. In this city and the neighboring area that made up the third Maryland electoral district, only 9 votes were cast for Crawford; for Crawford was championed by the conservative rural forces that kept the populous city from having full power in state affairs. The city gave 3,904 votes to Jackson and 3,004 to Adams; in the rural parts of the third district, Adams led Jackson by a majority of 506.[31] There are some indications that Jackson was the favorite of the plain people of Baltimore; Adams of the men of substance. If this were true, Jackson might not have won in this district had Maryland not abolished property requirements for voting some fourteen years earlier.

Clay's following in the South was restricted almost entirely to his own state and to Louisiana. All of his 14 electoral votes and all but about 1,000 of his 18,000 popular votes were won in Kentucky. Furthermore, some 6,000 voters in his own state registered a preference for Jackson. In the Louisiana legislature, Clay missed by a

[31] *Niles' Weekly Register*, XXVII (1824), 162; Annapolis *Maryland Gazette, and State Register*, November 11, 1824.

narrow margin winning the 2 electoral votes that went to Adams.[32]

Since no candidate received a majority of the electoral votes of the nation,[33] the lower House of Congress proceeded, under the provisions of the Twelfth Amendment, to ballot among the three highest, Jackson, Adams, and Crawford. Each Representative registered his preference as a basis for determining the vote of his state. Although there was some expectation that several ballots would be necessary, Adams was elected on the first ballot with the votes of thirteen states. Seven states were for Jackson and four for Crawford.

Although Jackson had received a good half of the popular and electoral votes of the South, in the Congressional ballot only one third of the Southern Representatives voted for him and only four of the ten Southern states were for him. Jackson's defeat and Adams' election have usually been credited to Clay on the theory that he diverted to Adams the electoral votes of the states that had been for Clay. He was doubtless responsible for putting Kentucky in the Adams column, although he was not strong enough to keep four of the twelve Kentucky Representatives from voting for Jackson; and his influence probably counted in giving Louisiana to Adams.

But it is not easy to find the hand of Clay shaping events in some other states. In Maryland, Clay could scarcely have had much influence, for he had polled less than 700 popular votes. Maryland's turn to Adams, even though Jackson had received 7 of the 11 electoral votes, was probably related to the fact that Adams had received a slight majority of the prior popular vote. Likewise, Clay had nothing to do with the loss of North Carolina. The Jackson-Adams People's party had carried the state and given its electoral vote to Jackson, but in the Congressional ballot ten of the thirteen North Carolina Representatives voted for Crawford.[34] In short, Adams was helped and Jackson was injured by two forces. In the West, Clay aided the New Englander. In the Southeast, notably in

[32] Louisiana *House Journal*, 1824–1825, p. 8; New Orleans *Louisiana Gazette*, November 9, 17, 23, 1824.

[33] For the entire United States, the electoral vote stood: Jackson 99, Adams 84, Crawford 41, Clay 37.

[34] But it should be noted that they would probably have voted for Jackson had they known that the election would be settled on the first ballot. Newsome, *Presidential Election of 1824 in North Carolina*, 168–70.

North Carolina, Jackson suffered from the hostility of the entrenched political leaders who were accustomed to control legislatures, Congressional delegations, and caucuses. For a long time they had governed without the people. Now, when the people had shown a preference for Jackson, these leaders of the old order refused to heed the popular voice.[35]

Clay's decision to throw his influence to Adams instead of to Jackson was dictated by political expediency as well as by the similarity of their views on public questions. Clay could have gained little by an alliance with Jackson, whose strength, like his own, was greatest in the West; on the other hand, Clay's Western support might be joined with Adams' New England following to the advantage of both men. Furthermore, despite great differences in moral attitudes and personal habits, Clay and Adams saw things much alike, and their views could be worked into a platform that would meet with much favor in the Northeast and the West though it would arouse bitter opposition through the South. Thus, platforms and principles were important in the conclusion of this campaign as they had also been in its early stages.[36]

The events of this campaign caused many men in the Southeast to give much thought to problems inherent in democratic government. There was discussion of whether long experience in statecraft was essential to high office or whether it was desirable for the people to elect a candidate because of his personal popularity. At the campaign's conclusion, a basic question of representative government was raised by the fact that in several states the people had voted one way and their Representatives had voted another. The old question of whether Eastern planters should be able to overrule a greater number of Western farmers became more critical and active.

One aspect of the last question deserves closer scrutiny. In most of the South Atlantic states a man could vote, if he was fortunate enough to vote at all, in only three elections of any importance; for members of his state legislature, for members of the lower House

[35] In Virginia there was a stronger majority for Crawford among the Congressmen (19 for Crawford, 1 for Adams, 1 for Jackson) than the popular vote of the state had warranted.

[36] For an account of the relations between Adams and Clay during the campaign, see Everett S. Brown, "The Presidential Election of 1824–1825," in *Political Science Quarterly* (Boston, New York), XL (1925), 384–403.

of Congress, and for Presidential electors. In the first of these three elections and sometimes in the second, the scales were weighted against the man in the upcountry. Only in Presidential elections was a Westerner certain of being fully equal to an Easterner in the South Atlantic states; and it went hard with him in 1824 to see himself cheated in this, the most democratic election in which he could participate.

And so the election of 1824 closed with the democratic movement well under way. The people had been aroused to the extent of participating in political discussions and assemblies; they had felt the excitement of a campaign; they had voted as never before in a Presidential election; and democracy had become for many of them a cause that was greater than a mere technique for settling questions and gaining selfish ends. The movement was not to be lost in emotional vapor, for there were definite tasks yet to be done: Jackson must be elected President; Congressmen who had not bowed to public opinion must be punished; and undemocratic features of state government must be ended. The events and results of this election served as a sharp spur to those who were working for constitutional reform in the South Atlantic states, particularly by pointing to the evils resulting from Eastern dominance in state government.

Among the immediate results of this election, and one of much significance, was the termination of Virginia's long leadership in American political affairs, including a virtual monopoly of the presidency. The candidate whom Virginia had backed was defeated, and Virginia was in no position to regain its lost power. Its political leadership during the campaign had been inept and ultra-conservative; the spirit of revolt had entered its former satellites, making them unwilling longer to "continue to drag along in the trail of Virginia"; [37] and the new democratic movement found its strength and leaders south and west of the Old Dominion.

The destruction of the old leadership brought on a troubled and chaotic period in Southern political history. There was no organized political party in the nation, and in this fluid and formless condition the South had neither a man nor a state that it was willing to follow as it had been following Virginia. At the moment,

[37] Quoted in Newsome, *Presidential Election of 1824 in North Carolina*, 117.

Jackson and the Southwest seemed to be in the ascendancy, but it remained to be seen whether the seaboard South would be willing to submit to Southwestern leadership. The answer would depend partly on whether Jackson could devise a platform that would satisfy both the Southeast and the Southwest. The campaign revealed greater tension between them than between the South and the North, and the critical question was whether the areas represented by Jackson and Calhoun could be held in some form of political partnership.

CHAPTER VIII

THE LOWER SOUTH ADOPTS
STATE RIGHTS

DURING the 1820's the conservative, state-rights philosophy that hitherto had been chiefly evident in Virginia swept over the lower South, thus obliterating one of the differences between the cotton and the tobacco kingdoms. Yet, uniformity was not altogether established; for the lower South, with the zeal of a new convert, soon carried the state-rights doctrines into more extreme and radical forms than they had ever assumed in Virginia.

The most notable change of sentiment occurred in South Carolina. It was the opinion of Governor James Hamilton, Jr., that nineteen twentieths of the citizens of South Carolina shifted from approval of loose construction in 1821 to disapproval in 1830.[1] At the beginning of the decade, the state was under the sway of Calhoun, Lowndes, Cheves, McDuffie, and other young politicians who were closely identified with the nationalistic program of the Young Republicans.[2] Although their views were not unopposed, the legislature nominated Calhoun for the presidency during the campaign of 1824 even though he was regarded as the champion of protection and of Federal expenditures for internal improvements and even though he had committed himself to loose constitutional construction. Furthermore, the lower house of the legislature, while considering the tariff of 1824:

"Resolved: That the People have conferred no power upon their State Legislature to impugn the Acts of the Federal Government or the decisions of the Supreme Court of the United States.

[1] Charleston *Courier*, August 23, 1830.
[2] David F. Houston, *A Critical Study of Nullification in South Carolina* (New York, 1896), 6, 8 ff.

"Resolved: That any exercise of such power by this state would be an act of usurpation.

"Resolved: That the Representatives of the People in Congress are responsible under God to the People themselves." [3]

But already the tide was rapidly turning in the opposite direction. In 1823 Thomas Cooper, president of South Carolina College, assumed the task of instructing the state in the evils of nationalism. In a pamphlet entitled *On the Proposed Alteration of the Tariff,* he questioned the constitutionality of protection and he marshaled laissez-faire economic arguments against it. The next year he published a second essay, entitled *Consolidation,* in which he attacked the nationalizing tendencies of the times, especially in respect to internal improvements. He declared that "the power of the President of the United States, the power of the Congress of the United States, and more than all, the power of the Supreme Court of the United States (the most dangerous body in the Union) *has increased, is increasing and ought to be diminished.*" [4] Singling out the Secretary of War as the leader of the detested trends, he sarcastically observed that "Mr. Calhoun himself, has been lately surveying some of the creeks in the Allegany [*sic*] mountains, no doubt for some great national object hereafter to be explained." [5]

Cooper was the most cogent and learned of the early South Carolina opponents of nationalism, but he was not alone. Judge William Smith had spoken in Congress against Calhoun's measures, and in 1823 and 1824 Thomas R. Mitchell and James Hamilton, Jr., opposed protection in the House while Robert Y. Hayne advocated state sovereignty in the Senate. By 1825 the sentiment of the state had reached such a point that the legislature which met in November adopted a set of antibank, anti-internal-improvement, and anti-tariff resolutions which had been introduced by Judge Smith. [6]

Events in the early months of Adams' presidency caused the

[3] Ames, *State Documents on Federal Relations,* 138.

[4] Thomas Cooper, *Consolidation. An Account of Parties in the United States, from the Convention of 1787, to the Present Period* (Columbia, 1824), 6.

[5] *Ibid.,* 11. An immediate object of *Consolidation* was to support Crawford in the Presidential election by showing that Calhoun as well as Adams and Jackson was committed to the program which Cooper labeled "consolidation." *Ibid.,* 12, 14.

[6] Houston, *Nullification in South Carolina,* 53–57; Chauncey S. Boucher, *The Nullification Controversy in South Carolina* (Chicago, 1916), 1–2.

South Carolina legislature to adopt these resolutions. Before his term was ended, the policies of his administration had aroused opposition in many parts of the South and had brought the South to a degree of sectional unity never before attained.

Adams stated his platform in his first message to Congress on December 6, 1825. He advocated, among other things, the building of roads and canals, the establishment of a national university, the erection of an astronomical observatory, the sending out of scientific expeditions, and the maintenance of a strong navy. Waxing enthusiastic over his nationalistic program, he wrote: "The spirit of improvement is abroad upon the earth"; great undertakings like the opening of the Erie Canal "have been accomplished in the compass of a few years by the authority of single members of our Confederation, [and] can we, the representative authorities of the whole Union, fall behind our fellow-servants in the exercise of the trust committed to us for the benefit of our common sovereign by the accomplishment of works important to the whole and to which neither the authority nor the resources of any one State can be adequate?" [7]

A brief paragraph in this message was the occasion of the first attack by Adams' opponents. He announced that a congress of representatives from several Latin-American states was to be held at the Isthmus of Panama, and that the United States had been invited to send ministers. "The invitation has been accepted," he said, "and ministers on the part of the United States will be commissioned to attend those deliberations." [8] His critics, among whom Southern Congressmen were prominent, charged that Adams should have consulted Congress before deciding to send representatives to Panama, and that this usurpation of authority by the executive coupled with proposals to expand the activities of the national government constituted a distinct threat to constitutional government and to the interests of the states. Old Republicans like John Randolph were in the vanguard of this attack. [9]

In the second place, participation in the Panama Congress was said to endanger slavery. Senator Benton, referring to Haiti, de-

[7] James D. Richardson (comp.), *Messages and Papers of the Presidents, 1789–1902* (Washington, 1903), II, 882. [8] *Ibid.*, 868.
[9] For Randolph's opinions, see *Register of Debates*, 19 Cong., 1 Sess., 394 ff., 403.

clared: "We purchase coffee from her, . . . but . . . receive no mulatto consuls, or black ambassadors from her . . . to parade through our country, and give to their fellow blacks in the United States, proof in hand of the honors which await them, for a like successful effort on their part." [10] Congressmen from Virginia, the Carolinas, Georgia, Tennessee, and Alabama voted against the appropriation bill for the mission and delayed its passage so long that the ministers from the United States did not arrive while the congress was in session.

While it would be a mistake to credit Adams with much influence over Congress, nevertheless, the course of legislation during his administration was in general accord with his views. The Federal government spent about as much money for internal improvements in the four years of his presidency as it had spent during the previous twenty-four years. Furthermore, it multiplied the number and increased the variety of projects in contrast with the previous concentration upon the Cumberland Road.[11]

As appropriations increased, so did the opposition thereto within the Southern states. Part of this opposition was due to hostility to the tariff, for one pretext for maintaining high duties was to provide funds for building roads and canals. Another reason for hostility was the fact that the internal-improvement program was bringing little benefit to the South except for three canals near its upper edge. These three were the Chesapeake and Ohio (to which Congress had appropriated $200,000) which extended along the north bank of the Potomac; the Louisville and Portland ($233,500) which served to move goods around the falls of the Ohio River at Louisville, Kentucky; and the Dismal Swamp ($200,000) which gave an outlet from the North Carolina sounds to Chesapeake Bay.

Excluding expenditures for these canals, for the Cumberland Road ($2,500,000), and for the Chesapeake and Delaware Canal ($450,000), Federal expenditures for internal improvements had amounted, by the end of the year 1829, to $251,000 in the Middle Atlantic states, $318,000 in New England, and $586,000 in the

10 Thomas Hart Benton, *Thirty Years' View: or, A History of the Working of the American Government for Thirty Years, from 1820 to 1850* (New York, 1854–1856), I, 69.

11 *Reports of Committees of the House of Representatives*, 21 Cong., 2 Sess., No. 77, "Internal Improvements," 37–67.

Northwest; while in the Southwest only $152,000 had been spent and in the South Atlantic states only $37,000. Except for the Dismal Swamp Canal, only $80 had been spent in Virginia for internal improvements. Not a dollar of Federal funds had been spent in South Carolina.[12]

Leaders of opinion in the Southern seaboard recognized the bitter fact that natural obstacles excluded their region from sharing in the wave of prosperity induced in the Northwest and the Middle Atlantic states by the expanding network of canals and roads. They therefore insisted that transportation improvements ought to be paid for by the states that would profit from them rather than by the Federal government.

In December, 1824, Governor John L. Wilson of South Carolina warned the legislature that the recently enacted survey bill would be "but an entering wedge which will be followed, no doubt by the expenditure of millions," and, he added, "the day, I fear, is not far distant, when South Carolina shall be grievously assessed, to pay for the cutting of a canal across Cape Cod." [13] Twelve months later the legislature resolved "That it is an unconstitutional exercise of power, on the part of Congress, to tax the citizens of one State to make roads and canals for the citizens of another State," and that "Congress does not possess the power, under the constitution, to adopt a general system of internal improvements as a national measure." [14]

Disturbed by the nationalistic tone of Adams' first message to Congress, Jefferson decided that the time had come to brush the dust off the Virginia Resolutions of 1798 and apply them to the present situation. He drafted a "Solemn Declaration and Protest" against the internal-improvement program of the Federal government, but he withheld it on Madison's advice [15] and because the South Carolina legislature strongly protested against Adams' philosophy of government. However, when the legislature of Maryland opposed South Carolina, the Virginia legislature came to

12 *Ibid.*, 66–67. Expenditures in Missouri ($24,000) and in the territories of Michigan, Arkansas, and Florida have not been included in this analysis.

13 Ames, *State Documents on Federal Relations*, 137.

14 *Ibid.*, 139–40.

15 Madison to Jefferson, December 28, 1825, in *Letters and Other Writings of James Madison* (Philadelphia, 1865), III, 511–14.

South Carolina's support and made use of lengthy quotations from the earlier Virginia Resolutions. In the year 1827 both Virginia and South Carolina entered new protests against national expenditures for roads and canals, and Georgia joined them with the declaration "that this State ought to *oppose,* in every possible shape, the exercise of the power, on the part of the General Government, . . . to promote internal improvement." [16]

About the time these protests were being made, the Supreme Court of the United States delivered a series of decisions holding that certificates issued by state loan offices and receivable for taxes and salaries were unconstitutional. Since these cases had arisen from the states of Kentucky, Georgia, and Missouri, it was natural for the decisions to excite resentment in those areas, against the Supreme Court and against the doctrine of broad constitutional construction.[17]

But this was a minor and transitory irritation as compared with the contemporary question of Indian removal. In 1802, Georgia ceded its western lands to the national government on condition that the Indians should be removed from its bounds as soon as practicable. Twenty years later ten million acres of Georgia land were still in possession of the Creeks and Cherokee, and Georgia's patience was thin. Troup became governor in 1823 with the avowed purpose of ridding the state of the Indians; and, with the hearty backing of his legislature, he demanded of the national government that it carry out at once the terms of the 1802 agreement. When President Monroe declared that "there is no obligation on the United States to remove the Indians by force," [18] Troup responded that the President's position "involves the destruction of the compact between Georgia and the United States, makes it null and void, and leaves no alternative to Georgia but acquiescence or resistance." [19]

[16] Ames, *State Documents on Federal Relations,* 140–43, 145, 147, together with the numerous letters and papers cited on these pages.

[17] Dewey, *Financial History of the United States,* 160–61; Bank of the United States *v.* Planters' Bank of Georgia, 9 Wheaton 904 (1824); Bank of the Commonwealth of Kentucky *v.* Wister *et al.,* 2 Peters 318 (1829); Craig *v.* The State of Missouri, 4 Peters 410 (1830).

[18] Richardson (comp.), *Messages and Papers of the Presidents,* II, 804.

[19] Edward J. Harden, *The Life of George M. Troup* (Savannah, 1859), 210.

Surely, this controversy was no pleasant heritage for Adams, and the situation was brought to a crisis just a month before he entered office by the negotiation of a treaty of cession which, according to many of the Indians, did not represent the will of the tribe. Adams concurred in their opinion, but the state of Georgia took steps to survey the land even before the date set in the treaty for the removal of the Indians. Adams protested and arranged for the negotiation of a second treaty; but Troup, assured of the backing of the Georgia legislature, ordered the survey to proceed and called on the state militia to be prepared to defend the state against possible invasion.[20]

Adams laid the facts before Congress on February 5, 1827, with the remark that "if the legislative and executive authorities of the State of Georgia should persevere in acts of encroachment upon the territories secured by a solemn treaty to the Indians," the President would be compelled to resist even to the point of using, as a last resort, "the arm of military force."[21] Twelve days later Troup returned a blunt and sarcastic answer in which he rested his case on the sovereign rights of the state of Georgia and denied that the Supreme Court of the United States was competent to decide controversies involving questions of sovereignty between a state and the United States.[22] His communication, addressed to Secretary of War James Barbour, included the following bellicose sentence: "From the first decisive act of hostility, you will be considered and treated as a public enemy; and, with the less repugnance, because you, to whom, we might constitutionally have appealed for our own defense against invasion, are yourselves the invaders, and, what is more, the unblushing allies of the savages whose cause you have adopted."[23]

But whereas the Georgia legislature stood firmly behind the Governor, Congress gave no encouragement to the President. A Senate committee advised Adams "to continue his exertions to obtain, from the Creek Indians, a relinquishment of any claims to lands within the limits of Georgia."[24] In short, the Governor van-

[20] *Ibid.*, 481–85.
[21] Richardson (comp.), *Messages and Papers of the Presidents*, II, 939.
[22] McLaughlin, *Constitutional History of the United States*, 426–27.
[23] Harden, *George M. Troup*, 485.
[24] *Ibid.*, 488.

quished the President; the state triumphed over the nation.

According to President Adams, American history contained the record of many "collisions" between "General and State Governments" with regard to the extent of their respective powers. "But never before," so he remarked, had "collision been urged into a conflict of actual force." He might have added, had he written on this unpleasant subject in later years, that in no previous conflict had a state gained its purposes so well as Georgia when it invoked state rights, assumed a blustering, defiant position, and threatened to fight for its alleged rights.[25]

Alabama and Mississippi likewise wanted to be rid of Indians, and it is instructive to observe Alabama's changing attitude toward what was going on in Georgia. In 1825, Alabama newspapers roundly denounced their neighbor to the east for presuming to think that one state could upset the operations of the national government, and they characterized both Adams and Troup as rash and intemperate. But in 1828 the legislature of Alabama passed a resolution which asserted that the state had jurisdiction over the Indians within her borders and that the national government had no right to interfere; and, for the purpose of coercing the Creeks, it extended the jurisdiction of the state over them.[26]

The state of Mississippi set foot upon the same defiant course. By laws passed in 1829 and 1830 state authority was extended over "the persons and property" of Indians within the state, tribal government was abolished, and penalties were provided for "any person . . . who shall assume" to exercise "the office of chief." [27] Georgia declared that all laws of the Cherokee tribe would be void after June 1, 1830, and created a constabulary to enforce state law within the Indian country.[28]

During Adams' administration these states of the far South reached the conclusion that the best way of ridding themselves of the Indians was by appealing to state rights and by threatening to defend their rights with force. Hitherto they had shown scant in-

[25] Ulrich B. Phillips, *Georgia and State Rights*, in American Historical Association, *Annual Report*, 1901, II (Washington, 1902), 39–142, treats the Indian question as well as other issues that contributed to the growth of state-rights sentiments in Georgia.

[26] Abernethy, *Formative Period in Alabama*, 116–19.

[27] Mississippi *Acts*, 1829, pp. 81–83; *ibid.*, January, 1830, pp. 5–6.

[28] Georgia *Acts*, 1829, pp. 98–101; *ibid.*, 1830, pp. 114–17.

terest in the fulminations in the Southeastern states against John Marshall's decisions, and they had not loudly echoed the state-rights sentiments of the upper South during the controversies over the admission of Missouri, protective tariff, and internal improvements. There had been a few men like Bolling Hall of Alabama who stood for strict construction of the Constitution, but it was only when the Indian problem reached an acute stage in the late 1820's that the lower South discovered the practical value of this doctrine.[29]

In the year 1827 it was again proposed that Federal funds be appropriated to further the work of the American Colonization Society. A number of Northern states endorsed the suggestion; within the Southern states opinion was divided. Kentucky, Tennessee, and Maryland were in favor; South Carolina, Georgia, and Missouri were opposed. Several of the opinions of the Georgia legislature merit quotation. It was asserted that Georgians had earlier supported the Colonization Society under the belief that its object "was limited to the removal beyond the United States of the then free people of color and their descendants, and none others." But, continued the legislature, "it is now ascertained that this impression was false; and its officers, . . . now boldly and fearlessly avow, that its object is, and ever has been, to remove the whole colored population of the Union to another land; and . . . they ask, that the general fund, to which the slave holding States have so largely contributed, should be appropriated for a purpose so especially ruinous to the prosperity, importance, and political strength, of the southern States." In short, Georgia was asserting, as the lower house of South Carolina had asserted in 1825, that it had no intention of considering any scheme for ending slavery. During the Missouri debates, Southern spokesmen had labeled slavery as an evil which must be endured because a way out of the difficulty could not be found; now, when a solution was proposed, the Georgia legislature spurned it. It spurned it with an affectation of self-righteous scorn, declaring that it could not "avoid reprobating the cold-blooded

[29] As a sidelight on the transmission of ideas, it is worth noting that it was Bolling Hall's nephew and political disciple who persuaded the Alabama legislature to adopt resolutions in 1826 condemning the use of implied and unconstitutional powers by the Federal government and in 1828 denying the right of the Federal government to interfere with the state in its handling of the Indian problem. Abernethy, *Formative Period in Alabama*, 118–19.

selfishness, or unthinking zeal, which actuates many of our fellow-citizens in other states, to an interference with our local concerns and domestic relations, totally unwarranted either by humanity or constitutional right. . . . The result of such interference, if persevered in, is awful and inevitable." [30]

Within the same year, 1827, the tariff question was again brought before Congress. The issue was raised by the manufacturers of woolen goods who were asking for increased duties on imported woolen cloth on the ground that they were compelled to pay more for materials because the tariff of 1824 had increased the duties on raw wool. This petition made a significant disclosure: increased protection for one group might make a tariff objectionable to others who would normally favor protection. The friends of free trade did not forget this lesson.

The legislative history of the Woolens Bill, as this measure was called, revealed other facts. It raised the question of whether Calhoun was deserting his earlier advocacy of protection; for the bill failed to become law by his casting ballot in the Senate. Furthermore, it showed that Martin Van Buren was trying to damage the political future of the South Carolinian; for he it was who so managed the course of the bill in the Senate that Calhoun, the presiding officer, was compelled to vote on this controversial question.[31]

The following year the friends of protection introduced a general tariff measure into Congress. The opposition, remembering that they had accomplished nothing by arguments in 1820, 1824, and 1827, now adopted a set of tactics which they may have learned from the history of the Woolens Bill. They offered amendments that were deliberately designed to make the bill highly objectionable. New England, whose opinion on previous tariffs had been divided, was the point of attack. Higher duties were placed on molasses, thereby injuring New England rum makers and those who imported molasses from the West Indies. Likewise, New England shippers, who preferred to outfit their vessels with Russian rather than with Kentucky hemp, were harmed by an increase in the duties on hemp.

[30] Ames, *State Documents on Federal Relations*, 145, 209–13.

[31] The course of the bill in the House may be followed in *Register of Debates*, 19 Cong., 2 Sess., 732–1099, *passim*. *Ibid.*, 496, records its death in the Senate by Calhoun's adverse vote.

While piling these and other injuries upon New England, the relief asked by its woolen manufacturers was withheld.

Besides trying to destroy this measure, some of its opponents had a second object in view: to weaken the political power and Presidential prospects of Henry Clay. His enemies charged in Congress that he supported protection to gain the votes of "the moneyed aristocracy of the East," and that his ambition for the presidency could "only be gratified by bribing the East, and by deluding the West." [32] By amending the original bill into such form that it would be discredited in the East, Clay could be injured. Jackson's friends were active in this maneuver. John Randolph remarked that "the bill referred to manufactures of no sort or kind except the manufacture of a President of the United States." [33]

In spite of the bitterness of this mixture concocted by antitariff Southerners and New Englanders, and by Jackson men, the protectionists swallowed it. The bill passed the House by a vote of 105 to 94, and the Senate by a vote of 26 to 21. New England continued to be divided, but Webster, who was an excellent barometer of the sentiments of his region, was now willing to vote for protection. The rest of the North plus Kentucky and western Virginia voted for the bill; the South and Southwest were against it.

While the Woolens Bill and the Tariff of Abominations were before Congress a great number of memorials and resolutions for and against protection were drafted by public meetings and state legislatures throughout the nation.[34] The most notable meeting of friends of protection convened at Harrisburg, Pennsylvania, on July 30, 1827, and lasted for five days. A hundred delegates from thirteen states, including Maryland, Virginia, and Kentucky, drew up a memorial to Congress requesting specific amendments to the tariff law, particularly in respect to wool and woolen goods.[35]

Except in Kentucky and Louisiana, where there was legislative approval of protection, the Southern states were virtually unanimous in their disapproval. In the opinion of the Virginia legisla-

[32] *Ibid.*, 20 Cong., 1 Sess., 2187–88.
[33] Stanwood, *American Tariff Controversies*, I, 290.
[34] *American State Papers, Finance*, V, contains several hundred pages of these documents.
[35] Stanwood, *American Tariff Controversies*, I, 264–68.

ture, the protective tariff was "unconstitutional, unwise, unjust, unequal and oppressive." [36] Georgia concluded its remonstrance with the caustic observation that "It will detract nothing from the firmness or wisdom of the Congress to listen to the voice of State Legislatures, while it is considering the memorials of *manufacturing companies*." [37] Senator Nathaniel Macon of North Carolina wrote to a friend that due to the tariff "We must wear old cloathes, & put patch upon patch, & not be ashamed, provided we owe nothing, though we may not be dressed in the fashion, there is no better fashion, than to be out of debt." [38]

The legislature of Alabama referred to the Harrisburg Convention as "the allied powers of avarice, monopoly and ambition" who "call for a further subsidy on the labor of the South and Southwest, in the shape of [the] woolens bill, to pamper the gentlemen woolgrowers and wool-carders of the Northeast; and this, too at a time when agriculture is languishing . . . and manufactures . . . flourishing. . . . Let it be distinctly understood, that Alabama . . . regards the power assumed by the General Government to control her internal concerns, by protecting duties, beyond the fair demands of the revenue, as a palpable usurpation of a power not given by the Constitution; and the proposed woollens [*sic*] bill, as a species of oppression little less than legalized pillage on the property of her citizens." [39]

It was in South Carolina that protest reached its most extreme form and that opposition to the tariff came closest to unanimity. A newspaper editor ventured the guess in 1830 that there were not 150 South Carolinians outside the city of Charleston who did not regard the tariff as unjust, unequal, and oppressive.[40]

Of the many antitariff pronouncements in South Carolina, one of the most radical was expressed at Columbia on July 2, 1827. At a meeting called to protest against the proposed Woolens Bill,

[36] Ames, *State Documents on Federal Relations*, 143–63.

[37] *Ibid.*, 147.

[38] Nathaniel Macon to Weldon N. Edwards, March 3, 1828, in Nathaniel Macon Papers (North Carolina Department of Archives and History).

[39] Ames, *State Documents on Federal Relations*, 150–51.

[40] Camden (S.C.) *Journal*, August 7, 1830, cited in Boucher, *Nullification Controversy in South Carolina*, 80. For a concurring opinion, see the estimate of James Hamilton, Jr., in Charleston *Courier*, August 23, 1830.

Cooper declared that through the operation of the tariff "Wealth will be transferred to the North, and wealth is power. Every year of submission rivets the chains upon us, . . . we shall, before long, be compelled to calculate the value of our union; and to enquire of what use to us is this most unequal alliance? by which the south has always been the loser, and the north the gainer? Is it worth our while to continue this union of states, where the north demand to be our masters, and we are required to be their tributaries? Who with the most insulting mockery call the yoke they put upon our necks the *American System!* The question, however, is fast approaching to the alternative, of submission or separation." [41]

The ominous choice between submission and disunion was likewise offered by Robert J. Turnbull in a series of essays published in the Charleston *Mercury* in August and September, 1827.[42] On June 19, 1828, the Charleston *City Gazette* opened its editorial column with the words: "The question of Disunion is at last seriously and openly submitted to the consideration of the people of South Carolina."

The most influential and thorough of the South Carolina pronouncements on the tariff was the South Carolina Exposition and Protest. This document was published in February, 1829, by order of the lower house of the legislature; thus it was given currency and the appearance of authority although it was not formally adopted by the legislature. It was the work of Calhoun. His authorship, however, was kept secret because it would have been politically unbecoming and unwise for one who was then Vice-President and who wished soon to become President to be known as the author of such a document.[43]

Nearly half of the Exposition was devoted to proving that the burden of the protective tariff fell exclusively upon the South while its benefits accrued to the North. More briefly, Calhoun disposed of the constitutionality of protection by asserting that the Constitution did not grant to Congress the power to give protection and that "The advocates of the Tariff have offered no such proof." For

---

[41] Charleston *Mercury*, July 18, 19, 1827, quoted in Malone, *Thomas Cooper*, 308–10.
[42] *Ibid.*, 325.
[43] Frederic Bancroft, *Calhoun and the South Carolina Nullification Movement* (Baltimore, 1928), 34–40; Ames, *State Documents on Federal Relations*, 152–53; and, for the text of the Exposition, Crallé (ed.), *Works of John C. Calhoun*, VI, 1–59.

the argument that protection had been made constitutional by custom and precedent he was scornful, for "Ours is not a Government of precedents. . . . The only safe rule is the Constitution itself." Finally, he foreshadowed the philosophy and plan of nullification which he was to expand and polish in subsequent papers.

The fact that Calhoun wrote the Exposition and Protest proves that a great change was coming over him. Ten years earlier he was working to push the Federal government into new and broader fields of legislation and control; now he was penning a trenchant analysis of the unhappy results of expanding Federal power and of loose constitutional construction. While it is significant that he had changed, perhaps it is more significant that he had taken so long to change. Randolph and other Old Republicans had been able to foresee the results of enlarged Federal activity when it was first proposed. Lowndes and some other Young Republicans had revised their views early in the 1820's. Calhoun was one of the last converts. Perhaps his mind worked slowly for all of its logical skill; perhaps he had a persistent faith in the essential goodness and unselfishness of mankind; perhaps his ambition for high national office confused his thinking; or perhaps his conversion came earlier than he was willing to publish. Only a few close friends knew that he was the author of the Exposition; and if he was secretive about his views in 1828, the divergence between private opinion and public statement may have begun much earlier.

Thirty years before, Jefferson, under similar circumstances, had quietly collaborated with Madison in writing the Virginia and Kentucky Resolutions for the double purpose of protesting against the Alien and Sedition Acts and of bringing about the defeat of John Adams. Now, Calhoun was playing the same game and in the same secretive way. He was attacking the policies of John Quincy Adams—those policies which had aroused so much opposition throughout the South and had brought the lower South over to a state-rights, sectional viewpoint. And he was seeking to transform this hostility toward Adams into an approval of Jackson, to whom Calhoun referred in his Exposition as the "eminent citizen, distinguished for his services to his country, and his justice and patriotism." By promising, or at least voicing the hope, that Jackson's administration would witness "a complete restoration of the pure principles of our Government," [44] Calhoun was venturing to write for Jackson the platform that Jackson himself had not yet announced.

The Exposition was published shortly after the election of 1828. Jackson and Calhoun, with Van Buren as a member of this coalition, had defeated Adams and Richard Rush of Pennsylvania, with Clay as a close and powerful ally. Both groups claimed the name of Republican. The Adams wing, because of the character of its platform, was called National Republicans. Jackson's followers were known as Democratic Republicans, or simply as Democrats.

Inasmuch as Jackson's views on protection, internal improvements, and other current questions were not clearly known, they could be variously interpreted during the campaign. He had the further advantage in Georgia, Alabama, and Mississippi, of being known as an Indian fighter; and his opposition to Adams and support of Troup in the Indian controversy was interpreted in Virginia and the Carolinas as evidence of his soundness on the state-rights question. As events proved, the defenders of extreme state rights were to be disappointed; but at the moment this misapprehension worked to Jackson's advantage.[45]

In this election, as in the previous one, Adams was presented as a man of much experience in public affairs and as a great champion of "Civil Liberty." With such a candidate, so it was said, "It would be little less than madness to select for the highest *civil* office, one who has no qualifications to offer but *military* endowments." [46] A statement that Jackson had a robust constitution and that he was capable of bearing much fatigue, was derided as "a tacit admission . . . that General Jackson is not qualified for *civil* office." [47] To show that he was a rough, quarrelsome frontiersman, stories were told about his fights and duels; and, to demonstrate his autocratic

[44] *Ibid.*, 56.

[45] For a sample of the wishful guessing of a Virginia supporter, see "Letters of William C. Rives, 1823–1829," in *Tyler's Quarterly Historical and Genealogical Magazine* (Richmond), VI (1924–1925), 14. The Alexandria *Gazette* published the following shrewd analysis: "In Pennsylvania the Jacksonites cry out, . . . Huzza for Jackson and the Tariff! In South Carolina it is, Jackson and free trade: No Tariff! . . . either the Pennsylvanians or the South Carolinians will, in the event of his election, be most miserably taken in." Quoted in Washington *National Intelligencer*, October 8, 1828.

[46] Raleigh *Register, and North-Carolina Gazette*, October 28, 1828.

[47] *Ibid.*, October 14, 1828.

spirit, "Coffin Hand Bills" were published to tell the story that he had ordered the execution of six militiamen for insubordination.[48]

On the other side, Jackson's friends once more made capital of his military career and called on the voters to "rally around the *Hickory Tree,* and vote for the incorruptible patriot, the Hero of New Orleans and the Farmer of the Cumberland." [49] Furthermore, they revived the charge of the "corrupt bargain" between Adams and Clay. "In the last election," so it was alleged in Kentucky, "Mr. Clay transferred your vote to John Quincy Adams without your consent and contrary to your will. He now calls on you to ratify the bargain." The voters were warned against Adams, " 'the enemy of the West, the clumsy negotiator and the vindictive man,' to whom you were sold by Henry Clay." [50] North Carolinians were assured that it would now be "impossible to cheat them out of their choice as was the case in the last election," because there were now only two candidates before the people.[51] Attempts were made by the Jackson party to ally Adams with the discredited caucus system, with governmental autocracy, and with wealth. "Of all the various classes among mankind," a Jackson newspaper asserted, "a proud monied aristocracy is the most superlatively contemptible. These are the men who have been laboring by means of bribery and corruption to cheat the people out of their liberties." [52] The people were told that a major issue before them was the question *"of monarchy*—the Secretary succession. Since the accession of Jefferson, each President has appointed his successor. . . . the whole administration uses the patronage of the first four years to secure the election of the President for the second four, and of the second four to secure the succession; so that the country is filled with corruption." [53]

When it was reported that the following toast was drunk at a dinner in South Carolina: *"Adams, Clay & Co.—*Would to God

[48] Lexington *Kentucky Gazette,* November 7, 1828. For a copy of the Coffin Hand Bill, see John S. Bassett (ed.), *Correspondence of Andrew Jackson* (Washington, 1926–1935), III, 455–64.

[49] Frankfort (Ky.) *Argus of Western America,* October 29, 1828. The *Argus* belonged to Amos Kendall.   [50] *Ibid.*

[51] Raleigh *Star, and North Carolina State Gazette,* October 30, 1828.

[52] Lexington *Kentucky Gazette,* November 7, 1828.

[53] Frankfort *Argus of Western America,* October 29, 1828.

they were like Jonah in the whale's belly: the whale to the devil; the devil in hell; and the door locked, key lost, and not a son of Vulcan within a million miles to make another," a North Carolina Adams paper declared that "even party rage is no apology" for such "grossness and vulgarity." [54]

Every effort was made, perhaps by the Jackson forces more than by the supporters of Adams, to get the voters out. "Rush then to the polls," urged the Baton Rouge *Gazette*, "ride, walk, or swim to reach them, and let your song of triumph be *Jackson and our Country* forever." [55] Both parties made strenuous efforts to gain control over existing newspapers and to establish new ones. Interested lawyers, merchants, and bankers used their advertising, and state and national governments gave or withheld public printing to line up the press on the "right" side.[56] The voters came to the polls as never before—some 312,000 of them in the Southern states, which was twice as many as in 1824.[57]

The result was a great victory for Jackson. In the nation he won 178 electoral votes and lost 83 to Adams. Every Southern state gave him its entire electoral vote except Maryland, which gave 5 to Jackson and 6 to Adams. Of the popular votes of the South, Jackson received well over twice as many as his opponent.[58] He carried Tennessee, Georgia, Alabama, and Mississippi almost unanimously, and he was overwhelmingly victorious in North Carolina and Virginia. He won by heavy majorities most of the areas that had supported Crawford four years earlier: Georgia and the counties of the conservative tobacco kingdom in the Virginia–North Carolina Piedmont.

[54] Raleigh *Register, and North-Carolina Gazette,* October 14, 1828.

[55] Baton Rouge *Gazette,* October 25, 1828.

[56] Frankfort *Argus of Western America,* November 12, 1828. Immediately on the heels of the election some newspapers were sold or discontinued because they had served the purpose for which they had been established; others, because their owners had backed the wrong horse. For examples of changes in management, see Augusta *Chronicle and Georgia Advertiser,* November 26, 1828; Nashville *Republican and State Gazette,* December 12, 1828; Knoxville *Register,* November 26, 1828.

[57] In 1824 there had been 150,000 votes, but it must be remembered that between 1824 and 1828 Georgia and Louisiana provided for the popular election of Presidential electors. However, these two states added less than 26,000 votes to the total cast in 1828.

[58] There was no popular vote to count in South Carolina because electors were chosen by the legislature.

Calhoun, in his race for the vice-presidency, did about as well as Jackson except that he lost 7 of the 9 electoral votes of Georgia to William Smith of South Carolina.[59]

Adams' following was confined to the upper South and to a few coastal and urban areas in the lower states. He did nearly as well as Jackson in Kentucky, he carried Maryland by 1,000 votes, he led in a dozen or so counties of western Virginia and North Carolina, and he carried certain coastal counties in North Carolina, Virginia, and Louisiana.[60] Generally speaking, he carried such areas as he or Clay had carried in 1824. But there was one important exception. He lost heavily in the farming and planting counties of Alabama. This loss, together with his failure to win any appreciable amount of the Crawford following, amounted to a repudiation of the Adams and Clay combination by the influential conservative segment of Southern society.

Jackson's success in the planting counties of the Eastern seaboard, where the county courts were strong and where democracy had made little progress, is to be accounted for partly by the nationalistic platform of his opponents and partly by the lack of knowledge about Jackson's views. His opposition to Adams and his approval by Van Buren, a leader in the old Crawford party, created a presumption that he would oppose centralization and adhere to a state-rights program. Slavery was not much discussed, but it may be significant that Jackson and Calhoun, both slaveholders, carried the slave states.

Outside the South, Jackson carried Pennsylvania, over half of the Northwest, and part of New York. New England was the only section that strongly supported Adams. The country was divided politically about as it had been during the first two decades of the

[59] The first popular election of Presidential electors in Georgia was remarkable. Confusion reigned, for the state was inexperienced in this matter. Returns from a number of counties were discarded because of failure to comply with the complex legal requirements. Furthermore, the contest between the Troup and Clark factions was vigorous but rather pointless since both factions were for Jackson. The Troup faction repudiated Calhoun. *National Banner and Nashville Whig,* December 2, 1828; Milledgeville *Georgia Journal,* November 24, 1828.

[60] See map of the election of 1828. In Georgia it was said that Adams would probably not get a hundred votes "with the exception of the northern merchants in Savannah, Augusta, Darien, and perhaps Macon." Augusta *Chronicle and Georgia Advertiser,* quoted in *National Banner and Nashville Whig,* December 2, 1828.

century—Adams had carried the ancient strongholds of Federalism; Jackson had succeeded to Jefferson's realm.[61]

But since Jefferson's day, the West had grown more rapidly than the South in population and political strength, and it was no longer the junior member of the partnership. It remained to be seen whether Jackson could keep his dual empire intact, and particularly whether the seaboard South would follow his Western leadership. Working in his favor were his popularity with the common man, the agrarianism of the South and West, the effects of the Panic of 1819, antipathy to the national bank, and the Jeffersonian political tradition. But Westerners had more faith in democracy, less regard for state rights, keener interest in the public-land question, and more zeal for Federal aid for internal improvements than did Southeasterners. The states above the Ohio differed from the South, and were like the Northeast, in their lack of slaves and their willingness to vote for protective tariffs. Should Jackson approximate a Crawford platform, he could easily lose the upper West to the East; if he shaped his policies too closely to the pattern of Western thinking, the seaboard South might fall away from him.

Jackson and Calhoun personified the Western and Southern elements in the coalition, and Jackson recognized the diverse character of his following in appointing several of Calhoun's friends to his cabinet. Inasmuch as Jackson had indicated a desire to retire from office after one term, his generosity toward Calhoun augured well for the Vice-President's future. But it was soon evident that Jackson did not set much store by his cabinet, which was, with the exception of Van Buren, composed of mediocre men. For advice he turned to an informal group of friends that came to be known as the Kitchen Cabinet. Van Buren and John H. Eaton of the cabinet were included. Most of the others were newspapermen, chief of whom were Amos Kendall, a shrewd politician and editor of Kentucky, and Duff Green, editor of the *United States Telegraph*, the party organ. In the Kitchen Cabinet only Green was friendly to the political aspirations of the Vice-President.

Calhoun's relations with Jackson were further impaired by the

[61] Compare plates 102 and 103 in Paullin and Wright, *Atlas of the Historical Geography of the United States;* tables of popular and electoral votes in Edward Stanwood, *A History of the Presidency from 1788 to 1897* (Boston, 193–?), 148–49.

Peggy Eaton affair. Peggy was the attractive daughter of the keeper of a Washington tavern where Jackson, Eaton, and other politicians frequently stayed. Her husband was a sailor; and Major Eaton, so said the Washington gossips, consoled Peggy in her loneliness while her husband was at sea. In time the husband died. It was rumored that he had learned of affairs at home and killed himself. Thereupon, Eaton gave thought to marrying Peggy. He consulted Jackson, whom he did not wish to embarrass on the eve of his inauguration. Jackson advised him to go ahead, on the theory that marriage would stop the wagging of tongues, and the marriage took place on January 1, 1829.

But Mrs. Eaton was received with a marked lack of cordiality in Jackson's official family. The cabinet members and their wives were barely polite. Only Van Buren, who was a widower and had no mentor in social affairs except his own political interests, was friendly. Jackson was highly incensed. It was bad to have unpleasantness in his cabinet; it was worse to have it occur over the wife of his close friend; but his feelings were perhaps more deeply stirred by his recollection of events in his own life. He himself had married a divorced woman, and, as in Peggy's case, there had been ugly stories which had not been quieted through all the years that he and Rachel had lived in decency and with every appearance of happiness. They had been repeated during the recent Presidential campaign, to Jackson's anger and to Rachel's sorrow; and a month after the election, Rachel had died. Soon after becoming President, Jackson wrote to a friend in Tennessee, "I find myself a solitary man, deprived of all hope of happiness this side the grave, and often wish myself at the Hermitage there to spend the remnant of my days, and daily drop a tear on the tomb of my beloved wife." [62]

Jackson was convinced that vile slander had hastened the death of Rachel. And now, hardly was she buried before a similar hue and cry was raised against the wife of his good friend Eaton. Jackson's wrath was great. He called his cabinet together and gave them a lecture on good manners. He was especially irritated at the Calhouns, whose leadership in the official family and whose social position made them in his eyes the chief persecutors of Mrs. Eaton. And Van Buren went up greatly in Jackson's estimation. He is "one of

[62] Bassett (ed.), *Correspondence of Andrew Jackson*, IV, 33.

the most frank men I ever knew," Jackson wrote, "*a true man* with no guile." In January, 1830, he threatened to remove Calhoun's friends from the cabinet.[63]

While questions of social propriety were estranging Jackson from Calhoun and drawing him closer to Van Buren, the Senate, like a Greek chorus echoing the words of the principal actors, entered upon a lengthy debate that revealed some of the differences between Jackson's West and Calhoun's South. The debate was precipitated by a resolution introduced on December 29, 1829, by Senator Samuel A. Foot of Connecticut, which had as its object the restriction of the sale of public lands. Since this resolution reflected the attitude of most New Englanders, Foot was acting as an authentic spokesman of his constituency; but he was most unwise in raising the question, because it was unlikely that he could accomplish his desires, and it was certain that he would antagonize the West. Benton of Missouri spoke with great vigor against the Foot resolution and advocated liberalizing rather than restricting Federal land policy. Others joined the debate which soon turned into a verbal battle between the Northeast and the West.

Southerners had no great interest in the land question, but those who were politically shrewd saw that this rift afforded an opportunity to estrange the West from the Northeast. Southern Senators therefore reminded the West that its desires had frequently been opposed and sometimes thwarted by New Englanders. The obvious goal of Southern political strategy was to strengthen the alliance between the South and the West and to return New England to the minority status it had occupied during the first quarter of the century. Thus the debate moved into a second stage: public lands were forgotten and New England recalcitrance and obstructionism were the subject of Southern and, to a less extent, of Western discussion.

New England, to extricate itself from this difficult position, steered the debate into a third stage. Instead of defending its own course of action, it opened an offensive against its critic, the South, on the subject of state rights, particularly against the theories advanced in the South Carolina Exposition and Protest. It charged

[63] *Ibid.*, 260. For Calhoun's version of this affair, see Crallé (ed.), *Works of John C. Calhoun*, VI, 435–45.

the strict constructionists of the South with holding to a narrow, restrictive constitutional interpretation that was injurious to Western interests. Further, it charged that the Exposition looked to a weakening of the powers of the national government if not to the destruction of the very Union. And it reminded the West that it had frequently been unable to obtain its objectives because of Southern zeal for strict construction.

At this point the Southern Senators made a grave tactical error. Instead of disregarding constitutional questions and pushing ahead into the breach between East and West, they accepted the challenge and rushed to the defense of state rights. Whether Daniel Webster or Robert Y. Hayne won the great debate on the nature of the Union was of little consequence from the standpoint of immediate political advantage. The important fact is that the South let New England escape the trap of Senator Foot's making; the South—more anxious to prove the correctness of its constitutional interpretation than to win in the game of practical politics—failed to take advantage of the quarrel between East and West.

As this debate developed through the early months of the year 1830, it clearly revealed the sectional nature of the contemporary political structure. No one of the major sections was able by itself to govern the nation; only by coalition could a working majority be created, and no two had identical interests. The desires of the sections, stated in order of their importance, were as follows: "The Northwest—low-priced public lands, internal improvements, high tariff; the Southwest—low-priced public lands, low tariff, internal improvements; the seaboard South—a low tariff, no internal improvements at federal expense, high-priced public lands; the North Atlantic States—a high tariff, high-priced public lands, internal improvements." [64]

Jackson's hostility to Calhoun suggested that he was more willing to sacrifice the interests of the Southeast than those of Van Buren's part of the country. By February of 1830 a Boston newspaper was publishing the statement that "The Vice-President already sees and feels that he is *dehors du combat*. He . . . tries to look cheerful and

[64] Raynor G. Wellington, *The Political and Sectional Influence of the Public Lands, 1828–1842* (n. p., 1914), 9.

manly, . . . but it is all in vain." The paper remarked, significantly, "Van Buren . . . is secretly pulling the strings." [65]

It became clear to politicians whose future depended on maintaining the alliance between West and Southeast that it was high time to take positive steps to strengthen it. With such thoughts in mind, Benton of Missouri, Hayne of South Carolina, and a number of other Southern and Western men attempted to tighten the bonds between their sections under the guise of a celebration of the birthday of Thomas Jefferson on April 13, 1830. Jefferson had once been popular in the same areas that had voted for Jackson and Calhoun in 1828; hence, the veneration of Jefferson might furnish an emotional bond for the elements of this new party, and the political principles of Jefferson might be made to serve as its platform. With this object in view, twenty-four "regular" toasts were arranged by a committee of which Benton was chairman. Some were platitudes; most of them were in favor of state rights, strict construction, and low tariff, or were opposed to internal improvements at Federal expense.

In two respects the plans for the love feast of Southern and Western leaders miscarried. In the first place, the platform implicit in the toasts was too Southern. As Webster wrote to Clay: "The object of those who originated the proceedings of the 13th was to give a state right anti Tariff tone and character to the whole party. It was to found the party on *Southern* principles, and such principles as should exclude, not only their avowed political opponents, but Mr. Van Buren's friends also." [66] The upper fringe of Jackson's following in the Northwest, in Pennsylvania, and in parts of New York, could not be expected to drink to low tariff and anti-internal-improvement sentiments. Politicians from those areas, getting a glimpse of the list of toasts, stayed away from the dinner, and some of them staged competing celebrations in their hotel rooms. In the second place, Van Buren, the man who would chiefly lose by the plans for the meeting, devised a shrewd counterattack. He suggested to the President that the antitariff character of the celebra-

[65] Boston *Columbian Centinel*, February 10, 1830, quoted in Richard R. Stenberg, "The Jefferson Birthday Dinner, 1830," in *Journal of Southern History*, IV (1938), 337.
[66] Quoted *ibid.*, 338.

tion stamped it as a nullification affair, and "that the proceedings and ceremonies of the day were portentous of danger to the Union." He urged Jackson to take the part of the "abrupt and defiant . . . ready guardian and Champion" of the Union against Calhoun.[67]

In this atmosphere of intrigue and counterintrigue, the guests began to assemble about five o'clock at the Indian Queen Inn in Washington. Cabinet members, Congressmen, and other prominent citizens took their places at the long table. Jackson and Calhoun faced each other from its two ends. The early part of the program carried out the theme of the love feast. Barbour of Virginia and Benton of Missouri spoke for the South and the West. Typical of their innocuous sentiments was the following sentence from Benton's speech: "This is the beginning only, the first in a series and multiplication of celebrations, which the friends and admirers of Jefferson will cherish and perpetuate, for the double object of shewing honor to him and preserving his principles for themselves." [68]

All went well, at least on the surface, until Jackson's toast. Rising, with glass in hand, and looking down the long table at Calhoun as though at a rebel, he pronounced the words: "Our Federal Union: it must be preserved!" Calhoun, as though accepting a challenge, responded: "Our Federal Union—next to our liberties most dear! May we all remember that it can only be preserved by respecting the rights of the States and distributing equally the benefit and burthen of the Union!"

The rest of the program was forgotten. Men were too busy talking of what had happened to listen to the remainder of the toasts. And there was, indeed, much to talk about. Tension between the President and the Vice-President had come to an open rupture; Jackson had refused to bind himself to the state-rights platform proposed by the Southern wing of his party; and Calhoun had become more clearly committed to such a program than heretofore. Less obvious, but equally as important, Van Buren, who had offered a noncommittal toast about "mutual forbearance and reciprocal

[67] John C. Fitzpatrick (ed.), *The Autobiography of Martin Van Buren*, in American Historical Association, *Annual Report*, 1918, II (Washington, 1920), 412–15.

[68] Quoted in Stenberg, "The Jefferson Birthday Dinner, 1830," *loc. cit.*, 340.

concessions," had stayed out of the limelight and had profited by the events of the evening.

From this point events moved rapidly to the complete destruction of the Jackson–Calhoun alliance. The Kitchen Cabinet arranged for Jackson to learn that Calhoun, while secretary of war under Monroe, had advocated censuring Jackson for alleged disobedience of orders in the Seminole campaign. Down through the years Jackson had thought that Calhoun had defended him at that critical moment in his career, and he was highly incensed when contrary evidence was produced in the form of a letter recently secured from Crawford. He at once requested an explanation from Calhoun. Calhoun answered at some length—at too great length, one is inclined to think—admitting that he had disapproved of Jackson's course in Florida. The answer was unsatisfactory to the General, who wrote on its back: "This is full evidence of the duplicity and insincerity of the man." To Calhoun, he sent a curt note terminating friendly relations. It included the words, as though the Old General had paused to strike a heroic pose: "Et tu Brute!"

The next step was for Jackson to clear all Calhoun influence out of the party and to set the facts before the country in their best light. Calhoun helped in his own undoing by publishing in pamphlet form his correspondence with Jackson.[69] Jackson brought Francis P. Blair to Washington to establish the *Globe* as the party organ, replacing the *Telegraph* of Calhoun's friend, Duff Green; and one of Blair's first jobs was to answer Calhoun and lead the hue and cry of the party press and politicians against the South Carolinian.

The purging of Calhoun's friends from the cabinet was delayed because Van Buren's future advancement had to be considered. For some time, possibly as far back as December, 1829, Jackson had looked upon Van Buren as his probable successor. A year later he proposed that they run on the same ticket in the next election and that he resign in Van Buren's favor early in the term. But Van Buren, with good judgment, suggested a slower and subtler plan

---

[69] *Correspondence between Gen. Andrew Jackson and John C. Calhoun, President and Vice-President of the U. States, on the Subject of the Course of the Latter, in the Deliberations of the Cabinet of Mr. Monroe, on the Occurrences in the Seminole War* (Washington, 1831).

of succession.[70] First, he convinced Jackson that the cabinet should be remade, omitting all Calhoun influence. This was done, the first steps being taken by Van Buren and Eaton who both resigned in April, 1831. Next, Jackson appointed Van Buren minister to England, where he could keep out of dangerous political crosscurrents. But the Senate refused to approve his nomination, Calhoun casting the deciding ballot against his enemy. Van Buren and Jackson were thus compelled to improvise another set of plans. Van Buren was written down for the vice-presidency in partnership with Jackson in the 1832 election, with the prospect of trying for the highest office in 1836.

Calhoun was ruined so far as his immediate political future was concerned. From the place of heir apparent in the major party early in 1829, he had fallen within two short years to the very bottom of the political abyss. Had the formless, unorganized political situation of 1824 prevailed, he might have nursed some hope. But now there were two well-organized parties, and he was completely out of them both.

[70] Fitzpatrick (ed.), *Autobiography of Martin Van Buren*, 506–507.

CHAPTER IX

BOLD ACTS AND BOLDER
THOUGHTS

THE events of Jackson's first administration laid the foundation for a more definite division between parties than had existed in the United States for at least two decades. The one-party era had been succeeded by a period of political chaos; now, with the approach of the election of 1832 the voters could weigh the merits of two distinct parties. Jackson's liberal use of the patronage had gone far toward imbuing the members of his party with a desire to remain in office, and his actions while President created something of a party platform. The National Republicans likewise had a platform in Clay's American System, and they had an impulse toward coherence in their opposition to Jackson. On the other hand, they were weak in respect to organization, largely because Adams had refused to use his executive power, especially his appointive power, to strengthen the party machine.

The creation of the national nominating convention during the campaign of 1832 gave a device for selecting candidates and an instrument for stirring up party enthusiasm. It was first used by the Antimasonic party, which met in Baltimore on September 26, 1831, and nominated William Wirt, who was now a resident of Maryland, and Amos Ellmaker of Pennsylvania. This party had little influence in the campaign and none whatever in the Southern states. Neither of the major parties needed any machinery for selecting its candidate, for it was certain that Jackson was the choice of the Democratic Republicans and almost as certain that Clay had the support of the National Republicans. Nevertheless, both parties held conventions in Baltimore, the National Republicans on December 12, 1831, and the Democratic Republicans on May 21 of the following year; and both conventions revealed significant facts about political attitudes in the South. The weakness of the National Republicans in the cotton states was suggested by the absence of any delegates from South Carolina, Georgia, Alabama, and Mississippi. The party chose John Seargent of Pennsylvania as Clay's running mate.

The chief revelation of the Democratic Republican convention was the unpopularity in the South of Jackson's choice of a running mate. While Jackson, by the use of strong pressure, managed to get Van Buren nominated with 208 votes, a considerable part of the South rebelled. Barbour of Virginia received 49 votes, and Richard M. Johnson of Kentucky received 26. All of the delegates from Virginia and South Carolina voted for Barbour, and he gathered 15 more votes from the Maryland, North Carolina, and Alabama delegations.[1]

Nowhere was dissatisfaction stronger than in South Carolina. Calhoun's bitterness toward the party that had expelled him and that was now nominating his supplanter for the vice-presidency gave some reason for thinking that he might be brought into an alliance with Clay. Jackson was not worried, believing that the contrariety of their views on public questions made them "antipodes in politics." [2] A further obstacle was Clay's belief that Calhoun could be of little help except in South Carolina. He therefore fought his battle without Calhoun's help, though a conciliatory spirit was evident between them during the campaign. South Carolina, refusing to choose between the lesser of the two evils, Clay or Jackson, entered a lonely path of political isolation by giving its electoral votes to John Floyd of Virginia.[3]

While neither party formally adopted a platform in convention, the differences between them were in part expressed by a convention of National Republican young men in May, 1832. It favored tariff protection for American industry and Federal support for internal improvements, and it criticized Jackson's record.[4]

The major issue of the campaign, the question of rechartering the national bank, unexpectedly entered the campaign when it was well

[1] Stanwood, *History of the Presidency from 1788 to 1897*, pp. 151–61; William MacDonald, *Jacksonian Democracy, 1829–1837* (New York, 1906), 195–96.

[2] Jackson to Van Buren, December 6, 17, 1831, Van Buren MSS., quoted in Arthur C. Cole, *The Whig Party in the South* (Washington, 1913), 15.

[3] E. Malcolm Carroll, *Origins of the Whig Party* (Durham, 1925), 53–55.

[4] Stanwood, *History of the Presidency from 1788 to 1897*, pp. 157–59.

under way. It was not raised by the deliberate choice of either party. For some years Nicholas Biddle, president of the Bank of the United States, had sought means of overcoming Jackson's hostility to banks, but Biddle had always exercised great care to avoid entangling the bank question with party politics. After a careful survey of the situation, he decided near the beginning of the year 1832 to attempt to secure a renewal of the bank's charter, believing that Jackson would take a neutral course provided certain amendments were made in the charter.

Clay and Webster were well pleased by Biddle's decision, for they calculated that Jackson would lose Pennsylvania if he vetoed a bank bill, and that he would lose in the South and Southwest if he signed it. The bill passed the Senate on July 11 by a vote of 28 to 20, and the House on July 3 by a vote of 107 to 85. Seven days later Jackson returned the measure to the Senate with his famous and emphatic statement of economic and constitutional objections.

Despite Biddle's careful planning, the bank measure was now in the middle of party politics in an election year. To save the bank, Jackson must be defeated; for he would regard a favorable verdict at the polls as a mandate to proceed to its destruction. The vote on the rechartering bill indicated that Southern hostility to the bank continued strong. In the Senate every state south of Maryland and Kentucky registered its disapproval except Louisiana. The Mississippi and Kentucky Senators were divided. No other states opposed the measure except New York. The bank question was clearly a sectional question, and Jackson's opposition to the bank promised to win votes for him in the slave states.[5]

Jackson won the election with 219 electoral votes to 49 for Clay. In the South he received all electoral votes except those of South Carolina and Kentucky and part of those of Maryland. In the last state, where the popular vote was extremely close, Jackson secured 3 electoral votes and Clay won 5.[6] Jackson won his states by enor-

[5] Catterall, *Second Bank of the United States*, 169–242, deals with this episode. The Senate vote is tabulated on p. 235.

[6] According to one account, Clay's Maryland majority was 4 in a popular vote of more than 38,000. The illness of two Clay electors on the day set for the meeting of the electoral college in Maryland cut his electoral vote in that state from 7 to 5. Maryland was the only state that retained through this election the once popular district system of choosing Presidential electors. Stanwood, *History of the Presidency from 1788 to 1897*, p. 163; *Niles' Weekly Register*, XLIII (1832), 214, 250.

mous popular majorities. Except for a fairly close fight in Louisiana, his majorities ranged from 75 per cent in Virginia to 100 per cent in Georgia and Mississippi.[7] He polled nearly as many votes in Clay's own state of Kentucky as Clay garnered in all the rest of the South. Outside of Louisiana, Maryland, and Kentucky, Clay carried scarcely more than a dozen Southern counties.

Whether Jackson's success was due to his veto of the bank bill, to his personal popularity, or to antipathy to Clay's American System, it was an overwhelming victory, especially in the South.[8] His victory over Clay was much greater than that over Adams four years earlier.

Perhaps it is worth noting that virtually every one of the black-belt plantation counties outside of South Carolina—the Crawford counties of the 1824 election—supported Jackson with strong majorities. One is tempted to guess that they voted for him with little enthusiasm, for he was the symbol of the Western democracy that was even then assaulting the citadel of Eastern political control in several Southern states; and his opposition to the extreme school of state-rights interpretation had become evident in the early stages of the nullification controversy. But the results of the election show that the Eastern squires preferred Jackson with these drawbacks to Clay's American System and all that it implied of alliance with the interests of the Middle and Northern states.

[7] The Clark and Troup factions in Georgia once more offered competing electoral tickets, both committed to Jackson; but the Troup faction backed Van Buren for the vice-presidency while the Clark faction was for Barbour. A good commentary on the Georgia contest is in the Macon *Georgia Telegraph*, November 14, 1832.

Inclement weather on election day diminished the vote in North Carolina and Mississippi, according to the Raleigh *Register, and North-Carolina Gazette*, November 15, 1832; and "Returns of elections of State officials and Presidential electors . . . 1832" (Mississippi Department of Archives and History), Ser. F, No. 36.

[8] According to Cole, *Whig Party in the South*, 14, a minor influence in the campaign was the report that Van Buren had made agreements that rendered him more satisfactory to state-rights Southerners and the companion report that Barbour had withdrawn from the contest. Another factor of some importance in Presidential elections of this period was the lack of uniformity among the states as to the day for holding the election. Voting was staggered over a period of three weeks. News of election results in Ohio, Pennsylvania, and New York, which were among the first states to vote, was closely watched and was sometimes of influence in states that voted late. For sample comments on this subject, see *Niles' Weekly Register*, XLIII (1832), 214; Frankfort *Argus of Western Kentucky*, December 8, 1824; and Nashville and Knoxville newspapers during the campaign of 1828. A schedule of election dates in the several states is in Washington *United States Telegraph*, April 7, 1829.

In the same month that the nation was making its choice between Jackson and Clay, the state of South Carolina adopted the Ordinance of Nullification. This was not a precipitate act; it was the culmination of a trend that had been in process for some years. An important preliminary was the crystallization of antitariff sentiment. By the year 1830 there was virtual unanimity in the state on this point; nevertheless, there was sharp disagreement over the question of how to secure its reduction. There were many who had faith in the sense of justice and fair play of the American people and who therefore expected ultimate relief through the votes of Congress and the decisions of the Supreme Court, to which they were willing to leave all constitutional questions. These men were usually known as Unionists. Among their leaders were Joel R. Poinsett, Daniel E. Huger, James L. Petigru, James R. Pringle, and Joseph Johnson.

On the other hand there were many who had no hope for a redress of grievances except through some act of positive resistance. Some advocated nullification by the state legislature; others preferred outright disunion; yet others, more cautious, wanted to call a consultative convention of the Southern states.[9] This party was, for a time, weakened by these conflicting views, but the mere fact that it proposed to take some positive step attracted recruits. It chose to call itself, when it was organized in 1828, the State Rights and Jackson party. But subsequent events, particularly the disclosures at the Jefferson dinner in 1830, showed that Jackson sharply disagreed with the ideas of the South Carolina extremists. In May of that year they dropped his name from the party label and henceforth called their organization the State Rights and Free Trade party. Calhoun and McDuffie were regarded as its leaders.[10] The Union party was likewise an early supporter of Jackson, and its approval of him increased as the controversy developed.

It is not easy in brief compass to indicate the earnestness and the thoroughness of the contest between these two parties. Newspapers were enlarged to make space for the increasing volume of political material. The constitutionality of nullification, the meaning and

[9] Boucher, *Nullification Controversy in South Carolina*, 61–64, 67 ff.
[10] Houston, *Nullification in South Carolina*, 65–68; Boucher, *Nullification Controversy in South Carolina*, 122, 146–53.

implications of the Virginia and Kentucky Resolutions, the opinions of Jefferson and Madison, and certain phases of American history were explored with remarkable thoroughness in the search for precedents and arguments. Spokesmen for the Union party looked to the future, forecasting with much accuracy the probable results of a trial of nullification. The State Rights party preferred to emphasize the present, insisting that it was wiser and more manly to risk the dangers inherent in vigorous action than tamely to submit to injuries.[11]

The Unionists branded the state-rights movement as an "unholy crusade" stirred up "to gratify an unhallowed ambition, a fiendish lust of power" of a small group of disappointed politicians. The Unionists in turn were called "submission men," "cowards," "recreants," "tories," "luke-warm politicians," and the "Yankee party of Charleston." [12] Intimidation and corruption were employed; formal duels and rough-and-tumble fights occurred; and there were fatalities.[13]

The first important trial of strength came in 1830. The State Rights party proposed that the legislature, which was to be elected in October of that year, should issue a call for a state convention. While there was no clear statement of the purposes of the convention, it was generally supposed that its action would be vigorous. When the legislature assembled in December it was evident that a majority in both houses favored a convention but that the constitutional two thirds could not be mustered in either house. The extremists therefore had to content themselves with introducing a vigorous set of state-rights resolutions, and these were adopted by overwhelming majorities. In general, the votes in the legislature showed that the Unionist party was strongest in the western and northern counties where slavery had made least progress.

Two years elapsed before there was another legislative election. During this time both parties sought to perfect their organizations, to gain adherents within the state, and to win the approval and support of neighboring states. The State Rights party seemed to have

11 Boucher, *Nullification Controversy in South Carolina*, 136, n. 1, 172–93.

12 *Ibid.*, 83–86.

13 Descriptions of encounters, both formal and informal, are in Kibler, *Benjamin F. Perry*, 108–36. See also, Boucher, *Nullification Controversy in South Carolina*, 204–205, 131–33.

much success within South Carolina, but it found little encouragement beyond its boundaries. Virginia, which had earlier been the center of resistance to centralizing tendencies, would not rally to the cause. Ritchie insisted that South Carolina's nullification plans had no precedent in the Virginia doctrines of 1798.[14] John Tyler wrote to Hayne that "Upon the question of nullification there exists here among the republicans some diversity of opinion." [15] Madison, who knew more about the matter than any living man, asserted in 1830 that neither Jefferson nor himself meant by the proceedings of 1798 what Calhoun interpreted them to mean.[16] From southwest Virginia it was reported that the doctrine of nullification was looked on with horror because the people did not *feel* the weight of the oppressions of the General Government and when they are told of it and the ultimate tendency of the 'System' they stun you with all the slangwhangery of fourth of July patriotism, the greatness of the Union and the blood and thunder of civil war." [17]

From 1830 to 1832, South Carolinians held themselves in restraint, as it were, waiting to see what action Congress would take on the tariff. Some modification was a virtual certainty, for the tariff of 1828 was unacceptable to the friends as well as to the enemies of protection. Furthermore, the fiscal affairs of the government clearly indicated the need of a downward revision. The income of the Federal government was nearly twice as large as its current expenses, and customs duties provided six sevenths of the income. At the moment, the surplus could be used to retire the Federal debt; but at the present rate the debt would be liquidated in about four years, and the surplus would then become a serious problem.

A number of bills representing various points of view were presented to Congress. The tariff that was finally agreed upon in the act of July 14, 1832, differed from the tariff of 1828 on two main

14 Boucher, *Nullification Controversy in South Carolina*, 225.

15 This is from a long and interesting letter written at Gloucester-place, Gloucester County, Va., June 20, 1831 (Division of Manuscripts, Library of Congress, but not in the main collection of John Tyler Papers).

16 Letters of Madison to Edward Everett, Nicholas P. Trist, and Henry Clay, written in August, September, and October, 1830, in *Letters and Other Writings of James Madison*, IV, 95–117.

17 John S. Preston to James H. Hammond, Abington, Va., April 17, 1831, in James H. Hammond Papers (Division of Manuscripts, Library of Congress).

counts. It pruned away most of the "abominations" of the previous tariff, and it reduced nonprotective schedules by the probable amount of several million dollars a year. On the other hand, the protective features of the tariff were virtually unimpaired. The average level of duties, nonprotective as well as protective, was reduced from 41 per cent to 33 per cent. The bill provided for the new schedule to go into effect on March 4, 1833.

The Congressional vote on this measure closely resembled the division of previous years. The only important exception was the affirmative vote of the Congressmen from Virginia and North Carolina who, presumably, regarded the new tariff as at least a step in the right direction.[18] In the House, New England and the Southeast were each evenly divided; the Middle states, the West, and the Southwest were heartily in favor.[19]

News of the terms of this bill reached Charleston while the State Rights and Unionist parties were holding their separate Fourth of July celebrations, for neither this year nor the year before were they willing to join each other in memorializing the independence of the United States. Both parties professed joy at the news. The Unionists expressed gratitude over such reductions as had been made, interpreting them as an omen of further reductions in the future; the State Rights party rejoiced that all men now had convincing proof that protection was the settled policy of the nation. It denounced as "betrayers of the state" the three South Carolinians who had voted for the measure, and it appropriated the sentiments expressed by American Revolutionists when they spurned British offers of conciliation with the words: "We have counted the cost, and find nothing so intolerable as voluntary slavery." [20]

Once more the convention issue was raised in connection with the approaching legislative election. The fight was more bitter than it had been two years earlier, and the issue was clearer, for now the members of the State Rights party admitted that their object was to

18 The growing power of the western parts of these two states also had some influence.

19 Stanwood, *American Tariff Controversies*, I, 359–85; MacDonald, *Jacksonian Democracy*, 153–54. A tabulation of the vote is in Dewey, *Financial History of the United States*, 185.

20 Boucher, *Nullification Controversy in South Carolina*, 169. See also, *ibid.*, 146–49, 162–69.

nullify the tariff, and some of them were willing to admit that nullification might lead to disunion and violence. The Unionists, sensing the weakness of a purely negative position, advocated a Southern rather than a state convention.[21]

The election was an overwhelming victory for the nullification forces, and events then moved rapidly. Governor Hamilton convened the legislature in extra session on October 22. Three days later, by votes of 96 to 25 in the house and 31 to 13 in the senate, a convention was called to meet on the third Monday in November. In the brief campaign for the election of convention members the Unionists put up only a halfhearted fight.[22]

The architect of the work done by the convention, which met at Columbia on November 19, 1832, was Calhoun, who had sketched his nullification plan together with an apologia for its use in the South Carolina Exposition and Protest. More recently he had polished and refined his arguments and plan in a letter of August 28, 1832, to Governor Hamilton.[23] In these papers, Calhoun discussed what he regarded to be a major danger to democratic government and proposed a plan for controlling it.

His reasoning began with two axioms: (1) that "Laws, so far from being uniform in their operation, are scarcely ever so," and (2) that human nature is so constituted "that the selfish predominate over the social feelings." Putting these two together, he reasoned that men would divide upon proposed legislation into those who anticipated advantage and those who anticipated injury, and that the majority would have its way regardless of the injury that the law would impose upon the minority. But this would not be the end. After the minority was made helpless, the majority would someday divide upon new issues into major and minor interests, a new controversy would begin, and the process would be repeated until democracy itself was destroyed. He ventured the prophecy that the manufacturing element of the nation, once it had finished destroying the planting interests, would break once more into opposing groups. Then, "the contests will be between the capitalists and

[21] *Ibid.*, 172–75, 196–203.
[22] *Ibid.*, 208–12.
[23] The Exposition is in Crallé (ed.), *Works of John C. Calhoun*, VI, 1–59; the letter to Hamilton, *ibid.*, 144–93.

operatives." [24] In view of this self-destructive tendency in democracy, Calhoun concluded that "No government, based on the naked principle that the majority ought to govern, however true the maxim in its proper sense, and under proper restrictions, can preserve its liberty even for a single generation."

In this part of his discussion, Calhoun made a distinct contribution to political thought. The great political philosophers of the seventeenth and eighteenth centuries had centered their attention upon an event, namely, the transfer of power from king to people. Assuming that democracy was better than monarchy, they had endeavored to justify the establishment of self-government. Calhoun, looking past the moment of creation, directed his attention to the long-run, continuing operation of democracy; and he detected, so he thought, an inherent disease that must be controlled if democracy was to survive. Even though his prescription was more likely to kill than to cure, his diagnosis of the tendency of majorities to oppress minorities has eternal validity.

To save democracy, then, it was necessary for limits to be placed on the will of the majority, and in America these had been placed by the Constitution. Calhoun's discussion of this subject was exhaustive, and it has often been summarized. But for all of its brilliance and subtlety, in the last analysis it was only a refinement of the doctrines of strict construction, state rights, and state sentinelship that had been expressed time and again by spokesmen of various minorities. Like all previous discussions of the rights of states, it needed to become something more than an argument if it was to be effective. The majority that would not respect constitutional limitations could not be expected to respect a discussion of constitutional limitations.

If Calhoun was to have any better success than earlier champions of lost causes, he needed to discover a technique by which minorities could block majorities intent upon unconstitutional aggression. The technique he proposed is usually known as nullification, though he also spoke of it as interposition and state veto. Inasmuch as none of the earlier theorists had described such a process, the guess may

[24] Calhoun did not discuss the possibility of an alliance between this second minority and the earlier planting minority.

be ventured that Calhoun found his clue in the history of political action rather than in the history of political theory.

Recent history contained two instances in which states, contrary to the usual rule, had thwarted the nation. South Carolina had quarantined Negro seamen and Georgia was forcing the removal of Indians despite Federal opposition. In both instances state-rights arguments were used, but this could not have been the effective element because their use in other issues was not ordinarily followed by success. Another suggestion as to procedure lay in the bluster and threat of armed conflict by Georgia officials, but Calhoun had enough liking for orderly processes of government to want to settle questions of right within the realm of law.

There was one other and a more significant element common to these cases. South Carolina and Georgia, instead of attempting to convert Congress or some other branch of the Federal government to their way of thinking, each made its own decision, each directed state officers to enforce the will of the state, and each took measures to restrain agencies of the Federal government from interfering.[25] Each sought to compel its citizens to obey the state rather than the nation, and placed—Calhoun would have said interposed—the state between the nation and the individual. The Federal government was thus robbed of its power to coerce individuals and was compelled to accept a stalemate or proceed to the more difficult task of coercing a state.[26]

Calhoun's plan of nullification, set forth in careful detail in his letter to Governor Hamilton, began with the assertion, buttressed

[25] In the Indian cases, the state of Georgia denied the authority of the Federal Supreme Court in cases involving state sovereignty, and Georgia courts refused to honor writs of error or injunctions of Federal courts in Indian cases. Cherokee Nation v. The State of Georgia, 5 Peters 1 (1831); Worcester v. The State of Georgia, 6 Peters 515 (1832); McLaughlin, *Constitutional History of the United States*, 428–29.

[26] Georgia and South Carolina had cut into the line of authority between nation and citizen, established in the Constitution, and had created a situation such as had existed under the Articles of Confederation. In referring to South Carolina's actions in the Negro seamen case, Judge William Johnson remarked: "Where is this to land us? Is it not asserting the right of each state to throw off the federal Constitution at its will and pleasure? If it can be done as to any particular article, it may be done as to all; and like the old confederation the union becomes a mere rope of sand." Quoted in Hamer, "Great Britain, the United States, and the Negro Seamen Acts. 1822–1848," *loc. cit.*, 7.

with many arguments, that a state had the right to declare a Federal law which it regarded as unconstitutional to be null and void within the limits of the state. Should the Federal government refuse to respect this decision and attempt to enforce the law, Calhoun yet believed that "the State would be able to enforce, *legally and peaceably,* its declaration of nullification," because, every citizen of the state being bound to respect and obey this declaration, judges and juries must support the opinion of the state in all cases arising under the Federal law in question. To prevent Federal courts from reviewing the judgment of state courts, "the State would take the precaution to prevent, by proper enactments, any means of obtaining a copy" of the record.

To those who feared that nullification would lead to armed conflict, Calhoun said that this was to be "a legal and constitutional contest—a conflict of moral, and not physical force." And to those who thought that nullification would be abused, he answered that three fourths or more of the states could unite in amending the Constitution so as to make a clear statement of the point in question and, if it seemed wise, overrule the state that was using its power wrongfully.[27]

The South Carolina Convention, meeting at Columbia from November 19 to November 24, adopted an Ordinance of Nullification by a vote of 136 to 26. The critical part of this document was the declaration that the tariffs of 1828 and 1832 were "null, void and no law," and not "binding upon this state, its officers or citizens." To give effect to this pronouncement, the Ordinance prohibited the constituted authorities of South Carolina or of the United States from enforcing these tariff measures within the limits of South Carolina; it prohibited the appeal from state courts to Federal courts of any case questioning the authority of this Ordinance or the validity of any act of the legislature to give effect thereto; and it required all persons holding office under the state (except members of the legislature) to take oath under penalty of removal from office "to obey, execute, and enforce" this Ordinance and such legislation as should be enacted to support it. Finally, the Ordinance declared

[27] In effect, Calhoun was reversing the amending process so as to permit one fourth of the states to amend the Constitution for the purpose of diminishing Federal power.

that the people of South Carolina would be absolved from their existing political connection with the people of the other states if the United States attempted to enforce the tariff by the use of military or naval power, by closing the ports of the state, or in any other way except through civil tribunals. This Ordinance was to become effective on February 1, 1833, which was slightly more than a month before the tariff of 1832 was to become effective.

Three days after the adoption of the Ordinance the legislature met, and it promptly passed a body of supporting legislation. The Replevin Act sought to establish a legal course of action by which an importer could gain possession of his goods without paying duties, and it sought to block the customary channels by which cases were appealed from state courts to Federal courts. The Militia Act was designed to put the state in a position to defend itself should the "peaceable remedy" fail to function. Under its terms $200,000 was appropriated to purchase arms; an equal amount was placed at the governor's disposal in the contingent fund; and the governor was authorized to accept the services of volunteer companies "to suppress insurrection and repel invasion." The Test Oath Act, by providing for the removal from office of all who would not support nullification, was designed to give all phases of state government into the hands of men of the state-rights persuasion. It was bitterly resented by the Union men. Judge Huger indignantly asked: "Can I be called a freeman when I am to be tried by a *perjured Judge* and a *packed jury?*" [28] The Unionists began organizing into military companies, and their leaders, especially Poinsett, kept in close touch with President Jackson.[29]

Before the Convention assembled, President Jackson had begun taking steps to meet the emergency. Besides keeping informed about political and military developments in the state, he issued special instructions to collectors of customs at South Carolina ports, and

[28] Quoted in Kibler, *Benjamin F. Perry,* 147.

[29] For accounts of the work of the convention and of the legislature, see Houston, *Nullification in South Carolina,* 106–13, and Boucher, *Nullification Controversy in South Carolina,* 208–24. Documents on the nullification controversy emanating from the Federal government, the state of South Carolina, and from other states are numerous. The more important of them may be conveniently consulted in Ames, *State Documents on Federal Relations,* 164–89. Many that are not quoted in Ames may be traced through his editorial notes.

he increased the forces at the disposal of military and naval officers in that quarter. In his annual message to Congress on December 4 he spoke briefly of the situation, and six days later he issued a proclamation to the people of South Carolina. This paper combined a persuasive appeal to public opinion with a plain statement of his intention to perform "the duty imposed . . . by the Constitution 'to take care that the laws be faithfully executed.'" On December 20 the governor and the legislature of South Carolina made defiant answers to Jackson. Through the rest of the month and on into January, 1833, military preparations were accelerated.

As the critical day of February 1 approached, it became increasingly apparent that the Federal government was determined to collect customs duties regardless of South Carolina's resistance, that South Carolina's course was frowned upon by the other states, even by its nearest neighbors, and that there was a growing disposition in Congress to reduce the tariff. In the face of these facts South Carolinians decided to postpone the date when nullification should become effective so that Congress might have time to effect "a beneficial modification of the tariff." This temperate move was made in a most irregular and unofficial manner. The action of the state Convention was suspended by a meeting of the State Rights party of the Charleston Congressional and judicial district on January 21. Some of the leading members of the Convention dominated this party meeting.

With a reprieve granted, it proved possible for Congress to work out a compromise. On December 27, 1832, the Verplanck Bill, which had Jackson's approval, was reported in the House. Its proposed reduction was, however, too rapid for the protectionists, and it was soon amended into unmanageable form. On February 12, Clay presented a substitute measure, and with Calhoun's aid this compromise passed both houses two weeks later. It provided for a gradual reduction in the duties imposed by the act of 1832 until they should stand at the level of 20 per cent after July 1, 1842. The rate was to be slow in the early years and rapid in the latter part of the period.

While Congress was passing the Tariff Act of 1833 it was also considering a special message submitted by the President on January 16, which presented a circumstantial statement of the situa-

216

tion in South Carolina and requested enlarged powers for dealing with the emergency. In particular, Jackson requested authority to use the army, the navy, and the militia to protect customs officers in the discharge of their duties. This measure, commonly known as the Force Bill and in South Carolina called "The Bloody Bill," passed both houses on March 1, 1833.[30] The compromise tariff and the Force Bill became law with Jackson's signatures on the same day, March 2, 1833, thus offering to South Carolina the choice between peace and armed conflict.

The South Carolina Convention was reassembled on March 11 for the ostensible purpose of receiving Benjamin Watkins Leigh, commissioner from Virginia; but as Henry Middleton, a leading Unionist, was quick to observe, Leigh's mission "came very opportunely to afford the authors of all this mischief a decent pretext of abandoning their course." [31] Calhoun hastened down from Washington, traveling part of the way by wagon, to exert his influence on the Convention for acceptance of the compromise.[32] On March 11 the Convention rescinded the Nullification Ordinance by a vote of 153 to 4. But a spirit of meekness had not descended upon the nullifiers; they at once adopted a new ordinance nullifying the Force Bill!

John P. Kennedy, who was in Washington while the tariff of 1833 was under consideration, tried to force Calhoun to admit that he was inconsistent because he would "vote for a bill that retained and perpetuated discriminatory duties" when he was publicly known to be vehemently opposed to protection on constitutional principles. Refusing to answer the implied question, Calhoun merely remarked "that it was absolutely necessary to insure the success of the compromise . . . that he and Mr. Clay had conversed over the subject and had agreed to the terms." [33] Just as Calhoun at this moment refused to have his attention diverted from the practical results of his course, so shall we avoid questions of constitutionality and logical consistency, and turn to a discussion of the effects of the

[30] Houston, *Nullification in South Carolina,* 124–28.

[31] Henry Middleton to Benjamin F. Perry, February 23, 1833, quoted in Kibler, *Benjamin F. Perry,* 152.

[32] *Ibid.,* 152.

[33] John P. Kennedy Journal, 1829–1840 (microfilm in Duke University Library, original in Peabody Library), entry for July 13, 1833, recording an earlier conversation.

nullification episode. Before doing so, however, it will be useful to sketch briefly a contemporary and somewhat similar episode in Alabama.

During the South Carolina nullification controversy and for some months thereafter, the state of Alabama was engaged in a conflict with the national government. The issue was over the enforcement of the treaty of March 24, 1832, between the United States and the Creek Indians, the fifth article of which required the removal of intruders from the ceded land pending its survey and pending the selection of land by those Indians who chose to remain in Alabama.[34] Federal troops, who were called upon to remove the intruders, destroyed the squatter village of Irwinton and killed a man named Hardeman Owens, but enough settlers remained to undertake the organization of several new counties. Public excitement and a determination to resist had reached an extremely high pitch by the early fall of 1833. Governor John Gayle, who had earlier opposed the nullification theories of South Carolina, now became the champion of Alabama resistance. The conflict between Federal troops and Alabama squatters threatened to become a conflict between Federal troops and the militia of the state of Alabama.

The tension was finally broken by the virtual surrender of the Federal government under an arrangement made by Francis Scott Key who was sent to the state as a special commissioner. Federal soldiers in the Creek country were ordered to submit to the legal process that had been instituted in the state courts after the death of Owens, and the Federal government discontinued its efforts to remove intruders under the fifth article of the treaty.[35]

Events in Alabama and South Carolina and somewhat similar circumstances in Georgia and Mississippi made several things clear. They demonstrated that the elaborate, formal blueprint for nullification was unacceptable except in South Carolina. Most of the other Southern states, especially the cotton states, reiterated their hostility to protective tariffs, but they seemed to be equally hostile to nullification. The legislature of Georgia declared that "we abhor

---

[34] *United States Statutes at Large*, VII, *Indian Treaties*, 366.

[35] Thomas C. McCorvey, "The Mission of Francis Scott Key to Alabama in 1833," in Alabama Historical Society *Transactions* (Tuscaloosa, Montgomery), 1899–1903, IV (1904), 141–65; Theodore H. Jack, *Sectionalism and Party Politics in Alabama, 1819–1842* (Menasha, Wis., 1919), 37–56.

the doctrine of Nullification as neither a peaceful, nor a constitutional remedy, but, on the contrary, as tending to civil commotion and disunion." [36] Alabama declared it to be "unconstitutional and essentially revolutionary, leading in its consequences to anarchy and civil discord, and finally to the dissolution of the Union." [37] Mississippi, Virginia, and other Southern states expressed similar views.

But there was more to nullification than a plan for thwarting the operation of Federal law by civil processes. Should this fail, South Carolinians proposed to enlarge and use the military branch of state government and to separate from the Union. While Alabama and other Southern states developed no liking for the theory of nullification, they seemed to be as willing as South Carolina to use force to resist Federal laws or treaties. Furthermore, while nullification had failed as a peaceful remedy and had been discredited, resistance had succeeded. South Carolina had forced a reduction in the tariff,[38] and Alabama and other states had hastened the removal of the Indians and the acquisition of their lands by white settlers.

Thus, the elaborate theory of nullification was discredited, and there was no early occasion for further experimentation with techniques of state resistance. Nevertheless, the stream of Southern history did not entirely subside into its former channels. It was the opinion of some of the wisest men of South Carolina that during this episode the leading nullifiers had turned into secessionists. Benjamin F. Perry was convinced by the end of March, 1833, that there was a disposition among the leading nullifiers "to dissolve the Union and form a Southern Confederacy." One month later he wrote: "Nullification is not dead but *sleepeth*. The grand object is disunion, and it will be attempted again." [39] With this opinion Huger and Poinsett as well as Webster concurred. Furthermore, it was believed that the nullifiers were establishing a thoroughgoing form of discipline over the political life of South Carolina and that John C. Calhoun was at its head. Huger, who radically disagreed

[36] December 14, 1832, in Ames, *State Documents on Federal Relations,* 180.
[37] January 12, 1833, *ibid.,* 181.
[38] It is sometimes said that the tariff was lowered because the national debt was on the point of being extinguished and the need for national revenue was therefore decreasing. But this knowledge had been available when the tariff of 1832 was passed.
[39] Quoted in Kibler, *Benjamin F. Perry,* 156, 160.

with Calhoun, summed up the matter in these terse words: "I am the State says Mr. Calhoun; he who does not fight to make me *first* is a slave, and he who obeys my will 'to the death' is a freeman!" [40]

The test oath was the instrumentality devised by the nullifiers to reduce their opponents to political impotence. As this oath was originally worded, no Unionist could take it with a clear conscience; hence, every state office, except membership in the legislature, was reserved for the nullifiers. It was modified after the Ordinance of Nullification was rescinded, and in this form it was declared unconstitutional by the state Court of Appeals on June 2, 1834. Thereupon the nullifiers forced through the next legislature an act abolishing the Court of Appeals, and they established another test oath to trouble the consciences of the Unionists.[41]

The rank and file of Southerners was also feeling the effects of the excitement. Speaking before a North Carolina audience, Judge William Gaston said: "Threats of resistance, secession, separation, have become as household words. The public mind will soon be accustomed to the detestable suggestion of disunion." [42] Disunion was no new word in the American vocabulary. It and its synonyms had frequently been used in New England during the War of 1812 and earlier, and it had occasionally been heard elsewhere, even in the South, before 1832. After this date it may not have had a great number of Southern advocates, but it became a familiar part of Southern thinking.

But perhaps the chief product of the troublesome early 1830's was the strong charge of emotion added to matters that had hitherto been on the level of thought and calculation. In the previous decade, something of a Southern platform on national issues had evolved. Clashes over that platform convinced many Southerners that their interests were seldom respected by the rest of the nation and that the fabric of their way of life was being destroyed. A feeling of oppression, of defeat, and even of desperation was engendered. The dimensions and the quality of this state of mind cannot be precisely described; but it was sufficiently real and vigorous to abide after the Nullification Ordinance was withdrawn and after the

40 Quoted *ibid.*, 160.　　　　　　　　41 *Ibid.*, 153–55, 161–63, 169.
42 Quoted in Joseph H. Schauinger, "William Gaston: Southern Statesman," in *North Carolina Historical Review*, XVIII (1941), 122.

Indians had crossed the Mississippi. From this time onward, it is not always possible to explain Southern actions and attitudes by a rational analysis of the facts in each new episode. In addition to these facts one must take into account the emotional tension and the state of mind engendered in the earlier period.

CHAPTER X

PROLOGUE TO THE END
OF SLAVERY

THE issues that troubled the 1820's were nearly all quieted by the end of the nullification controversy. The Missouri Compromise had settled the question of slavery in the territories of the United States. The westward removal of the Indians left little ground for future quarrels between Southern governors and the nation over questions of Indian policy. Jackson's attitude toward internal improvements, particularly his veto of the Maysville Road Bill, brought to a close the series of arguments over the propriety of using Federal funds to supply the transportation needs of the nation. Likewise, his veto of the bill to recharter the national bank indicated that it would be fruitless for Congress to attempt to pass another such bill as long as he was President. As for the tariff, the measure that was passed in 1833 set forth a nine-year program, and there was a general agreement on both sides of the fence to respect this settlement. The doctrine of nullification had failed to gain substantial support outside the state of its origin, and there was no reason to think that the nation would soon be disturbed by its resurrection.

With these issues settled, most of them permanently, the rising tide of Southern sectionalism might have been expected to recede after 1833 just as New England sectionalism had ebbed after the War of 1812. But this was not to be. At the very time when the old issues were being quieted, the slavery question was entering a new and more disturbing phase.

In the late fall of 1829 a pamphlet was discovered in the hands of blacks at Savannah, Georgia, entitled *Walker's Appeal, in Four Articles, together with a Preamble to the Colored Citizens of the World, but in Particular, and Very Expressly to Those of the United*

States of America. Its author, David Walker, was a free-born Negro of Wilmington, North Carolina, who had recently moved to Boston and opened a shop for selling old clothes. The *Appeal* was published in Boston in September, 1829.

The essential points in the *Appeal* were that American Negroes had been reduced to the *"most wretched, degraded,* and *abject* set of beings that *ever lived* since the world began"; that slaveholders were exceedingly oppressive and cruel; that slaves were capable of attaining freedom by destroying their masters; and that it was their duty as men and as Christians to do so. Walker declared that white men would "take vessel loads of men, women and children, and in cold blood, and through devilishness, throw them into the sea, and murder them in all kinds of ways." He regretted that black men had not fought for their lives. He warned: "Get the blacks started, and if you do not have a gang of tigers and lions to deal with, I am a deceiver . . . let twelve black men get well armed for battle, and they will kill and put to flight fifty whites." He gave the stern counsel: "If you commence, make sure work—do not trifle, for they will not trifle with you—they want us for their slaves, and think nothing of murdering us in order to subject us to that wretched condition—therefore, if there is an *attempt* made by us, kill or be killed." [1]

Within a few months copies of this pamphlet were found in Virginia, North Carolina, South Carolina, and Louisiana as well as additional copies in Georgia. Its discovery caused great excitement. State legislatures—sometimes in secret session—passed laws to keep the slaves from getting possession of writings that might cause unrest or revolution. Georgia and North Carolina, copying the example of South Carolina at the time of the Denmark Vesey insurrection, passed laws to quarantine incoming Negro seamen. [2] Prohibitions were laid, or if already in existence were made more stringent, upon teaching slaves to read and write. North Carolina free Negroes were prohibited from peddling wares outside the counties in which they resided and from leaving the state and returning at will. [3]

[1] These quotations are from *Walker's Appeal* (3d ed., Boston, 1830), 9, 20–21, 29–30.
[2] Hamer, "Great Britain, the United States, and the Negro Seamen Acts, 1822–1848," *loc. cit.,* 12–16.
[3] The best study of *Walker's Appeal* is Clement Eaton, "A Dangerous Pamphlet in the Old South," in *Journal of Southern History,* II (1936), 323–34. See also, the

Although the discovery of the *Appeal* put the ruling class of the South on the alert and made laws governing black men more severe, little if any hostility was engendered toward the North,[4] for the revolutionary doctrines preached by Walker met with strong Northern disapproval.[5]

Before the excitement aroused by the Walker pamphlet had subsided, the press began to carry reports of a great debate in the British Parliament in August, 1830, over the abolition of slavery in the colonies. News that the British were bringing slavery to an end disturbed the planting states; on the other hand, this news stirred American opponents of slavery to more vigorous action and to more radical proposals. One of the individuals who was greatly influenced by the British debate was the twenty-four-year-old William Lloyd Garrison, who was then in Baltimore assisting Benjamin Lundy with the publication of his *Genius of Universal Emancipation*. On the first day of the following year he was in Boston bringing out the first issue of the *Liberator*.

In the second issue, Garrison distinguished between his own program and that advocated in the *Appeal*. "We deprecate," so he wrote, "the spirit and tendency of this Appeal. . . . *We* do not preach rebellion—no, but submission and peace." [6] Although Garrison appealed to conscience rather than to physical force, the violence of his invective, his distortion of facts, and the savagery of his indiscriminate attacks upon all slaveholders seemed more likely to lead to emotional and violent action than to a reasonable and peaceful solution. Furthermore, his demand for immediate action without regard to consequences, his bitter denunciation of all laws that gave a legal basis for slavery, including the Constitution of the United States, and his opposition to the use of political action left scarcely any way of settlement except by physical force. At times, the *Liberator* advocated action in this realm. On July 23, 1831, it

---

sketch of Walker's life in the *Dictionary of American Biography*, XIX, 340; John H. Franklin, *The Free Negro in North Carolina, 1790–1860* (Chapel Hill, 1943), 64–70; Joseph C. Carroll, *Slave Insurrections in the United States, 1800–1865* (Boston, 1938), 120–27.

4 Franklin, *Free Negro in North Carolina*, 70, concludes a discussion of *Walker's Appeal* with the remark that it "had done more than any other single thing to reduce the legal status of free Negroes in North Carolina."

5 Eaton, "Dangerous Pamphlet in the Old South," *loc. cit.,* 328.

6 Boston *Liberator,* January 8, 1831.

JOHN C. CALHOUN. From a lithograph of a silhouette cut from life by William H. Brown, a Charlestonian. The original plate, which is 10 by 13½ inches exclusive of margins, is in William H. Brown, *Portrait Gallery of Distinguished American Citizens, with Biographical Sketches, and Fac-similes of Original Letters* (Hartford, 1845).

"MELROSE," NATCHEZ, MISSISSIPPI. Built about 1840. Historic American Building Survey, Library of Congress; the negative is by Ralph Clynne.

"RIVERWOOD," NEAR NASHVILLE, TENNESSEE. An example of an old house, in this instance erected in 1799, that was brought into the current style by the addition (1850) of a classical-revival façade. Historic American Building Survey, Library of Congress, negative by Lester Jones.

WEST LAWN OF JEFFERSON'S "ACADEMICAL VILLAGE." Historic American Building Survey, Library of Congress, negative by Thomas T. Waterman.

CLASSICAL-REVIVAL INTERIOR. Part of the ballroom of "Gaineswood," Demopolis, Alabama, built in 1842. Historic American Building Survey, Library of Congress, negative by W. N. Manning.

ANDREW JACKSON, DANIEL WEBSTER, AND HENRY CLAY. Steel engraving by John Sartain prepared for *The Eclectic Magazine of Foreign Literature, Science, and Art* (New York), LIII (1861).

"NULLIFICATION OR A PEEP AT SOUTH CAROLINA IN 1832–3." This
political cartoon, measuring 14 by 18 inches, is in the George Washington Flowers
Collection at Duke University.

VALUABLE GANG OF YOUNG

NEGROES

By JOS. A. BEARD.

Will be sold at Auction,

ON WEDNESDAY, 25TH INST.

At 12 o'clock, at Banks' Arcade,

17 Valuable Young Negroes, Men and Women, Field Hands. Sold for no fault; with the best city guarantees.

Sale Positive and without reserve!

☞TERMS CASH.

New Orleans, March 24, 1840.

ADVERTISEMENT OF A SLAVE SALE. Joseph A. Beard was one of the greatest slave auctioneers of New Orleans. The original broadside, measuring 10 by 11¾ inches, is in the George Washington Flowers Collection at Duke University.

Charleston and Hamburg Rail Road Co.

Distance 136 *Miles, performed in daylight.*

President, T. Tupper. Directors, Wm. Bell, Alex Black, Wm Dawson, Geo Gibbon, B. J Howland, L. E. Holmes, Dr. Jos. Johnson, Robt. Martin, John Ravenel, T. Street, Robt. Wotherspoon, Wiswal Jones. Sec'ry and Treas. Henry Ravenel. Assist. Sec'ry. W. H. Inglesby Agent of Transportation, W. Robertson, jr. Master of Work-Shops, —— Ross. Chief Clerk, John King, jr. Agent up. George A. Ring Receiver of down Freight, James Smith, Agent at Hamburgh, —— Haig.

RATES OF PASSAGE.

From Charleston to	MILES.	$ CTS	From Hamburg to	MILES	$ CTS.
Woodstock, -	- 15	50	Aiken,	- - 16	75
Summerville, -	- 21	75	Blackville,	- - 46	2 25
Inabnets,	- - 32½	1 62½	Midway,	- - 64	3 25
Branchville, -	- 62	3 00	Branchville	- - 74	3 75
Midway,	- 72	3 50	Inabnet's	- - 103½	5 12½
Blackville	- - 90	4 50	Summerville, -	- 115	6 00
Aiken,	- 120	6 00	Woodstock, -	- 121	6 25
Hamburg,	- 136	6 75	Charleston,	- - 136	6 75

And from one intermediate Station to another, Five Cents per Mile.—Children under 12 years and Coloured Persons half price.

Regulations for the Passenger carriages.

1st. All baggage at the owner's risk—75 lbs allowed. 2d Servants not admitted, unless having the care of children, without the consent of all the Passengers. 3d. Passengers not allowed to stand on the outside platform. 4th. Smoking prohibited. 5th. No Gun or Fowling Piece shall be permitted to enter the Car unless examined by the Conductor. 6th. The feet not to be put on the Cushions, nor the Cars soiled, defaced or injured in any way. 7th. Dogs not admitted into the Passenger Cars. 8th At the ringing of the bell, Passengers will be allowed one minute to take their places 9th. Seats must be engaged and paid for fifteen minutes previous to the hour of departure. As a general direction, the conductors of the Carriages are instructed not to permit any conduct that is inconsistent with good order, or the comfort and safety of the Passengers: for which especial end these Rules have been established, and are required to be enforced with civility but strictly.

Hours of Departure and Arrival on the S. C. R. Road.
UPWARD PASSAGE.

LEAVE CHARLESTON, - - - - - - - 6 A. M.
To Woodstock running time and stoppages 1h 5m.
Not to arrive before 5m past 7 A M.
Breakfast 20 minutes.
LEAVE WOODSTOCK - - - - - half past 7 A. M.
To Branchville running time and stoppages 3h 30m.
Not to arrive before ¾ past 10 A M.
LEAVE BRANCHVILLE, - - - - - 11 A M.
To Blackville running time and stoppages 2h 20m.
Not to arrive before ¼ past 1 P. M.
Dinner 25 minutes.
LEAVE BLACKVILLE, - - - - - quarter before 2 P. M
To Aiken, running time and stoppages 2h 15m.
Not to arrive before ¾ past 3 P. M.

RATES, REGULATIONS, AND SCHEDULE OF AN EARLY SOUTHERN RAILROAD. Completed in 1833, the Charleston and Hamburg was then the longest railroad in the world and a pioneer in other respects. Four years after its completion, this advertisement was published in Daniel J. Dowling, *Charleston Directory, and Annual Register, for 1837 and 1838* (Charleston, S. C., 1837).

CENTRAL RAIL ROAD,
FROM SAVANNAH TO MACON, GEORGIA,

THIS road is open for the transportation of passengers daily, (Sundays excepted) from
Savannah to McCall's, a distance of 187½ miles. The
distance from McCall's to Macon is 2½ miles. The
whole line will be open in the month of October next.
The Mail and Passenger Trains leave Savannah and
McCall's at 7 o'clock, A M, and run through in 12 hours.

There is a Tri-weekly Line of Steamers between
Charleston and Savannah, leaving Charleston on Tues-
days, Thursdays and Saturdays, at 9 A M, and leaving
Savannah on the same days of the week, after the arrival of the Cars. There are Two Lines of Steamers
from Savannah to Florida, and Three Regular Lines
of Packets to New York.

FARE FROM SAVANNAH TO McCALL'S:—
In Passenger Car, - - $8 00 ;
In Baggage do, - - $5 00
Children under 12 Half-Price

For further particulars refer to
Messrs. ALFRED KEARNY & Co, New Orleans.
Savannah, August 1, 1843.   aug15 3m

MAIL STAGE ROUTE

FROM MOBILE TO MONTGOMERY, ALA.

THE Proprietors of the Daily Mail
Stage Line between Mobile and Montgomery,
have the pleasure of informing the travelling community, that their Four Horse Stage Coaches are now in
effective operation—carrying passengers
THROUGH IN THIRTY-SIX HOURS,
without delay. The road has been much improved,
and the Coaches are of the most comfortable and convenient character.
WM OSWALD PAPE, Agent,
may4 d&Wtf   Mansion House, Mobile.

Mobile to Montgomery, stage...................$15 00
Montgomery to Franklin, railroad, 35 miles...... 2 00
Franklin to Madison, 180 miles, stage.............15 00
Madison to Augusta, 165 miles, railroad 5 25
Augusta to Charleston, 136 miles, railroad....... 8 00
Charleston to Weldon, 320 miles, railroad & s. b. ..13 00
Weldon to Baltimore, 250 miles, railroad & st. boat.10 00
Baltimore to Philadelphia, 96 miles.............. 3 00
Philadelphia to New York, 86 miles 3 00

je8 $74 25

1843.   DETROIT AND CHICAGO.   1843.
Through in 39 hours,
BY THE
CENTRAL RAILROAD
MAIL LINE.

THE cheapest, safest and most expe-
ditious route to the West, being 48 hours quicker
than the Lake route.

The Railroad Cars leave Detroit daily (Sundays excepted) at 8 o'clock, A. M., arrive at Jackson, 80 miles,
same day, at 2 P. M.; leave Jackson at 3 P. M. in Coaches, arrive at St. Joseph at 5 P. M. next day ; leave St.
Joseph, on the arrival of the Stages, in Steamboats, 69
miles to Chicago, and arrive at 1 A. M.

This route was established at a great expense in 1842,
and its success warrants the proprietors in extending
the facilities for 1843. A new Steamboat of 270 tons
burthen, with a powerful low pressure engine, will
take the place of the steamboat Huron in July.

☞ Extras always in readiness.
Office in Chicago at the General Stage Office. In
Detroit, at the Railroad Ticket Office.
T. W. WELLS, Act. Com. C. R. R.
Z. TILLOTSON & CO, S. P.
E. B. & S WARD, S. B. P.
Jackson, May, 1843;   je7

RAILROAD AND STAGE-ROUTE ADVERTISEMENTS. From the New Orleans
Daily Picayune, October 10, 1843.

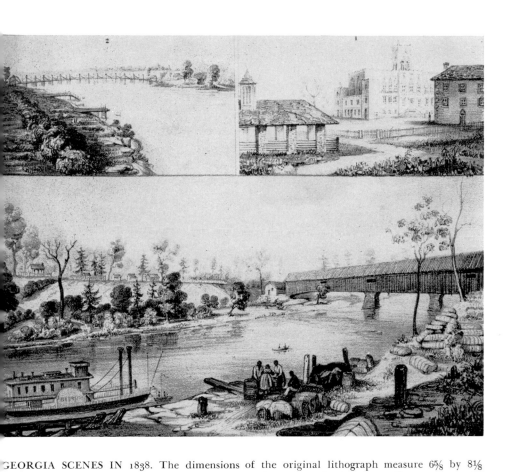

GEORGIA SCENES IN 1838. The dimensions of the original lithograph measure 6⅝ by 8⅛ inches, excluding margins. It is Plate 13 in Francis [Comte] de Castelnau, *Vues et souvenirs de l'Amérique du Nord* (Paris, 1842). Most of the plates in this work are based on sketches made on the spot by Castelnau, an experienced naturalist and traveler, who was in Georgia in 1838.

MEETING STREET, CHARLESTON, SOUTH CAROLINA, IN 1844. One of the better of the early lithographs of Thomas Addison Richards who later became a noted landscape artist. This plate is from Volume IV of *The Orion*, edited by William Carey Richards, brother of the artist.

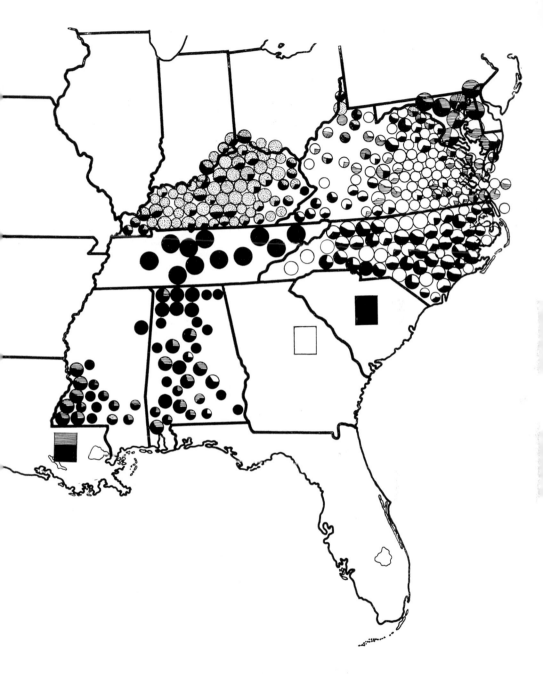

PRESIDENTIAL ELECTION OF 1824

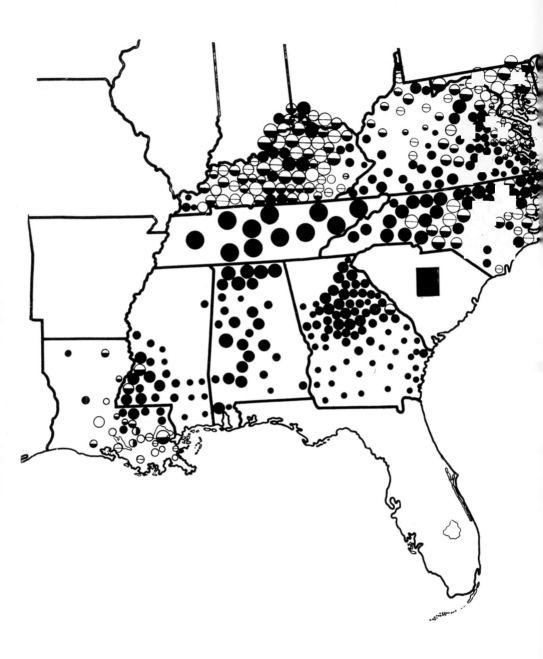

PRESIDENTIAL ELECTION OF 1828

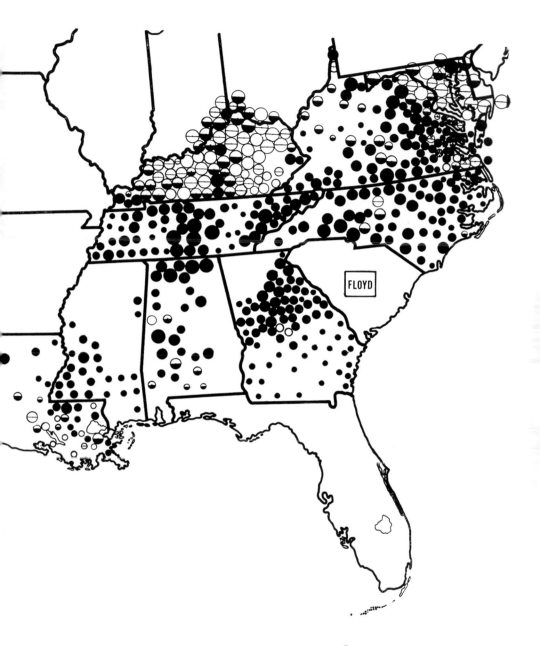

PRESIDENTIAL ELECTION OF 1832

published a "Song, Supposed to be Sung by Slaves in Insurrection," urging them to "strike for God and vengeance now." The following month a body of slaves struck in Southampton County, Virginia, under the leadership of Nat Turner.

Turner was born in Southampton County in the year 1800. His mother was a native African, and she brought him at an early age to believe that he possessed supernatural powers. As he grew to manhood he claimed that he could hear voices directing him, read signs in the heavens, and remember events that had transpired before his birth. By these and other means he gained considerable leadership among his fellow slaves. His influence was strengthened and extended to neighboring plantations by his being a Baptist preacher. Not much is known as to the motives behind his crime. Inasmuch as he later asserted that his master had treated him well, they cannot be explained on the ground of personal abuse. Neither was it ever proved that he had been influenced by Garrison or by the *Appeal,* although this was suspected because he had been taught to read by his master's son. But it is clear that he had been planning for several years before he finally struck, and according to his account he was pushed onward in his course by voices, visions, and an eclipse of the sun.

A singular blueness in the atmosphere in August, 1831, convinced Turner that the time had come. At a secluded spot in the woods he met with four confederates and two neophytes. With a barbecued pig for food and brandy for refreshment and stimulant, they laid plans. One of the new recruits had good reason for hating his owner, but Turner chose the home of his own master, Joseph Travis, as the place to begin. Striking before dawn on Monday, August 22, Turner and his followers slaughtered Travis' family. From then until the following morning they moved from plantation to plantation, killing between fifty and sixty persons without regard to age or sex. Nearly half were children, and more women than men were killed. Bodies were mutilated, and Turner sprinkled his followers with the blood of the dead. As he moved forward, he augmented his force by coercion as well as by persuasion. Estimates of its size have varied all the way from forty to two hundred.

On Tuesday morning the roles of hunter and hunted were reversed when a party of white men overtook, attacked, and scattered the band. Military units were soon scouring the countryside, and self-constituted patrols joined in the hunt. Some of them matched the brutality of Turner, torturing and killing innocent Negroes as well as guilty ones. Fifty-three Negroes were arrested and brought to trial. Of these, twenty-one were acquitted, twelve were transported out of the state, and twenty were hanged. Among the last was Turner who had eluded his pursuers more than two months—long after all the others had been killed or captured.[7]

The outbreak in Southampton County turned the thoughts of men in other parts of the South to the danger of similar disasters. The fact that Turner had been taught to read, that he had exercised the influence of a preacher, and that he might have been stirred by the writings of Walker or Garrison suggested that laws be passed to bind the minds and restrict the activities of slaves. Vigorous attempts were made to force free Negroes to leave the South.[8] There were many commentators who believed, however, that the chief need was for better law enforcement rather than for new laws. And there were some, especially in Virginia, who were convinced that the root of the trouble was neither in imperfect legislation nor inadequate enforcement, but in the fact that slavery was injurious to society and was dangerous, and that the danger increased as the ratio of slaves to whites increased.

When Turner struck, slaves outnumbered the white population in Southampton County three to two. In Virginia east of the Blue Ridge there were 81,000 more blacks than whites, and every previous census had showed that the blacks were increasing faster than the whites. Furthermore, reports that Louisiana and Georgia had closed their doors to the further importation of slaves for sale and that Mississippi was contemplating similar action, made it appear likely that the slave population of Virginia would increase at a yet more rapid rate.[9]

[7] Joseph C. Robert, *The Road from Monticello: A Study of the Virginia Slavery Debate of 1832* (Durham, 1941), 3–8, contains a brief account of the insurrection as well as extended and careful notes upon sources of information. See also, Carroll, *Slave Insurrections*, 129–61; and Aptheker, *American Negro Slave Revolts*, 293–304. Scarcely any two of the many accounts of the Nat Turner insurrection agree on the number of participants or the number killed.

[8] For a summary of these laws, see Carroll, *Slave Insurrections*, 165–69.

[9] Robert, *Road from Monticello*, 11–13; Sydnor, *Slavery in Mississippi*, 163.

With their minds filled with these and other disturbing thoughts, Virginians launched into a discussion of slavery that was more searching, thorough, and public than any other in her history. Some Virginians believed that slaves ought to be more closely controlled; others were of the opinion that no amount of patchwork would make the institution of slavery either beneficial or safe and that it therefore ought to be abolished. Governor Floyd was of the latter school of thought, and he noted in his diary that a law providing for gradual abolition ought to be passed during his administration.

The legislature convened in regular session on December 5, 1831. A few days later a select committee was appointed in the House of Delegates to consider questions relating to slaves and free Negroes. On January 11 a debate began which lasted for two weeks and which terminated in a series of votes expressing the opinion of that body on questions of the most fundamental character respecting the permanence of slavery in Virginia. This debate has been characterized as the "final and most brilliant of the Southern attempts to abolish slavery." [10]

A few of the advocates of abolition drew their arguments from the philosophy of natural rights and of human equality, but more of them began with mundane considerations. They asserted that slavery was a prime cause of Virginia's economic backwardness, that it was injurious to the manners and morality of the white population of Virginia, and—remembering the Southampton insurrection— that it was inherently dangerous. While abolition was advocated as an act of humanity and justice for the Negro, it was more often advocated as an act that would benefit the white man. Most of them agreed that abolition ought to be by gradual process, and that Negroes should be removed from Virginia as fast as they emerged from slavery. They preferred a plan that would in a measure cushion the economic shock of destroying so vast an investment. But they could not agree on a scheme to accomplish these purposes, and their failure to agree was a boon to their opponents.

The defenders of slavery countered with roseate descriptions of the prosperity and superior manners of Virginians as well as of the good treatment and contentment of the slaves. They also defended

[10] Robert, *Road from Monticello*, v, 12–18.

the right of private property, and they denied the right of the legislature to meddle with slave property.

The division of opinion closely followed the sectional division that had been a powerful force in Virginia history for many years. Most of the opponents of slavery lived west of the Blue Ridge Mountains—a land where there were few slaves, a land whose white inhabitants believed that they had been abused and misgoverned time and again by the politically dominant east. Most of the defenders lived in the Tidewater and Piedmont, where there were more blacks than whites. Nevertheless, opinion was not unanimous on either side of the Blue Ridge. Some of the leaders of the antislavery cause lived in the east, among them Philip A. Bolling, of Buckingham County, and Thomas Jefferson Randolph, of Albemarle County, grandson of Thomas Jefferson. Furthermore, the distinguished and powerful Richmond editors, Thomas Ritchie of the Richmond *Enquirer* and John Hampden Pleasants of the *Constitutional Whig,* gave much aid to the opponents of slavery.[11]

When the house finally came to the moment of decision, a motion that it was expedient for the present legislature to enact legislation for the abolition of slavery was lost by a vote of 73 to 58. Had representation been apportioned on the basis of white population instead of in the complex manner provided in the Constitution of 1830, the west would have had several more delegates and the vote would probably have been closer; but there is no reason to think that the decision would have been reversed. After two other related questions had been disposed of, the house by a vote of 65 to 58 decided that for the present the state of Virginia should direct its attention to the removal of free Negroes "and that a further action for the removal of slaves should await a more definite development of public opinion."[12]

Subsequent developments in Virginia public opinion were not in the direction of abolishing slavery. In legislative elections in the spring of 1832, several of the antislavery delegates were defeated in eastern Virginia. Powerful defenses of slavery began to be published, among them *The Letter of Appomat[t]ox to the People of Virginia,* ascribed to Benjamin Watkins Leigh, and a *Review of the Debate in*

11 *Ibid.,* 17–38; Eaton, *Freedom of Thought in the Old South,* 168–72.
12 Robert, *Road from Monticello,* 29–33.

the Virginia Legislature of 1831 and 1832 by Thomas Roderick Dew.[13]

Virginia's retreat from its high point of antislavery opinion was due to the subsiding of fears engendered by the Southampton insurrection; to the discovery that the domestic slave trade, contrary to gloomy anticipations, was drawing off large numbers of slaves into the cotton South to the great financial gain of Virginians; and to the distraction of other public questions. Chief of these was South Carolina's fight over the tariff, which was approaching a crisis at the time of the slavery debate. The Richmond *Whig* asserted that the economic distress of South Carolina was due to slavery much more than to the tariff, and Hezekiah Niles heartily agreed; but the *United States Telegraph* advised Virginians to cease considering emancipation and to join forces with South Carolina against the tariff—the chief cause of the lack of prosperity in the South.[14]

Northern opinion had little effect upon the genesis or the course of the Virginia slavery debate, but while this debate was in progress a movement was developing in the North that was soon to have tremendous influence upon the South. It began as a religious revival in upstate New York in the middle 1820's under the leadership of Charles G. Finney, an eloquent and powerful preacher, who exhorted Christians to "aim *at being useful in the highest degree possible*" by working for temperance, education, and the reformation of society.[15] His phenomenal success rested partly on his power to enlist young men, imbue them with his own fervor, and send them out to carry on the work. His ablest recruit was Theodore Dwight Weld, who by 1830 was the most powerful agent in the West for the American Temperance Society.

Sweeping over the West, Finney's revival reached its crest in the year 1830, with converts being won by the tens and hundreds of thousands; and at the crest Finney invaded New York City. The

---

[13] Reprinted under the title *An Essay on Slavery*, and later incorporated in his famous work, *The Pro-Slavery Argument*. Robert, *Road from Monticello*, 45–46.

[14] *Niles' Weekly Register*, XLI (1832), 445; Washington *United States Telegraph*, January 26, 1832.

[15] Gilbert H. Barnes, *The Antislavery Impulse, 1830–1844* (New York, 1933), 11–12. The following account of the abolition movement is drawn primarily from this scholarly and judicious study.

event was significant, for it brought the powerful religious impulse of the revival movement into close contact with a group of charitable and reformatory societies. Among their objectives were the distribution of Bibles and tracts, the establishment of Sunday schools, the advancement of education, the promotion of Christian missions, the salvation of sailors, and the attainment of temperance, prison reform, and peace among the nations. These organizations were then called benevolent societies, and New York was in some measure the capital of the benevolent empire. Most of the societies held their conventions each May in New York, and that city was the home of a small group of men who furnished the active leadership for most of these national societies. Chief of these men were Arthur and Lewis Tappan, wealthy New York merchants.

The Tappans welcomed Finney. To help him overcome opposition in New York and to assure him moral and financial support, they organized some of their business friends into an Association of Gentlemen. Thus there was formed a powerful alliance of religious fervor, reformatory zeal, organizational experience, and economic power.

This alliance was turned toward the abolition of slavery chiefly by the example and the propaganda of British antislavery forces. The British benevolent societies had been the models and inspiration of most of the American societies; and in 1831, while the question of slavery in the colonies was coming to a crisis in England, the Association of Gentlemen decided to establish an American antislavery society. However, they postponed action until they could take advantage of the high tide of interest which they expected America to feel when Parliament should take its final step against slavery.

When that time came, the Gentlemen hesitated; but they were forced to go ahead by Garrison, who was enjoying temporary prestige and power by having been feted and applauded in England as the self-appointed ambassador of American abolitionists. In December, 1833, the American Anti-Slavery Society was organized at Philadelphia. Although Garrison's influence in the Society was to be short-lived, his prominence in the meeting that created it invested the young organization with something of his reputation for fanaticism. Besides this unfortunate occurrence, the Society did itself great injury by making confused statements of its purpose It advocated immediate emancipation, but it hastened to explain that this term did not mean what an ordinary man would think it meant; rather it meant immediate emancipation gradually accomplished.

During the first year of its life the Society aroused Northern hostility toward abolitionists rather than toward slaveholders, and this hostility was strong enough to subject abolitionists to various forms of physical violence. To overcome these handicaps, the leaders of the Society tried to convince the public that Garrison was not the leader or the spokesman of their organization, and they strove without success to silence him. But though 1834 was a year of discouragements, it contained one event that was soon to turn the tide. The theological students at Lane Seminary at Cincinnati, many of whom were converts of Finney, considered the question of abolition in what was called a debate but was in reality more of a protracted revival meeting. Weld, who was one of their number, was mainly responsible for the wholesale transformation of this group of able young men into ardent abolitionists.

The Lane debate caused a great stir. President Lyman Beecher and the trustees sought to repress the abolition activities of the students. Instead, they drove them away to become the nucleus of Oberlin College. In the years 1835 and 1836, thirty of these young men were among the most effective of the missionaries of abolition. With the spirit of zealots and martyrs they endured "harsh words . . . stale eggs, and brick-bats and tar," but they won a hearing. They "precipitated another Great Revival in the nation, a revival in abolition." [16]

Weld was notably courageous and successful. When he entered a new community he usually met with all manner of indignities. While speaking before one audience, he was hit in the face by an egg. Before another, a large stone, hurled through the church window, struck him in the head and stunned him for several minutes. He earned the title of being "the most mobbed man in the United States." [17] But he kept going, usually for many nights in succession; and his calm spirit, his winsome personality, and his fervent eloquence often transformed enemies into abolitionists. By the end of 1835, he had planted the seed widely in Ohio. The next year he

[16] *Ibid.*, 77–78. [17] *Ibid.*, 80–87.

worked in Pennsylvania and New York State. Meanwhile, Garrison was keeping up the agitation in New England, antagonizing the clergy and other powerful groups, but winning some converts, notably Wendell Phillips, who respected Garrison for "the austerity of his life and his singleness of purpose." [18] Others, like William Ellery Channing, opposed slavery while remaining aloof from the activities of the American Anti-Slavery Society.

But it was the Society which gave form and much of the driving force to the abolition movement. In 1835 it issued a great stream of pamphlets and newspapers, most of which were given away and mailed in bundles to those who might be disposed to distribute them. In June it was planning to "issue gratuitously from 20,000 to 50,000 of some publication or other every week." [19] The mail-pouch invasion of the South came to grief in South Carolina. Citizens of Charleston, learning that a considerable quantity of abolition literature was in the post office awaiting distribution, forcibly seized the offensive publications and burned them on the Parade Ground. The New York postmaster, acting on the suggestion of Postmaster General Amos Kendall, announced that he would forward no more antislavery matter to Southern addresses. This event, together with the enactment in most of the Southern states of laws making the circulation of abolition literature a felony, effectively closed the South to the pamphlet campaign of the Society. [20]

Even in the North, the results of the pamphlet campaign were discouraging, and in 1836 the Society decided to shift its emphasis and resources back to the approach which had earlier proved more effective, namely, the use of zealous agents. Enough new recruits, "men of the most unquenchable enthusiasm and the most obstinate constancy," were carefully trained, and added to "Weld's ardent host" to bring their number up to the New Testament number of seventy. [21] Almost all were theological students or clergymen. A full measure of fervor and devotion was needed, for the abolition doctrine was still detested throughout most of the North. However, a development in Congress in the winter of 1835–1836 began to turn the tide, and the Society was quick to take advantage.

[18] *Ibid.*, 98.
[19] Quoted *ibid.*, 247. See also, *ibid.*, 46–47, 100–104.
[20] *Ibid.*, 100–101; McLaughlin, *Constitutional History of the United States,* 484.
[21] Quotations from Barnes, *Antislavery Impulse,* 104–105.

In the Congress that assembled in December, 1835, there was a sharp increase in the number of petitions praying for the abolition of slavery and of the slave trade in the District of Columbia. At the time, it was well understood that there were probably no more than one Representative and one Senator willing to vote for a change in the status of slavery in the District.[22] Nevertheless, Congressmen who did not favor such legislation continued to present petitions. The explanation for this curious situation lies chiefly in the political situation. Jackson was President, and his party controlled the House. The members of the newly formed Whig party, seeking in every way possible to discredit and obstruct the Democrats, soon struck on the presentation of abolition petitions as an effective instrument to sow dissension between Northern and Southern Democrats and to consume much time that the Democrats needed for carrying out the party's program. Whigs presented more than 95 per cent of the petitions that were brought to the House.[23]

Southern Congressmen were stung to the quick by the phrasing of some of the petitions which referred to slavery as "the foul stain of legalized plunder" and to slaveholders as "the villainous enslavers of souls." [24] On December 18, 1835, James H. Hammond of South Carolina exclaimed that: "He could not sit there and see the rights of the southern people assaulted day after day, by the ignorant fanatics from whom these memorials proceed." [25]

In an atmosphere of party conflict complicated by sectional feeling, much of the winter was spent by the Whigs in plaguing the Democrats with abolition petitions, and by the Democrats in trying to find a way to extricate themselves without running counter to the constitutional right of petition. It may be that the problem was insoluble, but both houses of Congress attempted to find a solution. The rule followed in the Senate was less objectionable and aroused less controversy than the rule adopted in the lower house.

On May 25–26, 1836, the House, after acrimonious discussion,

---

[22] *Ibid.*, 106–109, 111, 117–18, 130–32. The extent of the slave trade in the District of Columbia was greatly exaggerated by abolitionists. On this point, see William T. Laprade, "The Domestic Slave Trade in the District of Columbia," in *Journal of Negro History* (Lancaster, Pa., Washington), XI (1926), 17–34.

[23] Barnes, *Antislavery Impulse*, 118, 256.

[24] Quoted *ibid.*, 132.

[25] *Register of Debates*, 24 Cong., 1 Sess., 1967.

resolved that Congress had no authority to interfere with slavery in the states and that it ought not to interfere with slavery in the District of Columbia; that it was important to end agitation on the subject so as to restore tranquillity to the public mind; and that "all petitions, memorials, resolutions, propositions, or papers, relating in any way, or to any extent whatever, to the subject of slavery, or the abolition of slavery, shall, without being either printed or referred, be laid upon the table, and that no further action whatever shall be had thereon." [26] It should be noted that there was little difference between this rule and the previous custom in the House of laying such petitions upon the table after they were presented.

This rule, commonly known as the gag rule, utterly failed to end agitation. Former President John Quincy Adams was now a member of the House of Representatives. He characterized himself as the friend of "universal emancipation," and as the possessor of antislavery views so extreme that "the sturdiest of the abolitionists would have disavowed" them.[27] Adams took up the gauntlet with the solemn declaration: "I hold the resolution to be a direct violation of the constitution of the United States, the rules of this House, and the rights of my constituents." [28]

The question of whether the fateful resolution was in fact unconstitutional has been variously answered by subsequent students. At the time, some abolitionists believed that the logic of the argument permitted them to go no farther than to brand the rule as a "virtual" denial of the right of petition. But constitutional refinements were beyond the understanding of most men. The Northern public, overlooking the party issues at stake, accepted the half-truth that defenders of slavery stood opposed to the right of petition and that slaveholders were willing to subvert the Constitution to maintain their evil institution.

The American Anti-Slavery Society made it its business to keep abolition petitions pouring into Congress. It printed and sent them out by the millions, asking the abolition of the slave trade between the states, the abolition of slavery in the territories, and praying that Arkansas and Florida be denied admission to the Union as slave states. With lists of signatures pasted on, these petitions came back

[26] *Ibid.*, 4031, 4051–52. [27] Quotea in Barnes, *Antislavery Impulse*, 125.
[28] *Register of Debates*, 24 Cong., 1 Sess., 4053.

to Congress by the hundreds of thousands. More than 99 per cent of the petitions were printed. Between December, 1837, and April, 1838, enough of them were presented to Congress to fill "a room 20 x 30 x 14 feet, close packed to the ceiling." [29]

The Whigs, who had made such effective use of petitions to sabotage the Democratic administration, came into power in the election of 1840. Throwing consistency to the winds, they enacted gag resolutions more stringent than those against which they had been complaining. Even Adams for the moment forgot the constitutional scruples that had disturbed him, and through him the North; for he remarked that he could "not deny the right of the House to refuse to receive a petition when it is first presented." [30]

Both parties were in some measure now committed to the non-reception of antislavery petitions, and the controversy over the right of petition largely ceased. But during the years it raged, it enabled abolitionists to make Congress their sounding board and to compel even slaveholders to help the cause of abolition. Southern Congressmen, goaded into angry remarks, had fanned the fire that they wanted to extinguish. As one of the abolitionists sagely remarked: "Slaveholders are prime agitators." [31] The gag rule had put the South in an extremely bad light. And it had enhanced the prestige of the abolitionists. Instead of appearing as pious and meddlesome fanatics, they now appeared as the champions of a great constitutional right.

During the petition controversy, Weld prepared two books that were to have tremendous influence in the abolition crusade. One was designed to show the horrors of slavery; the other, to prove that emancipation would be followed by an agreeable state of affairs. Using material collected by two abolitionists who had been sent to the British West Indies, Weld edited so plausible a study of the satisfactory effects of emancipation [32] that the leaders of the American Anti-Slavery Society abandoned the complex formula of immediate emancipation gradually accomplished and announced that henceforth their goal was immediate abolition. The general public,

[29] Barnes, *Antislavery Impulse*, 266. See also, *ibid.*, 115–18, 133–45.
[30] Quoted *ibid.*, 119.
[31] Quoted *ibid.*, 110.
[32] James A. Thome and J. Horace Kimball, *Emancipation in the West Indies . . . .*, in *The Anti-Slavery Examiner*, No. 7 (New York, 1838).

whether hostile or friendly, had always believed that this was the object of the Society.[33]

The other study, entitled *American Slavery as It Is: Testimony of a Thousand Witnesses,*[34] was essentially a case study in the worst features of slavery. Weld, with the help of research assistants, combed thousands of Southern and other newspapers for atrocity stories, and he appealed to abolitionists to supply him with "facts never yet published, facts that would thrill the land with horror." [35] Within four months, 22,000 copies of his powerful indictment of slavery had been sold, and within the first year, nearly 100,000.[36] The influence of *American Slavery as It Is* went far beyond its many readers, for it was an easily accessible store of ammunition for subsequent campaigners. A large part of Charles Dickens' influential chapter on slavery in his *American Notes* was lifted bodily and without any expression of indebtedness from Weld's compilation,[37] and its service to Harriet Beecher Stowe in the preparation of *Uncle Tom's Cabin* was frankly acknowledged.[38]

At the end of the 1830's there occurred an important change in the management and the character of the abolition movement. The American Anti-Slavery Society was torn by quarrels among its leaders, and the Panic of 1837 brought these men and their organization to virtual bankruptcy. State societies revolted against the parent organization, and the women's-rights movement caused distraction and confusion of purpose.[39] But as the New York leadership declined, the empire that it had largely created found a new capital in Washington and a leadership in a small group of Congressmen, assisted by a lobby of their creation.

For a time these Congressmen were prohibited from speaking against slavery by the rule of silence that both parties adopted in the effort to avoid rifts within their ranks. When Thomas Morris, a Democratic Senator from Ohio, challenged this rule and spoke against Calhoun's 1837 resolutions he was refused re-election by

[33] Barnes, *Antislavery Impulse,* 138–39.

[34] [Theodore D. Weld], *American Slavery as It Is* (New York, 1839).

[35] Quoted in Barnes, *Antislavery Impulse,* 139.　　　　[36] *Ibid.,* 276.

[37] Louise H. Johnson, "The Source of the Chapter on Slavery in Dickens's *American Notes,*" in *American Literature* (Durham), XIV (1942–1943), 427–30.

[38] Harriet B. Stowe, *A Key to Uncle Tom's Cabin* . . . (Boston, 1853), 16, 21, 40–43 ff.

[39] Barnes, *Antislavery Impulse,* 146–64.

the Democratic legislature of his state.[40] Early in 1842, Adams, probably with the approval of the small but well-knit group of abolitionist Representatives, threw down the gauntlet to the Whig party with a bitter and powerful attack upon slavery. A caucus of Southern Whigs decided that he should be censured. Northern Whigs concurred. But when the attempt was made, Adams won a notable victory on the floor though, so it was rumored, at the price of promising to remain silent in the future.

Shortly afterward, the abolitionists commissioned Joshua R. Giddings, an Ohio Whig, to issue another challenge by speaking against slavery. He did so and was censured. Thereupon he resigned his seat, appealed to his constituency, and was re-elected by a large majority. Back in Congress, he resumed his attack upon slavery, and the Whig leaders knew that they could not stop him; for in the fight in Ohio over his re-election, the forces of abolition had proved stronger than the power of the Whig organization. The day had dawned when the Whig party could not forbid discussion of this issue even though its discussion was likely to rend the party into Southern and Northern factions. Abolitionists could now look to Congressmen to give them leadership and to speak and vote for their cause.[41]

This great turning point is a convenient moment for reviewing certain developments in the antislavery movement during the previous decade. In sheer numbers, its growth was phenomenal. Its respectability and influence had likewise increased. Instead of being scorned and stoned in Northern villages, abolitionists now had a great following among respectable folk, and they had vigorous leaders in Congress.

In respect to their goal, the abolitionists were singularly consistent throughout the years. Although they had abandoned the idea of gradualism, they never swerved from their essential goal of extinguishing slavery throughout the United States at the earliest possible date. Neither had they ever assumed responsibility for suggesting how to cushion the shock of emancipation or how to deal with the problems that would follow it. On the other hand, their

40 Dwight L. Dumond, *Antislavery Origins of the Civil War in the United States* (Ann Arbor, 1939), 85–86.
41 Barnes, *Antislavery Impulse*, 182–90.

strategy was somewhat modified. At first the abolitionists appealed both to Southerners and Northerners; but when the South barricaded itself against printed appeals and condemnations, the program of the abolitionists became primarily an attempt to convince Northerners, who neither owned slaves nor possessed the legal power to abolish slavery, that slavery was terrible and ought to be ended. An occasional abolitionist was worried by the impractical character of their approach. One of them implored Weld to supply him with "a plain common Sense view of . . . *how* emancipation and abolition are to be brought about by the correction of public sentiment at the North. . . . Can you not furnish . . . some *facts* pertinent to . . . the *effectiveness* of Northern abolition on the South?" [42] But most of the antislavery men, like the majority of the other reformers of their day, showed less zeal for reforming sinners than for persuading the righteous to denounce sinners.[43]

In the early days of the movement there were debates among abolitionists as to whether slavery was an evil or a sin; but the doctrine soon gained general acceptance among them that human bondage was contrary to the will of God. From this decision there flowed several important consequences. The slavery debate was turned into Biblical channels, with both sides in the controversy searching the Scriptures for proof that their views were in accordance with the revealed will of God. A second consequence was the condemnation of the slaveowner as a sinner; and while such a man as Finney thought the sinner ought to be reproved in a spirit of love and humility, the doctrine of the sinfulness of slavery led to a censorious attitude toward the slaveholder.

The doctrine that slavery was a sin was a natural outgrowth of the religious origin of the abolition movement. It was also natural that as the religious impulse diminished, as it did in time, the fight against slavery should lose some of its lofty, spiritual tone. Francis Wayland, president of Brown University and a strong opponent of slavery, agreed with "the late lamented Dr. [William E.] Channing, in the opinion that the tone of the abolitionists at the north has been frequently, I fear I must say generally, 'fierce, bitter, and

[42] Quoted *ibid.*, 248.   [43] *Ibid.*, 25.

abusive.' " It was, thought Wayland, "very different from the spirit of Christ." [44] Finney, watching the course of events, was much disturbed, fearing lest abolition without a foundation of sincere and genuine Christianity would bring the nation "fast into a civil war." [45]

But Weld was not fearful. At times he seemed to long for the appearance of "a storm blast with God in the midst." If slaveholders had refused to heed his warnings and reproofs, which he was sure were the warnings and reproofs of God, was it not inevitable and proper for them to be destroyed by insurrection and war? [46] Some twenty years earlier John Quincy Adams had looked upon disunion and civil war as sublime and glorious if for the purpose of ending slavery, and there is much to indicate that his mind was still filled with these thoughts during his great fight for the right of petition in Congress.

In spite of all that has been written about the abolition crusade, no one can tell with certainty how much it accelerated the ending of slavery in America, whether civil war could have been avoided without it, or whether in the long run it made the problem of race more or less acute. To take a broader sweep, no one can prove beyond question that the South, or the nation, or the Negro's status in America was made better or worse by the activities of the abolitionists. But on less important points, some of which bear upon these larger questions, something can be said about the effects of the abolition movement.

As for the slave, his lot was not much changed; certainly it was not improved. A thoughtful Scotch minister, who was no friend of slavery, came to the opinion after extended travel in America in 1844 that "Nowhere does the condition of the coloured people appear worse than in the slave States which border the free States. . . . Whatever may be the ultimate advantages, the immediate effect of the agitation for emancipation, and all the anxious, uncertain, suspicious, and angry feelings it engenders, is unfavorable to the improvement either of master or slave, making one more sus-

[44] Richard Fuller and Francis Wayland, *Domestic Slavery Considered as a Scriptural Institution* (New York, 1845), 13–14.
[45] Quoted in Barnes, *Antislavery Impulse*, 162.
[46] Dumond, *Antislavery Origins of the Civil War*, 110–11.

picious, and the other the more deeply to feel his chain." [47] The free Negro population of the South also suffered. In Maryland and Virginia, where the number had been increasing more rapidly than the number of slaves until there were more than 100,000 free Negroes in 1830, the rate of increase was thereafter sharply cut. In Louisiana and Mississippi there was an absolute decrease between 1840 and 1850.[48]

Travelers in the South began to find that they were objects of suspicion. The Reverend George Lewis was asked soon after he arrived at Savannah in the year 1844: "Are you come to be a spy here?" [49] Before entering Virginia in 1837 a British naturalist, Charles G. B. Daubeny, took the precaution of disposing of some antislavery writings that had been in his traveling bag.[50] The experiences of the prominent English Quaker, Joseph J. Gurney, illustrate the behavior and the treatment of the abolitionist in the South. In Virginia he freely stated his "views respecting the oppressed negro population" to Governor David Campbell. Although Gurney felt that he was kindly received, he recorded that Campbell "bitterly complained of what he called the violence of the Northern abolitionists" and asserted "that their proceedings had operated, in Virginia, as an effectual bar to the progress of emancipation." [51] In Charleston he asked Mayor Henry L. Pinckney to convene some of the principal persons of the city to hear his story of the favorable workings of freedom in the West Indies, but Pinckney thought it would be imprudent. On the other hand, Gurney was given free access to whatever he wished to inspect, including the jail, the Negro prison, and a plantation on Edisto Island. He left the city with the opinion that "we had certainly been received with much more kindness and polite attention, than we had ventured to expect." [52]

Slave traders in the neighborhood of Washington must have be-

[47] Rev. George Lewis, *Impressions of America and the American Churches* (Edinburgh, 1845), 143.

[48] *Compendium of the Ninth Census*, 1870, pp. 14–17.

[49] Lewis, *Impressions of America and the American Churches*, 127, 130.

[50] Charles G. B. Daubeny, *Journal of a Tour through the United States, and in Canada, Made during the Years 1837–38* (Oxford, 1843), 107.

[51] Joseph J. Gurney, *A Journey in North America, Described in Familiar Letters to Amelia Opie* (Norwich, 1841), 74–75.   [52] *Ibid.*, 373–81.

come accustomed to sight-seers and to persons collecting data on the evils of slavery, and they seem to have shown them about with an easy tolerance.[53] Planters occasionally submitted their estates to examination even at the risk of having to listen to private lectures on the evils of slavery or of having their visitors seek to create unrest among the slaves.[54]

But it was not the occasional visitor who disturbed the Southerner so much as the incessant attack in Northern press and pulpit and upon the floor of Congress. Despite the religious impulse behind the barrage of advice, warning, and denunciation, the slaveholder failed to see therein much evidence of the Christian virtues of truth, humility, and love. He was impressed, rather, by the holier-than-thou spirit of his mentors, a spirit which seemed to imply that Northern consciences were more enlightened than any to be found in the South.

Undoubtedly, the slaveholder did not give the abolitionists a fair hearing. His traditions, his economic interests, and his way of life all fought against his considering slavery in a detached, objective fashion; and his dealings with the North for some years past had destroyed any faith he may have had in Northern disinterestedness and fair dealing. As he looked to the region that was now inviting him to perform a costly and revolutionary act, he remembered that the opposition of this region to the extension of slavery in 1819 had been blended with a plan to increase New England's political power. As he recounted the contests in subsequent years over protective tariffs, over the expenditure of Federal funds for roads and canals, and over other issues, he could recall little but self-interest, and at times a very ruthless self-interest, in the words and votes of Northern Congressmen.[55]

[53] Ethan A. Andrews, *Slavery and the Domestic Slave-Trade in the United States* (Boston, 1836), 135–43; Joseph Sturge, *A Visit to the United States in 1841* (Boston, 1842), 45–47, 100–101; Edward S. Abdy, *Journal of a Residence and Tour in the United States of North America, from April, 1833, to October, 1834* (London, 1835), II, 179–80.

[54] "Extract of a Letter from James Cannings Fuller to Joseph Sturge," in Sturge, *Visit to the United States in 1841*, Appendix I.

[55] Southerners were not alone in suspecting that there were economic motives in the abolition crusade. William Kennedy, British agent in America, asserted in 1841 that Northern critics of slavery were seeking to discredit Southern advocates of free trade in England as well as in America. Kennedy, *Texas: The Rise, Progress, and Prospects of the Republic of Texas* (London, 1841), I, xxiv–xxvii.

Perhaps slaveholders should have distinguished between such men as Weld and Finney, who fought slavery because they considered it morally wrong, and Northern politicians, who voted for measures that would enhance Northern prosperity even at the expense of the South. But slaveholders failed to make that distinction; and after 1840, when the abolition movement entered politics with the formation of a bloc of antislavery Congressmen, the distinction largely ceased to exist.

As Southern opinion hardened toward abolitionists, Southern criticism of slavery waned. By the year 1837 there was not an antislavery society in all the South.[56] "In the general indignation," excited by abolitionists, wrote George Tucker of Virginia in 1843, "the arguments in favour of negro emancipation, once open and urgent, have been completely silenced, and its advocates among the slaveholders, who have not changed their sentiments, find it prudent to conceal them." [57] The careers of politicians were scrutinized to discover whether they were safe on this point. James McDowell, Jr., an antislavery spokesman during the Virginia debate over slavery, had his record flung against him when the legislature was considering him for the governorship in 1840; and although one of his friends assured the legislature that McDowell was hostile to Northern abolitionists, he failed of election at this time.[58]

The effect of abolitionism on Southern opinion is illustrated by the official statements of two Mississippi governors. In 1828, Gerard C. Brandon declared that slavery was "an evil at best" because it was harmful to the poor white man, it widened the gulf between rich and poor, and it kept the state from attracting a numerous white population and from enjoying the influence and power that such a population would bring.[59] Eight years later John A. Quitman, after reviewing and condemning the rise of the abolition movement, stated before the legislature: "It is enough, that we, the people of Mississippi, professing to be actuated by as high regard for the pre-

[56] *Life, Travels and Opinions of Benjamin Lundy,* 296.

[57] George Tucker, *Progress of the United States in Population and Wealth in Fifty Years, as Exhibited by the Decennial Census* (New York, 1843), 108.

[58] Richmond *Enquirer,* February 13, 1840, reporting proceedings in the House of Delegates for February 14, a misprint for February 11. Compare Virginia *House Journal,* 1839–1840, for these dates.

[59] Mississippi *House Journal,* 1828, p. 15.

cepts of religion and morality, as the citizens of other states, and claiming to be more competent judges of our own substantial interests, have chosen to adopt into our political system, and still choose to retain, the institution of domestic slavery." [60]

This was the sort of calm but determined statement proper in official messages, but it does not reflect the surging emotion aroused in the South. Southern hotheads threatened to lynch abolitionists if they came south of the Potomac River and offered rewards of thousands of dollars to anyone who would put them in reach of Southern vengeance.[61] A Mississippi newspaper declared that the quarrel over slavery had reached such a point that it would "not be settled by negotiation, but by the *sword,*—by balls and the *Bayonet.—We can do without the North.*" [62]

Although the abolition movement was followed by a decline of antislavery sentiment in the South, it must be remembered that in all the long years before that movement began no part of the South had made substantial progress toward ending slavery. The free and full discussion in Virginia in 1832 was promising, but the decision was in the negative. The trends are not clear enough to warrant prophecy as to what the South would have done about slavery had it not been disturbed by the abolitionists, but it is at least certain that before the crusade began Southern liberalism had not ended slavery in any state.

The Southern defense of slavery antedated the organization of the American Anti-Slavery Society. Shortly after the discovery of the Denmark Vesey plot at Charleston, Richard Furman, president of the Baptist State Convention, published a Scriptural defense of slavery together with a plea for better religious care of slaves.[63]

60 *Ibid.,* 1836, p. 15. For a set of vigorous resolutions supporting the proslavery views of the governor, see *ibid.,* 194–97.

61 W. Sherman Savage, *The Controversy over the Distribution of Abolition Literature, 1830–1860* ([Washington], 1938), 34–40. Fletcher M. Green, "Duff Green, Militant Journalist of the Old School," in *American Historical Review,* LII (1946–1947), 256–58, and Lloyd, *Slavery Controversy,* 120–22, give other examples of the development of Southern bitterness toward abolitionists.

62 Woodville (Miss.) *Republican,* August 22, 1835. During the next twelve months, this small paper gave an average of at least a column of each issue to discussions of abolition, slavery, and related subjects.

63 Richard Furman, *Exposition of the Views of the Baptists, Relative to the Coloured Population of the United States, in a Communication to the Governor of South-Carolina* (Charleston, 1823).

Dew and Leigh defended slavery against the attacks made upon it in the Virginia debate. Under the scourging of the abolition attacks, these defenses were much expanded and new arguments were evolved. To offset the harshly distorted descriptions of abolitionists, Southern champions depicted slavery as a kindly and altogether beneficial institution. They turned the pages of history, they dissected human cadavers, and they diligently searched the Bible for arguments to prove that the Negro was made for slavery and that slavery served a useful purpose in society.[64]

The intellectual defense of slavery failed to convert the North— it failed as completely as the abolitionists had failed to convince the South that slavery was sinful. One is tempted to believe that the appeal to reason was in this instance worse than a failure, for instead of bringing the problem nearer to solution, it served merely to convince each contestant of its own righteousness and of its opponent's wickedness, and to stir emotions for an ultimate contest in which reason would play little part.[65]

The strength of the contestants was determined by forces other than an array of facts and skill in argumentation. The chief advantage of the abolitionists consisted in their success in converting the North to the belief that slavery was wrong and must be ended. To check this powerful and growing offensive, the South had two modes of defense. One grew out of the circumstance that for a time the leaders of the Whig and Democratic parties agreed with Southern defenders that slavery ought to be kept out of politics. This line of defense was giving way in the early 1840's.

The bulwark of the South which promised a more permanent defense was the fact that law was on its side. This advantage was never explored more thoroughly nor pushed to greater extreme than in a set of resolutions introduced in the Senate in December, 1837, by Calhoun. In his first and less debatable proposition, Calhoun argued that the states when entering the Union had retained sole power over their own police and domestic institutions, including slavery, and that "any intermeddling of any one or more States,

---

[64] A systematic analysis of the Southern defense of slavery can be found in William S. Jenkins, *Pro-Slavery Thought in the Old South* (Chapel Hill, 1935), 200–85. See also, Lloyd, *Slavery Controversy*, Chaps. IV–VII.

[65] For an amplification of this idea, see Charles S. Sydnor, "The Southerner and the Laws," in *Journal of Southern History*, VI (1940), 19–23.

or a combination of their citizens, with the domestic institutions and police of the others, on any ground, . . . is an assumption of superiority not warranted by the Constitution . . . [and] subversive of the objects for which the Constitution was formed." [66]

His second and more advanced position was that the states had created the Federal government as their common agent and that the agent ought therefore to use its powers to safeguard the stability of their domestic institutions, once more including slavery. Reasoning from this general proposition, he argued that Congress ought to use none of the powers granted to it to restrict or damage slavery; it ought not to abolish slavery in the District of Columbia, or "refuse to extend to the Southern and Western States any advantage which would tend to strengthen, or render them more secure, or increase their limits or population by the annexation of new territory or States." [67]

Calhoun had earlier formulated another application of his general rule. During the discussion occasioned by the burning of abolition literature found in the Charleston post office he had asserted that the power delegated to the Federal government to establish a postal system ought not to be used to distribute abolition literature in the slave states where the circulation of such material was illegal.[68] In brief, he argued that the states had a constitutional right to retain slavery, and that the Federal government ought not to use the powers delegated to it to injure slavery but ought, rather, to safeguard it.[69]

Calhoun's second proposition was challenged during a discussion of the *Creole* case. In November, 1841, slaves being shipped on the *Creole* from Virginia to New Orleans revolted and managed to get into the British port of Nassau in the Bahamas, where slavery had been abolished. The United States demanded the return of the Negroes as criminals guilty of mutiny and murder. With these circumstances in mind, Giddings introduced a series of resolutions in

---

[66] *Cong. Globe*, 25 Cong., 2 Sess., 55.   [67] *Ibid.*

[68] McLaughlin, *Constitutional History of the United States*, 485–86.

[69] While Calhoun's position on this particular point has usually been attacked, subsequent developments have in large measure validated his opinion in regard to Federal reinforcement of state laws. Harold W. Thatcher, "Calhoun and Federal Reinforcement of State Laws," in *American Political Science Review* (Baltimore, Menasha, Wis.), XXXVI (1942), 873–80.

the House which began virtually with Calhoun's starting point, namely, that each state had full and exclusive jurisdiction over slavery and had delegated no part of this power to the Federal government. His other basic point was that slavery, "being an abridgment of the natural rights of man, can exist only by force of positive municipal law, and is necessarily confined to the territorial jurisdiction of the power creating it." [70] From these premises he reasoned that Virginia's laws maintaining slavery ceased to operate once the Negroes were taken on the high seas, and that the authority exercised at sea by the Federal government under the commerce clause did not extend to the maintenance of slavery because the states had given it no power to deal with slavery. He concluded, therefore, that the Negroes on the *Creole* ceased to be slaves as soon as they left Virginia and that they had infracted no Federal law in using force to maintain their natural right to personal liberty.[71]

Giddings had matched Calhoun in shrewd logic by pointing out that it was just as reasonable to insist that the delegated powers of the Federal government ought to be used to destroy slavery, because slavery was contrary to the will of the free states, as to insist that these delegated powers should be used to uphold the institution, because it was according to the will of the slave states. His resolutions brought into the open the essential weakness in the state-rights defense of slavery: if the Federal government had any authority over slavery, it could use that power to destroy it; but if it had no authority, how could it maintain slavery in the District of Columbia, in the territories, and on the high seas?

Another dilemma for those who relied on constitutional arguments for the protection of slavery was implicit in the case of Groves *v.* Slaughter which was decided by the Supreme Court of the United States on March 10, 1841.[72] The case involved the validity of a note given in purchase of slaves imported into the state of Mississippi and sold contrary to a prohibitory clause in the state constitution. It was well understood at the time that the Court might consider whether the prohibition in the Mississippi constitution was repugnant to the commerce clause in the Federal Con-

---

[70] *Cong. Globe*, 27 Cong., 2 Sess., 342.

[71] For the significance of Joshua R. Giddings' resolution in the development of the abolition movement, see above, p. 237.   [72] 15 Peters 449 (1841).

stitution. By deciding that slaves were property, the interstate slave trade could be regarded as interstate commerce; the prohibitory clause in the Mississippi constitution could be overruled; and the entire interstate slave trade could be subjected to Federal regulation. Regulation could, of course, be carried to the point of prohibition. On the other hand, if the slave were not property, was he not then to be regarded as a person endowed with those constitutional rights which are inconsistent with slavery? [73]

The implications in the case of Groves v. Slaughter, the resolutions of Giddings, and statements that were made on other occasions made it clear that slavery would be in a precarious position if Congress, the presidency, and the Supreme Court passed into control of the antislavery forces. Even though the constitutional right of the individual state to retain slavery were respected, slavery would be mortally wounded if slaves could not be sold from state to state, if slavery were abolished in the territories and in the District of Columbia, if no new slave states were admitted, and if the powers delegated to the national government—such as the power to tax and to distribute mail—were directed toward injuring slavery.

But there was no certainty that a government founded on abolition philosophy would respect even the most fundamental of the constitutional rights of the states, for the abolitionists, having discovered that the Constitution was an obstacle to the attainment of their goal, insisted that the Constitution was subordinate to other imperatives. In the Supreme Court of the United States an antislavery justice declared in 1841 that the right of a state "to protect itself against the avarice and intrusion of the slave dealer . . . is higher and deeper than the Constitution." [74] Various abolitionists insisted that the Declaration of Independence was a higher authority than the Constitution, and that its statements abrogated any part of the Constitution that seemed to be in conflict.[75] In the last analysis, the abolitionists set up their own ideas of right as the supreme law of the land, without, perhaps, quite realizing the revo-

[73] Charles Warren, *The Supreme Court in United States History* (Boston, 1923), II, 341–46; Sydnor, *Slavery in Mississippi*, 166–67. The opinions in this case constitute one of the best explanations of the relation of the slave trade to the Constitution.

[74] Justice John McLean of Ohio, in Groves v. Slaughter, 15 Peters 449 (1841). The quotation is from p. 508.

[75] Dumond, *Antislavery Origins of the Civil War*, 67–79.

lutionary and anarchistic implications of their position. Garrison was one of the few to follow the logic of this reasoning to its conclusion by preaching disobedience to all man-made laws.[76]

The higher-law doctrine, as it came to be called, of the abolitionists was detested by the slaveholders on two counts. It clearly implied that the Southern conscience was a corrupt and unreliable guide in comparison with the superior moral and religious insights of the abolitionists. It further implied that if abolitionists should gain political control, no law, not even the Constitution, would have permanence; for the abolition conscience, rather than legal enactments and the Constitution, would become the law of the land. This abolition conscience was neither weak nor abstract. Under its urgings, abolitionists committed various acts, especially in aiding slaves to escape, that were clearly contrary to the law of the land.[77] When they put conscience above law, these men obviously meant just what they said.

Thus it became evident in the 1840's that there was no effective defense of slavery available to the South against an abolitionized North. The abolition movement had not yet made sufficient headway to create an immediate danger, but it had become evident that the South could discover no way to stop its growth. The South had not been able to devise a secure defense against the power that Northern antislavery forces were in process of mustering.

[76] Barnes, *Antislavery Impulse*, 98.

[77] For an example, *ibid.*, 276. See also, Earl of Carlisle (Lord Morpeth), *Travels in America. The Poetry of Pope. Two Lectures Delivered to the Leeds Mechanics' Institution and Literary Society, December 5th and 6th, 1850* (New York, 1851), 35–37.

CHAPTER XI

VICISSITUDES OF AN
AGRICULTURAL ECONOMY

IN the early 1830's many persons in the South Atlantic states
were despondent over the economic condition of their region.
A member of the Virginia legislature of 1831–1832 compared
the original fertility of the land with the present "condition of the
slave-holding portion of this commonwealth—barren, desolate, and
seared as it were by the avenging hand of heaven." Another be-
moaned the fact that "Our towns are stationary, our villages almost
every where declining." A third asserted that "if you will go into the
credit stores and pop-shops, (with which the whole country is
thronged) you will find that, with very few exceptions, the slaveholder has there become very deeply entangled—the embarrassment mainly incurred to clothe and feed his slaves. The slave is
clothed and fed, that he may labor for victuals and clothes—a beautiful operation!—Thus, sir, the master of the slave absolutely be-
longs to the merchant, and has to labor—and labor hard—for their
benefit. He is literally their bondsman." [1]

Harriet Martineau, writing of conditions in South Carolina in
1835, declared that "Roads nearly impassable in many parts, bridges
carried away and not restored, lands exhausted, and dwellings for-
saken, are spectacles too common. . . . There is an air of rudeness
about the villages, and languor about the towns." [2] These strictures

[1] From speeches of Charles J. Faulkner, Thomas Marshall, and Philip A. Bolling.
Robert, *Road from Monticello*, 65, 77, 79.

[2] Harriet Martineau, *Society in America* (4th ed., New York, 1837), I, 75. The works
of Frederick Marryat, Charles Dickens, James S. Buckingham, and other travelers,
especially those of the 1840's, describe depressed conditions in the South, particularly
in Virginia. Few of them, however, are as reliable as Martineau; their adverse
conclusions are more often based on a priori reasoning about the evils of slavery
than upon close observation of actual conditions.

of a stranger were more than matched by Senator Robert Y. Hayne's gloomy description of the plight of Charleston and the South Carolina low country. "Our merchants," he wrote, are "bankrupt or driven away—their capital sunk or transferred to other pursuits— our shipyards broken up—our ships all sold! . . . our mechanics in despair; the very grass growing in our streets, and houses falling into ruins; real estate reduced to one-third part of its value, and rents almost to nothing. . . . If we fly from the city to the country, what do we there behold? Fields abandoned; and hospitable mansions of our fathers deserted; agriculture drooping; our slaves, like their masters, working harder, and faring worse; the planter striving with unavailing efforts to avert the ruin which is before him." [3]

While some denied the validity of these descriptions and many claimed that they were overdrawn, there was real ground for discouragement. The price of tobacco was prevailingly low from 1819 to 1833, and the size of the crop in Virginia, Maryland, and North Carolina had increased but little.[4] As for cotton, the price dropped from a range of 21 to 30 cents a pound between 1815 and 1818 to a range of 12 to 18 cents in the years 1819–1825. Then it went lower, never exceeding 10 cents a pound from 1826 to 1832.[5] Although there was a great increase in Georgia's production, the South Carolina crop increased only 25 per cent from 1821 to 1839, and South Carolina dropped from first to fifth place among the cotton-producing states.[6]

Commerce presented an equally discouraging aspect. The exports of Virginia, South Carolina, and Georgia were valued at no more in 1833 than they had been in 1819.[7] As for imports, customs duties collected at Charleston declined from a yearly average of $1,407,058 in the period 1815–1818 to $679,141 in the period 1819–1825.[8] In 1829 they amounted to $490,441 and in 1831 to $504,794.[9]

Population trends likewise indicated that something was wrong with the Southeast. From 1820 to 1830 the population of the United

3 *Register of Debates*, 22 Cong., 1 Sess., 80.
4 Robert, *Tobacco Kingdom*, 132–33, 140–43.
5 Gray, *Agriculture in the Southern United States*, II, 1027.
6 *Atlas of American Agriculture*, V, *The Crops. Sect. A. Cotton*, 16–18.
7 Albion, *Rise of New York Port*, 390.
8 Mills, *Statistics of South Carolina*, 168.
9 Charleston *Southern Patriot*, November 30, 1837.

States increased slightly more than 33 per cent. Georgia, with an increase of 51½ per cent, was the only South Atlantic state to exceed the national rate of increase. Neither in Maryland, Virginia, North Carolina, nor South Carolina did population increase as much as 16 per cent. In the next decade the record of the South Atlantic states was even worse. In Virginia, North Carolina, and South Carolina the increase of population amounted in no instance to as much as 2½ per cent, and in Maryland it was only 5 per cent.[10]

The picture of urban development was also dark. In the score of years that ended in 1840, Richmond increased from 12,067 to 20,153 and Charleston from 24,780 to 29,261.[11] But this modest growth did not keep Charleston from dropping from sixth to tenth place among American cities, or Richmond from twelfth to twentieth place.[12] Charleston could take no pride in its 20 per cent growth in a twenty-year period when New York, Buffalo, Rochester, Pittsburgh, Cincinnati, Louisville, St. Louis, New Orleans, and other cities had grown from ten to twenty-five times as much.[13] Furthermore, while Charleston, Richmond, and Savannah were barely holding their own in annual value of exports, New York increased its exports from thirteen million to twenty-five million dollars between the years 1819 and 1833, and New Orleans from nine million to eighteen million. By 1840 even Mobile was ahead of Charleston in value of exports.[14]

A Virginia legislator declared that if any of his fellow citizens was complacent about this state of affairs he ought to "extend his travels to the northern states of this union— . . . contrast the happiness and contentment which prevails throughout the country— the busy and cheerful sound of industry—the rapid and swelling growth of their population—their means and institutions of education—their skill and proficiency in the useful arts—their enterprise, and public spirit—the monuments of their commercial and manufacturing industry; and, above all, their devoted attachment to the government from which they derive their protection, with the

10 *Statistical View of the United States,* 1850, pp. 96–98.

11 *Ibid.,* 192.

12 *Twelfth Census of the United States, 1900, Statistical Atlas* (Washington, 1903), plate 22.

13 *Statistical View of the United States,* 1850, p. 192.

14 Albion, *Rise of New York Port,* 105, 390.

division, discontent, indolence and poverty of the southern country." [15]

All parts of the Southeast were not equally affected. In general, the cotton states fared worse than the tobacco states, and among the cotton states, none was so hard hit as South Carolina. Yet, the distress of the South Atlantic states was not so much an absolute decline as it was a leveling off while other areas were going ahead. Perhaps this leveling off was chiefly due to the fact that the economy of the region had approached the upper limits that could be reached under an agricultural regime. But whether the distress was relative or absolute, it hurt; and it stirred men to sober thought as to its cause and its cure.

Some Virginians declared that Negro slavery was the prime cause of that state's economic decadence.[16] South Carolinians preferred to emphasize the harmful effects of various policies of the Federal government, particularly the tariff. But neither of these partisan interpretations went unchallenged. There were South Carolinians with sufficient hardihood to assert that Southerners were idle, extravagant, and unskilled in business affairs, and that the nullification controversy wasted time, upset credit, and caused peaceful citizens to leave the state. Blame was also placed upon lack of trade connections with the West; upon expensive commercial dependence upon the North; upon ignorant and careless agricultural practices, with consequent soil depletion and dwindling returns; and upon the lure of vast quantities of Western lands which served both to drain off the population of the Southeast and to depress cotton prices by overproduction.[17]

Schemes for resuscitating the prosperity of the Southeast were fitted to most of these diagnoses. In Virginia there was the fruitless attempt to end slavery. In most of the South, but especially in South Carolina, there was the partly successful attempt to secure a reduction in the tariff. The price of cotton temporarily improved when Nicholas Biddle used his great financial power to keep a consider-

[15] Quoted in Robert, *Road from Monticello*, 77–78.

[16] *Ibid.*, 22, 65, 77–79, 85, 100. The evil effects of slavery on Southern economy were asserted from time to time by Southerners even after the rise of the abolition crusade. Kenneth M. Stampp, "The Southern Refutation of the Proslavery Argument," in *North Carolina Historical Review*, XXI (1944), 35–45.

[17] Boucher, *Nullification Controversy in South Carolina*, 189–93.

able part of the 1837 crop off the Liverpool market during the spring and summer of 1838. But relief by such measures was of brief duration. A group of Southern planters under the leadership of John G. Gamble of Florida and James Hamilton, Jr., failed in an attempt to concentrate the sale of the 1839 crop through a single Liverpool house.[18]

A more popular plan was to establish direct trade relations between the South and Europe [19] in order to stimulate the growth of Southern seaports and to save the fees and charges of Northern shippers and merchants. With declining incomes, planters were eager to reduce costs that they had paid in better times without much thought.

In 1831 a group of Charleston merchants investigated a project for establishing a line of ships to trade between their city and Great Britain and Le Havre. A local firm exhibited a model of a vessel proper for this run.[20] In the following years there were meetings to discuss commercial questions at Knoxville, Norfolk, Richmond, and elsewhere. The most notable of these were three conventions held at Augusta in 1837 and 1838, and a fourth that met in Charleston in 1839. Most of the delegates were from the South Atlantic states, especially from South Carolina and Georgia. Much use and misuse were made of statistics of foreign trade. It was asserted that South Carolina and Georgia imported goods to the value of $3,400,000 in the year 1836 though their exports amounted to $24,000,000, while New York, with exports of less than $20,000,000, imported goods to the value of $118,000,000. The conclusion was drawn that the cotton states were greatly injured and the Northern commercial states proportionately benefited by existing arrangements in respect to foreign trade.

The chain of costs between Southern interior markets and North-

[18] Thomas P. Govan, "An Ante-Bellum Attempt to Regulate the Price and Supply of Cotton," in *North Carolina Historical Review*, XVII (1940), 302–12.

[19] James S. Buckingham, who was in South Carolina when the movement was near its height, suggested that the South was seeking to withdraw its trade from channels controlled by Northern abolitionists. *Slave States of America*, I, 185, 566. John Quincy Adams believed the direct-trade conventions to be the "germ of a Southern Convention, with South Carolina at its head, which is to divide this Union into a Northern, a Southern, and a Western Confederacy." Adams (ed.), *Memoirs of John Quincy Adams*, IX, 421.

[20] Charleston *Courier*, June 1, 1931.

ern commercial houses was described by a committee of ten merchants, dealers, and planters. The Northern importer, after paying the duties on foreign goods, then added about 17½ per cent. Inasmuch as each importer tended to specialize in a distinct class of goods and received his goods in bales and packages that were usually too large for the retailer, the Southern merchant bought from a second class of dealers known as jobbers, who broke the importers' packages and made up orders in proper amounts and kinds. The markup of the jobbers was estimated at about 20 per cent. In addition to these costs, freight and insurance had to be paid for transporting goods from the Northern port to Charleston; there was a loss on exchange between the South and New York; and the Southern merchant had the expense of going to the North once or twice a year to select his goods. It was the opinion of the committee that the Southern purchaser could effect considerable savings by dealing with a Charleston importer.[21]

But despite some fact finding and much oratory and banqueting, the plan to revive Southern prosperity by establishing direct trade relations between the South and abroad was void of accomplishment. After 1839 it was virtually forgotten. Matthew Fontaine Maury, writing for the *Southern Literary Messenger*,[22] ascribed the failure to the tendency of the conventions to do nothing more than "to resolve and re-resolve to meet again," and to agree "not to buy northern goods when they can get southern, unless the northern are the cheapest; not to freight northern vessels when they can freight southern, unless the northern freight for less." He further reminded the Southern zealots that New York had several natural advantages, among them the fact that it was much nearer to Liverpool and Le Havre than any of the cotton ports, and that New York had a fund of commercial experience that could not be matched elsewhere in the United States. He held out no hope to the South unless it exerted itself greatly in action rather than in resolutions,

21 Most of the report of the committee is printed in Herbert Wender, *Southern Commercial Conventions, 1837–1859,* in Johns Hopkins University *Studies in Historical and Political Science,* XLVIII, No. 4 (Baltimore, 1930), 37–41. See also, John G. Van Deusen, *The Ante-Bellum Southern Commercial Conventions,* in Trinity College Historical Society *Historical Papers,* XVI (Durham, 1926), 14–21.

22 *Southern Literary Messenger,* V (1839), 3–12.

and not even then unless perhaps through developing steamships that could surpass the sailing packets of New York.

During the thirties there was no enthusiasm for developing Southern manufacturing which was thought to conflict with the established values of an agrarian society. But in the middle forties a change began to occur. William Gregg of South Carolina, who had an interest in a cotton mill and who was planning a more ambitious venture, published a defense of manufacturing.[23] In December, 1845, his Graniteville Manufacturing Company was chartered, and it soon became visible proof that a cotton mill could flourish in South Carolina to the profit of its owners and to the advantage of the community.[24] With the establishment of *The Commercial Review of the South and Southwest* at New Orleans in January, 1846, Southern industry and commerce found a vigorous champion in its editor, James D. B. De Bow.

While the Southeast was trying to escape from economic stagnation and depression, the Southwest enjoyed a period of remarkable growth and apparent prosperity during the 1830's. Removal of Indians from western Georgia, northern Alabama and Mississippi, and western Tennessee opened up vast quantities of new land.[25] More than two thirds of a million new inhabitants entered Alabama and Mississippi between 1820 and 1840, quadrupling their population. Louisiana also experienced some growth, and Arkansas's development was indicated by its admission to statehood in the year 1836.

The Southwest had strong attractions for ambitious young men who could see little prospect of advancement in their staid Eastern

23 First published as a series of articles in the Charleston *Courier*, beginning in the issue of September 20, 1844. It appeared in pamphlet form at the beginning of 1845 with the title, *Essays on Domestic Industry: or, An Enquiry into the Expediency of Establishing Cotton Manufacturers in South-Carolina* (Charleston, 1845).

24 Broadus Mitchell, *William Gregg: Factory Master of the Old South* (Chapel Hill, 1928), 34 and *passim*. William Thomson, a Scotch weaver, wrote an expert description of several cotton and woolen mills in the Carolinas and Georgia in *A Tradesman's Travels, in the United States and Canada, in the Years 1840, 41 & 42* (Edinburgh, 1842), 5, 112–18.

25 Bureau of American Ethnology, *Eighteenth Annual Report 1896–'97* (Washington, 1899), Pt. II, tabulates the various treaties and presents an excellent set of state maps showing the extent of the various cessions. Population growth in the Southwest is shown in *Twelfth Census of the United States, 1900, Statistical Atlas*, plates, 5, 6, and 7.

communities. One of these, John A. Quitman of New York, wrote to his father that he intended to seek his fortune in the "Southern States [because they] hold out golden prospects to men of integrity, application, and good acquirements. Money is there as plenty as it is scarce here, . . . their cotton, sugar, tobacco, and rice are always in demand, and the world will not do without them. They have, besides, facilities for transportation and avenues to market it at all seasons of the year." [26] These were the roseate hopes of a young man who had not yet seen the Southwest; but he came to it and he prospered.

New land was one of the principal bases for the boom times in the Southwest, affording to the speculator a quick road to wealth, and to the farmer a more permanent though a more laborious livelihood. Although cotton was selling at prices that caused complaint in South Carolina, the fresh lands of the West produced more bales for the same amount of labor. Furthermore, prices began to rise in the middle thirties, when the immigrant stream was at its peak, reaching more than fifteen cents a pound in 1834 and 1835.[27]

Excellence of natural waterways and of facilities for their use was another stimulus to the development of the Southwest. A large part of Alabama was served by the Coosa-Alabama-Tombigbee network of rivers. The Mississippi River and its tributaries carried the goods of a vast area down to the sea, and brought to the lower valley such upriver commodities as Kentucky hemp, Cincinnati pork, Kanawha Valley salt, and Pittsburgh ironware. The growing commerce of the river was reflected in the increase in the population of New Orleans from 27,176 in 1820 to 102,193 in 1840.

Steamboat design was radically modified in the West. To lessen the chances of disaster on sandbars, mudflats, and submerged trees, the draft of river boats was much reduced by building with light materials and by making hulls extremely flat. As the hold became too shallow to be of use, the engine was brought up to the first deck, and the horizontal high-pressure engine was generally adopted. To minimize damage to the propelling machinery, paddle wheels were used, usually as a pair of side wheels (instead of a single wheel at the

[26] J. F. H. Claiborne, *Life and Correspondence of John A. Quitman* (New York, 1860), I, 60–61. The letter was dated May, 1821.

[27] Gray, *Agriculture in the Southern United States*, II, 1027.

stern) so as to give maximum control in narrow and winding channels.[28]

One who traveled extensively in the early 1840's wrote that the Western boats "are of a very light draught of water—a steamer of 300 tons not drawing more than six feet. There is a smaller class that run when the river is low [and that go far up the smaller tributaries], of from 90 to 140 tons; these do not draw more than two feet. They have all two funnels, and have more resemblance to a house than a ship. They have no masts. . . .

"The lower decks of these boats are nearly flush with the water; but they are so top-heavy that in a windy day, or in turning short round, they swing about like a cart-load of hay on a rough road. They are built very slight; the timbers sawn out of plank—all gingerbread work;—and the hull of one is not reckoned to last more than four years." [29]

The lower deck was mostly open except for the supports and the engines. It was used for storing freight, and in the fall and winter it was often packed almost solidly with bales of cotton. The upper deck was devoted to cabins, lounges, and dining facilities. The fare for a deck or steerage passenger from Pittsburgh or Cincinnati to New Orleans was about $4.00 or $5.00 in the early 1840's with no provision of food. The cabin passenger, whose accommodations included three meals a day, paid from $15.00 to $25.00, which was scarcely half the fare that had been charged before the Panic of 1837.[30] On the best of the boats, cabin passengers enjoyed a degree of comfort and even of luxury in travel that could scarcely be matched at that time by any other form of conveyance in all the world.

Much of the commerce that came down the river to New Orleans was there converted into ocean commerce, and the city was a meeting point for various kinds of vessels. A Scotch Presbyterian minister, who visited New Orleans in the spring of 1844, wrote that "The shipping of Liverpool, half hid within its docks, is not so imposing a sight as this long line of vessels, forming the picturesque breastwork of the city. First we have a long range of steamers, the only

[28] Louis C. Hunter, "The Invention of the Western Steamboat," in *Journal of Economic History* (New York), III (1943–1944), 201–20.
[29] Thomson, *Tradesman's Travels*, 54–55.
[30] *Ibid.*, 56–57; Martineau, *Society in America*, II, 21–22.

vessels that can ascend the Mississippi and its tributaries against the stream, all ark-looking in their structure, but admirably adapted to these rivers. Then follow some thousand large flat boats, which have been floated down on the current, bringing the produce of the most distant regions thither, and which are broken up for their timber, the boatmen returning home by the steamer. . . . Last of all come the ocean vessels—the ships and barques, from all parts of the world, of which about 2000 arrived in 1842–3, and which extend, in lines of four, five, six, and seven deep, along the wharfs, presenting a forest of masts." [81] In the early 1840's, when steam navigation on the Mississippi-Ohio river system was some thirty years old, about four hundred steamboats were there afloat.[32]

Newcomers to the Southwest were likely to notice that conversations were always coming back to the subject of cotton and slaves. Joseph H. Ingraham wrote in the early 1830's that this Siamese-twin subject was "the constant theme—that ever harped upon, never worn out subject of conversation among all classes." [33] Well they might be talked about, for cotton more than any other article meant wealth to this region, and slaves were the instruments for creating much of this form of wealth.

The demand of the Southwest for slaves induced a great flow of black laborers out of the older South. In the 1830's, when the flow reached its peak, some 118,000 slaves were exported from Virginia, 23,230 from Kentucky, 67,707 from South Carolina, and large numbers from Maryland and North Carolina. Mississippi imported an estimated 102,394, thus increasing its slave population 197 per cent within the decade. Alabama's importations were about as large, and Louisiana, Arkansas, and Missouri were receiving considerable numbers.[34]

81 Lewis, *Impressions of America and the American Churches*, 201–202.

82 *The Louisville Directory for the Year 1843–'44* (Louisville, 1843), 196–205, lists the vessels by individual name—a total of 368 steamboats. Professor Louis C. Hunter suggests that this list, being privately compiled, may have missed some vessels. Buckingham, *Slave States of America*, II, 458–59, estimated about the same number in the late 1830's, but writers who spoke in general terms frequently overstated the number of steamboats on Western waters.

83 [Ingraham], *The South-West, by a Yankee*, II, 86. See also, *ibid.*, 67–68, 84–85.

84 Frederic Bancroft, *Slave-Trading in the Old South* (Baltimore, 1931), 382–406. It should be emphasized that this authority on the slave trade submitted these figures as mere approximations.

Some of the slaves who were swept southwestward in this great population movement were taken along by migrating masters. Others were purchased, either by traders or by planters who traveled to the older slave states to buy additional laborers.[35] The sale of slaves was worth millions of dollars yearly to Virginians, and it cost the Southwestern planters a large share of their annual income from cotton.

The greatest of the slave-trading firms in the early thirties was that of Franklin and Armfield. Their main collecting depot was at Alexandria under the direction of John Armfield, but the slaves were also purchased at other points in Virginia and Maryland with the help of agents and affiliated traders. Isaac Franklin, with headquarters at New Orleans and Natchez, was chiefly responsible for sales. This firm's annual shipment of slaves to the Southwest ranged from 1,000 to 1,200. Some were marched overland, but most of them were sent from Alexandria to New Orleans by boats which the firm owned. Armfield was reported to have made nearly half a million dollars in the business; and in 1841, six years after Franklin changed from slave trading to planting, his estate was appraised at three quarters of a million dollars.[36]

In the selling area, New Orleans was the greatest market, though much business was also done at Natchez, Mobile, Montgomery, and other places. It has been estimated that "more than 200, probably not less than 300," residents of New Orleans were engaged in slave trading in 1842.[37]

The time to sell slaves in the cotton and sugar kingdoms was in the winter when planters were receiving the income from their crops. But this income was usually insufficient to carry out their ambitious plans, and they often called on the sellers of Negroes to extend credit for part of the purchase price. In fact, a swollen demand for credit was a major characteristic of the Southwest, especially during the 1830's. Harriet Martineau saw signs of it on every hand in Mobile in 1835, and she was told that it was easy to

[35] *Ibid.*, 397–98, estimates that in the 1850's fully 70 per cent of the slaves taken to the Southwest were sold at some stage of the journey. He implies that the percentage had not been quite so high before 1850.

[36] Wendell H. Stephenson, *Isaac Franklin, Slave Trader and Planter of the Old South* (University, La., 1938), Chaps. III–VI.

[37] Bancroft, *Slave-Trading in the Old South*, 314.

obtain twice the legal rate of interest on money, even though the legal rate was 8 per cent.[38] The region was too young to have accumulated much ready capital, and its current income from cotton and sugar was insufficient for the real and fancied needs of an expanding economy—the desire of individuals to extend planting operations and the desire of society to secure transportation and other utilities. The most promising way of securing additional capital was to borrow from older societies, giving as security, mortgages on the land and slaves of the Southwest and, as added security, pledging the faith of the states.

The experience of Mississippi illustrates the way in which the Southwest secured capital from the East and Europe. Its first bank, the Bank of the State of Mississippi, was created in 1818. It was a conservatively managed and responsible institution, but its facilities, so it began to be said, were unequal to the needs of the people. In 1830 the state infringed upon its exclusive banking privileges by chartering the Planters' Bank with a capital stock of $3,000,000. Two thirds of the stock was bought by the state with state bonds which were sold within the next three years to Eastern capitalists. Almost at once there was a demand for still another bank, and the demand was sharpened when it became evident that the United States Bank would not be rechartered with a consequent closure of its Mississippi branch.

In 1837 and 1838 the legislature took a greater step by creating the Union Bank with a maximum authorized capital of $15,500,000. Payment for stock was to be by mortgages on the property of stockholders; but as a matter of fact, the mortgages were never delivered to the bank, and its capital was secured by the sale of $5,000,000 of 5 per cent state bonds. In addition to the remarkable expedient of giving the stockholders the right to the profits of the institution without incurring the slightest financial responsibility, there were irregularities in the process of chartering the institution and in the sale of bonds. Most of them found their way into the hands of English investors. The bank was operated in a reckless manner throughout its brief life.[39]

[38] Martineau, *Society in America*, II, 65–66.

[39] Reginald C. McGrane, *Foreign Bondholders and American State Debts* (New York, 1935), 193–99; Benjamin U. Ratchford, *American State Debts* (Durham, 1941), 90, 105–107.

Alabama, Arkansas, Florida, and Louisiana followed much the same course as Mississippi. Louisiana plunged deepest, but with better excuse because its economic orbit included the commercial activities of the city of New Orleans as well as the sugar and cotton plantations of the state. The first of its land banks was the Bank of Louisiana, chartered in 1824 with a capital of $4,000,000. Three years later the Consolidated Association of the Planters of Louisiana was chartered with a capital that was set at $2,500,000. In 1832 the Union Bank was created with a capital of $7,000,000; and the following year the Citizens Bank, with a capital of $12,000,000.[40] Alabama in 1837 borrowed $7,500,000 to enlarge the capital of the state bank it had created in 1824.[41] The Territory of Florida chartered several banks, among them the Union Bank of Florida, chartered in 1833, with a capital of $3,000,000 raised by the sale of territorial bonds.[42]

In all of these states—Mississippi, Louisiana, Alabama, and Arkansas—and in the Territory of Florida, the pattern of bank expansion was much the same. Most of the capital was supposed to be derived from mortgages on slaves and land; but in practice this obligation was either removed by law or was virtually unenforced. Actually, the capital was raised by the sale of bonds to which the faith of the state was pledged for payment of principal and interest. These bonds were sold chiefly to Eastern, English, and Dutch investors.

It is worth noting that bank capital imported into the Southwest in the 1820's and especially in the 1830's was less than the amount the region spent during this score of years for slaves. A labor system that required vast capital investments left scarcely anything for founding banks or for other public needs.

It is also notable that much of the credit of these Southwestern banks was monopolized by the directors, officials, and their friends. One who was qualified to know the facts stated in 1840 that there were men indebted to Mississippi banks for sums "of from one-half million to one million dollars, who, a few years previous, were not worth one dollar." Under the loose credit system, they had secured

[40] McGrane, *Foreign Bondholders*, 168–76.
[41] Ratchford, *American State Debts*, 81–82.
[42] McGrane, *Foreign Bondholders*, 223–36; Ratchford, *American State Debts*, 111–12.

bank loans to purchase property. Using this property as security for further loans, "from one bank they proceeded to another, extending their credit and increasing their property." [43]

A favorite object of speculation was the public land recently secured from the Indians. Bona fide settlers, local speculators, and agents of Eastern capitalists wanted the best of it, and some of them were able to pay good prices. An agent of the New York and Mississippi Land Company reported in January, 1836, that there were a million dollars for investment at Pontotoc, Mississippi. To keep prices down at government auction sales, noncompeting agreements were sometimes made; purchasers of large tracts would then sell almost at once at advanced prices.[44] A Senate committee charged with investigating alleged frauds in the sale of public land reported in 1835 that "The states of Alabama, Mississippi, and Louisiana have been the principal theatre of speculations and frauds in buying up the public lands, and dividing the most enormous profits between the members of the different companies of speculators." [45]

Inflation of credit, speculation in land and slaves, multiplication of banks, overproduction of cotton, and unsound practices in public and private finance made the Southwest extremely vulnerable to economic shock. Although outside events, such as the destruction of the Bank of the United States, Jackson's Specie Circular, and the unusual foreign demand upon America for specie, brought matters to a crisis, the Southwest had set the stage for its own tragedy.[46]

The shock came in the late 1830's in the form of a great decline in the price of cotton, in curtailment of credit, and in demands for specie in various commercial transactions. From 15 cents a pound in the year 1835, cotton declined 2 cents the following year and another 4 cents the next. While it recovered to 12 cents in 1838, it then dropped below 10 cents and did not return as high as that figure for a decade. For three years during this decade cotton sold

[43] Quoted in Reginald C. McGrane, *The Panic of 1837: Some Financial Problems of the Jacksonian Era* (Chicago, 1924), 25–26.

[44] *Ibid.,* 49–51.

[45] *American State Papers, Public Lands,* VII, 733.

[46] McGrane, *Panic of 1837,* pp. 40–42, 62–64; Ratchford, *American State Debts,* 80–100.

for less than 6 cents a pound.[47] While the great staple of the Southwest was declining in price, creditors began to press their debtors with such constancy that "some of the lawyers had their declarations in *assumpsit* printed by the quire, leaving blanks only for the names of the debtor, creditor and the amounts." [48]

Between the upper and nether millstones of curtailed income and demands for payment of debts, innumerable planters were ground to complete ruin. Others saved something by hard work and economy, and yet others escaped by chicanery and fraud. Some of the Mississippi planters who had bought slaves on credit during the boom years now refused to pay, claiming that their promissory notes were void because the state constitution of 1832 had prohibited the importation of slaves for trade after May 1, 1833. The supreme court of Mississippi supported this view in a series of decisions. Out-of-state traders, to whom Mississippians owed more than three million dollars, brought suit in Federal courts on the ground of diverse citizenship; and the Supreme Court of the United States ruled that the promissory notes were valid.[49] But the supreme court of Mississippi in a subsequent decision refused to change its former position. It was thus possible for a Mississippian to avoid payment to a slave trader of notes entered into after May 1, 1833, if the trader was a resident of Mississippi; but if the trader resided in some other state, the notes were collectible through the Federal courts.[50]

But notes that were collectible in law were often not collectible in fact, for the debtor and his property sometimes disappeared. Many a plantation was deserted during the darkness of a single night. "Every negro, every horse, every mule [would be] spirited away . . . the negro women and children on horses and mules, the men on foot, all in a double-quick march for Texas, then a foreign government. The first object was to get across the county line, the next to cross the Mississippi River, and the next to cross the line of

[47] Gray, *Agriculture in the Southern United States*, II, 1027.

[48] Jehu A. Orr, "A Trip from Houston to Jackson, Miss., in 1845," in Mississippi Historical Society *Publications* (Oxford), IX (1906), 175.

[49] This was the case of Groves *v.* Slaughter, 15 Peters 449 (1841), which was of some importance in the national controversy over slavery. See above, last pages of Chap. X.

[50] For a list of cases and a fuller discussion, see Sydnor, *Slavery in Mississippi*, 166–67.

the Republic of Texas. All this had to be done before the executions could issue and be placed in the hands of the sheriffs of the different counties." [51]

State government met hard times in ways that were equally censurable. With the collapse of mushroom banks, states became liable for bonds that had been issued to secure bank capital, Tennessee and Alabama met their obligations by vigorous measures which included the imposition of heavier taxes. But Mississippi, Arkansas, Florida, and Louisiana defaulted in interest payments in 1841 and 1842, and soon thereafter the first three of these states repudiated their obligations in whole or in part.[52] It is notable that the Panic struck the South with greatest force and was dealt with by more questionable methods in the Southwestern states where there had been less time for the accumulation of political and financial experience.

The Panic of 1837, by wiping out the lush prosperity and exuberant optimism of the Southwest, brought that region down toward the economic level of the Southeast. The Southeast, not having enjoyed enough prosperity before the Panic to be dragged into the upward spiral of the boom, escaped most of the subsequent ill effects. The price of tobacco was not affected as disastrously as the price of cotton, and Virginia had learned something from Edmund Ruffin and other agricultural reformers about how to increase the productivity of the soil.[53] The governor of South Carolina observed in 1840 that "Amid the general pressure of the times we have suffered but little," and his message breathed a confidence, that had been lacking in the state for some years, in the fundamental soundness of an agricultural economy. Instead of suggesting economic or political nostrums, he advised greater diversification on each plantation so that the income from cotton would not have to be spent for things that could be raised on the place.[54] Soon afterward, Ruf-

---

[51] Orr, "A Trip from Houston to Jackson, Miss., in 1845," *loc. cit.*, 176. While these words are from the recollections of an old man, they are well supported by contemporary documents. See, for example, McGrane, *Panic of 1837*, p. 118.

[52] Maryland and four of the free states also defaulted, and Michigan repudiated certain obligations. McGrane, *Foreign Bondholders*, especially pp. 265–66; Ratchford, *American State Debts*, especially p. 98.

[53] Craven, *Edmund Ruffin*, 63–64, 72.

[54] South Carolina *Senate and House Journals*, 1840 (published as one volume), 10–11.

fin was employed to make an agricultural survey of South Carolina.[55]

South Carolina's renewed zeal for agricultural improvement was but a part of a general movement that swept over the South in this period. Between the years 1837 and 1841 state agricultural societies became active in Maryland, South Carolina, Kentucky, Tennessee, Alabama, Mississippi, and Louisiana. Some of them were new; others were revivals of former organizations, for the previous crop, and most of the societies of this crop as well, had a way of dying after one or two meetings. In addition to the state societies, a good many county and local societies were formed. Furthermore, Southern agricultural promoters joined in the establishment of the United States Agricultural Society in 1841. In this same period, dozens of agricultural periodicals were established in the South. Like the societies, few of them lived many years. But in the aggregate, they published much information about agricultural trends and practices, while other information of this sort was published in the newspapers.[56] With the establishment of the *Southern Cultivator* at Augusta in 1843 by William S. and James W. Jones, the lower South acquired an ably edited agricultural journal which soon attained a primacy in the cotton states commensurate with that enjoyed by the *Farmer's Register* in the upper South.

The agricultural societies stirred the state agricultural and geological surveys into greater activity. Some that had been established in previous years continued to operate and publish reports; others were established in the 1840's and 1850's. The emphasis on agricultural subjects in the reports issued by the surveys bore witness to the fact that geology was widely regarded as the handmaid of agriculture rather than as a distinct science.[57] Crusaders for agricultural improvement published information about farm machinery and implements,[58] contour plowing, and ways of preparing the

[55] Edmund Ruffin, *Report of the Commencement and Progress of the Agricultural Survey of South-Carolina, for 1843* (Columbia, 1843), especially pp. 3–4.

[56] Gray, *Agriculture in the Southern United States*, II, 786–89; Blanche Henry Clark, *The Tennessee Yeoman, 1840–1860* (Nashville, 1942), 95–99; Sydnor, *Benjamin L. C. Wailes*, 158–60, 165–68.

[57] Sydnor, "State Geological Surveys in the Old South," in Jackson (ed.), *American Studies in Honor of William Kenneth Boyd*, 94–108.

[58] Gray, *Agriculture in the Southern United States*, II, 792–800; Clark, *Tennessee Yeoman*, 132; Sydnor, *Benjamin L. C. Wailes*, 155, 157.

soil, increasing its fertility, and tending the crops. In some areas, especially in Mississippi, the chief emphasis was upon supplementing the staple crop with foodstuffs and livestock; and there was a considerable importation of blooded sheep, hogs, and bulls. The need for agricultural professorships and agricultural schools was stressed.[59] Among the fads of the period were a revival of enthusiasm for silk production and a more novel interest in the chemical analysis of plants and soils—a zeal which outran the knowledge of the period.[60]

A notable feature of this agricultural improvement movement of the late thirties and early forties was its spread into the Southwest. Here could be found a large number of the state and local societies, and here resided some of the more active of the agricultural leaders. In Mississippi, Dr. Martin W. Philips was practicing and preaching "diversification and the employment of labor-saving devices to permit the planter to raise his supplies and improve his land while still maintaining a normal output of cotton." [61] Thomas Affleck, a Scotchman, came to the same state in the early forties, having previously served as junior editor of the *Western Farmer and Gardner* at Cincinnati. In Mississippi he established a nursery, sought to introduce bookkeeping into plantation management, and entered wholeheartedly into the movement for agricultural improvement.[62] Solon Robinson of New York traveled extensively in the South, and through conversation and the printed page he disseminated information about agricultural practices, societies, and journals.[63] Other agricultural promoters of this period were James M. Garnett of Virginia, Noah B. Cloud of Alabama, William Terrell and Thomas Spalding of Georgia,[64] and the able editors of the *Southern Cultivator.*

The sponsorship of fairs by the agricultural societies was another

[59] Gray, *Agriculture in the Southern United States*, II, 791.

[60] Demaree, *American Agricultural Press*, 66–69.

[61] Gray, *Agriculture in the Southern United States*, II, 781–82.

[62] Wendell H. Stephenson, "A Quarter-Century of a Mississippi Plantation: Eli J. Capell of 'Pleasant Hill,' " in *Mississippi Valley Historical Review*, XXIII (1936–1937), 355–56, n. 3; Sydnor, *Benjamin L. C. Wailes*, 159–60.

[63] Herbert A. Kellar (ed.), *Solon Robinson: Pioneer and Agriculturist* (Indianapolis, 1936), especially II, 115–31, 253–306, 334–68.

[64] E. Merton Coulter, *Thomas Spalding of Sapelo* (University, La., 1940), especially pp. 87–127.

innovation of this period. One was held at Macon, Georgia, in 1831. Ten years later twelve county fairs were reported for a single year in Tennessee, and fairs became popular and well attended elsewhere in the South.[65] They served to get the agricultural movement before the people; to make it a thing of sheep, hogs, cotton bolls, and farm machinery rather than of academic disquisitions; and they added a cheerful, friendly, and sociable element to the reform movement that had been born of hard times and depression.[66]

Through these years when the South was seeking to improve agriculture and was giving some thought to the development of other kinds of economic activity, it was also sharing in the movement that swept the United States for the improvement of transportation facilities. The South Atlantic states had made a serious effort in this direction around the year 1820, but the roads and especially the canals that were then built at considerable expense had proved, in most instances, useless. A new attack upon the transportation problem was launched in the 1830's. Georgia and the Carolinas concentrated upon railroads while Virginia and Maryland divided their support between canals and railroads.

South Carolina was a pioneer in experimenting with the newer method of transporting men and goods. In January, 1828, the South Carolina Canal and Railroad Company was chartered to connect Charleston with Hamburg, which was a South Carolina village across the Savannah River from Augusta, Georgia. The chief objective of the promoters was to rejuvenate the trade and commerce of Charleston, and to make that city, in the words of these enthusiasts, "the commercial emporium of the South and West." More specifically, they planned to secure to Charleston the wholesale supply trade of the towns that had grown up along the fall line in the state, and they expected it to bring to Charleston a large share of the upcountry Georgia and South Carolina commerce that had hitherto gone by water to Savannah.

In November, 1830, an engine made at West Point, New York,

<hr />

[65] Gray, *Agriculture in the Southern United States*, II, 785-86; Wayne C. Neely, *The Agricultural Fair*, in Columbia University *Studies in the History of American Agriculture*, II (New York, 1935), 76-82.

[66] An excellent description of a fair, written by J. F. H. Claiborne, is in *The Southern Planter* (Natchez, Washington, Miss.), I (1842), No. 4, pp. 13-14. Part of it is reprinted in Sydnor, *Benjamin L. C. Wailes*, 153.

began to operate upon the partly built line. This road was not only "the first to use an American-made locomotive, but it was the first definitely to replace horses with locomotives." [67] In October, 1833, the entire line had been finished from Charleston to Hamburg, a distance of 136 miles. At the time, it was the longest railroad in the world. Its cost, including seven locomotives, forty-six cars of various kinds, and some other properties, amounted to slightly more than $900,000. Most of the stock had been subscribed by civic-minded citizens of Charleston, $100,000 had been lent by the state for seven years without interest, and some of the landowners along the route had permitted the free use of their land and timber.[68]

The equipment and management of the road reflected the primitive stage of railroad construction. The rails were of wood surfaced with strap iron; the track was carried over low places on piles and trestling instead of on earth fills; and the entire mode of construction was as economical as possible with the consequence that much of the road had to be rebuilt almost at once.[69] A traveler of the early 1840's found his coach to be "very novel, very ugly, but not uncomfortable . . . [it] is nothing more than a huge cask—built in the usual way, and girded round with iron hoops—about ten or eleven feet diameter in the middle, thirty or thirty-five long, painted red, and the hoops black, with a large bunghold in the top, to give light and air. The passengers inside are seated in rows, facing each other, with an avenue down the centre, and a door at each end." [70]

According to rules and regulations published in 1837, trains were scheduled to leave Charleston at six in the morning and to arrive

---

[67] Meyer, *Transportation in the United States*, 310. Other important references on the railroad are Samuel M. Derrick, *Centennial History of South Carolina Railroad* (Columbia, 1930), and Phillips, *Transportation in the Eastern Cotton Belt*, 132–62.

[68] Meyer, *Transportation in the United States*, 424.

[69] *Ibid.*, 425.

[70] Thomson, *Tradesman's Travels*, 43. Thomson was usually a sober and careful commentator on his travel experiences, but he could not resist a "tall tale" about dining facilities on this road. "At some places," he wrote, "such as at Aiken, on the South Carolina Railroad, where the train can be seen for many miles, when there is an extra number of passengers, a signal is made to the clever and indefatigable Mrs. Schwats, who, *it is said*, can kill and cook a dozen chickens in ten minutes; but the chickens are as well up to the trick as she is, for no sooner do the cars make their appearance than they go scampering off in all directions, too sensible of the fate that would await them, on falling into the hands of the active old Dutch lady on such an occasion!" *Ibid.*, 44.

at Hamburg at five-thirty in the afternoon after stops for breakfast and the noon meal. The fare for the 136-mile trip was $6.75. Between intermediate stations the fare was calculated at five cents a mile.[71]

In 1835 the gross income of the road amounted to $249,754, and in 1839 to $422,842.[72] To the stockholders it was proving a profitable investment and to the city of Charleston it was bringing increased commercial activity and improved real-estate values. Perhaps the prosperity that was general in the United States in the middle 1830's was partly responsible for the profitableness of the road. Many Charlestonians interpreted the signs of the times as being auspicious for new ventures, and in 1836 they secured a charter from the South Carolina legislature for the Louisville, Cincinnati and Charleston Railroad to connect Charleston with the Ohio Valley. Charters were eventually secured from North Carolina, Tennessee, and Kentucky. Estimates of the cost ranged from $11,000,000 to $19,000,000.

Robert Y. Hayne, the president of the company, was the champion of the ambitious plan to penetrate the mountains by rail. Calhoun also desired to link Charleston with the West, but, believing that the engineering and financial difficulties in Hayne's plan were too great, he preferred an extension of the Charleston and Hamburg line south of the mountains through Georgia and thence to Memphis. Both men had political as well as economic ends in view. Hayne anticipated strengthening the political as well as the commercial ties between the Southeast and the Ohio Valley; Calhoun was seeking to strengthen the bond between the eastern and western parts of the lower South.

Amid expressions of unbounded optimism about the future growth and prosperity of Charleston, Hayne's plan was adopted. As a preliminary step, the Louisville, Cincinnati and Charleston Railroad purchased the South Carolina Canal and Railroad Company and began building a branch toward Columbia, South Carolina, with a view to eventually extending the line to Cincinnati. But the work progressed no farther west than Columbia, with short

71 Daniel J. Dowling, *The Charleston Directory, and Annual Register, for 1837 and 1838* (Charleston, 1837), advertisements, p. 24.

72 *Census of the City of Charleston, South Carolina, for the Year 1848* (Charleston, 1849), 169–70.

spurs to neighboring South Carolina towns. The financial stringency of the times, the scant support of Tennessee and Kentucky, and differences of opinion in South Carolina brought the work to a standstill. In 1843 the company was reorganized as the South Carolina Railroad Company.[73]

While the ambitious planning of South Carolina was coming to grief, its neighbor to the south was carrying toward completion one of the most notable programs of railroad building in the United States in this period. By the year 1846, 442 miles of railroad had been built in the state of Georgia. By 1850 lines had been built from Augusta to Atlanta, from Savannah to Atlanta, and from Atlanta to Chattanooga on the Tennessee River. Georgia thus became the first of the South Atlantic states to establish railroad connections with a tramontane waterway. Its success was due in part to its favorable location on the southern flank of the mountains and in part to the excellent management of the Central of Georgia Railroad and Canal Company, which was the most important of the Georgia companies. In one other respect the experience of Georgia was unusual. In contrast to the commercial spirit and financial resources of river and seaport towns, which were usually responsible for railroad building in this period, the principal force in Georgia was the striving of the interior towns for transportation outlets.[74]

North Carolina, lacking a major port along its coast, was under a great disadvantage in developing a major avenue of commerce from the Atlantic to the West. Only two railroad lines of any importance were built in the state before 1850. One began at Wilmington, the other at Raleigh, and they converged at Weldon near the Virginia boundary at the rapids of the Roanoke River.[75] Weldon was also a junction of some importance for Virginia railroads. One line went eastward to Portsmouth on Chesapeake Bay. A more important route was northward through Richmond and Fredericksburg to Aquia Landing on the Potomac where boats picked up the traffic and carried it on to Washington. Other Virginia railroads of

[73] Derrick, *History of South Carolina Railroad*, 128–89; Albert L. Kohlmeier, *The Old Northwest as the Keystone of the Arch of American Federal Union* (Bloomington, Ind., 1938), 22–30; Theodore D. Jervey, *Robert Y. Hayne and His Times* (New York, 1909), 383 ff.

[74] Meyer, *Transportation in the United States*, 438–57.

[75] *Ibid.*, 464–67; Ratchford, *American State Debts*, 87; Boyd, *North Carolina: The Federal Period*, 230.

some importance connected Richmond with Charlottesville and Winchester with Harpers Ferry.

Virginia's commitment to the project for connecting Richmond with the Ohio River by canal militated against extensive railroad building in the state. In 1835 the James River and Kanawha Company was transformed into a private corporation, but the state at once subscribed $2,000,000 to it over and above its previous expenditures on this project.[76] It thus became the major stockholder, and it continued to dominate the undertaking. The city of Richmond was also a heavy subscriber and was the chief promotional center. By 1840 the canal had been pushed up the James to Lynchburg, and soon afterward it was extended somewhat farther to the west. But three years later this Virginia attempt to establish a water connection with the Ohio Valley collapsed. More than $7,000,000, chiefly of state funds, had been spent with little profit except to the planters of the James River Valley. Western Virginians continued to be dissatisfied, Richmond had failed to become an outlet for the trade of the Ohio Valley, the state debt had been much increased, and Virginia, in proportion to its wealth and its needs, had fallen behind in the construction of railroads.[77]

Maryland, like Virginia, divided its resources between canals and railroads, and its planning was confused by local rivalries. The merchants of Baltimore wanted a canal northward to the Susquehanna to tap the waterways extending into New York state and westward toward Pittsburgh. Opened in 1840, this canal proved a strong stimulus to Baltimore commerce. The southern counties supported the plans of the Chesapeake and Ohio Company for a canal along the Potomac River to bring the produce of the valley, and perhaps someday the goods of the Ohio country, to deep water at Georgetown. But the commercial interests of Baltimore, dreading the loss of their western trade to Georgetown, developed the rival plan of building a railroad westward from Baltimore into the same area that the canal was to serve.[78]

The Baltimore and Ohio Railroad was chartered in 1827. Four years later it reached Frederick, a distance of seventy miles from

76 See Chap. IV.

77 Dunaway, *History of the James River and Kanawha Company*, 90–122, 132, 138–43, 147, 151.

78 Meyer, *Transportation in the United States*, 222–25, 266–69.

Baltimore, and in the same year it made its first successful attempt at using a locomotive. Hitherto it had relied upon horses with some use of stationary engines. After troublesome controversies with the canal company, Harpers Ferry was reached in December, 1834. In 1842 the railroad reached Cumberland and the near-by coal mines, but there was a disheartening delay before westward progress was resumed. It reached the Ohio River at Wheeling in 1853.[79] Meanwhile, the Chesapeake and Ohio Canal, trailing behind the railroad, eventually reached Cumberland.[80]

The first, and for some years the longest, railroad west of the Alleghenies was completed from Lexington to Frankfort, Kentucky, in 1835. A few years later it was extended to Louisville, making a total distance of ninety-eight miles. The novelty of some of its features was notable even in this experimental period of railroad construction. Its first cars held only four persons; later models were two-decker affairs, the top story for men and the lower for women and children; its first locomotive, built by a Lexington mechanic, had two projecting beams with hickory brooms attached for sweeping the tracks.[81]

There was virtually no railroad construction in Tennessee before 1850 although several companies were chartered and the legislature, in 1836, authorized the governor to purchase one third of the stock of any company incorporated to build railroads or macadamized roads. Over a quarter of a million dollars were invested within the next year.[82]

Most of the early railroads in the lower Mississippi Valley were short lines radiating inland from river-port towns. Seven or eight were built out from New Orleans in the 1830's, forming "a sort of street-car system extending from 1 to 8 miles into the surrounding country." [83] Other short lines were built in Louisiana from Port Hudson to Clinton and from St. Francisville inland to Woodville, Mississippi. In January, 1837, the Mississippi towns of Natchez, Vicksburg, Grand Gulf, and Port Gibson had built or were planning to build short inland lines to bring cotton to their water

[79] Ibid., 397–410.   [80] Ibid., 266–69.   [81] Ibid., 467–69.

[82] Ibid., 470–71; Stanley J. Folmsbee, Sectionalism and Internal Improvements in Tennessee, 1796–1845 (Philadelphia, 1939), 126.

[83] Meyer, Transportation in the United States, 477.

fronts.[84] The road east from Vicksburg was the only one to attain importance. By 1840 it reached Jackson, forty-seven miles inland; and within the next decade plans were formulated to extend it farther eastward toward Montgomery, Alabama. The only other Alabama road worthy of note before the middle of the century was built from Tuscumbia to Decatur, around the shoals in the Tennessee River.[85]

In Texas there was considerable interest in a proposed railroad from Harrisburg to Houston, but nothing was accomplished until the 1850's. In Florida a twenty-three-mile railroad was completed in 1835 from Tallahassee to the Bay of St. Mark's, or Apalachee.[86]

Except in Virginia and Maryland, Southern canal building was virtually ended by the year 1830. By 1840 some 455 miles of canals had been built in the South Atlantic states, and 68 miles had been built west of the Alleghenies and south of the Ohio River. But this was a small accomplishment in comparison with what had been done in the North. Three Northern states, Pennsylvania, Ohio, and New York, each had built more miles of canals than had been built in all of the slave states.[87]

In respect to railroads the slave states, despite their pioneering efforts, also trailed the North. On January 1, 1848, some 2,012 miles, slightly more than one third of the national total, were reported in operation in the South. The five coastal states from Maryland to Georgia had each built more than 200 miles; none other of the slave states had built as much as 100 miles. Georgia led with 602 miles. Virginia was next with 406 miles. New York, Pennsylvania, and Massachusetts exceeded Georgia in railroad mileage at this date.[88]

[84] Woodville *Republican,* January 7, 1837.

[85] Meyer, *Transportation in the United States,* 472–75.

[86] *Ibid.,* 479.

[87] The canal mileage of the South Atlantic states in 1840 was: Maryland, 136; Virginia, 216; North Carolina, 13; South Carolina, 52; Georgia, 28—a total of 445 miles. The mileage of the three highest Northern states was: Pennsylvania, 954; Ohio, 744; New York, 640. The figures for the other slave states were: Kentucky, 2; Alabama, 52; Louisiana, 14; with none reported for Florida, Tennessee, Mississippi, and Arkansas. The canal mileage for the nation in 1840 was 3,326. Meyer, *Transportation in the United States,* 573.

[88] The railroad mileage reported for the South Atlantic states as of January 1, 1848, was: Maryland, 253; Virginia, 406; North Carolina, 255; South Carolina, 204, Georgia, 602—a total of 1,720 miles. The corresponding figures of the four highest Northern states were: New York, 744; Pennsylvania, 721; Massachusetts, 705; Michigan, 264. The

Although state governments seldom received dividends on their transportation investments, many of the people of the South were greatly benefited by the investment of public funds in steamboats. True enough, one could not travel across the South from east to west or, except on the Mississippi River, from north to south without numerous complications and discomforts.

But the South had little need for long trunk lines. Its primary need was to get its upland staples down to the port towns, and the businessmen of these towns were deeply interested in seeing that this need was met. In consequence, most of the transportation improvements were short lines. The commercial rivalry of the towns worked against connecting these lines into a far-flung system, and the economic sameness of the region created little need for such a system. The staples of the region were destined for transatlantic and Northern markets; no part of the South needed much of the product of any other part.

The North, in contrast, was developing a complex network of canals and railroads for exchanging the various products of its factories and farms. This system contributed mightily to the growth of cities and to the evolution of a complex, interrelated economic society that was increasingly different from the old-fashioned, staple-crop agricultural order that prevailed through much of the South. Furthermore, this expanding transportation system was binding the Northwest closer to the Eastern states while divorcing it from its earlier alliance with the South. Transportation developments in the first half of the nineteenth century increased the differences between slave and free states and contributed to the isolation of the South.

---

figures for the other slave states that had railroads in operation on January 1, 1848, were: Kentucky, 28; Mississippi, 95; Alabama, 92; Louisiana, 51; Florida, 26—a total of 292 miles. The railroad mileage of the nation at this date was 5,589. *Ibid.*, 572.

CHAPTER XII

MOVEMENT TOWARD POLITICAL DEMOCRACY

S ELDOM if ever have the governments of the Southern states been subjected to more vigorous domestic criticism than during the 1820's or to more thoroughgoing constitutional reformation than during the 1830's. The principal goal was a broader and more equitable distribution of political power, and this goal was in large measure gained. While there were doubtless some threads connecting this phase of Southern history with contemporary reform movements in the North and in England, the more obvious roots ran back into the local situation in the South.

Some of the reformers were liberals who believed in democracy and sought its extension for humanitarian and philosophical rather than for personal reasons, others were poor men who were disfranchised by property-holding or taxpaying prerequisites to voting, and yet others were residents of the upcountry and of certain cities like Baltimore that were underrepresented in the state legislatures. Of these groups, the politically underprivileged of the South Atlantic upcountry were the most energetic champions of constitutional reform.

The chief cause of dissatisfaction was their inability, due to underrepresentation in state government, to secure the laws that they wanted. This dissatisfaction was of long standing, but it was becoming stronger as the western population grew while its representation remained fixed, and as the western spirit and ambition expanded. Furthermore, control over government was becoming more important because the powers of government were increasing. The depression that began in 1819 drove home the lesson that political power led to economic advantage. In the attempts to secure relief by stay laws and by banking and paper-money experiments, the debtors sometimes succeeded and sometimes failed; but in either case it was transparently clear that economic salvation might be worked out with votes. Such being the case, no man wanted his vote to be diminished to a small fraction of its worth by a constitutional clause.

Similar lessons were taught by increased state activity in transportation improvements. The west favored an ambitious program because its need was great. The east, with better natural facilities for trade and commerce, was loath to spend huge sums for canals and highways, particularly since it feared that its greater wealth would have to supply the lion's share of the taxes. Furthermore, the east had local projects to match those of the west. Rightly or wrongly, the upcountry believed that its interests were sacrificed; that its products were kept from market by the political dominance of the eastern counties.

Likewise, there was rivalry between the western and eastern parts of the states over whether the state should support common schools or colleges, and over the location of colleges, hospitals, asylums, and other public institutions. In some of the younger states the location of the state capital was still a sectional issue. In respect to taxes, there were quarrels over whether to place the heavier burden upon slaves who were held chiefly in the east, or upon land which was the chief form of western property. In national politics the westerner found that his power was reduced because of eastern dominance in the legislature which elected United States Senators and constituted the caucus. Finding himself thwarted at every turn by the political subordination of his region, the westerner increasingly translated his economic, social, and political grievances into hostility to the existing system of state and local government.[1]

Reformers were able to point to corruption as well as to undemocratic features in government. In Kentucky, for example, the office of sheriff was sometimes farmed out. The constitution required the county court to nominate two of its senior members for the sheriffship, one of whom the governor was required to commission. But in order to secure the rewards of office without incurring its burdens

[1] A condensed and sprightly version of the conflict in Virginia between those who lived on opposite sides of the Blue Ridge is in [James K. Paulding], *Letters from the South, Written during an Excursion in the Summer of 1816* (New York, 1817), I, 111–15.

and responsibilities, the court's first choice sometimes informed the governor that he waived his rights provided the commission was issued to a person whom he designated and from whom he had collected $1,000 or $2,000. Thus a man who was not a magistrate became sheriff contrary to the plain provisions of the constitution.[2]

A more universal abuse in county government was the multiplication of justices past the needs of the county. Men sought the office for its prestige and power, and the courts created new members for personal and political considerations. As a result, county governing bodies became ridiculously large, often consisting of forty or fifty men, and sometimes of as many as ninety. Obviously, this was too many for the efficient management of county business, and it was far too many to function as a court of law. Men who knew little or no law were made justices, and judicial decisions of the courts were all-too-frequently founded on whim or so-called common sense rather than upon law.[3] But the greatest objection to the county courts was their undemocratic character. Naturally enough, men believed that the unpopular decisions and actions of the courts could be reversed if only there were more democracy, and to inject more democracy into local government it was necessary in most states to make constitutional revisions.

The desires of the reformers, and their usual fate before 1830, are illustrated in a resolution presented in the North Carolina senate in 1819 by Duncan Cameron of Orange County. He proposed a number of reforms, among them that the governor and other state officers and the sheriffs should be popularly elected, and that representation in the senate and house of representatives should be made "conformable to the principles of Republican Governments" instead of remaining "greatly unequal and highly unjust." The senate, after striking out one after another of Cameron's proposals, finally tabled the entire resolution by a vote of 36 to 23.

This vote deserves close examination. Every one of the twenty-three who wanted change represented the western counties; their thirty-six opponents were all from the eastern counties. The division followed the eastern edge of Person, Orange, Chatham, Moore, and Richmond counties. There is another fact of great significance

[2] Lexington *Kentucky Gazette*, December 2, 1824.
[3] *Report of the Revisors of the Code of Virginia*, I, 266 n.; and Chap. II above.

about this vote. The twenty-three defeated western senators represented a white population of 223,000; the larger number of victorious easterners represented only 173,000 white persons. However, the easterners represented a somewhat larger total population, for there were 311,000 persons, slave as well as free, in the eastern counties as against 284,000 in the western. On the basis of total population, the eastern counties were somewhat overrepresented; on the basis of white population, they were greatly overrepresented.[4]

Except for minor differences, the other South Atlantic states were like North Carolina. Their western citizens wanted constitutional revision; the eastern counties, being strong through overrepresentation, obstructed the march of democracy.

The defensive position of the easterners was strong. Standing behind constitutional ramparts and possessing political experience, they sought to identify the established order with ancient traditions and accepted values. When the citizens of Baltimore asked for legislative representation in proportion to their numbers, the rural conservatives scorned them as "the Merchants, the Bank Speculators, the Lottery Office keepers, the Foreigners, and the Mob of Baltimore," while boasting of "the honour, the dignity and independence of the *Cultivators of the Soil.*" [5] A Baltimorean, so it was said, "can climb to the top of the *new Shot Tower,* and overlook, at one sweep of the eye, *seven thousand voters,* rich and poor, old and young, lame, halt and blind, all of whom may put their ballots in the box in less time than an old farmer could saddle and bridle his horse, to ride off ten miles or more to the polls; and should the election, which lasts but one day, happen on a rainy one, Baltimore city would counterbalance the voters of *half the State of Maryland.*" [6] It was a contest of *"Baltimore* against *the State! A Populace against the People!"* [7]

Property qualifications for voting and overrepresentation of the wealthy eastern counties were defended in good British style by

4 North Carolina *Senate Journal,* 1819, pp. 40–41, 44; and, for population statistics, *Compendium of the Ninth Census,* 1870.

5 Annapolis *Maryland Gazette and Political Intelligencer,* September 23, 1819.

6 *Ibid.,* December 18, 1823.

7 *Ibid.,* January 29, 1824. The country "People" won this contest which was over a proposal to choose Presidential electors by general ticket.

asserting that it was only proper for men of wealth to have much weight in political affairs. Analogies were drawn between the position of the eastern counties in the state and of the Southern states in the nation. How, it was asked, could Southerners expect to count slaves in Congressional apportionments—and the three-fifths clause had often been under Northern fire [8]—if they were to disregard the slave population in state legislative apportionments?

As tension between North and South increased, the Southern conservatives sometimes charged their upcountry opponents with accepting and spreading Yankee errors. A conservative delegate in the Virginia Constitutional Convention of 1829–1830 affirmed that "if any plague originate in the North, it is sure to spread to the South and to invade us sooner or later: the influenza—the small-pox —the varioloid—the Hessian fly—the Circuit Court system—Universal Suffrage—all come from the North—and they always cross above the falls of the great rivers." [9]

One of the arguments evolved in these local quarrels was later to do yeoman service in debates over the nature of the Federal government. When John C. Calhoun presented his theory of the concurrent majority he might have used as his text the words of a Maryland conservative. Writing in the year 1819—long before Calhoun became a sectionalist—it was affirmed in Maryland *that government alone is securely free, where the rights and interests of all the parts are equally well guarded against the encroachment of the others.*" [10] Ten years later, in the Virginia Constitutional Convention, former President Madison declared: "In republics, the great danger is, that the majority may not sufficiently respect the rights of the minority. . . . The only effectual safeguard to the rights of the minority, must be laid in such a basis and structure of the Government itself, as may afford . . . a defensive authority." [11]

Finally the conservatives argued, and with some reason, that the

[8] Simpson, "The Political Significance of Slave Representation, 1787–1821," *loc. cit.,* 315–42.

[9] *Proceedings and Debates of the Virginia State Constitutional Convention, of 1829–30* (Richmond, 1830), 407.

[10] Annapolis *Maryland Gazette and Political Intelligencer,* September 9, 1819.

[11] *Proceedings and Debates of the Virginia State Constitutional Convention, of 1829–30,* pp. 537–38. Similar statements can be found *ibid.,* 63–79, and in Jesse T. Carpenter, *The South as a Conscious Minority, 1789–1861* (New York, 1930), Chap. IV.

march of democracy ought to be halted until the voters could be educated. As Governor Daniel Martin of Maryland said when advocating public education, "If there be danger in popular elections, as has been conceived by some, the sure correction is to be found in moral instruction." [12] It ought to be said to the credit of the conservatives that the larger appropriations for education in the 1820's were made in the states where their control was strongest.

The weak point in the armor of the conservatives was that they were defending an undemocratic form of government in a day when democracy was an accepted good. Some of them met the issue squarely by denying the validity of the democratic dogma,[13] but usually they fought in silence, relying upon their power rather than upon appeals to reason. The governors of the South Atlantic states, who were the capstones of the old order, scarcely mentioned the much-agitated question of constitutional revision in their messages to the state legislatures, though they discussed at length many other current questions. With the established order of government on their side, the conservatives needed only to guard the ramparts and repel assaults. It would have been fatal to their power in Maryland, Virginia, and North Carolina for new counties to spring up in the west and reverse the balance of power in the legislature. But eastern politicians were careful. Only five counties, all toward the west, were established in these states in the ten-year period that began in 1820 whereas in the other seven Southern states, where the number of counties had little political significance, eighty-seven were created in the same decade.

The disfranchised and underrepresented advocates of a more complete democracy could draw upon the full arsenal of democratic dogma and arguments. But these weapons, though intellectually impressive, were ineffective against a foe that was more disposed to use its power than to argue. Luckily, they did not have to rely entirely upon appeals to reason. They found a few allies in easterners whose impulses and theories made them espouse the cause of political underdogs even though they themselves were tied to the conservatives by personal and economic interests.

12 Message of December 30, 1829, in Maryland *Senate Journal*, 1829–1830, p. 12.

13 William G. Bean, "Anti-Jeffersonianism in the Ante-Bellum South," in *North Carolina Historical Review*, XII (1935), 103–24.

Furthermore, western radicals had an advantage over eastern conservatives in the use of novel techniques for influencing voters and for getting into office. The contrast between the old and the new ways of getting votes was well described by a Tennessean. Writing of conditions in the early part of the nineteenth century, he said: "if a candidate for office had left his home to traverse the country and solicit votes, instead of securing his election he would most certainly have occasioned his defeat, no matter what his personal popularity might have been. Nor would this have been the only consequence of his imprudent temerity; he would have met with an insult from every individual whose vote he solicited, and in all probability would have been knocked down before he had solicited the suffrages of twenty men. But now [about the year 1840], how changed are the feelings, manners and customs of the people in relation to this subject! A candidate for office in these enlightened days . . . is not only permitted to electioneer for votes, but if he does not do so—nay, if he is not very industrious, and also, very skilful in the science of flattery—he is certain to be defeated." [14]

This practice of vigorously and brazenly soliciting votes was no new thing in history, but it was breaking forth with new virulence in the South. The South Atlantic states had seen very little of it during the first quarter of the nineteenth century. Close-knit oligarchies of county courts, state legislatures, and caucuses had nominated candidates and sponsored them before the voters while the candidates themselves maintained an aloof and almost reluctant attitude, often alleging that they had entered the race only on the insistence of their friends. In Kentucky and Tennessee, where universal manhood suffrage was closely approached, where elective offices were numerous, and where party discipline was imperfect, candidates began at an early date to nominate themselves, to acclaim their own virtues (since they had no political patrons to do it for them), and to go after the votes with all the energy and ingenuity they could muster. These practices of an active and turbulent democracy became more evident in the seaboard South during the Presidential campaign of 1824 when the Republican organization was shattered by quarrels among its leaders and party

14 J. W. M. Breazeale, *Life as It Is* . . . (Knoxville, 1842), 152–53.

discipline dissolved. Candidates began to nominate themselves in unorthodox ways, and most of them were compelled to appeal straight to the voters because they had no established political machine to work for them. For the first time in a dozen years, votes were sought and votes had influence in a Presidential election; and the voters were greatly stirred and exhilarated by the experience.

In using the new technique of vote getting, the old political leaders of the Southeast were at a disadvantage. They knew their way around in county courts, in the legislature, and in party caucuses, but they had not had to rely on demagogic speechmaking and personal canvassing to control the plain folk, and they showed little skill in acquiring the new arts. In contrast, some of the reformers quickly adopted and developed these arts, and they used them to lure plain people away from their old masters, forging something of a political army out of the hitherto unorganized mass of discontented men.

Generally speaking, the contestants in the struggle for constitutional change were closely matched. On the one side were custom, wealth, experience, constitutional advantages, and control over the instruments of government; on the other were the weight of numbers, hope for a new day, the spirit of change, and threats of extralegal action if reform could not be won by orderly processes. It should be said to the credit of the conservatives that they knew when to surrender; they did not suppress the champions of more radical democracy to such an extent that they resorted to violence and revolution.[15]

In a few states the conservatives held their power unimpaired; more often they were compelled to compromise; and in some states the radicals won a complete victory. Where the revolution ran its full course, voting and officeholding qualifications were ended, the ballot was lengthened particularly by making the governor an elective officer, governors' councils were abolished, legislatures were reapportioned, democracy was introduced in county government, and judges were given limited instead of life terms

[15] Fletcher M. Green, "Democracy in the Old South," in *Journal of Southern History*, XII (1946), 12–13.

of office. In a few instances they were subjected to popular election.[16]

Between 1830 and 1837 four new state constitutions were adopted in the South. One was the constitution of the new state of Arkansas; the other three were revised constitutions adopted in Virginia, Mississippi, and Tennessee. All four were ratified by popular referendums. Maryland and North Carolina made important amendments to their constitutions, and less radical changes were made in several other states either by law or by constitutional amendment. All of these revisions and amendments provided for more democracy in state government.

Alabama, the most democratic of the Southern states in 1819, found little to change in its form of government except to reduce the terms of office of judges from life to six years.[17] By the end of the 1830's its extreme democracy ceased to be unique. Several of its neighbors moved up to its position by small steps or great, depending on how much of privilege their constitutions had contained; and others came close to complete democracy though they did not go the whole way. Tennessee, by its constitution of 1834, totally divorced property from voting and, what was more important, made county government thoroughly democratic. Thereafter, justices of the peace, constables, sheriffs, trustees, and registers were popularly elected for limited terms. The most revolutionary change in any Southern state was made in Mississippi, which became, by its constitution of 1832, the most democratic state in the whole South. Universal manhood suffrage was established, property qualifications for voting were abolished, the state treasurer and the state auditor became elective officers, and the undemocratic county courts were replaced by boards of police whose five members, to-

16 The changes themselves are mostly embedded in the new constitutions and constitutional amendments, which may be conveniently consulted in Thorpe (comp.), *Federal and State Constitutions*. The journals of the constitutional conventions throw much light on the alignment of the opposing forces as well as on the array of arguments. Other important sources are contemporary newspapers and a few files of private letters, such as the Campbell Papers, which illuminate the Virginia Convention of 1829–1830 and the Tennessee Convention of 1834.

17 Amendment of 1830. In this discussion, it is understood that reform in government was accomplished by constitutional amendment or revision unless specific laws are cited.

gether with nearly all other county officers, were elected for two-year terms. Mississippi went farther into democracy than any other Southern state by granting to the people the right to elect all their judges, even the three members of the High Court of Errors and Appeals, for limited terms of office.[18] Another state joined the ranks of democracy when Texas entered the Union in 1845. As a republic it had already employed most of the democratic devices of government under its constitution of 1836.

Thus, instead of the single state of Alabama, there came to be before the middle of the century five states in which government was thoroughly democratic; and most of the change was brought about in the first half of the 1830's. In each of these states—Alabama, Mississippi, Tennessee, Arkansas, and Texas—the governor was popularly elected, there was universal manhood suffrage, legislative apportionment in both houses was based on white population, with provision for periodic reapportionments, and county government was democratic.

In three other states, all in the lower South, democracy was closely approximated. Georgia made its governorship an elective office in 1824.[19] Subsequently it abolished all property qualifications for officeholding though tax payment was retained as a prerequisite for voting. No great change was made in the apportionment of seats in the legislature. In the lower house, Federal population was to serve as the basis (with provision for periodic reapportionment), but no county was to have more than two representatives nor less than one; in the upper house each county was given equal representation.[20] Florida entered the Union with a constitution that was about as democratic as any of the day except for the retention of the undemocratic county court and for the fact that apportionment in both houses was according to Federal population. However, local govern-

[18] The advocates of this clause were known in the convention as "whole hogs"; those who favored electing the lesser judges and appointing superior judges were the "half hogs"; while the "aristocrats" preferred that all judges should be appointed. Stephen Duncan to Levin Wailes, September 14, 1832, in Wailes Papers (Mississippi Department of Archives and History, Jackson), Ser. N, No. 30.

[19] The law making this change was enacted in 1824; the first popular gubernatorial election was in 1825.

[20] Constitutional amendments of 1824, 1835, 1840, 1843, and 1847.

ment was made democratic in 1845.[21] In that same year Louisiana adopted a constitution which abolished property qualifications for office and ended tax payment as a prerequisite for voting. As for legislative apportionment, white population was made the basis for the lower house while senatorial seats were divided according to the whole population. Fifteen years earlier the police jury had been made entirely elective by excluding the appointed parish judge from membership.[22]

Despite some differences among these states—Georgia, Florida, and Louisiana—in all three the governorship was elective, county government was democratic, property qualifications for office were abolished, and legislative seats were to be reapportioned from time to time. These states differed from the five that were more democratic by counting, in various ways, slaves as well as white people in apportioning seats in the legislature; and in one of the three only taxpayers were allowed to vote. But these were minor differences; it seems reasonable to say that state and local government closely approached democracy in these three states as well as in the five previously considered.

Five more states remain to be examined, Kentucky and the four seaboard states above Georgia. None of them instituted democracy in county government during the first half of the century. Two of the five underwent no important change in government during the period under consideration. Kentucky continued to be democratically governed except in its counties, and South Carolina retained without change its highly centralized system in which almost every power was vested in its legislature.

North Carolina, in its lengthy constitutional amendment of 1835, made no important concessions to democracy in respect to the franchise. On the other hand, eastern power was somewhat diminished in the legislature. Equal representation of the counties was ended; instead, seats in the lower house were apportioned among the counties according to their Federal population, and senatorial

---

[21] See Florida's constitution of 1838, and Leslie A. Thompson, *A Manual or Digest of the Statute Law of the State of Florida* (Boston, 1847), 62, 70–71, 126–27. Florida had adhered to the county-court system through its territorial period.

[22] Bullard and Curry (comps.), *New Digest of the Statute Laws of the State of Louisiana*, 647.

apportionment was based on the amount of taxes paid into the state treasury. In both houses there were to be periodic reapportionments. A considerable gain for democracy consisted in taking the power of choosing the governor from the legislature and giving it directly to the voters.

Maryland's governmental reforms, accomplished by constitutional amendment in 1837 and by several important laws, were somewhat similar to those in North Carolina. Federal population was made the basis of apportioning seats in the lower house, with provision for periodic reapportionments; but in the senate each county and the city of Baltimore were assigned one senator. The governorship was made elective, but with a unique proviso: the state was divided into three districts from which, in rotation, the governor was to be chosen by vote of the people of the whole state. Just as the North Carolina changes strengthened the power of the numerous farmers of the upcountry, so in Maryland the people of Baltimore gained more power than they had earlier enjoyed.

In Virginia the old order retained essential power even though it made several concessions. By the constitution that was framed in the winter of 1829–1830 the suffrage was broadened, but voting continued to depend on property holding or, in certain circumstances, on taxpaying. The east, in spite of some concessions to the west, retained legislative dominance through a complex arrangement. Seats in the two houses were apportioned among the counties in approximate proportion to their white population, and the two houses were to be reapportioned at ten-year intervals; but democracy was hedged about by fixing the total representation of each of the four great areas: Tidewater, Piedmont, Valley, and trans-Allegheny. To the first two divisions, which were east of the Blue Ridge, the constitution allocated 19 of the 32 senators and 78 of the 134 representatives, and it distinctly stated that these totals should not be changed in future apportionments. In short, one county might gain in representation and another might lose, but the east must control both houses as long as this constitution remained in force. When this arrangement was made in 1830, it was not unfair to western Virginia, whose white population was somewhat smaller and whose total population was considerably smaller than that of the east. But before ten years had passed, the white population of the west was much greater than that of the east, and the west continued to grow more rapidly after 1840.[23]

Whenever a state, such as North Carolina, provided for the popular election of its governor while retaining inequalities in legislative apportionment, the governor became a more accurate reflector of state-wide white opinion than the legislature. Theoretically, the governor represented the white voters, whereas the legislature was weighted in favor of the eastern planters—an arrangement which constituted something of a political check between the powers of these economic-social groups and which foreshadowed conflicts between governor and legislature.

Democracy was advanced in those states which ended the autocratic powers of the county courts. In the early 1820's only three of the ten Southern states had had democracy in local government, and those three states contained only one fifth of the counties of the South. By the middle of the century eight of the thirteen states of the South—and those eight contained three fifths of the Southern counties—let the voters of each county elect their petty rulers.

Even in those states where the county court continued to be undemocratic, its powers were sometimes diminished. The choice of constables and sheriffs was taken from the North Carolina courts and given to the people.[24] The Virginia squires lost the power to appoint school commissioners in 1846.[25] Some of the courts lost judicial as well as appointive powers. In Virginia, judicial power was shifted from county courts to judges who were not members of those bodies.[26] In other states, judicial power was vested in a small minority of the members of the county court. In Tennessee, for instance, each court could elect three of its members who were to "proceed with the trial of the civil and criminal business in the same manner and . . . the same jurisdiction . . . that the justices of the county

[23] The counties in each of the four districts are listed in the constitution of 1829-1830. County populations are presented for every census in the *Compendium of the Ninth Census, 1870*.

[24] In 1838 and 1848, respectively. James Iredell, *A New Digested Manual of the Acts of the General Assembly of North Carolina* (Raleigh, 1851), 114, 360.

[25] Historical Records Survey, *Inventory of the County Archives of Virginia, No. 21. Chesterfield County*, 24, 124.

[26] *Ibid.*, 25-26. This change was made by an act of 1831 passed under authority granted in the constitution of 1830.

courts now possess." These three justices were designated as justices of the quorum.[27]

The states that resisted the democratic movement most effectively were South Carolina and Virginia. Both of them retained property qualifications for officeholding, undemocratic local government, eastern dominance in the legislature, and the choice of the governor by the legislature. Furthermore, they possessed economic and social qualities that set them off from their neighbors. As compared with North Carolina, for example, each had a more numerous and powerful body of eastern planters, a larger per cent of slaves, and a stronger tradition of class distinction. Neither had so large a city as Maryland, and they were older and more settled than the states that bordered them to the west and south. The small farmers of western Virginia and South Carolina had less influence in state policies than in the other Southern states.

South Carolina resisted change even more than Virginia. Perhaps this was because its western region of hills and mountains, where the banner of constitutional reform was usually raised, was smaller than in the other South Atlantic states; because its geography was such that cotton culture had spread over most of the state, and thus effected homogeneity in economic interests; because its county governing bodies had less autonomy than in Virginia; and because its political leaders preached the doctrine that internal dissension must be curbed so that the state could present a united front to the nation. But whether or not these are the correct explanations, the fact remains that after 1820 there was little tension between upcountry and seaboard and little demand for constitutional reform in South Carolina.

South Carolina was ruled through an efficient, unified, and highly centralized governmental system that was almost devoid of checks and balances. Men of wealth had much power because of property qualifications for officeholding and because taxes as well as white population were the basis of legislative apportionment.

Before the year 1840 these two states, despite their differences, stood somewhat alone in respect to governmental forms. Previously they were part of a broad plateau of aristocratic government that

[27] Acts of 1823 and 1829, in Haywood and Cobbs, *Statute Laws of the State of Tennessee*, I, 199–200.

had spread over the eastern and upper South; now they stood like two peaks. Time and circumstance had worn down some of the power of the conservatives in the near-by states of Maryland and North Carolina. In them and in Kentucky, government was held above the level of democracy chiefly by the county courts. Farther away, in the eight states of the lower South and Southwest, local government was completely democratic and state government was practically so.

Democracy covered more of the land of the South than formerly. It covered an even greater part of the people of the South, for it was the democratic states that had experienced the greater increases in population and, consequently, in political power. No longer could Virginia and the Carolinas control one half of the Southern votes in the lower house of Congress. Between the apportionments based on the census of 1820 and that of 1850 the number of Virginia's Representatives declined from 22 to 13, of North Carolina's from 13 to 8, and of South Carolina's from 9 to 7. By the latter date, these three states elected only one third of the Representatives of the Southern states. Virginia's share of Southern Representatives had dropped from one fourth to one sixth. The significance of all this is that political power was moving away from the old tobacco kingdom, where aristocratic government had prevailed and where Revolutionary leaders and Founding Fathers had been produced, and was moving into the land of cotton where (excepting South Carolina) democracy was rampant and where the secession movement was to find most of its strength. It must be remembered, however, that the black man was not allowed to share in the democratic movement in any part of the South.

In these politically democratic states society was marked by great inequalities in culture, in wealth, and in intellectual attainments. Inasmuch as political leaders were seldom drawn from the upper brackets of the social and economic hierarchy, tensions and cross-purposes developed. But the result of the conflict was confusion and inaction rather than social revolution or equalization of economic privilege. There was some enthusiasm, it is true, on the part of the new leaders for educating the common people; but too often it happened in the democratic states that almost no state aid was given to education for either the many or the few. Attempts were made to destroy banking monopolies; but attempts to democratize banking and credit facilities were seldom successful, and sometimes a few of the new masters of government enriched themselves while grievously damaging the financial structure and reputation of the state. In brief, political democracy was vigorous, active, and noisy; but the people gained little in return for their votes. To use a phrase attributed to David Crockett: the social program of the democrats was like shearing a pig: big squeal and little wool.

Why was this the case? Perhaps the people, after translating their economic and social grievances into political and governmental programs, lost sight of their original goals. Or perhaps conservatism had been growing in the South: some of the areas that had previously contained much discontentment were now becoming more prosperous, and frontier regions were maturing. Again, the rise of the antislavery movement in some measure checked the Southern reform movement. When the abolitionists began their attack upon slaveholders, one might have expected them to win the support of the Southern radicals who were already trying to destroy the political power of the planters. Instead, the radicals turned to attack abolitionism. They became the loudest defenders of slavery, outdoing even the planters. Henry S. Foote declared that the slaveholders of Mississippi were "more discreet and moderate in spirit and in action than the noisy and, in general unscrupulous *nonslaveholding* champions who assumed to represent them." [28]

Although Southern society was not remade as a result of the democratic revolution, the new fashions in the art of getting office became an accepted part of political life except in the few states like South Carolina where democracy had made little progress. If a man wanted to be elected he had to electioneer for the votes of the people; it was not enough to offer a platform that ought to appeal to the people. Those who refused to get into the rough and tumble of political life were pushed off the field of action. Democratic government seemed to have no need for the great planters, who in everything except government were the men of chief influence. Held to the side lines, some of them scoffed at the follies of the democrats, and most of them gave their attention to private business and social life. They lost the sense of responsibility, which had characterized

[28] Henry S. Foote, *War of the Rebellion* (New York, 1866), 256.

the earlier planters of the Tidewater, for the maintenance of government. Thus, large parts of the South entered a period filled with critical political problems, bereft of a considerable part of its ablest leadership. John H. B. Latrobe of Maryland summarized the trends of the times in a conversation with Alexis de Tocqueville in the year 1831.

"There existed with us formerly," he said, "a race of proprietors dwelling on their estates. They were, on the whole, the most distinguished men of the region; they had received an excellent education, had the manners and ideals of the English upper classes. This class was, in general, a nursery for distinguished men for the legislature and the army. They formed our best statesmen, our finest characters. All the great men of the Revolution, in the South, came from this class. We still have a certain number of these *gentlemen farmers,* but the inheritance law and 'democracy' is killing them, in two or three generations they will have disappeared." [29]

Whether there were men in the South in the 1830's and 1840's of the caliber of Washington, Jefferson, Madison, Charles Carroll, or Edward Rutledge is an unanswerable question, but it is certain that not many of this sort were in places of political power. The odds were against their attaining office except perhaps in South Carolina or Virginia. Elsewhere, political power was going to men who were untainted with aristocracy and who were willing to court the common man.

The transformation in the lower brackets of officeholders was as important as the changes at the top. Before the democratic revolution, those who governed the counties and sat in the legislatures were mostly planters. Nearly all of them were men of substance. They were accustomed to managing men and conducting business, often on a large scale. Those who replaced them in political power were, in many instances, unaccustomed to managing anything, and this fact goes far toward explaining the mistakes of their regime and their failure to accomplish many of the social and economic reforms to which the movement was dedicated. Two contemporary opinions help to explain why so little was done.

[29] Quoted from Pierson, *Tocqueville and Beaumont in America,* 497. The sentences in this quotation have been rearranged without, it is believed, changing the meaning.

"I have always discovered," it was said of Tennessee, "that ignorant men however bold they may be, when before the people, in projecting reforms when electioneering, are usually timid when clothed with power, and they go to put their plans of reform into execution. They are more apt to do too little, than too much at last."[30]

A thoughtful young lawyer of Alabama, who believed that universal suffrage had filled the legislature of his state with ignorant flatterers of the people, was nevertheless convinced that the laws they passed were not so bad as one might expect. His explanation was that "there are always, in our assemblies, some men of talent; from the first days [of the session] these overwhelm the others and dominate business entirely. It's really they who make and discuss the laws; the others vote blindly." [31]

While there was some comfort in reflections such as these, the general tenor of contemporary observation was to the effect that the democratic revolution had brought much evil and little good, and that the chief of its evil results was a decline in the quality of political leadership. Of the Tennessee Constitutional Convention which met in 1834, it was said: "*In confidence,* it will be a hell of a body for so important a trust with some exceptions." [32]

Even though conservatives found solace in thinking that the results were not so bad as they had feared, they were convinced that the quality of Southern political leadership had declined during the first half century of national independence. They were, of course, not without bias in forming this opinion, because they had been forced out of power by the chieftains of the rising democracy. Even so, there seems to have been some validity in their strictures. Men with little or no political experience came into office after the destruction, chiefly during the Presidential campaign of 1824, of the party organization for selecting candidates. Close on the heels of this event, large numbers of men who had never before voted

[30] James Campbell to John Campbell, Winchester, Tenn., May 1, 1834, in Campbell Papers.

[31] Pierson, *Tocqueville and Beaumont in America*, 639–41. See also, *ibid.*, 507–508, for the opinions of Charles Carroll of Carrollton, the venerable signer of the Declaration of Independence, and of his son James, on the rise of democracy and its effects.

[32] James Campbell to John Campbell, Winchester, Tenn., May 1, 1834, in Campbell Papers. See also, David Campbell to William B. Campbell, Abingdon, Va., August 29, 1834, *ibid.*

were enfranchised. Many of them were not prepared for political responsibility. Over much of the South illiteracy was widespread, communications were poor, intellectual horizons were narrow, and few men had had the healthy experience of participating in local government. It was not to be expected that such men would show discrimination in choosing candidates or wisdom in determining public policy, and wisdom was sorely needed because state government was becoming more complex and national problems more critical.

But blame lies in the last analysis not at the door of the ignorant voters who chose ignorant leaders, nor does the experience of this time and place constitute a general indictment of democracy in government. The trouble sprang in the first place from the suddenness of the democratic revolution. In Mississippi, for example, where great change was telescoped into a brief moment of time, there was a sharper decline in the quality of political leadership than occurred in Virginia, where the movement was more gradual.

Secondly, and of greater significance, the new political sovereigns had not been prepared for their responsibilities. In earlier years no doctrine had been preached more frequently and more fervently throughout the South than that democracy could survive only if the citizens were educated. But the generality of Southern people had not been educated either in the academic or in the broader sense for self-government. There had been much talk, great plans, and self-sacrificing effort by many devoted and intelligent men; but common-school education for common people had not been adequately provided.

If any one group is to be held responsible for this grievous condition it must be the aristocratic, privileged, eastern planters. They had possessed wealth, influence, and political power for a long time, but they had failed to develop and execute a plan that would prepare the disenfranchised for the duties of citizenship. There is no use in citing the considerable progress that had been made in college education, or the real difficulties in the way of providing universal education. When all this is said, the fact remains that great numbers of the newly enfranchised were unprepared for the responsibility of self-government, and blame must be placed on those who had been in power rather than on those who were coming to power.

293

CHAPTER XIII

REGIONALISM IN MIND
AND SPIRIT

THROUGH the years that the abolitionists were discovering the "depravity" of the South, the region was becoming—if church membership be any guide—increasingly religious. Between 1820 and 1850 the membership of the Methodist church in Virginia, the Carolinas, and Georgia increased from 93,000 to 223,713 and of the Baptist church from 99,000 to 246,000, while the aggregate population of these four states increased only one third. The Episcopalians and Presbyterians were also growing, though not in such numbers; and west of the mountains the churches were making great gains.[1] A part of this growth was the fruit of a movement, instigated in large measure by William Capers, to bring the gospel to the slaves. Giving up the amenities of life on a South Carolina plantation to enter the Methodist ministry, Capers began his missions among the plantation Negroes of his state in the late 1820's, and he was notably successful in making this a popular cause in the churches.

As the churches grew in numbers, they adhered closely to their ancient beliefs. Among the Presbyterians, James H. Thornwell came into leadership and helped to cast into more logical and systematic form the conservative Calvinism of Old School American Presbyterianism.[2] Richard Furman attained great influence among the Baptists. One is tempted to believe that these and other stalwart defenders of the faith brought Southern churchmen to theological positions that were more conservative than those of earlier

[1] Compare the membership figures in Chap. III above with those in Joseph Belcher, *Religious Denominations in the United States* (Philadelphia, 1854), 242, 604, and *passim*.

[2] Paul L. Garber, *James Henley Thornwell, Presbyterian Defender of the Old South* (Richmond, 1943), "Reprinted from *Union Seminary Review* . . . February, 1943."

times. But Southern change, if there was any, was far less significant than its comparative steadfastness, while the stern theology of colonial New England was giving way to Unitarianism, liberalism, and transcendentalism, with a fringe of curious religious and social experiments, especially in upstate New York. Whether the South eschewed these innovations because some of their champions were abolitionists or because of an intellectual conviction that the old beliefs were the more correct, the fact remains that the South and New England were in process of swapping their colonial positions in respect to religious conservatism. The South, whose deistic liberalism had shocked conservative New Englanders at the time of the Revolution, was becoming the citadel of conservative theology. Its religious leaders, in turn, were shocked at the unorthodoxy of New England.

Religion in the South was also becoming more dignified. Ranting and ignorance still characterized some of the preachers, and unseemly emotional upheavals occurred at some of the revivals; but the brush arbors and campgrounds of the back country and frontier were being supplemented if not replaced by buildings of brick or wood, and religious services were becoming more orderly. A demand for a better-educated ministry was beginning to be felt in the popular Methodist and Baptist churches. Although the Methodists lagged behind the other major denominations in the establishment of theological seminaries, the General Conference that met in 1816 took steps for providing a course of required readings for young ministers in which the writings of John Wesley naturally occupied an important place.[3]

The other major denominations established theological seminaries in the South in the 1820's, though some of them amounted to no more than a chair of theology in a church college. Between the years 1821 and 1831 the Presbyterians established Southwestern Theological Seminary at Maryville, Tennessee, Union Theological Seminary in Prince Edward County, Virginia, and Southern Theological Seminary at Columbia, South Carolina. The Episcopalians concentrated their efforts upon a single institution, the Episcopal Theological School of Virginia, established at Alexandria in 1822. The Baptists established five seminaries in the score of years that

[3] Godbold, *Church College of the Old South*, 34.

began in 1826: Virginia Baptist Seminary at Richmond, Virginia, Furman in South Carolina, Mercer in Georgia, Howard in Alabama, and Western Baptist Theological Institution in Kentucky.[4] Thereafter it was easier for a young Southern man with a call to the ministry to secure a professional education, and the number of educated ministers increased. But, as an offset to these gains, subsequent generations of Southern preachers in large measure lacked the experience of having lived for a time in another part of the nation. Theological schools in the South and in the North could more easily reflect sectional viewpoints as their student bodies became increasingly sectionalized.

The same years also witnessed the multiplication of religious periodicals, and it is likely that many churchmen gained much of their knowledge about political questions from the summaries of secular news in denominational papers. In these papers, emphasis upon foreign events declined in the 1840's; thereafter, most space was given to domestic news, drawn in large measure from Richmond and Charleston papers and from the *National Intelligencer.*[5] Since religious papers were in most cases the official or semiofficial organs of particular denominations, they urged the establishment and support of colleges, seminaries, and other denominational institutions; and, unfortunately, they fostered sectarian rivalries and carried on unseemly quarrels between denominations.

"Moral evils" received much attention in the church papers, especially during the 1830's. Intemperance in the use of intoxicants was at the head of the list, and dueling was perhaps second. Among the others were lotteries and other forms of gambling, divorce, dancing, the theater, Sabbathbreaking, and novel reading. In addition to expressing disapproval of these things that were regarded as evil, approval was given to plans to help the poor, both white and slave, and the cause of education received the blessing of most of the papers.[6]

---

[4] *The American Almanac and Repository of Useful Knowledge, 1849* (Boston, 1848), 188. Godbold, *Church College of the Old South*, 15–16, 19–29, gives details about the establishment of most of these institutions. During the 1830's the Episcopal church sponsored a small theological seminary at Lexington, Kentucky. Henry Caswall, *America and the American Church* (London, 1839), 214–16.

[5] Stroupe, "Religious Press in the South Atlantic States," 336.

[6] *Ibid.*, Chaps. V, VIII, IX.

Some of the Baptists vigorously objected to this early phase of the social gospel, roundly condemning temperance, Bible, tract, educational, and especially missionary societies. They wanted the church to avoid entanglement with organizations for the improvement of society and to remain entirely separate from the state. The controversy between missionary and antimissionary Baptists was heated, and peace was not restored to many parts of the Baptists' empire until the antimission elements had withdrawn into separate organizations.[7]

The Baptist church again lost heavily, especially in Kentucky, when the Disciples of Christ became a separate organization. Alexander Campbell, who spent much of his life at Bethany, Virginia (now West Virginia), gained many followers within the Baptist church, and led them out of that fold by the end of the year 1832. Before this time he had held many of the views of the antimission Baptists. In addition to this basis for dissension, there were differences of opinion on theological questions and in respect to the emphasis that should be placed upon denominationalism.[8]

However, the abolition crusade was the chief schismatic force. The Presbyterian church was the first to be affected by it, largely because much of the early work of the abolitionists was carried on within this church. Charles G. Finney was a Presbyterian minister from his ordination in 1824 until he withdrew from his presbytery in 1836; Lewis and Arthur Tappan were prominent Presbyterian laymen; and Weld used this church for his purposes. He worked two weeks among the commissioners to the General Assembly at Pittsburgh in 1835 with such success as to enable him to report that forty-eight commissioners are "with us in sentiment on the subject of slavery," of whom twenty-seven were ministers and six of them were from the slave states.[9]

Slavery, however, was but one of several issues that divided the Presbyterians into the Old School and the New School factions. Some were doctrinal questions, and there was a sharp difference of opinion over the maintenance of the long-standing Plan of Union

[7] Sweet, *Religion on the American Frontier: The Baptists*, 63–76.

[8] Sweet, *Religions in America*, 343–44; Sweet, *Religion on the American Frontier: The Baptists*, 26, 70–72.

[9] Gilbert H. Barnes and Dwight L. Dumond (eds.), *Letters of Theodore Dwight Weld, Angelina Grimké Weld, and Sarah Grimké, 1822–1844* (New York, 1934), I, 224.

with the Congregational church.[10] In the General Assembly which met in Philadelphia in 1837, the Old School party was able to muster sufficient strength to abrogate the Plan and to exscind several synods and presbyteries, especially in upper New York, where the abolition movement had made much headway. The following year the New School commissioners, after failing to win admission to the body which had cut them off, created a separate organization.[11]

With the Methodists, the separation was more clearly tied to the single question of slavery. They had long been disturbed by it, and after 1840 it seemed more than probable that the church could not be held together much longer. The major uncertainty was whether the deflection would be of the Southern or of the Northern extremists. Contrary to the procedure in the Presbyterian church, the aggressive act within the Methodist church was taken by the antislavery faction. A resolution was introduced in the General Conference in May of 1844 to restrain Bishop James O. Andrew of Georgia from exercising his episcopal office as long as he had any connection with slavery. His connection with the institution was not intimate. It consisted chiefly in the fact that his wife owned slaves whom she had inherited, but Andrew had legally renounced all rights of ownership in them.

Andrew was disposed to resign his bishopric to preserve the peace of the church, but the Southern delegates counseled otherwise, being unwilling to accept the dictation of the antislavery faction. After long and earnest debate a "Plan of Separation" was adopted. The first General Conference of the Methodist Episcopal Church, South, assembled in 1846.[12]

During these same years the Baptists also came to the parting of

[10] The Plan of Union, inaugurated in 1801, provided for close co-operation between these two denominations in several respects, particularly in their program of westward expansion.

[11] A convenient summary is in the Introduction to Sweet, *Religion on the American Frontier: The Presbyterians*, 99–125.

[12] *Journal of the General Conference of the Methodist Episcopal Church, Held in the City of New York, 1844* (New York, 1844), 63–76, 81–87, 109, 111–13, 117–21, 128, 130–37, 186–210; *Journals of the General Conference of the Methodist Episcopal Church, South, Held 1846 and 1850* (Richmond, 1851), 5–9, 15, 52–53, 104–18; several manuscript letters and papers in the Eugene R. Hendrix Papers (Duke University Library). Secondary accounts are in William W. Sweet, *Methodism in American History* (New York, 1933), 229–53, and the sketch of Bishop James O. Andrew, in *Dictionary of American Biography*, I, 277–79.

the ways. This more loosely organized church lacked so authoritative a body as the General Conference of the Methodist church; the chief co-operative action of the Baptists throughout the nation consisted in control over several boards organized to manage certain activities of the denomination. One of these, the Board of Foreign Missions, was reported to have forced the resignation of John Bushyhead, a highly respected Indian Baptist preacher, because he was a slaveholder. Thereupon, Richard Fuller, a prominent South Carolina clergyman, published an article attempting to demonstrate that slavery was sanctioned in the Bible. Francis Wayland, president of Brown University and the author of a popular textbook on moral philosophy, answered him; and in 1845 their arguments were published as *Domestic Slavery Considered as a Scriptural Institution.* Meanwhile, the Board of Foreign Missions, in answer to a memorial from the Alabama Convention, stated that it would not appoint a slaveholder as a missionary nor would it ever "be a party to any arrangement which would imply approbation of slavery." [18] Following this pronouncement, Baptists within the slave states withdrew from the existing organization of the church; and in May, 1845, the Southern Baptist Convention was organized in Augusta, Georgia.

The spirit of those who presided over the dismemberment of the churches appears to have been dominated by feelings of sorrow more than of bitterness. It was proper for good men to grieve over this event, but wise men could hardly be surprised by it; for once a considerable part of the American churches became convinced that slavery was sinful in the sight of God, the time for compromise between Northern and Southern churchmen was past. In dealing with economic and political questions, men of contrary views may often come to middle ground, perhaps unhappily but nevertheless with clear consciences. But if religion means anything, it means that God will not condone compromise between moral right and moral wrong; and once abolitionists had catalogued slavery as sinful and Southern defenders had catalogued it as a thing that was right in the sight of God, compromise was impossible.

The division of the churches was something more than an ecclesiastical event. The churches were among the great cohesive forces

[18] Albert H. Newman, *A History of the Baptist Churches in the United States* (6th ed., New York, 1915), 445-47.

in America, serving along with the Whig and Democratic parties, business organizations, and other institutions to reinforce the Federal government in the maintenance of the American Union. The snapping of any one of these bonds under the stress of sectional tension inevitably increased the strain upon the others. The churches were the first to break; and when they did, tension upon other national organizations was brought nearer to the danger point.

The growth of the Southern state universities in numbers of students and in resources was disturbing to many churchmen during the 1820's and 1830's, because the universities were outstripping the church colleges, and ecclesiastical influence in the larger and more influential of the universities was decreasing. It was especially small in South Carolina College, Transylvania, and the University of Virginia. Denominational leaders began to complain of the irreligious and immoral atmosphere of the state institutions, and they widened their attack by alleging that universities were patronized chiefly by the children of men of considerable property and that the students indulged in a round of wild, reckless extravagance.

While Presbyterians and Episcopalians were somewhat disturbed by this state of affairs, they at least had colleges of their own to which they could send their children. Methodists and Baptists, however, had none in the South before the year 1830,[14] and they claimed that very few of their members were placed on the faculties or the boards of trustees of the universities.[15]

These considerations, together with the growth of the churches in membership, in influence, and in denominational pride, were responsible for the establishment of a considerable number of church colleges in the 1830's—a larger number than had been founded in all previous Southern history. The Methodists and Baptists, despite the determined opposition of some of their members, were extremely active. In Virginia the Methodists established Randolph-Macon and Emory and Henry; in Georgia, Emory and Wesleyan; in North Carolina, Greensboro and, in co-operation with the Quakers, Union Institute, progenitor of Trinity College and Duke University. The Baptists founded Mercer in Georgia, Wake

14 Columbian College (now George Washington University) established by the Baptists in 1821 constitutes an exception.
15 Godbold, *Church College of the Old South*, 149.

Forest in North Carolina, and Richmond College in Virginia. The Presbyterians expanded southward by establishing Davidson in North Carolina and Oglethorpe in Georgia. Only in South Carolina, where the legislature was extremely loyal to the state institution, did the churches fail to establish any colleges in the 1830's.[16]

West of the seaboard states, the Catholics established Spring Hill in Alabama and St. Mary's in Kentucky. The Baptists founded Howard in Alabama, Union in Tennessee, Georgetown in Kentucky, and Baylor in Texas. The Disciples of Christ founded Bacon, which developed into the state university, in Kentucky, and Bethany in western Virginia. The Presbyterians established Austin in Texas, and Maryville and Cumberland in Tennessee.[17]

The Methodists showed considerable interest in the education of women, establishing Wesleyan and Lagrange in Georgia and Greensboro in North Carolina. An innovation of this period occurred in 1838 when the College of Charleston became a responsibility of the city, and eight years later another municipal institution, the University of Louisville, was chartered in Kentucky.[18]

Most of the colleges were beset by serious financial difficulties. Attempts to get money from the state rarely succeeded. The lack of adequate funds caused the founders of most of the colleges of the 1830's to begin their institutions as "manual labor" colleges. But in spite of their claims that a union of labor with study would lower the cost of education, dignify labor, teach scientific farming, and develop sound bodies and spiritual humility, the manual-labor system seldom survived more than a year or two.[19]

Just how the colleges of the 1830's did survive is something of a mystery; but the task was not much greater for the new institutions than it was for some of the older ones. Income from students was often the only source of revenue, and if catalogues can be trusted,

[16] The chartering of several South Carolina colleges in the early 1850's was the delayed fruit of this movement of the 1830's. *Ibid.*, 148.

[17] The last was located at Lebanon. The earlier Cumberland College at Nashville was called the University of Nashville after 1826. For charter dates and other information about these colleges, see Tewksbury, *Founding of American Colleges and Universities before the Civil War*, especially pp. 38–44; Godbold, *Church College of the Old South*, 3–45.

[18] Tewksbury, *Founding of American Colleges and Universities before the Civil War*, 34–44.

[19] Godbold, *Church College of the Old South*, 56–60.

tuition, board, and room at the state universities ranged in general from $125 to $200 a year, whereas these expenses at the church colleges averaged from $100 to $150.[20] The colleges seem to have been kept alive chiefly by the Spartan simplicity of academic life, by the hard and ill-paid labor of the presidents and teachers, and by the sacrifices of churchgoing folk, especially those living near the college, who believed that education was worth all that it cost.

While church colleges were being founded in the 1830's and 1840's, new state universities were springing up in the Southwest. The states of Alabama and Mississippi received Federal land grants for the support of higher education; but part of the proceeds from land sales was lost during the Panic of 1819, and the states, in effect, spent what was left of the principal. The legislatures then agreed to make annual payments to higher education. The net result was more generous support than in most of the seaboard states, but a less generous support than the land grants should have provided. Furthermore, the arrangement left the universities subject to the whims of the legislatures.

In Mississippi there was debate over whether to create a university *de novo* or to graft it upon an existing small college; whether to divide available funds among several small institutions or to use all to develop one large university; and whether to locate the university in this, that, or the other rival part of the state. In Alabama, where these problems were less acute, the university was opened at Tuscaloosa in April, 1831; the University of Mississippi was opened at Oxford in 1848. In curriculums, both institutions were colleges rather than universities, and neither added schools of law or medicine before 1850.

Louisiana made but slow progress toward the establishment of a state university. After maintaining the College of Orleans, which offered a classical collegiate course, until 1826, it then spread thin its support among three colleges of scarcely more than academy rank. Finally, after much discussion, the University of Louisiana was chartered in 1847. It was to include the Medical College of New Orleans, which had been operating as a private institution for some twelve years, a collegiate department, and a law school. Little prog-

[20] *Ibid.*, 198–201.

ress was made by the college for some years, but the law school, unique among American institutions in its emphasis upon civil law, attracted a number of students, and in May, 1848, conferred the degree of Bachelor of Laws upon sixteen graduates.[21]

All three of these Southwestern states had been slow in founding universities, and Texas and Arkansas lagged even further behind. J. D. B. De Bow explained Southwestern apathy toward literary matters on the ground that the inhabitants had been too busy "struggling with the wilderness, subduing soil into cultivation, opening trade and creating for it avenues. . . . The physical want precedes, in the order of time, the intellectual." [22] Because of the business activity of the Mississippi Valley and particularly of New Orleans, he thought that the University of Louisiana ought to prepare students for commercial careers; and to that end he advocated the establishment of a professorship of public economy, commerce, and statistics.[23]

The universities, more than the colleges, added utilitarian courses to their curriculums, and they paraded the practicality of their education for something more than it was worth. The colleges, making a virtue out of necessity, championed the classical curriculum, which could be taught with a small faculty. They also emphasized their affiliation with the church. Thus they created the impression that there was a necessary relationship between religious orthodoxy and educational conservatism.

According to the census of 1850, there were 113 colleges in the South. The average college had 7 faculty members and 117 students, and had an annual income of $8,220. In the entire nation, there were 239 degree-granting institutions—law, medical, and theological schools, women's colleges and men's colleges, with a preponderance of men's colleges.[24] In addition, Southern youth continued to patronize the colleges of the North. From 1820 onward, one third

21 For the three universities of the Southwest, see Foerster, "State University in the Old South," Chap. VI.

22 De Bow's Review (New Orleans), I (1846), 3.

23 Ibid., III (1847), 502–16; IV (1847), 44; V (1848), 237–39.

24 Statistical View of the United States, 1850, p. 141. For other information about schools and colleges, see American Almanac and Repository of Useful Knowledge, 1849, pp. 184–89, and other editions of this reference work.

of the students at Princeton came from the South, and in 1850 there were over 250 Southern students at Princeton, Yale, and Harvard.[25] The number who went to the North for medical training was especially large. In the session of 1845–1846 at the University of Pennsylvania, 265 of the 432 students were from the South.[26]

Leaving out of account this migration of students, the South, in proportion to its population, led the nation at mid-century in number of colleges, of faculty members, and of college students. If comparison be made on the basis of white population, the per cent of Southern youth in college was twice as high as in the rest of the United States.[27]

The rapid expansion of provisions for college education was not matched by improvements at the lower educational levels. If one may rely on the census of 1850, the great majority of the public schools in the South were one-teacher schools, with an average of about 30 students in each school. In Arkansas, 353 schools were taught by 355 teachers,[28] and in South Carolina there were 737 teachers for the 739 free schools.[29] Inasmuch as students were of various ages and degrees of progress, the effectiveness of even the good teachers could not have been great. In the average academy, conditions were slightly better, with perhaps two teachers to instruct approximately 40 students.[30]

Poor as such schooling must have been, a great number of children did not receive even this much of elementary education. Most of the Southern states continued to subsidize the education of those who could not pay for it, but this system never worked well. The South Carolina legislature of 1847 was informed that the state was paying for the education of less than 9,000 children, and these, with few exceptions, attended less than half the year. It was further said that there were about eight times this many South Carolinians be-

[25] Thwing, *Higher Education in America*, 254–55.

[26] Edward Ingle, *Southern Sidelights: A Picture of Social and Economic Life in the South a Generation before the War* (New York, 1896), 144.

[27] The above facts are calculated from *Statistical View of the United States*, 1850, p. 141 for college data, and pp. 40, 45 for population data.

[28] *Ibid.*, 141–43. The census defined a public school as one which received its support in whole or in part from taxation or public funds.

[29] "Abstract of the Several Boards of Commissioners of Free Schools in South Carolina—1847," in South Carolina *Reports and Resolutions*, 1847, p. 245.

[30] *Statistical View of the United States*, 1850, pp. 142–43.

tween five and twenty years old who were not attending school.[31] One member of the legislature bluntly stated that "the Free School System was a *failure*." [32] Another declared: "There is scarce a State in the Union, in which so great apathy exists on the subject of the education of the people, as in the State of South-Carolina. . . . her sister States . . . [have] outstripped her in this career of glory. We have been talking and they have been acting." [33] Although the historian can agree that conditions in South Carolina were deplorable, he can see little reason for placing this state below the rest of the South, though he can find ample reason for placing the South below the rest of the nation. According to the census of 1850, 8.27 per cent of the adult white population of the slave states was illiterate as compared with 3.36 per cent in the nonslaveholding states.[34]

Yet there were some signs of a brighter future. Southerners were reading and discussing the writings of Horace Mann in New England, and, through the writings of Mann and the work of Francis Lieber at South Carolina College and of others, they were learning about German experiments in education.[35] There was much discussion of ways to provide more and better teachers, and, in 1851, Union Institute in North Carolina changed its name to Normal College as an indication of its intention to try to supply a part of the need for teachers.[36]

It was in the cities that most progress was made in the establishment of tax-supported schools that were free to rich and poor alike. In 1830 the city of Louisville erected the Centre School House, a three-story brick building to accommodate from 600 to 700 students. There were classes designed to give "a good English Education for Females," primary and grammar classes for boys, and a night school. Teachers' salaries were paid by the city treasurer, and students were at no expense except for quarterly fees of from one to two dollars "for the incidental expenses of the School." [37] By 1848 there

---

[31] South Carolina *Reports and Resolutions*, 1847, p. 217.

[32] *Ibid.*, 196. [33] *Ibid.*, 207–208.

[34] *Statistical View of the United States*, 1850, p. 152. For other data on illiteracy in the South, see Eaton, *Freedom of Thought in the Old South*, 64–66.

[35] Foerster, "State University in the Old South," 240–56, 303.

[36] *Ibid.*, 372, 456; Nora C. Chaffin, "Trinity College, 1839–1892: The Beginnings of Duke University," in *Southern Association Quarterly* (Durham), IX (1945), 314.

[37] Gabriel Collins, *The Louisville Directory, for the Year 1836* . . . (Louisville, 1836), 94–95.

were seven public schools in the Lower District of Louisville, six in the Middle District, and nine in the Upper District.[38] In Baltimore, four tax-supported schools were opened in 1829, two for boys and two for girls, and the system was considerably expanded in the 1840's.[39] By this time New Orleans had a well-developed public-school system,[40] and a city no larger than Natchez supported a public school, opened in 1845, that had an average enrollment of 618 pupils during the first six years of its life.[41]

Education and letters were not closely allied in the Old South; for the arduous life of the teacher left little time or energy for writing, and colleges were related to the church rather than to literary circles. Neither was literature a profession unto itself. Few there were in the South who thought that a man could or should make his living by turning out poetry or novels. The casual attitude assumed by many of the authors is indicated by the fact that they frequently published their product anonymously. Most of the writers lived in or near the towns, and most of them were professional men—lawyers, doctors, preachers, and, especially, journalists. One of the few planter-writers was William Elliott of South Carolina, whose *Carolina Sports, by Land and Water; Including Incidents of Devil-fishing* was published at Charleston in 1846 and was republished in several later editions.

Most Southerners were less willing to buy books and read them than to hear the oratory of Henry Clay or Seargent S. Prentiss or to read their favorite church or secular papers. And who can say that they were wrong? In the use of the spoken word the orators were artists, and in their generation American oratory was at a high level. As for the newspapers, Thomas Ritchie of the Richmond *Enquirer,* John Hampden Pleasants of the *Whig,* George D. Prentice of the Louisville *Journal,* and George W. Kendall of the New Orleans *Picayune* frequently had something to say, and they knew how to write, sometimes wittily and sometimes seriously. They opened their columns to local literary efforts and to essays on sub-

[38] John B. Jegli, *Louisville Directory for 1848* . . . (Louisville, 1848), 28–29.

[39] Clayton C. Hall (ed.), *Baltimore: Its History and Its People* (New York, 1912), I, 139.

[40] Lewis, *Impressions of America and the American Churches,* 195 ff. Information about education in some other Southern towns can be found in this work.

[41] Sydnor, *Benjamin L. C. Wailes,* 219.

jects of public interest, and they gave much space to reprinting good literature. The newspapers in some measure took the place of journals of discussion and of literature.

During the first half of the nineteenth century a large number of journals were established in the South, especially at Charleston, Richmond, and New Orleans. Others were born in Southern towns of only a thousand or two inhabitants, and a few of these, like *The Orion: A Monthly Magazine of Literature, Science, and Art,* contained material of some significance.[42] Some of the periodicals were written for physicians, or farmers and planters, or the members of some one of the churches. Others were edited for women or for children. Yet others discussed public questions and gave much space to literary productions and to weighty reviews and criticisms. One of the most substantial literary journals was the *Southern Review* which was published at Charleston from 1828 to 1832. For a time it was edited by the distinguished linguist and student of the history of law, Hugh Swinton Legaré,[43] with the assistance of Stephen Elliott, Sr., who was a planter, naturalist, enlightened legislator, and banker as well as a man of letters. A later literary venture was the *Southern Quarterly Review,* which was founded in New Orleans in 1842 and was moved to Charleston in 1844, where it remained until its death in 1857. William Gilmore Simms was the ablest of its editors. *The Commercial Review,* begun at New Orleans in 1846 by J. D. B. De Bow, and usually called *De Bow's Review,* was the leading business journal of the Old South. But chief among all the periodicals of the region was the *Southern Literary Messenger,* which was founded in Richmond in 1834 and remained there throughout its extraordinary life span of thirty years. Among the better of its editors were Benjamin B. Minor, John R. Thompson, and George W. Bagby. Edgar Allan Poe was a brilliant member of its editorial staff from 1835 to 1837. During those years, the circulation of the *Messenger* rose from 500 to 3,500 or more.

[42] *The Orion* was established at Penfield, Georgia, in 1842. It was moved to Charleston in March, 1844, and died within the year. It was edited with some ability by William Carey Richards, and it contained the earliest published drawings and engravings of his brother Thomas Addison Richards, who later became one of the leading landscape painters in America.

[43] Linda Rhea, *Hugh Swinton Legaré, a Charleston Intellectual* (Chapel Hill, 1934), 91–130.

The best remembered of the literary productions of the Old South are some of its poems, especially those of Poe, Richard Henry Wilde's "My Life Is Like the Summer Rose," and Theodore O'Hara's "The Bivouac of the Dead." Some of the poems of Thomas Holley Chivers deserve to be better known. The lyrics of Edward Coote Pinkney of Maryland and a single volume of poems by Philip Pendleton Cooke of Virginia suggest that a measure of fame might have been won by these two men had they not died young.[44] But Southern poetry of this period, whether good or bad, was not close-tied to the land where it was written, and Poe, the greatest of the poets, was the least Southern of them. It is only when one turns from his poems and his tales to his literary criticisms that much evidence can be found of his relationship to the South.

In prose, however, much of the life and manners of the South was reflected. The form of the writing was of course determined in large measure by current literary styles, but the material compressed into this form was part and parcel of the region.

The first work of John Pendleton Kennedy, *Swallow Barn, or, A Sojourn in the Old Dominion*, was published in 1832. It follows the leisurely and almost plotless style of Washington Irving's *Sketch Book*,[45] but its substance, to use Kennedy's own words, exhibited "a picture of country life in Virginia" in the early nineteenth century: "the mellow, bland, and sunny luxuriance of her old-time society—its good fellowship, its hearty and constitutional *companionableness*, the thriftless gayety of the people, their dogged but amiable invincibility of opinion, and that overflowing hospitality which knew no ebb." [46]

Kennedy could write of Virginia with a perspective that few Virginians could attain, for he was bound by ties of marriage, business,

[44] Philip Pendleton Cooke was the older brother of the better known though less gifted John Esten Cooke and the cousin of John Pendleton Kennedy. For studies of the older Cooke, see David K. Jackson, "Philip Pendleton Cooke: Virginia Gentleman, Lawyer, Hunter, and Poet," in Jackson (ed.), *American Studies in Honor of William Kenneth Boyd*, 282–326; and John D. Allen, *Philip Pendleton Cooke* (Chapel Hill, 1942).

[45] Earlier but less important than Kennedy's *Swallow Barn* was *The Valley of Shenandoah, or, Memoirs of the Graysons* (New York, 1824), by George Tucker (1775–1861), who is best remembered as a political economist.

[46] From "A Word in Advance, from the Author to the Reader," which precedes the text of the second edition (New York, 1851), 8.

and politics to Maryland and the urban centers of the North. At the same time, he knew his rural Virginia intimately, somewhat as one knows a place where he has spent long and happy vacations. He avoided the harsher aspects of plantation life, without falling into the romantic extravagances of many later writers on this subject. He had sound taste and much ability. Vernon L. Parrington believed that "Few Americans of his day were so generously gifted; none possessed a lighter touch." [47]

Following the trend of the times, Kennedy abandoned the essay-sketch and formed his next two works on the pattern of the romance of love and adventure, but he did not desert the Southern locale for the setting of these stories. *Horse-Shoe Robinson: A Tale of the Tory Ascendency* (1835) is laid in Virginia and the Carolinas in the Revolutionary period; *Rob of the Bowl: A Legend of St. Inigoes* was placed in seventeenth-century Maryland. In 1840 he was stirred to publish a satire on Jacksonian democracy under the title *Quodlibet,* and nine years later he brought to completion his life of William Wirt, to whom he had dedicated *Swallow Barn.*[48]

William Alexander Caruthers, a cultured and widely traveled Virginian, was similar to Kennedy in his amiable outlook, in his treatment of Southern subjects, and in his transition from an older to a newer form of writing. Caruthers' *Kentuckian in New York, or, the Adventures of Three Southerns* (1834) is in the form of letters between Southern young men visiting in different parts of the nation, and through these letters Caruthers manages to say some wise things about the understanding and toleration of regional differences. The adventure and romance that are thrown in to spice this work become the main diet in his next two stories, the first of which is laid in the time of Bacon's Rebellion and the second is Governor Alexander Spotswood's day.[49]

Down in the Southwest there was a third writer who turned out

[47] Vernon L. Parrington, *Main Currents in American Thought* (New York, 1927–1930), II, 56.

[48] An account of Kennedy's life and works, with considerable attention to his friendships with Edgar Allan Poe and William Makepeace Thackeray, is in Jay B. Hubbell's Introduction to the American Authors Series edition of *Swallow Barn* (New York, 1929).

[49] *The Cavaliers of Virginia, or the Recluse of Jamestown* (1834–1835); *The Knights of the Horse-Shoe; a Traditionary Tale of the Cocked Hat Gentry in the Old Dominion* (1845).

historical romances after first trying his hand with a more sedate literary form. Joseph Holt Ingraham came to the region as a Yankee schoolteacher, and soon thereafter he published a description of New Orleans, Natchez, and the surrounding plantation country under the title *The South-West, by a Yankee* (1835). His was not the first description of the region, but he was the first that saw it as something more than a fertile land, a mighty river, and trees laden with Spanish moss. Coming from Maine and coming after the society of the lower Mississippi Valley had evolved from the pioneer into the plantation-slavery stage, he saw and described a culture as well as a geography, and he helped to make the people of the Natchez region aware of their cultural distinctiveness.

Following the familiar pattern of his time, Ingraham turned next to historical novels, beginning with preposterous stories about Lafitte the pirate (Ingraham spelled the name Laffite) and about Aaron Burr and later ranging far afield in search of scenes and characters. His novels were hurriedly done and extravagantly romantic, but he turned them out in great profusion and he sold them. He succeeded perhaps better than any Southern writer of his generation in making a living with his pen. In 1846 he told Longfellow that he had written eighty novels, twenty of them within the past year.[50]

The land across the Mississippi River, in frontier Arkansas and in the wilder regions farther west, was described in a host of novels by Gustave Aimard, a Frenchman, and by Friedrich W. C. Gerstäcker, a German. Both of them lived in the Southwest in the 1830's and 1840's, and both of them were facile and popular writers, chiefly for the European market, of "thrillers" of Western adventure and pioneer life. At one time Aimard's publishing schedule called for a novel each month.[51]

[50] Sketch in the *Dictionary of American Biography*, IX, 479–80; Sydnor, *Benjamin L. C. Wailes*, 131–33. Later, Ingraham became an Episcopal clergyman and a pioneer in the writing of historical novels constructed about Biblical characters. His son, Prentiss Ingraham, became the most prolific of all American dime-novel writers.

[51] There is no adequate biography or appraisal of the work and influence of either man. A sketch of Friedrich W. C. Gerstäcker is in *Der Grosse Brockhaus*. For Gustave Aimard, whose real name was Oliver Gloux, see Virgil L. Jones, "Gustave Aimard," in *Southwest Review* (Dallas), XV (1929–1930), 452–68, and the bibliography and note in Frank Monaghan, *French Travellers in the United States, 1765–1932* (New York, 1933), 1–4.

In contrast to these tellers of good stories about various parts of the South stands Nathaniel Beverley Tucker. He also told a story, and he followed the style of the time in injecting into it much romance, intrigue, and swordplay. But Tucker was not trying to pass away the idle hour or amuse his reader, but to warn him and arouse him to defensive action. Perhaps because he was half brother to the gloomy John Randolph of Roanoke, he had long brooded over Virginia's ill treatment by the North, and he was depressed by the apathy of Virginians. Convinced that war and disunion must come, he wrote *The Partisan Leader: A Tale of the Future* (1836) to stir them to action. He laid the scene some ten years too soon, which was no great error; and he ends with the triumph of Virginia, which was a wider miss. Otherwise, *The Partisan Leader* is not bad prophecy.

William Gilmore Simms of South Carolina cannot be pressed into a neat and simply-labeled package or be judged by one or two works. The enormous quantity of his writing included poetry, biography, history, geography, criticism, plays, and novels; and he gave much time to editorial work and to delivering orations. The quality of his product ranged from much that has been properly forgotten to some that was the work of "a good writer judged by any standard."[52]

The uneven quality of his work was due in some measure to the crosscurrents that influenced him. Unlike most Southern writers of his generation, he sought to make letters a profession rather than a gentleman's avocation. He ground out many books under the hard compulsion of making a living, and he squandered much of his enormous energy in trying to develop a distinctive Southern literature and to provide a magazine to publish the writings of Southerners. Furthermore, there was a conflict between his veneration for the aristocratic society of the low country—a society which he loved and defended even though it was slow in fully accepting him—and his instinctive liking to write, with "a rich picaresque energy, of the rogues whom he magnificently enjoyed drawing to the life with all their eccentric vulgarity and swaggering ruthlessness."[53] It was

[52] Carl Van Doren, in *Dictionary of American Biography*, XVII, 171–74. Parrington, *Main Currents in American Thought*, II, 125–36, is in essential agreement. See also, William P. Trent, *William Gilmore Simms* (New York, 1892), especially pp. 324–32.

[53] Van Doren, in *Dictionary of American Biography*, XVII, 173.

this vein that is the best of Simms's work, and it crops out in a number of his books, especially in *The Partisan* (1835) and his other romances of the Revolutionary period in South Carolina. He did for the frontier type of the lower South what Kennedy did for the plantation life of the upper South, and each in a style that was well suited to the subject.

In the year that Simms published *The Partisan*, Augustus Baldwin Longstreet brought out a book entitled *Georgia Scenes*. The sketches that composed it had been appearing in the newspapers of the state for several years, some of them in the *States Rights Sentinel* which Longstreet was editing in Augusta.[54] Longstreet's favorite characters were the Crackers, and he wrote of them in their native habitat, or in the bewildering surroundings of a town, with as little sympathy and with as much objective merriment as though they were monkeys in a cage. The humor that runs through the *Scenes* is frequently rough; it is a humor that appeals to men more than to women though it is not of the sort that needs to be labeled "for men only." His sketches are usually called realistic. They are certainly down to earth, but in his search for the ludicrous he probably deviated from reality in the direction of caricature as far as Kennedy did in the direction of idealization. Longstreet's writings are kin to some of Simms's partisan stories. They were also similar to Seba Smith's Jack Downing letters that appeared in New England in the early 1830's, and to the Western yarns and tall tales that were contemporaneously developing in the David Crockett myths. In widely separated areas, humorists were appearing as pioneer local colorists and as forerunners of realism in American literature.

The *Scenes* were popular enough to go through several editions and to embarrass the author after he became a Methodist preacher and a college president. Furthermore, they started a vogue for that kind of writing. William Tappan Thompson, who had been associated with Longstreet in issuing the *States Rights Sentinel*, was the first to follow in this freshly blazed literary trail. In 1840 Thompson published *Major Jones's Courtship*, and he subsequently wrote two more books about the Major. Johnson Jones Hooper of Alabama, who was also a newspaperman, put strong doses of humor and local color into *Some Adventures of Captain Simon Suggs, Late of the*

[54] Wade, *Augustus Baldwin Longstreet*, 149.

Tallapoosa Volunteers (1846) and into *The Widow Rugby's Husband* (1851), and he achieved somewhat more unity than Longstreet and Thompson had achieved. In 1851, Joseph B. Cobb published his *Mississippi Scenes; or Sketches of Southern and Western Life and Adventure, Humorous, Satirical, and Descriptive.* Two years later Joseph G. Baldwin produced *The Flush Times of Alabama and Mississippi,* a vivid and humorous description of the turbulent life of the Southwest as it was when he moved into it in the middle thirties.

Professor Arthur P. Hudson has suggested that the originality of Longstreet, Baldwin, and the rest consisted chiefly in their having "the wit to realize that something old in talking might look new in writing." [55] Their stories were of the sort that men liked to hear and to tell. Once the style of putting them on the page began, it spread rapidly. Hard-riding young bloods, who would have scorned association with elegant literature, were yet willing to contribute to William T. Porter's New York *Spirit of the Times, a Chronicle of the Turf, Agriculture, Field Sports, Literature and the Stage.*[56]

Only three years separated the appearance of *Georgia Scenes* from the crisis of South Carolina's controversy over the tariff; Southern regionalism gave birth at nearly the same time to nullification and to the humorous, local-color story. In the one case, the differences between the several parts of the nation developed into economic and political conflict and fruited in threats of disunion. In the other, they produced a reflection in literature of subspecies of the genus *Americana* whose variations could be labeled by words of rich connotation such as Suckers, Hoosiers, Crackers, and Yankees.[57] Literary regionalism was far pleasanter and less dangerous than the contemporary political sectionalism.

One other relationship deserves notice. Literary sketches of uneducated backwoodsmen began to appear in the very decade that a greater share of political power was being won by the common man. Furthermore, this literary vogue ran its course chiefly in the lower South and the Southwest, where political democracy was reaching

[55] Arthur P. Hudson, *Humor of the Old Deep South* (New York, 1936), 16–17.

[56] *Ibid.,* 11–12.

[57] See the penetrating article by Thomas D. Clark, "Hoosiers, Suckers, and Red Horses," in Wabash College, *The Wabash Bulletin* (Crawfordsville, Ind.), XLI, No. 1; and, by the same author, *The Rampaging Frontier* (Indianapolis, 1939), 25 and *passim*.

its most extreme form. Perhaps it was the political behavior of the backwoods sovereign that won for him a place in literature. His lingo and antics attracted the attention of journalists, lawyers, and travelers and suggested to them the idea of describing these things for cultivated, sophisticated readers in the seaboard states.

CHAPTER XIV

PARTY ALLEGIANCE OR
SECTIONAL PATRIOTISM?

DURING the years that have been passed in review, the South came a long way on the lonely road from nationalism to sectionalism. Along this way, the ultimate landmark presented itself in varying aspects. In the 1820's, sectionalism was chiefly observable in Congressional controversies over internal improvements, public lands, the national bank, and tariffs. Most of these issues were obviously rooted in economic differences; they were chiefly manifest in speeches and votes of Congressmen who were reflecting the divergent interests of the areas they represented. In some measure, candidates and parties divided on these issues during the Presidential elections of 1824, 1828, and 1832.

In the 1830's and 1840's, especially about the middle of the 1830's, sectionalism became chiefly evident in other and widely differing areas of life. In religion, the liberal movement in New England and the conservative tendencies in the South fostered misunderstanding; and under the strain of the slavery controversy, several of the churches split into Northern and Southern branches. In education, the establishment of Southern colleges and theological seminaries fostered intellectual provincialism, and the presidents and trustees of these institutions occasionally tried to recruit students by stirring up sectional prejudice. In literature, the local-color sketch appeared, regional literary and religious journals multiplied, and Simms and others appealed to local pride in their efforts to create a Southern literature. In industry and commerce, Southerners were aware that their region was being outdistanced by the North, and they talked of establishing factories and direct trade relations with Europe as a means of attaining economic parity with the North. Above all else, the abolition crusade startled and angered Southerners, embittering them against the North and increasing the sentiment of Southern unity.

Thus, in the 1830's and 1840's, sectionalism was more deeply charged with emotion, and it was reaching out into intellectual, spiritual, and cultural, as well as economic, phases of life. On the other hand, it was becoming less conspicuous in politics than it had been in the 1820's. This condition, the decline of sectionalism in politics at the very time when it was becoming more pronounced in nearly every other aspect of life, must now be examined and its causes must be explored.

The formation of the Whig party early in Jackson's second administration introduced the only thoroughgoing two-party period in all Southern history. But this event, with its connotation of political healthfulness, did not inaugurate an era in which Southerners could express their opinions in party platforms and settle their differences by votes. Neither Whigs nor Democrats offered a program that was thoroughly satisfactory to large segments of Southern political thought. Consequently, party conflict south of the Potomac, from nullification to the late 1840's, had the hollow sound of a stage duel with tin swords. To understand this period, one must remember that major Southern hopes and fears found no champion in either party.

Industrial developments in the North were at the root of much of the political conflict. On the one hand, liberals and labor leaders sought to limit working hours, advocated various social reforms, and fought against the national bank. In the opposing camp, the wealthier and more conservative segments of society clung to the benefits they had won through the Federalist and National Republican programs. In this conflict, which formed a major issue between the Democratic and Whig parties, the agrarian South felt little interest. True enough, there was a contemporary democratic movement of large proportions among the upcountry farmers of the South, but their hopes and aspirations were unlike those of the urban workers of the North. These two dissatisfied groups were not to become political partners.

While most of the South was apathetic toward the class-struggle elements of the Whig-Democratic conflict in the North, one small but influential body of Southern opinion was able to find for itself a satisfactory niche in the Whig party. Kentucky hemp growers, Louisiana sugar planters, and the businessmen of Maryland gravitated to the Whig party because they felt an instinctive alliance with Northern champions of economic and social stability and because it was to their advantage to retain a national bank and a protective tariff.

The larger body of Southern opinion disliked the Whig party because it contained Clay and his American System. At the same time, it feared the Democratic party because of the radical ideas and reformatory zeal of some of the party's leaders. Herein lay the dilemma that faced many a Southern voter: the necessity of choosing between two parties each of which contained disagreeable elements.

Furthermore, neither party took a clear and satisfactory stand on the question that was now of greatest importance to the South, namely, the maintenance of slavery. Obviously, neither party could support slavery without losing much of its Northern support. While Southerners disliked neutrality toward slavery, it is clear that if parties should reflect sectional interests, the Southern party would be distinctly weaker than the Northern. The Southern voter, unable to see much difference between Whigs and Democrats, therefore made his choice on the basis of minor events and insignificant words. He was often dubious about the wisdom of his decision, and he was likely to vote for one party in one election and for the other party four years later.[1]

These considerations form the backdrop for Southern action in the election of 1836. On the one hand was Van Buren, whose party had enjoyed the support of most of the South in the previous election. But Van Buren lacked the magnetism of Jackson, Van Buren's home was in the land of abolition, and some of the Northern Democrats had a penchant for social reform that might not stop short of meddling with slavery. South Carolinians and other Southern extremists, embittered by Jackson's course during nullification, were in no mood to vote for the man to whom Jackson had given his political mantle.

[1] The dilemma of the South is well stated in Arthur M. Schlesinger, Jr., *The Age of Jackson* (Boston, 1945), 242-49. Useful accounts of this period of Southern political history are Cole, *Whig Party in the South*, and Carroll, *Origins of the Whig Party*.

The alternative was not much better. Northern Whigs were bringing tons of abolition petitions into Congress, and Clay's American System was unacceptable. While the old National Republican element in the South—sugar planters and hemp growers and commercial leaders—could easily vote for Clay or one of his protégés, this was impossible for men of the South Carolina stripe.

In the election of 1836, South Carolina met the dilemma by refusing to grasp either horn, giving its vote to Willie P. Mangum of North Carolina. Georgia and Tennessee followed nearly as lonely a course in voting for Hugh L. White of Tennessee. These men were sound enough on Southern principles, but they had no following outside the South. Only Maryland and Kentucky voted for William H. Harrison of Ohio, who was acceptable to Northern Whigs. The other Southern states voted for Van Buren, giving him nearly as many electoral votes as Harrison, White, and Mangum received. The closeness of the popular vote in nearly all the Southern states was remarkable. In Mississippi, Van Buren received 9,979 votes to White's 9,688, and in several other states the vote was nearly as close. Except in Arkansas, where Van Buren defeated White by a vote of two to one, no candidate received as much as 60 per cent of the popular vote in any Southern state. There is no way of determining the division of public opinion in South Carolina where electors were chosen by the legislature. Outside of Calhoun's state, the Southern vote for Van Buren was 215,135, while the combined vote of the other candidates was 200,598.[2]

Generally speaking, the Whigs were strongest in the planting counties, and it was sometimes said that they owned three fourths of the slaves in the South. But in North Carolina the situation was reversed, with the democratic upcountry generally voting for Whig candidates. Perhaps this area, which had long desired better transportation facilities, was attracted by Whig enthusiasm for internal improvements.

Local conditions in other areas threw light on political diversities, but one should not forget that ambitious politicians were

[2] Election statistics may be consulted in Stanwood, *History of the Presidency from 1788 to 1897,* and election maps in Cole, *Whig Party in the South,* and Paullin and Wright, *Atlas of the Historical Geography of the United States.*

calculating their chances of advancement and were throwing their influence to the party that held out the better prospects. The chief activity of Southern politicians in the 1830's and 1840's consisted in struggles for local place and power rather than in contests over any principles that differentiated the national parties.

Inasmuch as the political complexion of any Southern state could be changed by a shift of no more than a few thousand votes, both parties began making overtures. The Democrats, sensing that Jackson's actions were chiefly responsible for their losses in the South, confessed their sins and offered to reform. The *United States Magazine and Democratic Review* admitted that the executive power of the Federal government had been overexpanded in recent years. It reminded its readers, however, that Jackson was no longer President, and it promised that Van Buren would follow a more careful course. Furthermore, it expressed sympathy with minorities and declared that minority rights should have "a high moral claim on the respect and justice of majorities." [8]

Lured by these blandishments, Calhoun of South Carolina, followed by R. M. T. Hunter of Virginia and a number of other Southern politicians, cut free from the Whig party and joined the Democrats. In South Carolina and Alabama the migration was substantial enough to attach those states firmly to the Democratic standard in subsequent elections. Justification for the change of party affiliation—perhaps it was no more than an excuse—was found in the fight over Van Buren's independent treasury scheme.

The Whigs, taking stock of their Southern losses, also began to make pronouncements with a view to improving their position in that closely balanced region. They began to speak of the American System as an outmoded program. Clay, realizing that most Southerners disliked a high tariff, expressed a willingness to see the compromise tariff continue in force as a permanent arrangement. In February, 1839, he spoke against abolition agitation in the South. The Whigs also made a strong bid for the Southern vote by nominating a perfect representative of strict-construction views, John Tyler of Virginia, as the junior member of the ticket headed by

---

[8] *United States Magazine and Democratic Review* (Washington), I (1837), 1–3; III (1838), 9.

Harrison. The renomination of Van Buren by the Democrats was expected, and his campaign was largely a defense of his administration.

Conflicting views among the Whigs made it impossible for them to agree on a platform. They therefore appealed to emotion rather than to reason, making much use of processions and barbecues and of tirades against the Democrats. While the incongruity of such a campaign on the part of the conservative party was noted by the Democrats, it proved highly profitable, winning many votes for the Whigs among those who had been newly enfranchised by the constitutional reforms of the previous decade.

The Whigs carried seven Southern states, losing only Virginia, South Carolina, Alabama, and Arkansas. They won 75 Southern electoral votes to 44 for the Democrats, and 345,991 popular votes. The Democrats received 284,621 popular votes in addition to carrying South Carolina. Although the Democrats were defeated, their position was not hopeless in any Southern state. Even in Kentucky, where the odds against them were greatest, they had received more than a third of the popular votes.

The death of Harrison greatly altered the political position of the state-rights ultra Southerners. Hitherto, both parties, aware of Southern discontent, had treated the region with deference and had tried to buy its votes with a conciliatory policy. This position was not a commanding one or a source of much pride to Southerners, but it enabled them to exert a moderating influence on the policy of the two great national parties.

When Tyler became President, moderation and compromise were thrown to the winds. With notable and perhaps noble refusal to alter his philosophy of government, Tyler used all the power that was now his to write into the Whig party a platform that was acceptable only to conservative Southerners. The attempt was a total failure. Tyler was virtually expelled by the Whigs, with Clay showing great and almost unseemly zeal to that end.

More important than Tyler's fate was the fate of his cause. It was perfectly clear that the antibank, anti-internal-improvement, anti-tariff, proslavery, and strict-construction platform of ultra Southerners had not the ghost of a chance of being made the platform of the Whig party. Evidence of the declining influence of Southern

Whigs can be found in the strongly protective tariff of 1842, which was passed despite the adverse votes of eight Whig Senators from the slave states. On the other hand, it also became evident that no large number of Southerners was willing in the early 1840's to rally to the banner of a separate Southern political party. Tyler raised such a banner after the resignation of the cabinet he had inherited from Harrison. Calhoun later accepted the secretaryship of state and other Southern politicians joined the official family, but the attempt to create a Southern state-rights party failed. Perhaps Southerners were wise enough to see the advantage of retaining some influence in each of the national parties instead of withdrawing into a separate party.[4]

Clay, once he was rid of Tyler, set about repairing the damage to his party in the South. Taking advantage of the fact that a large body of Southern opinion had come to accept the bank and that even in the cotton kingdom a considerable number of Southerners had developed a more temperate view toward the tariff,[5] especially since a period of prosperity had accompanied the protective measure of 1842, he strove to unify the party that had hitherto been distinguished for its contrarieties. He gave much attention to its Southern wing, making an extensive tour in the South early in 1844. His popularity reached its zenith as the election of 1844 approached, and the Whig party attained a high degree of unity. But before the election could be held, Clay's good prospects were destroyed by the question of slavery, which re-emerged when the question of annexing Texas was raised. Tyler was chiefly but by no means solely responsible for injecting the Texan question into politics.

The annexation of Texas had been long delayed because it could not be done without agitating the question of slavery; and the leaders of both parties endeavored to suppress discussions of slavery lest the political organizations to which their fortunes were tied be split into Northern and Southern wings. Only extremists like Calhoun and the abolitionists would risk shaking the political order to its foundations by raising that question in Congress. Inas-

[4] Oliver P. Chitwood, *John Tyler, Champion of the Old South* (New York, 1939), 197–289.
[5] Cole, *Whig Party in the South*, 93–99.

much as annexation would add another slave state to the Union, no public man could advocate it without risking the loss of many Northern votes. President Jackson would not support it in the summer of 1836 when it was requested by the newly established Republic of Texas because he did not wish to jeopardize Van Buren's chances in the fall election. Throughout Van Buren's administration both of the national parties skirted this politically dangerous question.

The South was not of one mind in respect to annexation. In 1837 and 1838 Senator William C. Preston of South Carolina tested that sentiment with resolutions favoring annexation, but Southern Senators would not unite in supporting them. The possibility of invoking war with Mexico, a tendency to leave the existing political equilibrium undisturbed, and fear that stimulation of cotton production in Texas would injure the Eastern cotton kingdom made many Southerners oppose any steps in the direction of immediate annexation. On the other hand, annexation had strong Southern supporters. A sample of their thoughts and sentiments can be found in a bitter and vigorous resolution introduced in the Mississippi legislature denouncing abolitionists and demanding the immediate acquisition of Texas in order that slave states might secure "an *equipoise* of influence in the halls of congress . . . which will furnish . . . a permanent guarantee of protection . . . against the tide of fanaticism which is rapidly setting against us."[6]

The stalemate in respect to Texas continued until after the rupture between Tyler and Clay. Then Tyler, freed from the restraining influence of a party connection, negotiated a treaty of annexation. Every Southern Whig Senator except John Henderson of Mississippi voted against it, and the treaty was defeated on June 8, 1844. Nevertheless, Tyler had accomplished something that no regular party adherent could have accomplished at that moment: he had forced the Senators to consider and commit themselves on the twin questions of annexation and slavery.

While Tyler was bringing this question to the center of the political stage, Clay and Van Buren, the leaders of their respective parties, were trying to force it back into the wings. In April these

[6] Mississippi *House Journal*, April–May, 1837, pp. 157–58.

two men, who were regarded as the probable candidates in the election to be held later in the year, announced their opposition to immediate annexation.

It was not so easy to seal off the Texan question in 1844 as it had been in the late 1830's. Since 1842 the growing inhumanity of Mexico to American citizens and her truculent dealings with the United States had brought the relations of the two countries close to the breaking point. American irritation was strongest in the Southwest, whose residents were more often affected by Mexican actions. Anti-Mexican feeling was especially bitter in New Orleans. George W. Kendall, the able editor of the New Orleans *Picayune*, spent several months in Mexican prisons in 1842, and his descriptions of his own and his companions' sufferings helped to arouse American hostility.[7] By the year 1844 there was a widespread feeling in the United States that Mexico might soon precipitate an armed conflict. There was also a belief that England had designs on Texas and that the United States must annex Texas in the near future or perhaps lose it for all time.

The Democratic party took advantage of the ground swell of sentiment by passing over Van Buren and nominating James K. Polk of Tennessee, an ardent expansionist whose candidacy had the blessing of the aged Jackson. To counterbalance the proslavery aspect of this proceeding, the party advocated expansion in the Northwest as well as in the Southwest under the slogan "the re-occupation of Oregon and the re-annexation of Texas."

Clay, who had hoped to maintain a neutral position toward the Texan question, was much embarrassed by this turn of events. He modified his antiannexation pronouncement, and thereby he confused his followers; but he was unable to repair the damage. Whig journals in the South supported him, and some of them insisted that annexation might become desirable should existing obstacles be removed. A major obstacle was the risk that annexation might be followed by war with Mexico. Southern Democratic papers enthusiastically welcomed the expansionist platform of their party, some of them demanding "Texas or Disunion."

[7] George W. Kendall, *Narrative of the Texan Santa Fé Expedition, . . . with an Account of the Sufferings . . . and Final Capture of the Texans, and their March, as Prisoners, to the City of Mexico* (New York, 1844).

Polk won the Presidential election by a narrow margin. In the South he received 60 electoral votes to 44 for Clay, and he carried all the Southern states with the exception of Maryland, North Carolina, Kentucky, and Tennessee. He made a much better showing than Van Buren had made in 1840. Even so, there is no evidence that the South was overwhelmingly in favor of annexation. In a total Southern vote of more than 700,000, Polk's majority over Clay was less than 14,000; [8] and Polk carried no state except Arkansas by as much as 60 per cent of the popular vote.

The annexation issue won votes for the Democrats in the South, but in the North a growing number of voters were dissatisfied with the refusal of either of the two major parties to take a positive stand against slavery. Many of them turned to the Liberty party. It had polled only 7,069 votes in the election of 1840 but in 1844 this antislavery party won 62,300 votes. It tipped the scales in New York from Clay to Polk, thus giving the presidency to the candidate whose views were less acceptable to the abolitionists.

Of more significance than this perverse working of fate was the long-range movement inaugurated by this episode. Slavery and related sectional questions, which had been consciously excluded from party warfare in recent years, were now breaking across the barriers that party leaders had set up, and they were disrupting the existing political order just as experienced politicians had foreseen and dreaded. When the Democratic party favored the opinions of its Southern members on questions intimately tied to slavery, it changed in some measure from a national party into a sectional party. At the moment, the Whigs were more successful in retaining their national character, but they did so at the cost of avoiding commitment on questions that an increasing number of Americans regarded as of fundamental importance. The contrary choices and experiences of these two parties on this occasion illustrate the general dilemma that faced them both during all the years that slavery was an important issue. On the one hand, a party could overlook the main question of the age and busy itself with matters of relatively little consequence. On the other hand, it could take a position for or against slavery and thereby convert itself into either a Southern or a Northern party. There seemed to be no way for a

[8] Polk also carried South Carolina where election was by the legislature.

national party to face squarely the chief issue of the day and to survive as a national party.

The election having gone in favor of the Democratic program of annexation, Congress passed a joint resolution in the last days of Tyler's term providing for its accomplishment. Party lines held fairly close in both houses, but enough Southern Whigs joined the Democrats to carry the resolution. Sectional feeling as well as party politics influenced the voting. Tyler, who had urged annexation primarily on the ground of broad national policy, nevertheless placed the question in a sectional light by alluding to England's desire to abolish slavery in Texas and to the advantages that would accrue to the South as a result of annexation. Calhoun in the State Department went even farther than the President in talking of slavery and abolition and in emphasizing the sectional implications of the Texas question. These remarks only emphasized what Americans already knew, namely, that the political power of the South would be strengthened and that of the North weakened by the addition of slave territory. Annexation was therefore regarded with more favor in the South than it was in the North.[9]

Although annexation had received Congressional approval before Polk was inaugurated, Polk still had a definite program, and he was notably successful in accomplishing it. A few days after his inauguration he stated that: "There are four measures which are to be the measures of my administration: one, a reduction of the tariff; another, the independent treasury; a third, the settlement of the Oregon boundary question; and lastly, the acquisition of California."[10]

These four measures interested Southerners in varying degrees. The Oregon boundary question was of minor concern to them. They had greater interest in the independent treasury, which was re-established in 1846, but political as well as economic considerations split Southern opinion widely. Even the tariff had lost some of its sectionalizing force; in Polk's administration it could be regarded by Southerners with more diversity of opinion and with more moderation than had been possible twenty years earlier.

[9] Chitwood, *John Tyler*, 353–54, 358.
[10] Eugene I. McCormac, "James Knox Polk," in *Dictionary of American Biography*, XV (1935), 37.

On the subject of protection, both major parties had made cautious and even ambiguous utterances during the campaign of 1844. The Democrats had shrewdly if not slyly strengthened themselves in Pennsylvania by nominating George M. Dallas, a protectionist, for the vice-presidency. But Polk, once his election was secured, clearly committed his administration to a downward revision of the tariff by statements in his inaugural address and by the appointment of Robert J. Walker as secretary of the treasury. The measure that was passed in July, 1846, closely followed Walker's recommendations. It substituted *ad valorem* for specific duties, and it placed the tariff substantially on a revenue basis. Protection was not abolished, but it was much reduced below the level of 1842. Neither the high tariff of 1842 nor the low tariff of 1846 caused the distress that was prophesied by its opponents; therefore, the leaders in this controversy had difficulty in convincing the rank and file of Americans that the level of protection was supremely important.

The Walker tariff, which remained in effect from 1846 to 1857, was passed by a Democratic Congress just as the previous tariff was the work of the Whigs. Nevertheless, eighteen Democratic Representatives, most of them from Pennsylvania and New York, voted against the tariff of 1846. In the South, party lines held fast. With very few exceptions Democratic Representatives and Senators voted for the measure while Southern Whigs voted against it. In the House there were 56 Southern votes for the bill and 20 against it, of which 11 were from Kentucky and Tennessee. Alexander H. Stephens and Robert Toombs of Georgia were among the opponents.[11]

Obviously, the tariff was less of a sectional and more of a party issue than it had once been. In the 1820's the fight over protection had played a large part in creating sectional feeling in the South; by the administrations of Tyler and Polk it had lost much of its dangerously divisive force. Nevertheless, enough interest remained to cause a considerable number of Northern Democrats to vote against the program of the Democratic administration. In Tyler's administration the Whig party had attained greater unity by shaking off Southern extremists; now the Democratic party was losing its hold on some of its Northern members. Both episodes illustrate

11 Stanwood, *American Tariff Controversies*, II, 69–76.

the difficulty of maintaining national parties in this period, and the difficulty was increased when the more critical question of slavery was raised.

In striving to accomplish the fourth of his objectives, the acquisition of California, Polk worked with a complicated set of circumstances growing out of the annexation of Texas. Among the main facts before him were the injured feelings of the Mexicans, a dispute over the lower boundary of Texas, the financial embarrassment of the Mexican government, some two million dollars of unpaid claims of American citizens against that impoverished government, and, of course, his own strong desire for westward expansion. Except for the fact that he disregarded the feelings and temper of those with whom he was to deal, the plan that Polk worked out took due account of the various elements in the situation.[12]

John Slidell of Louisiana was chosen to present the proposals of the United States to the Mexican government. Although that government, which had withdrawn its minister from Washington in protest against the annexation of Texas, had consented only to the reception of a commissioner, Slidell was sent as envoy extraordinary and minister plenipotentiary. His reception would have implied the full restoration of diplomatic relations between the two countries. Slidell's instructions required him to insist on a speedy adjustment of the claims of American citizens against Mexico. Inasmuch as Mexico was in no position to pay in money, Slidell was instructed to propose that the United States assume responsibility for paying those claims and that Mexico compensate the United States by territorial concessions. The minimum proposal was that Mexico relinquish claim to all lands lying above the Rio Grande, but Slidell was to secure, if possible, New Mexico and California as well. For these he was authorized to offer additional sums of money over and above the amount needed to pay the claims of American citizens.

When the Mexican government refused to receive Slidell, Polk decided to recommend to Congress a resort to arms. His case before

[12] The following summary of the Mexican War period follows closely the interpretations of Justin H. Smith, *The Annexation of Texas* (New York, 1911), and *The War With Mexico*, 2 vols. (New York, 1919). Smith's revisionist views were generally corroborated by Eugene I. McCormac, *James K. Polk, A Political Biography* (Berkeley, 1922).

Congress and the American people was strengthened when American soldiers were killed in consequence of the advance of the American army toward the Rio Grande. On May 11, 1846, he informed Congress that a state of war existed, and he recommended that prompt and energetic measures be taken for bringing it to a speedy and successful conclusion.[18] Both houses gave their approval to his recommendations.

The campaigns of the Mexican War need not be described in these pages, but some of their results must be noted. They gave to the junior officers an experience in actual warfare which enhanced the skill of some of them in the subsequent conduct of large-scale operations in the Confederate and Union armies. General Zachary Taylor gained for himself a reputation which helped to place him in the presidency. The United States won such decided victories on the field of battle that it was able to dictate peace terms of its own choosing. By the Treaty of Guadalupe Hidalgo, the Rio Grande was recognized as the boundary of Texas; New Mexico and Upper California were ceded to the United States; and the United States agreed to pay fifteen million dollars to Mexico and to assume payment of claims of American citizens against the Mexican government.

One other effect of the Mexican War was a marked increase in the tension between North and South. Abolitionists in Congress, most of whom belonged to the Whig party, charged that Polk and the Democrats instigated and waged the war for the extension and and preservation of slavery. The allegation was politically shrewd; but it was false. Polk may have been too aggressive an expansionist, but the facts do not support the charge that his goal was the extension of slavery. It was generally recognized that most of the territory in question was unsuited for slavery, and many of the stanchest defenders of slavery were opposed to the war and to the acquisition of additional territory. Calhoun, for example, had refused to vote for the declaration of war. John A. Campbell of Alabama, who was later a justice of the United States Supreme Court, reasoned that any large acquisition of Mexican territory would upset the balance of power in the United States to the disadvantage of the South. His conclusion was based on the belief that the territory in question was wholly unfit for a Negro population, and that expansion would

18 Milo M. Quaife (ed.), *The Diary of James K. Polk* (Chicago, 1910), I, 382–90.

therefore result in "an increase of the strength of the nonslaveholding states and a corresponding diminution of our own." [14] There
are strong indications that a movement to annex all of Mexico was
chiefly supported by antislavery men and was chiefly opposed by
proslavery Democrats led by Calhoun.[15]

But though the war and the acquisition of additional territory
were not the products of a proslavery conspiracy, the charges of the
abolitionists embarrassed Northern Democrats, making them appear to be supine supporters of an aggressive Southern leadership
in their party. The case was doubly hard for those who had voted
for lowering the tariff in 1846. Such a one was the Pennsylvania
Democrat David Wilmot. To prove that a Northern Democrat
could be independent, Wilmot seriously embarrassed the administration's attempt to secure funds for making peace by proposing
that slavery should be excluded from any territory that might be
acquired from Mexico. In the fight over the Wilmot Proviso, party
lines broke.[16] Northern Whigs joined Northern Democrats in supporting it. Southerners of differing party affiliations rallied against
it. Calhoun, who had opposed the war with Mexico, presented a
set of resolutions in the Senate asserting that a Federal law pro-
hibiting slavery in any territory of the United States would be a
"violation of the constitution . . . and would tend directly to
subvert the Union itself." [17] This statement met with wide approval
throughout the South.

Although the Wilmot Proviso was not adopted, leaving the question of slavery in the Mexican territory for future settlement, the
debate over Wilmot's proposal widened the rift between North and
South. The debate also revealed that the opposing camps were ready
to fight even when little or nothing was at stake; it was generally
recognized that slavery would make little progress in the Mexican
territory regardless of any law that Congress might pass. This tend-

[14] John A. Campbell to John C. Calhoun, Mobile, November 20, 1847, in J. Franklin Jameson (ed.), *Correspondence of John C. Calhoun,* in American Historical Association, *Annual Report,* 1899 (Washington, 1900), II, 1140.
[15] John D. P. Fuller, "The Slavery Question and the Movement to Acquire Mexico,
1846–1848," in *Mississippi Valley Historical Review,* XXI (1934–1935), 31–48.
[16] Richard R. Stenberg, "The Motivation of the Wilmot Proviso," *ibid.,* XVIII
(1931–1932), 535–41.
[17] *Congressional Globe,* 29 Cong., 2 Sess., 455.

ency for party lines to break whenever the question of slavery was raised was extremely hazardous for the South. Since the early 1830's the South had protected its interests chiefly by making the two national parties bid for Southern support. In recent years this policy had paid rich dividends, as in securing the Walker tariff and the annexation of Texas. The South was undoubtedly winning more in this kind of game than it could win if national parties should be replaced by sectional political alignments. Perhaps it was overplaying its strength and contributing to the destruction of the national parties by asking Northern Whigs and Democrats to make too great concessions. In any event, there was an increasing tendency for questions about slavery to occur, and on such occasions patriotism to section was usually stronger than allegiance to party.

This early evidence of the disintegration of the national parties was dangerous to the nation as well as to the South, for national parties were among the chief ties holding the nation together. Before many more years had passed, the flood tide of sectionalism was to sweep the Whig party into oblivion and to split the Democratic party into Northern and Southern wings.

CHAPTER XV

THE AFFIRMATION OF
SOUTHERN PERFECTION

HOW far the South had come toward sectionalism or nationalism by the late 1840's depends on the meaning ascribed to these words. But this much is clear. To the South's ancient economic and social distinctiveness there had been added, chiefly in the 1820's, something of a political platform. In the 1830's, regional self-consciousness and hostility toward the North became evident in many aspects of Southern thought and expression. By the late 1840's, there were those who desired a separate South.

While the relationship of the South to the nation was deteriorating and the power of the South in Congress was declining, changes were taking place within the region itself. Most noticeable, perhaps, was its southwestward expansion, engulfing the Indian lands of the lower South and sweeping across the Mississippi River into eastern Texas. The declining strength of the Southern states in Congress between the 1820's and the 1840's is measured by the loss of three seats by the South while the rest of the nation gained twenty-two seats. Within this same period the southwestward shift of Southern population caused the seaboard states to lose fifteen seats in the lower house of Congress while the rest of the South gained twelve seats.

Beyond the realm of statistical measurement, a more significant political shift had occurred. The strong and nationally respected leadership of Virginia in early years had vanished. By the 1840's, the leading Southern politicians were in the cotton states, and few of them had much influence outside the South. Much of the cotton South, stretching from South Carolina to Texas, was newly settled— a blend of the South and West—and most of it was in the vanguard of the democratic movement. On several counts, the cotton-kingdom politicians were too aggressive, and their viewpoint was too sectional, for the older and more conservative tobacco South.

Nonpolitical changes were also occurring in the region. Railroads and steamboats were introduced, a few factories were established, colleges increased in numbers, evangelical churches multiplied, significant literary developments occurred, and democracy made much progress. These were important, but the sum total of them all was probably less important than the relative changelessness of the South in a nation that was changing fast. The booming cities, the factories, the multiplying railroads, the expanding population, and the changing attitudes and viewpoints above Mason and Dixon's line account for tension between North and South far better than any changes that were taking place in the South.

The South of the 1840's, like the South of the previous century, was a land of farms and plantations, of few towns and of scattered population, of internal waterway transportation, and of a great export trade to foreign markets. Through all of this period Negro slavery continued. In the formation of the Union and in its early years, the South was accepted as a respectable part of the nation; by the 1840's it was regarded by many Northerners as an obstacle to American social and economic progress and as a moral pariah. The explanation of this change in attitude is to be found in part in the long series of conflicts between the diverging sections, and sectional divergence was due chiefly to those forces that were transforming the North. Because of this fact, the student of this period of Southern history must rely heavily on the student of Northern economic, social, and religious movements; for these were the forces that remade the North and that in a large measure gave to the North a new and more critical attitude toward the South.

As the South declined in political power and as it experienced the growing force of the antislavery movement, the mind of the South was transmuted into something very different from what it had been a generation earlier. This mental change, in its various aspects, was one of the most notable developments in the South between 1819 and 1848.

To speak of the mind of the South implies, perhaps, a unity in the thinking of Southerners when, as a matter of fact, there was much diversity. They disagreed about the merits of the Whig and Democratic parties, about slavery, about the Union, and about a host of other subjects. But within the area of Southern thought and expression, certain traits and qualities had developed which if not universal in the region or even dominant were at least influential and significant.

Some of the changes that had come within a generation are suggested by the contrasting impressions made by James Madison and John C. Calhoun on Harriet Martineau. She wrote of the aged former President, after visiting him in 1834, "the finest of his characteristics appeared to me to be his inexhaustible faith; faith that a well-founded commonwealth may, as our motto declares, be immortal; not only because the people, its constituency, never die, but because the principles of justice in which such a commonwealth originates never die out of the people's heart and mind. This faith shone brightly through the whole of Mr. Madison's conversation" except in his discussion of slavery. He talked of slavery freely and at length, "acknowledging, without limitation or hesitation, all the evils with which it has ever been charged." But he could muster little hope for an improvement.

Except for his deep pessimism about slavery, Madison's opinions were an authentic echo into the 1830's of views that were widely held by the Revolutionary generation of Virginians. In sharp contrast to his tolerance, communicativeness, faith in democracy, and optimism, is the impression that Calhoun made at nearly the same time upon this shrewd though biased English observer. Of him she wrote: "His mind has long lost all power of communicating with any other. I know of no man who lives in such utter intellectual solitude. He meets men, and harangues them by the fireside as in the Senate; he is wrought like a piece of machinery, set a going vehemently by a weight, and stops while you answer; he either passes by what you say, or twists it into a suitability with what is in his head, and begins to lecture again." [1]

The difference between Madison and Calhoun in the 1830's was not altogether a matter of personal temperament. Calhoun's mind had been more open, more willing to exchange ideas with others, more favorable toward experimentation, less tense and severe, and more amicable in the early years of his career than it was in the

[1] Harriet Martineau, *Retrospect of Western Travel* (London, 1838), I, 148, 191.

1830's and 1840's. A great change had come over him and over many of his generation of Southerners. In the first place, he and they had lost faith in some of the fundamental premises of democracy. Perhaps they had never thoroughly believed that all men were created free and equal and that all had an inalienable right to liberty, but neither had they denied these tenets until the slavery controversy forced them to face the contradiction between slavery and the Declaration of Independence. Compelled to make a choice, they denied the accuracy and validity of the Revolutionary doctrines; and Jefferson, the personification of democratic idealism, they repudiated as a theoretical and dangerous visionary.[2]

Going beyond theories, Calhoun's contemporaries pointed to evils in the actual operation of democratic government. They believed, and with good reason, that grave injuries had been done to the substantial interests of the South during the 1820's within the framework and through the procedures of democratic government. The conclusion was inescapable that a democracy could and often did oppress minorities within itself. Much thought was therefore given to devices for limiting and controlling self-government so as to protect smaller parts against the tyranny of the majority. The doctrine that the will of the majority ought always to be followed was utterly repudiated.

Inasmuch as the government to be held in check operated under a written constitution, the discussion turned into constitutional rather than philosophical channels. Champions of the South seldom began with the nature of man or with the good of man and society. Their arguments usually started with the written words of the fundamental document, and thence they proceeded by close reasoning and logical skill that was sometimes amazingly subtle. As one follows their mental operations he feels at times that he is watching intellectual giants struggling with very real and very profound problems of constitutional government, but at other times they seem to be no more than medieval scholastics working in an unreal world where little matters except logical technique.

The narrow but brilliant operation of the Southern mind on questions of government was accompanied by a restricted and abstract concept of humanity. Although the object of Southern

2 Bean, "Anti-Jeffersonianism in the Ante-Bellum South," *loc. cit.,* 103–24.

political thought was to afford protection to the individual, far less attention was given to man than to checks and limitations on the machinery of government. It had not been so at an earlier period of Southern history. Jefferson and Madison knew, as Calhoun seems finally to have forgotten, that man is a creature of many parts, compounded of good as well as of bad, and that government must be fitted to man rather than man to government; they had tried to build democracy on such elements of goodness and wisdom as could be found in humanity. Calhoun, in contrast, limited himself to the task of devising a system of government that would hold in check the destructive tendencies of man. Yet, the last word must be said for Calhoun. The grim, narrow, pessimistic spirit that had come over him was not altogether and perhaps not mainly of his own creation. The selfish and reckless tendencies in human nature which he was trying to place under legal and constitutional limitations were the forces that had in large measure placed his region on the defensive and made him the champion of a minority.

Along with its concern about problems of government, the mind of the South was becoming preoccupied with the problem of its own social organization. For a long time the South had possessed a distinctive social order, compounded of such elements as ruralism, the plantation system, Negro slavery, and a complex pattern of customs and conventions. To this way of life Southerners had conformed without much thought that they were odd persons living in a curious and different society. But by the 1830's the Southern mind was turned inward to a consideration of its own society. Among the forces that engendered this regional self-consciousness were Southern writers, like Kennedy and Simms and the school of local-color humorists, who described aspects of the Southern scene; foreign and Northern travelers who commented on distinctive Southern characteristics; and Northern opponents of slavery who extended their criticisms to include the whole fabric of Southern society. The bitter and extravagant antislavery attack was the major force in making Southerners aware that their region had a way of life that was far different from the rest of the United States, and the shock of the attack was aggravated because it came at a time when there was deep concern in the region over its failure to keep pace with the North and West in the march of progress.

The first response of Southerners to the vigorous onslaught was frequently one of startled amazement. This reaction was especially noticeable in the early stages of the Missouri debate. But defensive forces were soon rallied, and something of a plan of campaign began to emerge. It consisted in small measure of an attack upon the enemy's country, and this was aimed at the Northern characteristic that was most unlike the South, namely industrialism. One of the earliest American critiques of an industrial society, with emphasis on its exploitation of labor, was evolved in the South as a counter-attack against Northern critics of slavery.[3]

But the master plan of the South in this war of words called for a defensive instead of an offensive war. It denied the validity of Northern criticisms, and it evolved into a remarkable apologia of virtually every aspect of the Southern way of life. Inasmuch as the attacking forces charged that Southern life was blighted throughout by slavery, Southern defenders rallied to this point. They claimed that slavery was good, that slavery had a beneficent influence upon Southern life, and that the South like ancient Greece had evolved a noble civilization because the institution of slavery was an integral part of it.

In 1835 Governor George McDuffie of South Carolina utterly repudiated the opinions earlier expressed "in a mischievous and misguided spirit of sickly sentimentality" by "some of our own statesmen," to the effect that slavery was "a moral and political evil, much to be deplored, but incapable of being eradicated." Instead, he affirmed that no human institution was "more manifestly consistent with the will of God," better designed to enhance the happiness of the Negro, or a firmer "corner stone of our republican edifice."[4] The following year Senator James H. Hammond said: "It is no evil. On the contrary, I believe it to be the greatest of all the great blessings which a kind Providence bestowed upon our glorious region. . . . it has rendered our southern country proverbial for its wealth, its genius, and its manners."[5] Somewhat later he claimed that slavery was responsible for the superiority of the

[3] Wilfred Carsel, "The Slaveholders' Indictment of Northern Wage Slavery," in *Journal of Southern History*, VI (1940), 504–20.

[4] South Carolina *Journal of the General Assembly*, 1835, pp. 6–8.

[5] *Register of Debates*, 24 Cong., 1 Sess., 2456.

moral code, the educational system, the religious beliefs and practices, and other attributes of Southern life. Pointing with pride to Southern religious conservatism, especially to its freedom from "Mormonism and Millerism," as well as from "Shakers, Rappists, Dunkers, Socialists, Fourierists, and the like," he concluded: "You may attribute this to our domestic slavery if you choose. I believe you would do so justly. There is no material here for such characters to operate upon."[6]

The effect of slavery upon the character of slaveholders was praised. It was claimed that many of the "highest, manliest and most admirable qualities in the Southern character have been preserved in their pristine strength, if not engendered by our peculiar, social and domestic system."[7] It set apart and gave a vigorous individuality to Southern men. Accustomed to commanding, they became leaders wherever they went, demonstrating their prowess in all acquisitions of national territory, and displaying their capacity for political leadership in the predominance of Southerners in the presidency of the United States.

It was also claimed that slavery was the only perfect and permanent foundation for democracy. Because of a servile population, citizens of the Southern states were said to be equal, and "Equality among its citizens is the corner-stone of a republic."[8] Again, it was said that slavery, as it existed in the South, was the only safeguard against anarchy and aggressive skepticism, and that "the destruction of African slavery would be the destruction of republicanism."[9] As proof of this remarkable claim, it was argued that under a system of universal suffrage all political power must eventually fall into the hands of men without education or property, and that property was the great conservative force in government.[10]

In sharp contrast to current pessimism about the economic plight

[6] J. D. B. De Bow (ed.), *The Southern States, Embracing a Series of Papers Condensed from the Earlier Volumes of De Bow's Review* . . . (Washington, New Orleans, 1856), 245.

[7] William P. Miles, *Oration Delivered before the Fourth of July Association* . . . *1849* (Charleston, 1849), 25.

[8] *Congressional Globe*, 27 Cong., 2 Sess., Appendix, 337.

[9] Lawrence M. Keitt, *Address on Laying the Corner-Stone of the Fire-Proof Building, at Columbia, Dec. 15, 1851* (Columbia, 1851), 7.

[10] William Harper, *Anniversary Oration; Delivered* . . . *in the Representative Hall, Columbia, S.C., Dec. 9, 1835* (Washington, 1836), 10.

of the South, regional defenders boasted of the indispensable character of Southern staples in the commerce of the world and of the essential importance of the South as a market for the manufactured goods of the North. But their greatest claim to economic excellence was that slavery abolished the usual feud between capital and labor. Thus, the South could escape the discontentment and turbulence of the North because the Southern laborer was freed from the uncertainty and misery of the Northern laborer, especially in depression years.

From this point the argument sometimes moved into a sweeping defense of the social fabric of the South. The Southern laborer was said to be an integral part of the economic and social life of his region whereas his Northern counterpart floated loosely on the surface of society without belonging to it. Having so small a stake in society, the great body of Northern labor was "easily, on any occasion of excitement, formed into a mob—so easily swayed by artful and designing demagogues." [11] The impermanent and granular quality of Northern society allowed its members to have much freedom but it gave them little security. In contrast, Southern society was stable because each person, rich and poor, black and white, was firmly rooted in a close-knit, organic social order.

The Reverend Iverson L. Brookes swept into the pages of a single essay many of the claims of Southern perfection. It bore the significant title: *A Defense of the South against the Reproaches and Encroachments of the North: in Which Slavery is Shown to be an Institution of God Intended to Form the Basis of the Best Social State and the Only Safeguard to the Permanence of a Republican Government.*[12] Here we have it. The champions of the Old South claimed that theirs was the ideal social order and the only permanently founded democracy, all because it had, with God's blessing, slavery. Surely, Southerners had come a long way from Jefferson and a long way out of reality. Fighting to defend their way of life they had taken refuge in a dream world, and they insisted that others accept their castle in the sky as an accurate description of conditions in the South.

11 Miles, *Oration Delivered before the Fourth of July Association,* 24; Charleston *Courier,* April 4, 1849.

12 Hamburg, S.C., 1850.

The ancient Hebrews looked back to the Garden of Eden and the Greeks to a Golden Age. Early in the twentieth century, zealous and uncritical devotees of evolution looked into the distant future for the ideal society. The ante-bellum defenders of the South, rare among mortals, claimed that their own age was the golden age, and they claimed that its main foundation was Negro slavery.

It would be fruitless to point to fallacies in their reasoning and to the great contrast between the perfections they described and the imperfections that lay all about them. It would be impossible to guess how many Southerners agreed with these spokesmen in their extravagant claims and boastings about the perfect society of the Old South. It is enough to recognize that before the middle of the century there were some Southerners whose minds, under the impact of a long train of bitter criticism of their region and with a realization that the power of their opponents was growing, had turned into this curious, psychopathic condition. And one thing else must be recognized. Even though the idealized portrait of the South was false, it was to be a strong and living force in the years ahead. In the long run, the vision of the perfect South was to supply a substantial element in the construction of the romantic legend about the Old South. In the nearer future, it was to give the Confederate soldier something to die for.

APPENDIX

NOTE CONCERNING MAPS OF
PRESIDENTIAL ELECTIONS
OF 1824, 1828, AND 1832

THE primary purpose of these maps is to indicate the areas of strength and weakness of each of the Presidential candidates in the elections of 1824, 1828, and 1832, and to show gains and losses from one election to the next. The maps in Arthur C. Cole, *Whig Party in the South,* afford a basis for continuing such comparisons in the elections of 1836 and thereafter. To achieve the second purpose of these maps, a mode of plotting data was devised which would distinguish between areas of heavy and light voting.

For a background map, the earliest of the series of outline maps of the United States published by the Department of Agriculture was used. This map is for the year 1840; but better than any other map that could be found it could be adapted to present needs.

A more difficult task was the location of county election returns. At one stage of the work, the publication of these records was contemplated, but their extensiveness compelled a negative decision. Only the sources where they were found will be given. In some instances the total state vote for the Presidential candidates as revealed by these sources differs somewhat from the votes published in Edward Stanwood, *History of the Presidency from 1788 to 1897,* but the differences are not important enough to warrant publishing another set of tables.

Except in a few cases, and these will be noted, each circle represents the vote of a single county. Where the vote was heavy and the counties small, a few of the circles fall beyond the bounds of the appropriate county. A cross within a circle shows the vote of a town. Where electors were chosen by the legislature instead of by popular election, the state vote is indicated by a rectangle with the relative strength of the candidates, so far as this can be found, shown within the rectangle.

A single set of symbols was used in plotting the elections of 1828 and

340

1832. The lighter vote in 1824 permitted the use of larger circles, and these were needed because of the greater number of candidates.

MAP OF 1824 ELECTION

In the election of 1824 the smallest circle indicates a vote of less than 300; the next, 300–1,000; the third, over 1,000; and the largest, used in Maryland and Tennessee, shows votes in electoral districts rather than in counties. Within each circle the share of the vote received by the several candidates is shown with an error of less than 10 per cent by the following symbolism:

⬤ Jackson   ⊜ Adams

◯ Crawford   ⬤ Clay

MAPS OF 1828 AND 1832 ELECTIONS

In these two elections the smallest circle indicates a vote of less than 200; next, 200–500; the third, 500–1,000; the fourth, over 1,000; and the largest, used for Tennessee in 1828, represents electoral districts, in each of which there were more than 3,000 votes. In these two elections the symbolism is as follows:

⬤ Jackson majority of more than 2 to 1

◖ Jackson majority of less than 2 to 1

◑ Tie vote

⊖ Adams (1828) or Clay (1832) majority of less than 2 to 1

◯ Adams (1828) or Clay (1832) majority of more than 2 to 1

SOURCES FOR DATA USED IN PLOTTING 1824 ELECTION MAP

ALABAMA. "Complete Presidential Electoral Returns," in *Cahawba Press and Alabama State Intelligencer,* November 22, 1824.

GEORGIA. *Senate Journal,* November-December, 1824, p. 34, records the election of the state's nine electors on November 4, without indicating whether there were other candidates and without recording the vote. The Georgia electors voted unanimously for Crawford.

KENTUCKY. Lexington *Kentucky Reporter,* November 22, 29, 1824; Lexington *Kentucky Gazette,* December 2, 1824; Russellville *Weekly Messenger,* November 20, 1824.

LOUISIANA. *House Journal,* 1824–1825, p. 8, records the choice by the legislature of the five electors, showing the number of votes received by each of the five and by each of the unsuccessful candidates. From the *Journal* and from comments in the New Orleans *Louisiana Gazette,* November 23, 1824, the following facts are evident: three of the electors were for Jackson and two for Adams; each of these five candidates received nearly the same vote; two Clay candidates failed of election by small margins; there was no evidence of a Crawford party in Louisiana.

MARYLAND. The popular vote in each of the nine electoral districts (together with the names of the counties composing each district) is given in *Niles' Weekly Register,* XXVII (1824), 195–96. *Ibid.,* 162, shows the number of electors to which each district was entitled.

MISSISSIPPI. Returns from all but four of the counties are in Natchez *Mississippi State Gazette,* November 20, 1824, and a less perfect set of returns in Natchez *Mississippi Republican, and Literary Register,* November 17, 1824. The original manuscript return from Perry County, which is one of the four not recorded in the *Gazette,* is filed in Series F, Number 29, Mississippi Department of Archives and History.

NORTH CAROLINA. Albert R. Newsome, *Presidential Election of 1824 in North Carolina,* 156, gives the popular vote by counties for the Crawford ticket and the People's ticket. Votes for the People's ticket are counted as Jackson votes even though a minority preferred Adams.

SOUTH CAROLINA. The manuscript "Journal of the Senate of South Carolina, 1824" (in South Carolina Historical Commission) records on pages 48, 50, 57, the election by the legislature on November 30 of the state's eleven electors. The entries do not suggest any division of opinion, and the electors voted unanimously for Jackson and Calhoun.

TENNESSEE. The original county returns could not be found in the archives of the State Library, nor could returns be found in available newspapers. According to Stanwood, *History of the Presidency from 1788 to 1897,* p. 136, the Tennessee popular vote was as follows: Jackson, 20,197; Adams, 216; Crawford, 312; and according to *Niles' Weekly Register,* XXVII (1824), 216, all of the Crawford votes and 200 of the Adams votes were cast in Davidson, Williamson, and Rutherford counties. Since Crawford and Adams received less than 10 per cent of the popular votes even in this area, the map shows no popular votes except for Jackson. The 20,725 popular votes cast in this election have been distributed over the state, according to electoral districts, on the basis of the white population of the districts.

VIRGINIA. "Votes for President and Vice President of the United States," a manuscript table which accompanies the original county returns in the election of 1824, is in the Division of Archives of the Virginia State Library.

SOURCES FOR DATA USED IN PLOTTING 1828 ELECTION MAP

ALABAMA. Manuscript "Returns of the Vote for the Electors of the President and Vice President of the United States in Alabama 1828," in Executive Files of the Alabama Department of Archives and History.

GEORGIA. Although a "consolidated return" of the 1828 election was laid before the legislature on November 21 (*House Journal, 1828*, pp. 132–33), it cannot now be found. The following newspapers contain pertinent information: Milledgeville *Georgia Journal*, November 24, 1828; *National Banner and Nashville Whig*, December 2, 1828, quoting Augusta *Chronicle*; and various issues for November and early December, 1828, of the Augusta *Constitutionalist*, Augusta *Georgia Courier*, Athens *Athenian*, and Savannah *Republican*.

The Clark faction offered an electoral ticket pledged to vote for Jackson for President and for Calhoun for Vice-President. The highest number of votes received by any Clark elector was 7,991. The Troup electoral candidates also favored Jackson but opposed Calhoun, and the highest of these candidates received 9,712 votes. Some 600 Georgians, chiefly "northern merchants in Savannah, Augusta, Darien, and perhaps Macon," voted for an Adams ticket. Accurate returns were found for only a minority of the Georgia counties. The remaining popular vote was plotted over the other counties in proportion to white population.

KENTUCKY. "The complete official return" is in Frankfort *Kentuckian*, November 20, 1828, and Lexington *Kentucky Reporter*, November 26, 1828.

LOUISIANA. Returns in Baton Rouge *Gazette*, November 22, 1828, with unimportant corrections in issues of November 29 and December 6.

MARYLAND. Washington *United States Telegraph*, April 7, 1829.

MISSISSIPPI. Manuscript tabulation entitled "Jackson-Adams" together with original county returns in Series F, Number 31, Mississippi Department of Archives and History.

NORTH CAROLINA. "Official returns" in Raleigh *Register, and North-Carolina Gazette*, December 5, 1828, and Raleigh *Star, and North Carolina State Gazette*, November 27, 1828.

SOUTH CAROLINA. Manuscript "Journal of the House of Representatives, of South Carolina, 1828" (in South Carolina Historical Commission), pp. 60, 62, records election on December 2 of the state's eleven electors. No division of opinion in the legislature is indicated. The electors voted unanimously for Jackson and Calhoun.

TENNESSEE. Popular vote by electoral districts is in Washington *United States Telegraph,* April 10, 1829.

VIRGINIA. Original county returns and a tabulation in the Division of Archives of the Virginia State Library.

SOURCES FOR DATA USED IN PLOTTING 1832 ELECTION MAP

ALABAMA. Manuscript "Returns of the Vote for the Electors of the President and Vice President of the U.S.," in Executive Files of the Alabama Department of Archives and History.

GEORGIA. The highest electoral candidate on the Troup ticket received 13,398 votes. This ticket supported Jackson for President and Van Buren for Vice-President. The highest on the Clark ticket, which was for Jackson and Philip P. Barbour, received 7,352 votes. As was usual in this period, the Georgia returns were confused and records poorly kept. The vote was discovered for thirteen counties; the remainder of the popular vote was distributed over the other counties in proportion to white population. Information was found in Savannah *Georgian,* November 8, 9, 10, 12, 15, 16, 1832; *Daily Savannah Republican,* November 6, 8, 26, 1832; Macon *Georgia Messenger,* November 8, 1832; Macon *Georgia Telegraph,* November 14, 1832; Milledgeville *Georgia Journal,* November 12, December 10, 1832; Columbus *Enquirer,* November 10, 1832; Augusta *Chronicle,* October 13, November 10, 1832.

KENTUCKY. Manuscript "true & correct statement of the Polls from each & every County in the State of Kentucky except the County of Jefferson which was excluded. Novr. 22nd, 1832," in Box 48, Jacket 340, Kentucky State Historical Society.

LOUISIANA. A "return of the late Presidential Election in this State, copied from the official documents in the office of the Secretary of State," in Baton Rouge *Gazette,* December 8, 1832.

MARYLAND. Popular vote by counties, in *Niles' Weekly Register,* XLIII (1832–1833), 214. In this election Maryland chose ten electors in four unequal districts, but since the vote was found on a county basis, it has been so mapped.

MISSISSIPPI. Manuscript county returns are in Series F, Number 36, Mississippi Department of Archives and History. Two tickets were before the voters, both supporting Jackson. The largest number of votes received by any candidate on the electoral ticket favoring Van Buren for Vice-President was 4,399; the largest for a Barbour for Vice-President electoral candidate was 1,547.

NORTH CAROLINA. Raleigh *Register, and North-Carolina Gazette,* November 23, 1832; Raleigh *North-Carolina Constitutionalist and People's Advocate,* November 21, 1832. The Jackson–Van Buren ticket received 21,007 votes; the Jackson-Barbour ticket, 3,855; and the Clay-Sergeant ticket, 4,563.

SOUTH CAROLINA. Manuscript "Journal of the Senate of South Carolina, 1832" (South Carolina Historical Commission), p. 49, records the election on December 4 of eleven electors. They voted unanimously for John Floyd of Virginia for President and for Henry Lee of Massachusetts for Vice-President.

TENNESSEE. Manuscript county returns are in the Tennessee State Library. Each shows the number of popular votes for each electoral candidate, but the commitments of the candidates are usually not indicated. The Jackson–Van Buren candidates and the votes cast for them can be determined with a high degree of accuracy. It is not always easy to distinguish between Jackson-Barbour and Clay-Sergeant candidates. Despite lack of exactness on minor points, it is certain that the Jackson–Van Buren ticket carried every county by a large majority.

VIRGINIA. Manuscript county returns are in the Division of Archives of the Virginia State Library. Jackson and Van Buren received 33,727 votes; Jackson and Barbour, 235; and Clay and Sergeant, 11,331.

CRITICAL ESSAY ON AUTHORITIES

PHYSICAL REMAINS

MUSEUMS are good, but travel guided by historical knowledge is better if one would see the physical remains of life in the South in the first half of the nineteenth century. Off the paved highways, the kind of roads in common use a hundred years ago are easily discovered, and some of them follow ancient roadbeds. A few tollgate houses yet stand. Most of the canals are in ruins, but a section of the Chesapeake and Ohio Canal west of Washington, D.C., is kept in order by the National Park Service. The old-fashioned river steamboat is almost extinct, but trips by canoe or houseboat on the rivers will bring one closer to the Old South than travel by train, automobile, or plane. The fields of cotton, tobacco, sugar, and corn that one sees today are often much as they were a hundred years ago; but hemp and tidewater rice fields are about gone.

Many log and frame homes of the plain folk, built more than a hundred years ago, are standing, but it is usually hard to document their age. Public buildings of the period of this study, often modified past recognition, can be found in some of the towns. For example, very early railroad stations are in Lexington, Kentucky, and in Woodville, Mississippi. Clues to the location of Greek-revival town and country mansions and academic buildings are given in Chapter III. Photographs of many of these buildings are in the Historic American Buildings Survey in the Library of Congress.

MAPS

The most useful of the maps published during the years of this study are those of Henry C. Carey and Isaac Lea, 1822, and of Henry S. Tanner, 1829. An excellent set of large maps, usually containing two states to the sheet, especially valuable for data on post roads and post offices, was published in 1839 by David H. Burr, topographer to the Post

Office Department. Less detailed are the numerous editions of Samuel A. Mitchell maps. In the field of local maps, Texas is especially well represented in guidebooks published in the 1840's.

Of recent maps, Charles O. Paullin and John K. Wright, *Atlas of the Historical Geography of the United States* (Washington, 1932), is the most valuable single work. It is supplemented at several important points by Clifford L. Lord and Elizabeth H. Lord, *Historical Atlas of the United States* (New York, 1944). Maps showing canals and railroads in this period are in Balthasar H. Meyer, *History of Transportation in the United States before 1860* (Washington, 1917); and maps, summaries of treaties, and other data about land cessions by Indian tribes are in United States Bureau of American Ethnology, *Eighteenth Annual Report, 1896–97*, Part II (Washington, 1899). Arthur C. Cole, *The Whig Party in the South* (Washington, 1913), contains maps showing the vote in each county in the South in Presidential elections from 1836 through 1852.

MANUSCRIPTS

A thorough discussion of the manuscript sources of this period of Southern history would far exceed the space that is here available. It must suffice to say that notable collections of plantation records have been assembled at the University of North Carolina, at Duke University, and at Louisiana State University. Guides to the manuscript holdings for all three of these institutions have been published. Much unpublished material is in state archives, and these differ in respect to the quantity and condition of their holdings and in respect to the facility with which manuscripts can be located and made available to scholars. In this study considerable use was made of unpublished election returns in Virginia, Mississippi, Alabama, Kentucky, and Tennessee archives. Some of the governors' papers were useful, among them the papers of John Breathitt and Joseph Desha of Kentucky. South Carolina is extraordinary among Southern states in that its legislative journals were not published for a considerable span of years prior to 1831, and these must be consulted in manuscript at the South Carolina Historical Commission at Columbia. Rare and valuable materials in the Virginia State Library are the collection of manuscript registers of county officers and the annual tax returns by counties. Fragmentary data of the former kind are in the Kentucky State Historical Society at Frankfort.

Considerable bodies of older county records—deeds and will books, marriage registers, order and minute books of county courts, and other materials—have been assembled in some of the state archives either by transfer of the original records from the counties or by film or photostatic copies. Vast quantities of such material, much of it never examined by any historian, remain at the county seats. County Court Minutes, 1823–1831, of Pasquotank County, North Carolina, and records of a number of Virginia counties were closely examined in the present study.

Although collections of the letters and papers of John C. Calhoun, Henry Clay, and Andrew Jackson have been published, some of their writings can be consulted only in manuscript. Of such materials, the Clay Papers in the Library of Congress are probably the most important. In the present study, the more useful collections of unpublished papers were those of less important men. Among these are the William C. Rives Papers in the Library of Congress and at Duke University; the David Campbell Papers at Duke University; the large collection of James H. Hammond Papers at the Library of Congress, which illuminates many phases of South Carolina history; and, in the same repository, a letter from John Tyler to Robert Y. Hayne, June 30, 1831, discussing the theory of nullification and appraising Virginia sentiment on this subject.

The Benjamin L. C. Wailes Diary and Papers at Duke University and the Mississippi State Department of Archives and History throw light on many phases of Mississippi social and intellectual history, and the Eugene R. Hendrix Papers at Duke University illuminate a number of points in Methodist history. The Journal of John P. Kennedy, at the Peabody Library in Baltimore, contains pertinent material, and the Willie P. Mangum Papers and the Nathaniel Macon Papers in the North Carolina Department of Archives and History are valuable for political history in the 1820's.

GOVERNMENT DOCUMENTS: FEDERAL

Federal law of the period of this study can be consulted in the first nine volumes of *Statutes at Large of the United States* (Boston, 1845–1851). Volume VII contains treaties between the United States and Indian tribes, 1778–1842. Congressional proceedings and debates were imperfectly reported during these years, especially during the earlier of them. Three series must be consulted; the last two of them overlap several years: (1) *Debates and Proceedings in the Congress of the United States, 1789–1824*, 42 vols. (Washington, 1834–1856), which is customarily cited by its cover title as *Annals of Congress*; (2) *Register of Debates in Congress*, 14 vols. (Washington, 1824–1837), which covers the years of its publication; and (3) *Congressional Globe, 1833–1873*, 46 vols. (Washington, 1834–1873).

Despite defects in compilation, editing, and indexing, James D. Richardson (ed.), *A Compilation of the Messages and Papers of the Presidents, 1789–1902*, 10 vols. (Washington, 1903), is helpful.

The *Reports of Cases Argued and Adjudged in the Supreme Court of the United States* are usually cited by the name of the reporter. For the years of this study the reporters were: 1 Wheaton (1816) to 12 Wheaton (1827); 1 Peters (1828) to 17 Peters (1843); 1 Howard (1843) to 24 Howard (1860). The following cases have been cited in the present study: Bank of the Commonwealth of Kentucky *v.* Wister *et al.*, 2 Peters 318 (1829); Bank of the United States *v.* Planters' Bank of Georgia, 9 Wheaton 904 (1824); Cherokee Nation *v.* The State of Georgia, 5 Peters 1 (1831); Craig *v.* The State of Missouri, 4 Peters 410 (1830); Groves *v.* Slaughter, 15 Peters 449 (1841); McCulloch *v.* Maryland, 4 Wheaton 316 (1819); Osborn *v.* Bank of the United States, 9 Wheaton 738 (1824); Worcester *v.* The State of Georgia, 6 Peters 515 (1832).

The titles of the fourth through the seventh censuses are as follows: *Census of 1820* (Washington, 1821); *Fifth Census; or Enumeration of the Inhabitants of the United States* (Washington, 1832); *Sixth Census or Enumeration of the Inhabitants of the United States . . . in 1840* (Washington, 1841); *The Seventh Census of the United States: 1850, Embracing a Statistical View of Each of the States and Territories* (Washington, 1853). Abstracts of most of these were published; that of the census of 1850, entitled *Statistical View of the United States, . . . Being a Compendium of the Seventh Census, to Which are Added the Results of Every Previous Census . . .* (Washington, 1854), is especially useful because of its tabulation of earlier returns. These early censuses deal almost solely with population; but in 1820 and 1840 data on other aspects of American life were published in *Digest of Accounts of Manufacturing Establishments in United States, and Their Manufactures* (Washington, 1823), and *Statistics of the United States of America, as Collected and Returned . . . June 1, 1840* (Washington, 1841). Among the subsequent publications of the Census Office that contain data and calculations of much value for studies in the earlier period are *The Compendium of the Ninth Census* (Washington, 1872), which gives county populations for all previous census years; and the *Twelfth Census of the United States, 1900, Statistical Atlas* (Washington, 1903), which indicates the comparative population of American cities. A study of trends that seemed to be evident from the first five Federal censuses is George Tucker. *Progress of the United States in Population and*

Wealth in Fifty Years, as Exhibited by the Decennial Census (New York, 1843). Here and elsewhere in the discussion of primary sources, it seems wise to mention a few closely related studies, guides, and bibliographies.

Four of the ten divisions of the great documentary series known as *American State Papers. Documents, Legislative and Executive, of the Congress of the United States,* 38 vols. (Washington, 1832–1861), were useful, namely: *Indian Affairs,* II, for its many documents relating to the attempts of Georgia, Alabama, and Mississippi to rid themselves of the Indians within their boundaries; *Finance,* III, IV, and V, for numerous memorials and resolutions for and against protective tariff in the 1820's; *Public Lands,* especially VII, for information on this subject at the time of the Panic of 1819 and in subsequent years; and *Commerce and Navigation,* II, for statistical and other material on imports, exports, and related matters. A more detailed mass of information on the last subject is presented in the annual reports of the Secretary of the Treasury on *Commerce and Navigation of the United States.* These reports were made pursuant to a Congressional act of February 10, 1820; the first of them covers the year ending September 20, 1821.

Other Federal documents that have proved useful are the *Report of the Commissioner of Patents for the Year 1855: Agriculture* (Washington, 1856); a segment of an incompleted work entitled United States Department of Agriculture, *Atlas of American Agriculture, V, The Crops, Section A. Cotton* (Washington, 1918); and two important compilations of material about Federal laws and expenditures for improvement of transportation. One of these can be found in *Reports of Committees of the House of Representatives,* 21 Cong., 2 Sess., No. 77, "Internal Improvements"; and the other in *Senate Miscellaneous Documents,* 49 Cong., 2 Sess., II, No. 91, "Laws of the United States Relating to the Improvements of Rivers and Harbors from August 11, 1790, to March 3, 1887, with a Tabulated Statement of Appropriations and Allotments."

GOVERNMENT DOCUMENTS: STATE

Francis N. Thorpe (comp.), *The Federal and State Constitutions, Colonial Charters, and Other Organic Laws,* 7 vols. (Washington, 1909), is a convenient compilation of the texts of state constitutions and constitutional amendments. For discussions and votes that preceded the constitutional changes of this period one must consult the journals of the several conventions. Of especial importance is the *Proceedings and Debates of the Virginia State Convention, of 1829–30* (Richmond, 1830).

For data on social as well as political phases of this study, the laws of the Southern states were indispensable. A list of statutes, compilations, digests, and codes is available in Grace E. Macdonald, *Check-List of Statutes of States of the United States of America* (Providence, 1937). The following have been cited: William Kilty *et al., The Laws of Maryland,* 7 vols. (Annapolis, 1799–1820); Benjamin W. Leigh, *Revised Code of the Laws of Virginia,* 2 vols. (Richmond, 1819); Joseph Tate, *A Digest of the Laws of Virginia* (Richmond, 1823); *Report of the Revisors of the Code of Virginia,* 5 reports, variously bound (Richmond, 1847–1849); Henry Potter *et al.* (revisors), *Laws of the State of North-Carolina,* 2 vols. (Raleigh, 1821); James Iredell, *A New Digested Manual of the Acts of the General Assembly of North Carolina* (Raleigh, 1851); Bartholomew F. Moore and Asa Briggs, *Revised Code of North Carolina* (Boston, 1855); Joseph Brevard, *An Alphabetical Digest of the Public Statute Law of South Carolina,* 3 vols. (Charleston, 1814); *The Statutes at Large of South Carolina, 1682–1866,* 13 vols. (Columbia, 1836–1875); Oliver H. Prince, *A Digest of the Laws of the State of Georgia* (2d ed., Athens, 1837); Leslie A. Thompson, *A Manual or Digest of the Statute Law of the State of Florida* (Boston, 1847); Charles S. Morehead and Mason Brown, *A Digest of the Statute Laws of Kentucky,* 2 vols. (Frankfort, 1834); John Haywood and Robert L. Cobbs, *The Statute Laws of the State of Tennessee,* 2 vols. (Knoxville, 1831); John G. Aiken, *A Digest of the Laws of the State of Alabama* (Philadelphia, 1833); [George Poindexter], *The Revised Code of the Laws of Mississippi* (Natchez, 1824); Henry A. Bullard and Thomas Curry (comps.), *A New Digest of the Statute Laws of the State of Louisiana,* only Volume I published (New Orleans, 1842).

To trace modification of the law between the issuance of successive codes, to learn dates of enactment, or for other reasons, it was often necessary to go to the session acts. The best guide to this great body of materials is Grace E. Macdonald, *Check-List of Session Laws* (New York, 1936). In locating state documents on nullification, internal improvements, the tariff, slavery, and some other subjects, the scholar is saved much trouble by Herman V. Ames, *State Documents on Federal Relations: The States and the United States* (Philadelphia, 1906), but it must not be forgotten that Ames did not publish all the available documents.

House and senate journals of the Southern states for the years of this study are imperfect on various counts, and especially in respect to the scantiness of their reports of debates. Nevertheless, in early years these journals are often the only place where one can find governors' messages, state treasurers' reports, and reports on penitentiaries, asylums, and other state institutions. Guides to this body of material are Grace E. Macdonald, *Check-List of Legislative Journals of States of the United States of America* (Providence, 1938), and William S. Jenkins, *Supplement Check List of Legislative Journals of the United States of America* (Boston, 1943). It is unfortunate that the location of copies is not given, for some of the journals are extremely rare. The Library of Congress collection, with film supplementing its printed holdings, is more nearly complete than any other. Inasmuch as libraries have followed various policies in respect to binding legislative journals—some of them binding house and senate journals together, and others binding them separately; some adding to the journal of one or the other house an appendix of reports and resolutions, and others binding this material separately—it may be well to say that nearly all of the citations to such materials are made to the Library of Congress collection. The *Reports and Resolutions of the General Assembly of the State of South Carolina, 1847* (Columbia, 1847), deserves special note because some of its documents, especially those on education, cover a considerable span of years.

Much material on social and political as well as on legal history is hidden away in reports of cases tried before the supreme courts of the several states. The indexes are almost useless to the historian, and often he must know much more than appears in the printed report if he is to understand the political or social significance of the material.

Among the semiofficial state documents that have proved useful are Archibald De Bow Murphey, *Memoir on the Internal Improvements Contemplated by the Legislature of North-Carolina; and on the Resources and Finances of That State* (Raleigh, 1819); the extensive collection of documents, some of which are otherwise very hard to find, by David Kohn (ed. and comp.), *Internal Improvement in South Carolina, 1817–1828* (Washington, 1938), compiled from the reports of the Superintendent of Public Works and from contemporary pamphlets, newspaper clippings, letters, petitions, and maps; and the *Thirteenth Annual Report of the Library Board of the Virginia State Library, 1915–1916* (Richmond, 1917), which lists the membership of the successive general assemblies of Virginia.

COUNTY RECORDS

The numerous inventories of county archives prepared by the Historical Records Survey of the Works Progress Administration are usually no more than lists and brief descriptions. Even so, they reveal much about the structure and activities of local government. The *Inventory of the County Archives of Virginia, No. 21. Chesterfield County* (Charlottesville, 1938), has the added value of containing a study by Lester J.

Cappon, "The Evolution of County Government in Virginia." Citation is also made to the mimeographed *Inventory of the Parish Archives of Louisiana, No. 35. Natchitoches Parish* (University, La., 1938).

URBAN DIRECTORIES AND STATE GAZETTEERS

Directories furnish a basis for making analyses of the occupational distribution of urban population. In addition, they as well as the gazetteers often contain unexpected odds and ends of information. A large number of directories have been examined, but only the following have been cited: Daniel J. Dowling, *The Charleston Directory, and Annual Register, for 1837 and 1838* (Charleston, 1837); *Census of the City of Charleston, South Carolina, for the Year 1848* (Charleston, 1849); Gabriel Collins, *The Louisville Directory, for the Year 1836: to Which are Annexed Lists of the Municipal and Bank Officers; Lists of the Various Societies and Corporations of Louisville, and Their Officers: an Advertiser . . .* (Louisville, 1836); *The Louisville Directory for the Year 1843-'44* (Louisville, 1843); and John B. Jegli, *Louisville Directory for 1848 . . .* (Louisville, 1848).

As for state reference works, the following proved useful: Colin McIver, *The North-Carolina Register, and United States Calendar, for the Year of Our Lord 1823* (Raleigh, 1822); Robert Mills, *Statistics of South Carolina, Including a View of Its Natural, Civil, and Military History, General and Particular* (Charleston, 1826); and Adiel Sherwood, *A Gazetteer of the State of Georgia* (2d ed., Philadelphia, 1829).

PRINTED CORRESPONDENCE, MEMOIRS, AND AUTOBIOGRAPHIES

Although the public careers of Thomas Jefferson, James Madison, and James Monroe belong chiefly to an earlier period, some of the comments of these elder statesmen give insight into the period of this study. Most of their published papers can be found in Paul L. Ford (ed.), *The Writings of Thomas Jefferson,* 10 vols. (New York, 1892–1899); Andrew A. Lipscomb (ed.), *The Writings of Thomas Jefferson,* 20 vols. (Washington, 1903–1904); Gaillard Hunt (ed.), *The Writings of James Madison, Comprising His Public Papers and His Private Correspondence,* 9 vols. (New York, 1900–1910); *Letters and Other Writings of James Madison,* 4 vols. (Cong. ed., Philadelphia, 1865); and Stanislaus M. Hamilton (ed.), *The Writings of James Monroe, Including a Collection of His Public and Private Papers and Correspondence,* 7 vols. (New York, 1898–1903).

Turning to the major political figures of the period, the most complete and carefully edited set of papers is the work of John S. Bassett (ed.), *Correspondence of Andrew Jackson,* 6 vols. and index (Washington, 1926–1935). Less scholarly and less complete is Calvin Colton (ed.), *The Life, Correspondence, and Speeches of Henry Clay,* 6 vols. (New York, 1857).

For the papers of Calhoun, one must use several sources. The basic collection is Richard K. Crallé (ed.), *The Works of John C. Calhoun,* 6 vols. (New York, 1851–1856), but this must be supplemented by J. Franklin Jameson (ed.), *Correspondence of John C. Calhoun,* in American Historical Association, *Annual Report,* 1899, II (Washington, 1900). Two small collections that contribute to an understanding of Calhoun's part in the campaign of 1824 are Albert R. Newsome (ed.), "Correspondence of John C. Calhoun, George McDuffie and Charles Fisher, Relating to the Presidential Campaign of 1824," in *North Carolina Historical Review* (Raleigh), VII (1930), 477–504; and Thomas R. Hay (ed.), "John C. Calhoun and the Presidential Campaign of 1824: Some Unpublished Calhoun Letters," in *American Historical Review* (New York), XL (1934), 82–96. The former deals largely with strategy in North Carolina; the latter, in New York. The exchanges between Calhoun and Jackson when they came to the parting of the ways were published by Calhoun in *Correspondence between Gen. Andrew Jackson and John C. Calhoun, President and Vice-President of the U. States, on the Subject of the Course of the Latter, in the Deliberations of the Cabinet of Mr. Monroe, on the Occurrences in the Seminole War* (Washington, 1831).

Charles R. King (ed.), *The Life and Correspondence of Rufus King; Comprising His Letters, Private and Official, His Public Documents and His Speeches,* 6 vols. (New York, 1894–1900), is indispensable in studying the controversy over the admission of Missouri. Would that we had equal access to the mind of James Tallmadge, Jr. "Letters of William C. Rives, 1823–1829," in *Tyler's Quarterly Historical and Genealogical Magazine* (Richmond, 1919–), V (1923–1924), 223–37; VI (1924–1925), 6–15, 97–105, presents a group of letters, chiefly political in character, by one of the chief of the Virginia supporters of Andrew Jackson. A document of fundamental importance for the Mexican War period is Milo M. Quaife (ed.), *The Diary of James K. Polk,* 4 vols. (Chicago, 1910).

Light is thrown on agricultural practices and theories by Herbert A. Kellar (ed.), *Solon Robinson: Pioneer and Agriculturist,* 2 vols., in *Indiana Historical Collections,* XXI–XXII (Indianapolis, 1936); on education, especially in Tennessee, by Le Roy J. Halsey (ed.), *The Works of Philip Lindsley,* 3 vols. (Philadelphia, 1866); and on the slavery controversy by the notable collection, Gilbert H. Barnes and Dwight L. Dumond (eds.), *Letters of Theodore Dwight Weld, Angelina Grimké Weld, and Sarah Grimké, 1822–1844,* 2 vols. (New York, 1934).

Several of the most important memoirs for this period of Southern history were written by non-Southerners. Charles Francis Adams (ed.), *Memoirs of John Quincy Adams, comprising Portions of His Diary from 1795 to 1848,* 12 vols. (Philadelphia, 1874–1877), is an invaluable commentary on political events, the abolition movement, and various phases of the sectional struggle—invaluable despite the bias and the caustic comments of the diarist and despite the historian's uncertainty about the editor's omissions from his father's diary. Thomas Hart Benton, *Thirty Years' View: or, A History of the Working of the American Government for Thirty Years, from 1820 to 1850,* 2 vols. (New York, 1854–1856), has many of the defects common to memoirs; yet it throws much light on the activities of the Jackson forces and on the relations between politicians. John C. Fitzpatrick (ed.), *The Autobiography of Martin Van Buren,* in American Historical Association, *Annual Report,* 1918, II (Washington, 1920), interprets the events of these years from the viewpoint of Calhoun's successful rival for Jackson's favor and for party leadership.

Other memoirs and autobiographies of the period are Reuben Davis, *Recollections of Mississippi and Mississippians* (Boston, 1889); Henry S. Foote, *War of the Rebellion* (New York, 1866); William H. Sparks, *The Memories of Fifty Years* (Philadelphia, 1870); James Champlin, *Early Biography, Travels and Adventures of Rev. James Champlin, Who Was Born Blind* (Columbus, Ohio, 1842); and John S. Wise, *The End of an Era* (Boston, 1899).

CONTEMPORARY BOOKS AND PAMPHLETS

The records of the governing bodies of the various churches are numerous and important. Indispensable in a study of their divisions over slavery are the *Journal of the General Conference of the Methodist Episcopal Church, Held in the City of New York, 1844* (New York, 1844), and the *Journals of the General Conference of the Methodist Episcopal Church, South, Held in 1846 and 1850* (Richmond, 1851). A brief report on the growth of the Roman Catholic church in the West during the first third of the nineteenth century is in *Mémoire présenté à Son Éminence le cardinal Fransoni préfet de la propagande par les ordres du souverain pontife, dans lequel j'expose l'état de mon diocèse en 1810, et celui où il est en 1836* (n.p., n.d., photostatic reproduction in New York Public Library).

355

Illustrative material about higher education has been taken from *Laws of Jefferson College, Located in the Town of Washington, State of Mississippi* (Natchez, 1820), and from the following collections of source materials: Charles L. Coon (ed.), *The Beginnings of Public Education in North Carolina: A Documentary History, 1790–1840*, 2 vols. (Raleigh, 1908); Alfred J. Morrison, *The College of Hampden-Sidney: Calendar of Board Minutes, 1776–1876* (Richmond, 1912); Hampden-Sydney College, *General Catalogue of Officers and Students, 1776–1906* (Hampden-Sydney, Va., [1908]). The spelling of the name of this college has been changed through the years.

Much was written with a view to economic improvement. Among the most influential works on agriculture were [John Taylor], *Arator; Being a Series of Agricultural Essays, Practical & Political. By a Citizen of Virginia* (Georgetown, D.C., 1813), which went through a number of editions; and Edmund Ruffin, *An Essay on Calcareous Manures* (Petersburg, 1832), which was likewise republished several times. A forceful plea for Southern industrialization, but a plea that was little heeded, was William Gregg, *Essays on Domestic Industry: or, An Enquiry into the Expediency of Establishing Cotton Manufactures in South-Carolina* (Charleston, 1845). Edmund Ruffin, *Report of the Commencement and Progress of the Agricultural Survey of South-Carolina, for 1843* (Columbia, 1843), is a sample of the kind of material that is listed in some detail in Charles S. Sydnor, "State Geological Surveys in the Old South," in David K. Jackson (ed.), *American Studies in Honor of William Kenneth Boyd, by Members of the Americana Club of Duke University* (Durham, 1940).

Among the books and pamphlets that were most influential in arousing Southern opposition to the national bank, internal improvements, and protective tariffs, and in creating state-rights sentiments in the South were John Taylor, *Construction Construed, and Constitutions Vindicated* (Richmond, 1820), and *Tyranny Unmasked* (Washington, 1822); and Thomas Cooper, *Two Tracts: On the Proposed Alteration of the Tariff; and on Weights & Measures* (Charleston, 1823), and *Consolidation. An Account of Parties in the United States, from the Convention of 1787, to the Present Period* (Columbia, 1824).

Slavery was the most widely discussed subject in the 1830's and 1840's. In one book, Richard Fuller and Francis Wayland, *Domestic Slavery Considered as a Scriptural Institution* (New York, 1845), two eminent Baptist ministers presented their opposing views on this question. Most of the books and pamphlets, however, were altogether on one side or the other.

Among the more notable of the proslavery writings were Richard Furman, *Exposition of the Views of the Baptists, Relative to the Coloured Population of the United States, in a Communication to the Governor of South-Carolina* (Charleston, 1823); *The Letter of Appomatox* [sic] *to the People of Virginia: Exhibiting a Corrected View of the Recent Proceedings in the House of Delegates, on the Subject of the Abolition of Slavery; and a Succinct Account of the Doctrines Broached by the Friends of Abolition, in Debate: and the Mischievous Tendency of Those Proceedings and Doctrines* (Richmond, 1832); and Thomas R. Dew, *Review of the Debate in the Virginia Legislature of 1831 and 1832* (Richmond, 1832). With a change of title to *An Essay on Slavery,* this work appeared in two editions in 1849, and it was again published as the concluding part of *The Pro-Slavery Argument; as Maintained by the Most Distinguished Writers of the Southern States, containing the Several Essays, on the Subject of Chancellor Harper, Governor Hammond, Dr. Simms, and Professor Dew* (Charleston, 1852), and in later editions.

Some of the writers, going beyond a narrow defense of slavery, attempted to show that many aspects of Southern life were far superior to life in nonslaveholding communities. Much of this kind of thing can be found in Congressional debates, resolutions of Southern state legislatures, and newspapers. Among the pamphlets that illustrate this development in Southern thought are: William Harper, *Anniversary Oration; Delivered . . . in the Representative Hall, Columbia, S.C., Dec. 9, 1835* (Washington, 1836); William P. Miles, *Oration Delivered before the Fourth of July Association . . . 1849* (Charleston, 1849); Iverson L. Brookes, *A Defense of the South against the Reproaches and Encroachments of the North: in Which Slavery is Shown to be an Institution of God Intended to Form the Basis of the Best Social State and the Only Safeguard to the Permanence of a Republican Government* (Hamburg, S.C., 1850); Lawrence M. Keitt, *Address on Laying the Corner-Stone of the Fire-Proof Building, at Columbia, Dec. 15, 1851* (Columbia, 1851).

Antislavery books or pamphlets that have been cited are David Walker, *Walker's Appeal, in Four Articles, together with a Preamble to the Colored Citizens of the World, but in Particular, and Very Expressly to Those of the United States of America* (Boston, 1829), and two subsequent editions published at the same place in 1830; James A. Thome and J. Horace Kimball, *Emancipation in the West Indies. A Six Months' Tour in Antigua, Barbadoes, and Jamaica, in the Year 1837,* in *The Anti-Slavery Examiner,* No. 7 (New York, 1838), a report on West Indian emancipation written to aid the cause of abolition in America; [Theodore D. Weld], *American Slavery as It Is: Testimony of a Thousand*

Witnesses (New York, 1839), a powerful indictment of American Negro slavery; and Harriet Beecher Stowe, *A Key to Uncle Tom's Cabin; Presenting the Original Facts and Documents upon Which the Story is Founded. Together with Corroborative Statements Verifying the Truth of the Work* (Boston, 1853).

A welcome relief from the serious and often distorted polemics for and against slavery can be found in the writings of those who were content to describe the Southern scene, often with a touch of broad humor. In addition to the travelers, who will be mentioned separately, the following deserve note, together with others who are discussed in the text of Chapter XIII: [Augustus B. Longstreet], *Georgia Scenes, Characters, Incidents, etc. in the First Half Century of the Republic, By a Native Georgian* (Augusta, 1835); J. W. M. Breazeale, *Life as It Is; or, Matters and Things in General* (Knoxville, 1842); Joseph B. Cobb, *Mississippi Scenes; or, Sketches of Southern and Western Life and Adventure, Humorous, Satirical, and Descriptive* (Philadelphia, 1851); Joseph G. Baldwin, *The Flush Times of Alabama and Mississippi* (New York, 1854); and [John P. Kennedy], *Swallow Barn, or, A Sojourn in the Old Dominion*, 2 vols. (Philadelphia, 1832). The American Authors Series edition of *Swallow Barn* (New York, 1929), contains an introduction by Professor Jay B. Hubbell. Kennedy wrote a satirical description of the habits and manners of the Democrats under the title, *Quodlibet: Containing Some Annals thereof, with an Authentic Account of the Origin and Growth of the Borough and the Sayings and Doings of Sundry of the Townspeople* . . . (Philadelphia, 1840).

Several compilations of this kind of material have been made. They serve the scholar well in their introductory comments and by making available rare and out of the way materials. Among these are Arthur P. Hudson, *Humor of the Old Deep South* (New York, 1936); and Thomas D. Clark, *The Rampaging Frontier; Manners and Humors of Pioneer Days in the South and the Middle West* (Indianapolis, 1939), which should be read in connection with an essay by the same author entitled "Hoosiers, Suckers, and Red Horses," in Wabash College, *The Wabash Bulletin* (Crawfordsville, Ind.), XLI, No. 1. [Denis Corcoran], *Pickings from the Portfolio of the Reporter of the New Orleans "Picayune"* (Philadelphia, 1846), is a collection of humorous sketches of characters who appeared in the Recorder's Court of New Orleans. A more recent exploitation of the columns of the *Picayune* is E. Merton Coulter, *The Other Half of Old New Orleans: Sketches of Characters and Incidents from the Recorder's Court of New Orleans in the Eighteen Forties as Reported in the "Picayune"* (University, La., 1939).

TRAVEL

The best edition of Alexis de Tocqueville, *Democracy in America,* was published in 2 vols. (New York, 1945), with introduction, editorial notes, and bibliographies by Phillips Bradley. *Democracy in America* is one of the greatest of commentaries on America by a foreigner, and it contains a number of thoughtful observations about the South. George W. Pierson, *Tocqueville and Beaumont in America* (New York, 1938), includes generous excerpts from the notes from which Tocqueville worked, and it gives in Tocqueville's own words much of the detail that is missing in *Democracy in America.*

Other important travelers were James S. Buckingham, whose long shelf of books included *The Slave States of America,* 2 vols. (London, [1842]), and whose work might have been better if he had been less of a reformer and if he had made more use of his eyes instead of relying so heavily on guidebooks, city directories, and newspapers; Harriet Martineau, *Retrospect of Western Travel,* 2 vols. (London 1838), and *Society in America,* 2 vols. (New York, 1837), whose deafness did not keep her from hearing much, and who had a sharp eye and a keen mind; and Sir Charles Lyell, *Travels in North America; with Geological Observations on the United States, Canada, and Nova Scotia,* 2 vols. (London, 1845), and *A Second Visit to the United States of North America,* 2 vols. (London, 1849). The second work contains somewhat more about the South than the first. Despite the fact that Lyell's primary interest was in geology—or perhaps for the very reason that he was primarily a scientist—his analyses of such contemporary problems as abolition, slavery, and race relations in America are among the most thoughtful, temperate, and careful of his generation.

A famous artist-naturalist who spent much time in the South in these years was John J. Audubon. Howard Corning (ed.), *Journal of John James Audubon Made during His Trip to New Orleans in 1820–1821* (Boston, 1929), tells about travel on the Mississippi River and about life in New Orleans. Many of the plates in Audubon's monumental *Birds of North America,* 4 vols. (Edinburgh, 1827–1838), are based on drawings made by Audubon while he was living in Louisiana and Mississippi.

Among the better of the less famous travelers of this period are the Reverend George Lewis, *Impressions of America and the American Churches* (Edinburgh, 1845); William Thomson, *A Tradesman's Travels, in the United States and Canada, in the Years 1840, 41 & 42* (Edinburgh, 1842); Lester B. Shippee (ed.), *Bishop* [Henry B.] *Whipple's Southern Diary, 1843–1844* (Minneapolis, 1937).

359

A considerable number of travelers came to the South to investigate slavery, and in some cases it is hard to decide whether to classify their writings as travel accounts or as antislavery propaganda. Among these are Edward S. Abdy, *Journal of a Residence and Tour in the United States of North America, from April, 1833, to October, 1834*, 3 vols. (London, 1835); Ethan A. Andrews, *Slavery and the Domestic Slave-Trade in the United States* (Boston, 1836); John R. Godley, *Letters from America*, 2 vols. (London, 1844); Joseph J. Gurney, *A Journey to North America, Described in Familiar Letters to Amelia Opie* (Norwich, 1841); Joseph Sturge, *A Visit to the United States in 1841* (Boston, 1842); and Charles Dickens, *American Notes for General Circulation*, 2 vols. (London, 1842). Dickens' influential chapter on slavery should not be used without reading Louise II. Johnson, "The Source of the Chapter on Slavery in Dickens's *American Notes*," in *American Literature* (Durham), XIV (1943), 427–30.

Other travel accounts that have been cited are the Earl of Carlisle (Lord Morpeth), *Travels in America. The Poetry of Pope. Two Lectures Delivered to the Leeds Mechanics' Institution and Literary Society, December 5th and 6th, 1850* (New York, 1851); Charles G. B. Daubeny, *Journal of a Tour through the United States, and in Canada, Made during the Years 1837–38* (Oxford, 1843); William Kennedy, *Texas: The Rise, Progress, and Prospects of the Republic of Texas*, 2 vols. (London, 1841); [James K. Paulding,] *Letters from the South, Written during an Excursion in the Summer of 1816*, 2 vols. (New York, 1817); Jehu A. Orr, "A Trip from Houston to Jackson, Miss., in 1845," in Mississippi Historical Society, *Publications* (Oxford, 1896–1914), IX (1906), 173–78. Henry Caswall, *America and the American Church* (London, 1839); Philip H. Gosse, *Letters from Alabama, (U.S.) Chiefly Relating to Natural History* (London, 1859); George W. Kendall, *Narrative of the Texan Santa Fé Expedition, . . . with an Account of the Sufferings . . . and Final Capture of the Texans, and their March, as Prisoners, to the City of Mexico*, 2 vols. (New York, 1844), a popular work that rapidly went through many editions and that stirred American hostility toward Mexico. [Joseph H. Ingraham], *The South-West, by a Yankee*, 2 vols. (New York, 1835), was written by an emigrant from New England who settled in the region he describes in this work. Some other works, though none of great importance for the South of this period, can be found in Reuben Gold Thwaites (ed.), *Early Western Travels, 1748–1846*, 32 vols. (Cleveland, 1904–1907).

NEWSPAPERS

Winifred Gregory (ed.), *American Newspapers, 1821–1936: A Union List of Files Available in the United States and Canada* (New York, 1937), can be consulted for periodicity, title variations, and location of files of newspapers that have been cited. Only those changes in title that occurred within the years the papers were used in this study are shown in this bibliographical note. In citations the title in use at the moment was used.

The series of administration organs, all of which were published in Washington, constitute one important category of newspapers. In order of time, these were the *National Intelligencer* (1800–1869?), edited by Joseph Gales and William W. Seaton, during the administrations of Monroe and John Quincy Adams; the *United States Telegraph* (1826–1837), edited by Calhoun's friend, Duff Green, which spoke for the Jackson-Calhoun alliance until its rupture; and, after that event, the *Globe* (1830–1845), which was established by Francis P. Blair to provide Jackson with an official organ.

Of the independent national papers, *Niles' Weekly Register* (Baltimore, Washington, Philadelphia, 1811–1849), which lies on the border line between newspapers and periodicals, was influential in its day and is now extremely useful to the historian. Inasmuch as Hezekiah Niles was a stanch advocate of protective tariffs, his paper helped to mold a national policy which had great influence upon the course of Southern history. To the historian, this paper supplies information about political events, it discusses economic and some social movements, it reprints national, state, and other documents, and it contains clippings from a large number of newspapers in various parts of the Union, including a number of Southern papers. Despite its name and its place of publication, the Georgetown, D.C., *National Messenger* (1816–1821) was, in contrast to the Washington papers that have been listed, essentially a local sheet.

During the 1820's the Virginia papers, especially the Richmond *Enquirer* (1804–1877), constituted the most important segment of the Southern press. One gains the impression that the *Enquirer* was more often quoted or commented upon than any other paper of the region. For more than forty years, and through most of the years covered by this study, it was edited by Thomas Ritchie. In social outlook, Ritchie was in many ways progressive: he advocated public schools, better means of transportation, the constitutional convention of 1829–1830, and the liberal side in the slavery debate of 1832. In politics, however, his sympathies in the early 1820's were with the Old Republicans. He had great influence in the Democratic Republican party in Virginia, and his power extended far past the boundaries of his state as long as the Virginia dynasty was in power. In the 1830's he supported Jackson and Van Buren, and he opposed nullification.

Ritchie's chief rival was John Hampden Pleasants, the able editor of the Richmond *Constitutional Whig* (1824–1888, with changes of title, the first in 1832). Pleasants founded this paper and edited it for more than twenty years. The *Whig* supported John Quincy Adams and Clay. During the nullification controversy it championed South Carolina, but it later came back to a more nationalistic position. The Richmond *Compiler* (1813–1853) was chiefly concerned with trade and commerce. Other Virginia newspapers that proved useful were the Alexandria *Herald* (1811–1826) and the *Norfolk and Portsmouth Herald* (1794–1861?).

In the Maryland contest between city and country, the urban spirit was reflected in the Baltimore *Patriot & Mercantile Advertiser* (1812–1861?). The views of the eastern planting counties were frequently championed in the Annapolis *Maryland Gazette* (1745–1839), a paper that was showing its age in its worn type and its conservative editorial policy. An unimportant variation of title occurred on January 1, 1824, when the name was changed from *Maryland Gazette and Political Intelligencer* to *Maryland Gazette and State Register*.

In North Carolina, where the chief division of opinion was a reflection of the struggle between the west and the east, the Salisbury *Western Carolinian* (1820–1844) was perhaps the most authentic spokesman for the west. In the Presidential campaign of 1824 its editor, Charles Fisher, strongly supported Calhoun. The opinions of the more conservative and, certainly until 1835, the dominant east were championed in some of the Raleigh papers, notably in the Raleigh *Register, and North-Carolina Gazette* (1799–), which was founded and edited until 1832 by Joseph Gales, the father of the editor of the *National Intelligencer*. Other Raleigh papers examined were the *Star, and North Carolina Gazette* (1808–?), the *North-Carolina Constitutionalist and People's Advocate* (1831–?), and the *Semi-Weekly Standard* (1850–1870?).

With the rise of the nullification movement, the South Carolina newspapers became of prime importance. The best list of these papers and commentary upon their frequent changes in editorship and policy is in Chauncey S. Boucher, *The Nullification Controversy in South Carolina* (Chicago, 1916), *passim*, especially pp. 367–73. Of the papers listed by Boucher, the following were consulted in this study: the Charleston *City Gazette and Commercial Daily Advertiser* (1783–1840), the Charleston

Courier (1803–), the Charleston *Mercury* (1822–1868), the Charleston *Southern Patriot* (1814–1848), the Columbia *State Gazette, and Columbian Advertiser* (1794–1830), the Columbia *Telescope* (1815–?), and the Greenville *Mountaineer* (1829–1911).

Georgia papers that proved useful were the Savannah *Georgian* (1818–1856), the *Daily Savannah Republican* (1802–1873), the Augusta *Chronicle and Georgia Advertiser* (1786–1910?), the Augusta *Constitutionalist* (1823–1877), the Augusta *Georgia Courier* (1825–1837?), the Macon *Georgia Telegraph* (1826–1906), the Macon *Georgia Messenger* (1823–1869), the Athens *Athenian* (1826–1832?), and the Milledgeville *Georgia Journal* (1809–1847). The following Alabama papers were used: the Cahawba *Press and Alabama State Intelligencer* (1819–1826), the Huntsville *Weekly Democrat* (1823–1919), and the Huntsville *Southern Advocate* (1825–).

Kentucky was distinguished among the Southwestern states by vigorous newspaper editorship. Amos Kendall conducted the Frankfort *Argus of Western America* (1808–1838?) from 1816 to 1828, first as a supporter of Clay and then of Jackson. In 1830 George D. Prentice, who came from Connecticut to Kentucky to collect material for a campaign biography of Clay, began to edit the Louisville *Daily Journal* (1830–1868). His courage, ability, and keen wit made it the most influential Whig paper in the South and West. The Lexington *Kentucky Gazette* (1787–1848) supported Jackson in the 1828 campaign although it was published in Clay's home town. Other Kentucky papers used were the Louisville *Public Advertiser* (1818–1828?), the Frankfort *Kentuckian* (1828–1833?), and the Lexington *Kentucky Reporter* (1808–1832).

With the possible exception of Prentice's Louisville *Daily Journal*, the Southern paper that was chiefly distinguished for its audacity and the bantering tone of its news reporting was the New Orleans *Picayune* (1837–). It strongly supported the war with Mexico; and George W. Kendall, one of the founders of the paper, participated as a war correspondent. The New Orleans *Louisiana Gazette* (1804–1826) and the Baton Rouge *Gazette* (1819–1874?) also proved useful.

Of Tennessee newspapers, the Nashville *Republican and State Gazette* (1824–1837), the Knoxville *Register* (1816–1863), and the Nashville *Whig* (1812–) were consulted. The last experienced several changes of name within the years of this study. In 1817 it was expanded to Nashville *Whig, and Tennessee Advertiser;* in August, 1819, it was returned to its original form; in 1826 it was merged with another paper to become the *National Banner and Nashville Whig;* and in 1832 it assumed the title of *National Banner, and Daily Advertiser.*

Three Mississippi papers have been cited: the Woodville *Republican* (1823–), the Natchez *Mississippi Republican, and Literary Register* (1812–1824?), and the Natchez *Mississippi State Gazette* (1813–1833). The last-named paper experienced several changes of title. The title given here was in use from 1818 to 1825.

PERIODICALS

The earliest antislavery journal in the South was founded by Elihu Embree at Jonesborough, Tennessee, in 1820. All of this scarce publication, known as *The Emancipator,* was reprinted as a single volume at Nashville in 1932. After Embree's death, Benjamin Lundy, who had been publishing *The Genius of Universal Emancipation* in Ohio, moved his paper to Tennessee and there published it until his removal to Baltimore in 1824. The *Abolition Intelligencer and Missionary Magazine* was published at Shelbyville, Kentucky, in 1822 and 1823. The most famous of the non-Southern antislavery papers was William Lloyd Garrison's *The Liberator.* The first number appeared in Boston on January 1, 1831, and there it continued to be published to the end of the year 1865.

The first important agricultural journal in the South and in the United States, the *American Farmer* (Baltimore, Washington, 1819–1897), was founded by John S. Skinner. It numbered among its early contributors some of the chief statesmen and some of the leading agricultural reformers of the South. Another early Southern agricultural journal was the *Southern Agriculturist and Register of Rural Affairs* (Charleston, 1828–1839; with a change of name and with some irregularity, it continued until 1846). Edmund Ruffin's *Farmer's Register* (Shellbanks, Petersburg, Va., 1833–1843) was probably the most influential agricultural paper in the South during the 1830's. Chief among agricultural periodicals founded in the 1840's were the *Southern Planter* (Richmond, 1841–), and the *Southern Cultivator* (Augusta, Athens, Atlanta, 1843–1935). The *Southern Cultivator* was the most influential farmers' and planters' journal in the lower South. The *Southern Planter* (Natchez, Washington, Miss., 1842), should not be confused with the Richmond journal with the same name. *The Western Farmer and Gardener* (Cincinnati, 1839–1845), was read in the lower Mississippi Valley, and other agricultural papers published above Mason and Dixon's line had much influence within the South.

Several of the leading literary journals of this period have been described in Chapter XIII. Others are described in Bertram H. Flanders, *Early Georgia Magazines; Literary Periodicals to 1865* (Athens, 1944), and in William S. Hoole, *A Check-list and Finding-list of Charleston Periodicals, 1732–1864* (Durham, 1936). Hoole's list is not restricted to literary journals. For guidance in the wide field of ecclesiastical publications, one should consult Henry S. Stroupe, "The Religious Press in the South Atlantic States, 1802–1865" (Ph.D. dissertation, Duke University, 1942).

Other contemporary journals that have been consulted are *United States Magazine, and Democratic Review* (Washington, New York, 1837–1859); *African Repository* (Washington, 1825–1892), the official organ of the American Colonization Society; *American Almanac and Repository of Useful Knowledge* (Boston, 1830–1861); and *De Bow's Review*, subtitle varies (New Orleans, Washington, Charleston, Columbia, Nashville, New York, 1846–1864, 1866–1870, 1879–1880). Selections from this journal were reprinted in J. D. B. De Bow (ed.), *The Southern States, Embracing a Series of Papers Condensed from the Earlier Volumes of De Bow's Review, upon Slavery and the Slave Institutions of the South, Internal Improvements, etc., together with Historical and Statistical Sketches of Several of the Southern and South Western States; Their Agriculture, Commerce, etc.* (Washington, New Orleans, 1856).

BIOGRAPHY

The older generation of political figures has received very unequal biographical treatment. Jefferson is in much need of a careful, full-length biography. Of present works, the longest, Henry S. Randall, *The Life of Thomas Jefferson*, 3 vols. (New York, 1858), is uncritical and eulogistic; one of the shortest, David S. Muzzey, *Thomas Jefferson* (New York, 1918), is probably the most judicious. Marshall has been adequately treated in Albert J. Beveridge, *The Life of John Marshall*, 4 vols. (Boston, 1916–1919); and there are two good one-volume studies of Madison: Gaillard Hunt, *The Life of James Madison* (New York, 1902), and Abbot E. Smith, *James Madison: Builder, A New Estimate of a Memorable Career* (New York, 1937). The most recent life of Monroe, William P. Cresson, *James Monroe* (Chapel Hill, 1946), is also the best, though its background of internal American history is in places faulty. For Randolph, one needs to consult both Henry Adams, *John Randolph* (Boston, 1882), and William C. Bruce, *John Randolph of Roanoke, 1773–1833*, 2 vols. (New York, 1922). John E. D. Shipp, *Giant Days: or The Life and Times of William H. Crawford* (Americus, Ga., 1909), is far from being an adequate study, but the scarcity of Crawford papers will be a handicap to anyone who would work on this misinterpreted

365

person. Among the studies of John Taylor are Henry H. Simms, *Life of John Taylor: The Story of a Brilliant Leader in the Early Virginia State Rights School* (Richmond, 1932); Eugene T. Mudge, *The Social Philosophy of John Taylor of Caroline* (New York, 1939); and Benjamin F. Wright, Jr., "The Philosopher of Jeffersonian Democracy," in *American Political Science Review* (Baltimore, 1906–), XXII (1928), 870–92. Biographies of Daniel Webster, John Quincy Adams, Rufus King, Martin Van Buren, Thomas Hart Benton, and other non-Southern figures have been consulted, but space is lacking for appraisals in this bibliography.

As for Calhoun, William M. Meigs, *Life of John Caldwell Calhoun*, 2 vols. (New York, 1917), is scholarly but defensive; briefer but more impartial is Gaillard Hunt, *John C. Calhoun* (Philadelphia, 1908); better than either for the prenullification period is Charles M. Wiltse, *John C. Calhoun, Nationalist, 1782–1828* (Indianapolis, 1944). A special phase of Calhoun's thought is treated in Harold W. Thatcher, "Calhoun and Federal Reinforcement of State Laws," in *American Political Science Review*, XXXVI (1942), 873–80.

Carl Schurz, *Life of Henry Clay*, 2 vols. (Boston, 1887), after serving as the standard biography for many years, is superseded by Glyndon G. Van Deusen, *The Life of Henry Clay* (Boston, 1937); George R. Poage, *Henry Clay and the Whig Party* (Chapel Hill, 1936); and Bernard Mayo, *Henry Clay, Spokesman of the New West* (Boston, 1937), which is the first volume of a projected three-volume biography.

Jackson has attracted many biographers. The best are John S. Bassett, *The Life of Andrew Jackson*, 2 vols. (New York, 1911); and Marquis James, *Andrew Jackson, The Border Captain* (Indianapolis, 1933), and *Andrew Jackson, Portrait of a President* (Indianapolis, 1937). Reissued together, these two volumes are entitled *The Life of Andrew Jackson* (Indianapolis, 1938). The colorful work of James Parton, *Life of Andrew Jackson*, 3 vols. (New York, 1860), is still of value.

Biographies of persons below the top bracket of political prominence reveal much about local conditions and political crosscurrents that are scarcely noticed in biographies of major figures or in secondary writings of other kinds. Oliver P. Chitwood, *John Tyler, Champion of the Old South* (New York, 1939), is an excellent biography of an extreme defender of state rights who became President. Eugene I. McCormac, *James K. Polk, A Political Biography* (Berkeley, 1922), is a scholarly and judicious study; it supports the better-known interpretations of Justin H. Smith. Theodore D. Jervey, *Robert Y. Hayne and His Times* (New

366

York, 1909), sympathetic but discriminating, throws much light on the economic and social history of South Carolina; while Lillian A. Kibler, *Benjamin F. Perry, South Carolina Unionist* (Durham, 1946), tells with rich detail the life of a leading opponent of the nullifiers. Edward J. Harden, *The Life of George M. Troup* (Savannah, 1859), and J. F. H. Claiborne, *Life and Correspondence of John A. Quitman,* 2 vols. (New York, 1860), reproduce much primary material while treating these Georgia and Mississippi politicians. William B. Hatcher, *Edward Livingston, Jeffersonian Republican and Jacksonian Democrat* (University, La., 1940), throws light on several phases of Louisiana history. Joseph H. Parks, *Felix Grundy, Champion of Democracy* (University, La., 1940), and James B. Ranck, *Albert Gallatin Brown, Radical Southern Nationalist* (New York, 1937), deal with representatives of radical democracy. A Whig who matched the Democrats in the art of oratory is described in [George L. Prentiss], *A Memoir of S. S. Prentiss,* 2 vols. (New York, 1855), and in Dallas C. Dickey, *Seargent S. Prentiss, Whig Orator of the Old South* (Baton Rouge, 1945).

Biographies of persons whose major activities were outside the field of politics trace bypaths and main roads of Southern history, some of which are otherwise unexplored. Three leading newspaper editors are treated in Fayette Copeland, *Kendall of the Picayune* (Norman, Okla., 1943); Charles H. Ambler, *Thomas Ritchie, A Study in Virginia Politics* (Richmond, 1913); and Fletcher M. Green, "Duff Green, Militant Journalist of the Old School," in *American Historical Review* (New York, 1895-), LII (1946–1947), 247–64. Educational, intellectual, and literary history is enriched by John D. Wade, *Augustus Baldwin Longstreet; A Study of the Development of Culture in the South* (New York, 1924); Dumas Malone, *The Public Life of Thomas Cooper, 1783–1839* (New Haven, 1926); Linda Rhea, *Hugh Swinton Legaré, A Charleston Intellectual* (Chapel Hill, 1934); John D. Allen, *Philip Pendleton Cooke* (Chapel Hill, 1942); and David K. Jackson, "Philip Pendleton Cooke: Virginia Gentleman, Lawyer, Hunter, and Poet," in Jackson (ed.), *American Studies in Honor of William Kenneth Boyd.* Helen M. Pierce Gallagher, *Robert Mills, Architect of the Washington Monument, 1781– 1855* (New York, 1935), is a competent biography of the leading Southern architect in the generation after Thomas Jefferson.

There is much about the agricultural reform movement, as well as about the subject suggested in the title, in Avery O. Craven, *Edmund Ruffin, Southerner: A Study in Secession* (New York, 1932). Agricultural history also has a large place in E. Merton Coulter, *Thomas Spalding of*

Sapelo (University, La., 1940); and industrial history, in Broadus Mitchell, *William Gregg, Factory Master of the Old South* (Chapel Hill, 1928).

One of the few works to which one may turn for information about the humanitarian movement in this period of Southern history is Helen E. Marshall, *Dorothea Dix, Forgotten Samaritan* (Chapel Hill, 1937). Charles S. Sydnor, *A Gentleman of the Old Natchez Region: Benjamin L. C. Wailes* (Durham, 1938), includes a good deal of Mississippi social history. Joseph H. Schauinger, "William Gaston: Southern Statesman," in *North Carolina Historical Review* (Raleigh, 1924–), XVIII (1941), 99–132, is a sketch of a liberal Catholic jurist of ante-bellum North Carolina. A queer Georgian is described in E. Merton Coulter, *John Jacobus Flournoy, Champion of the Common Man in the Antebellum South* (Savannah, 1942); and one of the largest operators in the slave trade, in Wendell H. Stephenson, *Isaac Franklin, Slave Trader and Planter of the Old South* (University, La., 1938). Florence R. Ray, *Chieftain Greenwood Leflore and the Choctaw Indians of the Mississippi Valley* (Memphis, 1936), is a biography of an Indian who became a large-scale planter. A leader in the early period of the antislavery movement is the subject of *The Life, Travels and Opinions of Benjamin Lundy, Including His Journeys to Texas and Mexico; . . . Compiled under the Direction and on Behalf of His Children* (Philadelphia, 1847). This work contains lengthy excerpts from Lundy's diaries and summaries of material in *The Genius of Universal Emancipation*.

It hardly needs to be said that one of the most useful reference works is Allen Johnson and Dumas Malone (eds.), *Dictionary of American Biography*, 20 vols. and index (New York, 1928–1937), and Harris E. Starr (ed.), Supplement, I (New York, 1944). For data about obscure Congressmen and for lists of Congressional membership, *Biographical Directory of the American Congress, 1774–1927* (Washington, 1928), was helpful.

GENERAL AMERICAN HISTORY

A number of standard works in American history treat the period of this study, but as a general rule the authors have failed to examine Southern newspapers, books, pamphlets, and manuscripts as much as they examined the historical sources of other parts of the United States. The more important of these works are: John B. McMaster, *A History of the People of the United States, from the Revolution to the Civil War,* 8 vols. (New York, 1883–1913); Edward Channing, *A History of the United States,* 6 vols. (New York, 1905–1925), of which Volume V covers the period of our study; John A. Krout and Dixon R. Fox, *The Completion of Independence, 1790–1830,* and Carl R. Fish, *The Rise of the Common Man, 1830–1850,* which are Volumes V (1944) and VI (1927) in Arthur M. Schlesinger and Dixon R. Fox (eds.), *A History of American Life,* 12 vols. (New York, 1927–1944); and Frederick J. Turner, *The Rise of the New West, 1819–1829,* and William MacDonald, *Jacksonian Democracy, 1829–1837,* which are Volumes XIV (1906) and XV (1906), in Albert B. Hart (ed.), *The American Nation: A History,* 28 vols. (New York, 1904–1918).

Although the recent book by Arthur M. Schlesinger, Jr., *The Age of Jackson* (Boston, 1945), gives relatively little space to the South, the author makes a good case for his thesis that Southerners were not greatly concerned with the liberal-conservative conflict with which his study largely deals. Frederick J. Turner, *The United States, 1830–1850: The Nation and Its Sections* (New York, 1935), contains chapters on "The South Atlantic States," "The South Central States," and on sectional controversy from Jackson to Polk. Justin H. Smith, *The Annexation of Texas* (New York, 1911), and *The War with Mexico,* 2 vols. (New York, 1919), are the standard works on these subjects.

AMERICAN HISTORY: SPECIAL TOPICS

More useful for our purposes than general studies are articles and books exploring topics and special phases of national history. The category of constitutional and political studies contains several works of great value. Among these are Andrew C. McLaughlin, *A Constitutional History of the United States* (New York, 1935); Charles Warren, *The Supreme Court in United States History,* 3 vols. (Boston, 1923); Homer C. Hockett, *The Constitutional History of the United States, 1826–1876* (New York, 1939); William O. Lynch, *Fifty Years of Party Warfare, 1789–1837* (Indianapolis, 1931); and Edward Stanwood, *A History of the Presidency from 1788 to 1897* (Boston, New York, 193–?). Among other data, the last work contains tabulations of votes and information about platforms.

There are useful monographs about various phases of economic history. On the tariff, there are Edward Stanwood, *American Tariff Controversies in the Nineteenth Century,* 2 vols. (Boston, 1903); and Frank W. Taussig, *The Tariff History of the United States* (8th ed., New York, 1931). On public lands, Benjamin H. Hibbard, *A History of the Public Land Policies* (New York, 1939); Payson J. Treat, *The National Land System, 1785–1820* (New York, 1910); and Raynor G. Wellington, *The*

Political and Sectional Influence of the Public Lands, 1828–1842 (n.p., 1914). On bankruptcy, F. Regis Noel, *A History of the Bankruptcy Clause of the Constitution of the United States of America* (Gettysburg, [1918]).

The history of money and banking is treated in Davis R. Dewey, *Financial History of the United States* (12th ed., New York, 1934), and by the same author, *State Banking before the Civil War* (Washington, 1910); William M. Gouge, *A Short History of Paper Money and Banking in the United States* . . . (Philadelphia, 1833); Albert Gallatin, *Considerations on the Currency and Banking System of the United States* (Philadelphia, 1831); Ralph C. H. Catterall, *The Second Bank of the United States* (Chicago, 1903); and Thomas P. Govan, "Banking and the Credit System in Georgia, 1810–1860," in *Journal of Southern History* (Baton Rouge, 1935–), IV (1938), 164–84. Arthur H. Cole, *Wholesale Commodity Prices in the United States, 1700–1861* (Cambridge, 1938), and its companion volume, *Statistical Supplement: Actual Wholesale Prices of Various Commodities* (Cambridge, 1938), constitute an indispensable source of information about the prices of the Southern staples; but considerable knowledge of seasonal movements and of grades is required of the user of these tables.

The panics of 1819 and 1837 are treated in Samuel Rezneck, "The Depression of 1819–1822, A Social History," in *American Historical Review,* XXXIX (1933–1934), 28–47; Joseph H. Parks, "Felix Grundy and the Depression of 1819 in Tennessee," in East Tennessee Historical Society *Publications* (Knoxville, 1929–), No. 10 (1938), 19–43; and Reginald C. McGrane, *The Panic of 1837: Some Financial Problems of the Jacksonian Era* (Chicago, 1924). Other economic studies of value are Reginald C. McGrane, *Foreign Bondholders and American State Debts* (New York, 1935); Benjamin U. Ratchford, *American State Debts* (Durham, 1941); and Joseph J. Spengler, "The Political Economy of Jefferson, Madison, and Adams," in Jackson (ed.), *American Studies in Honor of William Kenneth Boyd.*

The Missouri Compromise, a topic of critical importance in the present study, has been treated in several monographs; but the interpretation that most of them present needs a thorough overhauling. They usually explain the controversy in terms of subsequent Southern political frustration instead of beginning, as chronology requires, with previous New England political frustration. The most extended and thoughtful of the monographs, but one that is extremely careless in its quotations, is James A. Woodburn, "The Historical Significance of the Missouri Compromise," in American Historical Association, *Annual Report,* 1893

(Washington, 1894), 249–97. Other studies are Frank H. Hodder, "Side Lights on the Missouri Compromises," *ibid.*, 1909 (Washington, 1911), 151–61; Homer C. Hockett, "Rufus King and the Missouri Compromise," in *Missouri Historical Review* (Columbia, 1906–), II (1907–1908), 211–20; and Floyd C. Shoemaker, *Missouri's Struggle for Statehood, 1804–1821* (Jefferson City, 1916). An important contribution to understanding the origins of this controversy is Albert F. Simpson, "The Political Significance of Slave Representation, 1787–1821," in *Journal of Southern History*, VII (1941), 315–42.

WORKS DEALING CHIEFLY WITH THE SOUTH

Two generalizations may be ventured about most of the historical writings on the South. In the first place, more has been done on social and economic subjects than on constitutional and political history; and this paucity of constitutional and political monographs has been a serious handicap in treating a period in which these matters have an important position. In the second place, some of the general and many of the special works on the South are restricted to the South Atlantic region or give chief emphasis to it. Good studies have been published on the Gulf and Mississippi Valley segments of the South, but they are less numerous than studies on the eastern parts of the region.

Most of the larger treatises on the South are too well known to need more than brief mention. The most ambitious of these is *The South in the Building of the Nation; A History of the Southern States Designed to Record the South's Part in the Making of the American Nation; to Portray the Character and Genius, to Chronicle the Achievements and Progress and to Illustrate the Life and Traditions of the Southern People*, 13 vols. (Richmond, 1909–1913). It was the work of many scholars. Despite the uneven quality of their work and the revision of interpretation required by subsequent studies, many parts of this monumental endeavor are yet useful.

There are a number of one-volume works that treat the South with a broad sweep. Edward Ingle, *Southern Sidelights: A Picture of Social and Economic Life in the South a Generation before the War* (New York, 1896), was one of the earliest of this kind. It was exceedingly good for its time, and it repays reading even today. Thomas J. Wertenbaker, *The Old South: The Founding of American Civilization* (New York, 1942), although chiefly concerned with the colonial period, contains interpretations that are helpful in the early national period. William E. Dodd, *The Cotton Kingdom; A Chronicle of the Old South*, Volume XXVII

(1919), in Allen Johnson (ed.), *The Chronicles of America Series,* 50 vols. (New Haven, 1918–1921), is a brief but well-organized essay, full of bold generalizations. Ulrich B. Phillips, *Life and Labor in the Old South* (Boston, 1929), is chiefly concerned with the plantation and slavery; its strength is in description rather than in generalization. Robert S. Cotterill, *The Old South: The Geographic, Economic, Social, Political, and Cultural Expansion, Institutions, and Nationalism of the Antebellum South* (Glendale, Calif., 1936), treats a wider variety of topics than Dodd or Phillips and gives considerable space to political history. The first third of Avery O. Craven, *The Coming of the Civil War* (New York, 1942), deals thoughtfully with the period under review; and there are several pertinent essays in Jackson (ed.), *American Studies in Honor of William Kenneth Boyd.* Jesse T. Carpenter, *The South as a Conscious Minority, 1789–1861: A Study in Political Thought* (New York, 1930), marshals an impressive array of material. Its interpretations would have been sounder had more consideration been given to the West while discussing the North-South struggle for power. Finally, William B. Hesseltine, *The South in American History* (New York, 1943), devotes seven of its thirty-one chapters to the period of the present study.

Fletcher M. Green, *Constitutional Development in the South Atlantic States, 1776–1860: A Study in the Evolution of Democracy* (Chapel Hill, 1930), is the main and virtually the only work on Southern state constitutional history, and it does not include the western South. A recent and thoughtful essay by the same author is entitled "Democracy in the Old South," in *Journal of Southern History,* XII (1946), 3–23.

Extremely little work has been done on the history of local government in the South. Robert D. Calhoun, "The Origin and Early Development of County-Parish Government in Louisiana," in *Louisiana Historical Quarterly* (New Orleans, 1917–), XVIII (1935), 56–160; and Lester J. Cappon, "The Evolution of County Government in Virginia," in Historical Records Survey, *Inventory of the County Archives of Virginia, No. 21. Chesterfield County* (Charlottesville, 1938), are among the few useful studies. Brief and sketchy historical introductions can be found in Columbus Andrews, *Administrative County Government in South Carolina* (Chapel Hill, 1933); and in Paul W. Wager, *County Government and Administration in North Carolina* (Chapel Hill, 1928).

Ulrich B. Phillips was preparing a political history of the South to serve as a companion volume of his *Life and Labor in the Old South* when death cut short his career. The completed part of his political study was published under the editorship of E. Merton Coulter with the title, *The Course of the South to Secession* (New York, 1939).

Lacking full and integrated studies of Southern political history, one must either turn to general works of American history, or he must piece together special studies about Southern politics. Not many of these studies deal with the period before 1830; among the few in this category are Albert R. Newsome, *The Presidential Election of 1824 in North Carolina*, in the *James Sprunt Studies in History and Political Science*, XXIII, No. 1 (Chapel Hill, 1939), which is a careful study of the most critical of the Southern states in this election; Horace L. Bachelder, "The Presidential Election of 1824 in Virginia" (M.A. thesis, Duke University, 1942); Everett S. Brown, "The Presidential Election of 1824–1825," in *Political Science Quarterly* (Boston, New York, 1886–), XL (1925), 384–403; and Charles S. Sydnor, "The One-Party Period of American History," in *American Historical Review*, LI (1945–1946), 439–51, which treats party history in the decade prior to this important election.

Favorite topics in the period after 1830 are nullification and the Whig party. Chauncey S. Boucher, *The Nullification Controversy in South Carolina* (Chicago, 1916), is the best account of this episode. The older work of David F. Houston, *A Critical Study of Nullification in South Carolina* (New York, 1896), gives more attention than Boucher to the preliminaries of nullification. Frederic Bancroft, *Calhoun and the South Carolina Nullification Movement* (Baltimore, 1928), is a careful and scholarly work by one who was no admirer of Calhoun. Major studies of the Whig party are Arthur C. Cole, *The Whig Party in the South* (Washington, 1913); and E. Malcolm Carroll, *Origins of the Whig Party* (Durham, 1925).

Other studies of importance to Southern political history are Thomas P. Abernethy, "Andrew Jackson and the Rise of Southwestern Democracy," in *American Historical Review*, XXXIII (1927–1928), 64–77; Ulrich B. Phillips, *Georgia and State Rights: A Study of the Political History of Georgia from the Revolution to the Civil War, with Particular Regard to Federal Relations*, in American Historical Association, *Annual Report*, 1901, II (Washington, 1902); Clarence C. Norton, *The Democratic Party in Ante-Bellum North Carolina, 1835–1861* (Chapel Hill, 1930); Richard R. Stenberg, "The Jefferson Birthday Dinner, 1830," in *Journal of Southern History*, IV (1938), 334–45, and "Jackson's 'Rhea Letter' Hoax," *ibid.*, II (1936), 480–96; and Culver H. Smith, "The Washington Press in the Jacksonian Period" (Ph.D. dissertation, Duke University, 1933), which explores the relation between politics and journalism with emphasis on the years 1826–1830. Robert S. Cotterill, "Federal Indian Management in the South, 1789–1825," in *Mississippi*

Valley Historical Review, XX (1933–1934), 333–52, sketches an important segment of the background of the removal of Southern Indians.

Several works deal with the relationship between the South and the Ohio Valley. Albert L. Kohlmeier, *The Old Northwest as the Keystone of the Arch of American Federal Union* (Bloomington, Ind., 1938), emphasizes commercial and political connections. John D. Barnhart, in the three following articles, deals chiefly with personal and population relationships: "Sources of Southern Migration into the Old Northwest," in *Mississippi Valley Historical Review,* XXII (1935–1936), 49–62; "The Southern Element in the Leadership of the Old Northwest," in *Journal of Southern History,* I (1935), 186–97; and "The Southern Element in the Formation of Ohio," *ibid.,* III (1937), 28–42.

There is space to mention only those state histories, and studies restricted to single states, that have been cited. These are Albert B. Moore, *History of Alabama* (University, Ala., 1934); Thomas P. Abernethy, *The Formative Period in Alabama, 1815–1828* (Montgomery, 1922); Theodore H. Jack, *Sectionalism and Party Politics in Alabama, 1819–1842* (Menasha, Wis., 1919); and Thomas C. McCorvey, "The Mission of Francis Scott Key to Alabama in 1833," in Alabama Historical Society *Transactions* (Tuscaloosa, Montgomery, 1899–1903), IV (1904), 141–65. For Mississippi, J. F. H. Claiborne, *Mississippi as a Province, Territory and State* (Jackson, 1880); and Dunbar Rowland, *History of Mississippi: The Heart of the South,* 2 vols. (Chicago, 1925). For North Carolina, William K. Boyd, *History of North Carolina: The Federal Period, 1783–1860* (Chicago, 1919); and Fred N. Cleaveland, "Service Legislation of the North Carolina General Assembly from 1777 to 1835" (M.A. thesis, Duke University, 1942). For South Carolina, David D. Wallace, *The History of South Carolina,* 3 vols. (New York, 1934). For Tennessee, Stanley J. Folmsbee, *Sectionalism and Internal Improvements in Tennessee, 1796–1845* (Philadelphia, 1939); and *History of Tennessee* (Nashville, 1887).

There is a dearth of histories of the towns of the Old South. Thomas J. Wertenbaker, *Norfolk: Historic Southern Port* (Durham, 1931); and Gerald M. Capers, *The Biography of a River Town: Memphis, Its Heroic Age* (Chapel Hill, 1939), are good. Clayton C. Hall (ed.), *Baltimore: Its History and Its People,* 3 vols. (New York, 1912), is poorly organized but rich in material. A dramatic episode in the history of a town that deserves a full-length study is described in E. Merton Coulter, "The Great Savannah Fire of 1820," in *Georgia Historical Quarterly* (Savannah, 1917–), XXIII (1939), 1–27.

SLAVERY

Scarcely any subject in Southern history has attracted more investigation than slavery, both as an institution and as a controversial issue. Among the studies that chiefly describe and analyze the institution of slavery are Ulrich B. Phillips, *American Negro Slavery* (New York, 1918); Ralph B. Flanders, *Plantation Slavery in Georgia* (Chapel Hill, 1933); Charles S. Sydnor, *Slavery in Mississippi* (New York, 1933); J. Winston Coleman, Jr., *Slavery Times in Kentucky* (Chapel Hill, 1940); and John S. Bassett, *The Plantation Overseer as Revealed in His Letters* (Northampton, Mass., 1925). The trade in slaves is discussed in Frederic Bancroft, *Slave-Trading in the Old South* (Baltimore, 1931); and William T. Laprade, "The Domestic Slave Trade in the District of Columbia," in *Journal of Negro History* (Lancaster, Pa., Washington), XI (1926), 17–34. Slave insurrections, in Joseph C. Carroll, *Slave Insurrections in the United States, 1800–1865* (Boston, 1938); and Herbert Aptheker, *American Negro Slave Revolts*, in Columbia University *Studies in History, Economics and Public Law*, No. 501 (New York, 1943). The free Negro, in John H. Franklin, *The Free Negro in North Carolina, 1790–1860* (Chapel Hill, 1943); Luther P. Jackson, *Free Negro Labor and Property Holding in Virginia, 1830–1860* (New York, 1942); Charles S. Sydnor, "The Free Negro in Mississippi before the Civil War," in *American Historical Review*, XXXII (1926–1927), 769–88; and J. Merton England, "The Free Negro in Ante-Bellum Tennessee," in *Journal of Southern History*, IX (1943), 37–58.

Another large group of studies are primarily concerned with the slavery controversy, and in some instances they continue it. The best work on the movement to end slavery is Gilbert H. Barnes, *The Antislavery Impulse, 1830–1844* (New York, 1933), and it would have been better had more attention been given to antislavery forces in New England. Other studies are the interpretative essay of Dwight L. Dumond, *Antislavery Origins of the Civil War in the United States* (Ann Arbor, 1939); Arthur Y. Lloyd, *The Slavery Controversy, 1831–1860* (Chapel Hill, 1939); W. Sherman Savage, *The Controversy over the Distribution of Abolition Literature, 1830–1860* ([Washington], 1938); Kenneth W. Stampp, "The Southern Refutation of the Proslavery Argument," in *North Carolina Historical Review*, XXI (1944), 35–45; Wilfred Carsel, "The Slaveholders' Indictment of Northern Wage Slavery," in *Journal of Southern History*, VI (1940), 504–20; Clement Eaton, "A Dangerous Pamphlet in the Old South," *ibid.*, II (1936), 323–34; Stephen B. Weeks, "Anti-Slavery Sentiment in the South," in Southern History Association

Publications (Washington, 1897–1907), II (1898), 87–130; and William S. Jenkins, *Pro-Slavery Thought in the Old South* (Chapel Hill, 1935), which is a systematic analysis of the Southern apologia.

Special phases of the history of slavery are treated in Philip M. Hamer, "Great Britain, The United States, and the Negro Seamen Acts, 1822–1848," in *Journal of Southern History*, I (1935), 3–28; and in Early L. Fox, *The American Colonization Society, 1817–1840*, in Johns Hopkins University *Studies in Historical and Political Science*, XXXVII, No. 3 (Baltimore, 1919). It is unfortunate that this study ends in the middle of the history of the colonization movement. Two studies of relationships between the slavery question and the Mexican War are John D. P. Fuller, "The Slavery Question and the Movement to Acquire Mexico, 1846–1848," in *Mississippi Valley Historical Review*, XXI (1934–1935), 31–48; and Richard R. Stenberg, "The Motivation of the Wilmot Proviso," *ibid.*, XVIII (1931–1932), 535–41.

AGRICULTURE, MANUFACTURING, COMMERCE, AND TRANSPORTATION

The most important single work on Southern agricultural history is the great compilation of Lewis C. Gray, *History of Agriculture in the Southern United States to 1860*, 2 vols. (Washington, 1933). The best study of any one of the major crops is Joseph C. Robert, *The Tobacco Kingdom: Plantation, Market, and Factory in Virginia and North Carolina, 1800–1860* (Durham, 1938). The Kentucky tobacco belt needs investigation. Nothing professing to be a full-length study of rice is in print, but James H. Easterby (ed.), *The South Carolina Rice Plantation as Revealed in the Papers of Robert F. W. Allston* (Chicago, 1945), presents a large body of significant documents, an introduction that sketches the history of rice culture in South Carolina, and an extensive bibliography. Percival Perry, "Naval Stores Industry in the Antebellum South, 1789–1861" (Ph.D. dissertation, Duke University, 1947), treats a subject that Gray touches only lightly.

Other phases of agricultural history are treated in Charles S. Davis, *The Cotton Kingdom in Alabama* (Montgomery, 1939); Wayne C. Neely, *The Agricultural Fair*, in Columbia University *Studies in the History of American Agriculture*, II (New York, 1935); Albert L. Demaree, *The American Agricultural Press, 1819–1860*, ibid., VIII (New York, 1941); Avery O. Craven, *Soil Exhaustion as a Factor in the Agricultural History of Virginia and Maryland, 1606–1860*, in University of Illinois *Studies in the Social Sciences*, XIII, No. 1 (Urbana, 1926); Avery O. Craven, "John

Taylor and Southern Agriculture," in *Journal of Southern History,* IV (1938), 137–47; Wendell H. Stephenson, "A Quarter-Century of a Mississippi Plantation: Eli J. Capell of 'Pleasant Hill,' " in *Mississippi Valley Historical Review,* XXIII (1936–1937), 355–74. Several of these studies deal with attempts to improve agricultural practices, and several of the biographies earlier listed throw light on this subject. The agricultural reform movement in the lower South has received less study than the movement in the upper South. Blanche Henry Clark, *The Tennessee Yeoman, 1840–1860* (Nashville, 1942), deals somewhat with this subject as well as with the distribution of land among Tennessee farmers and planters.

Kathleen Bruce, *Virginia Iron Manufacture in the Slave Era* (New York, 1931); Broadus Mitchell, *The Rise of Cotton Mills in the South,* in Johns Hopkins University *Studies in Historical and Political Science,* XXXIX, No. 2 (Baltimore, 1921); and Fletcher M. Green, "Gold Mining: A Forgotten Industry of Ante-Bellum North Carolina," in *North Carolina Historical Review,* XIV (1937), 1–19, 135–55, deal with types of subjects that have not attracted much historical attention.

Studies of Southern trade and commerce and of attempts to improve existing commercial arrangements are Lewis E. Atherton, "Itinerant Merchandising in the Ante-bellum South," in *Bulletin of the Business Historical Society* (Boston, 1926–), XIX (1945), 35–59; Thomas P. Govan, "An Ante-Bellum Attempt to Regulate the Price and Supply of Cotton," in *North Carolina Historical Review,* XVII (1940), 302–12; J. Carlyle Sitterson, "Financing and Marketing the Sugar Crop of the Old South," in *Journal of Southern History,* X (1944), 188–99. Herbert Wender, *Southern Commercial Conventions, 1837–1859,* in Johns Hopkins University *Studies in Historical and Political Science,* XLVIII, No. 4 (Baltimore, 1930), summarizes at some length the proceedings of the commercial conventions and discusses opinion about them. A briefer treatment of the same subject is John G. Van Deusen, *The Ante-Bellum Southern Commercial Conventions,* in Trinity College Historical Society *Historical Papers,* XVI (Durham, 1926).

The best insight into the foreign trade of the South in the period of this study is through Robert G. Albion, *Square-Riggers on Schedule: The New York Sailing Packets to England, France, and the Cotton Ports* (Princeton, 1938), and *The Rise of New York Port* (New York, 1939). Both volumes contain valuable appendixes.

Three studies not primarily concerned with the South nevertheless are important to an understanding of transportation history in the period of the present study. These are Balthasar H. Meyer, *History of Transpor-*

tation in the United States before 1860 (Washington, 1917); Leland D. Baldwin, *The Keelboat Age on Western Waters* (Pittsburgh, 1941); and Louis C. Hunter, "The Invention of the Western Steamboat," in *Journal of Economic History* (New York, 1941–), III (1943–1944), 201–20.

The following studies pertain more directly to transportation in the South: Ulrich B. Phillips, *A History of Transportation in the Eastern Cotton Belt to 1860* (New York, 1908); Survey of Federal Archives, Louisiana, *Ship Registers and Enrollments of New Orleans, Louisiana* (University, La., 1941–1942), I (1804–1820); II (1821–1830); Wayland F. Dunaway, *History of the James River and Kanawha Company*, in Columbia University *Studies in History, Economics and Public Law*, No. 236 (New York, 1922); William E. Martin, *Internal Improvements in Alabama*, in Johns Hopkins University *Studies in Historical and Political Science*, XX, No. 4 (Baltimore, 1902); Samuel M. Derrick, *Centennial History of South Carolina Railroad* (Columbia, 1930); and Cecil K. Brown, *A State Movement in Railroad Development: The Story of North Carolina's First Effort to Establish an East and West Trunk Line Railroad* (Chapel Hill, 1928).

CULTURAL HISTORY

The following works deal with the classical revival in Southern architecture. Fiske Kimball, *Thomas Jefferson and the First Monument of the Classical Revival in America* [Harrisburg, Pa., Washington, 1915], establishes the importance of the Virginia state capitol in this movement. Talbot F. Hamlin, *Greek Revival Architecture in America* (New York, 1944), relates architectural history to social history. J. Frazer Smith, *White Pillars: Early Life and Architecture of the Lower Mississippi Valley Country* (New York, 1941), deals with an area that has been less closely studied than the Eastern seaboard. The second lecture, entitled "The Universalism of Thomas Jefferson," in Lewis Mumford, *The South in Architecture* (New York, 1941), treats thoughtfully the period of our investigation. James C. Bonner, "Plantation Architecture of the Lower South on the Eve of the Civil War," in *Journal of Southern History*, XI (1945), 370–88, is a warning against overemphasizing the vogue for Greek-revival mansions.

Sectarian bias runs through much religious history. Among the more objective and scholarly studies in this important field are several by William W. Sweet, *The Story of Religions in America* (New York, 1930), *Methodism in American History* (New York, 1933), and three volumes in

378

his *Religion on the American Frontier* series: *The Baptists, 1783–1830* (New York, 1931), *The Presbyterians, 1783–1840* (New York, 1936), and *The Methodists, 1783–1840* (Chicago, 1946). Others of high merit are Clarence Gohdes, "Some Notes on the Unitarian Church in the Ante-Bellum South: A Contribution to the History of Southern Liberalism," in Jackson (ed.), *American Studies in Honor of William Kenneth Boyd;* Paul L. Garber, *James Henley Thornwell, Presbyterian Defender of the Old South* (Richmond, 1943), "Reprinted from *Union Seminary Review* . . . February, 1943"; and the previously mentioned unpublished dissertation of Henry S. Stroupe, "The Religious Press in the South Atlantic States, 1802–1865." Useful statistical data are in Joseph Belcher, *Religious Denominations in the United States* (Philadelphia, 1854). Albert H. Newman, *A History of the Baptist Churches in the United States* (6th ed., New York, 1915), is helpful in explaining the sectional fracture of the Baptists.

Charles F. Thwing, *History of Higher Education in America* (New York, 1906); and Donald G. Tewksbury, *The Founding of American Colleges and Universities before the Civil War,* in Teachers College, Columbia University *Contributions to Education,* No. 543 (New York, 1932), have been helpful in dealing with the history of higher education. The following studies, relating more directly to the South, have proved of greater value: Alma P. Foerster, "The State University in the Old South: A Study of Social and Intellectual Influences in State University Education" (Ph.D. dissertation, Duke University, 1939); Albea Godbold, *The Church College of the Old South* (Durham, 1944); Donald R. Come, "The Influence of Princeton on Higher Education in the South before 1825," in *William and Mary Quarterly* (Williamsburg, 1892–), third series, II (1945), 359–96.

For information about education below the college level one may consult William A. Maddox, *The Free School Idea in Virginia before the Civil War,* in Teachers College, Columbia University *Contributions to Education,* No. 93 (New York, 1918); Edgar W. Knight, *Public Education in the South* (Boston, 1922); and Charles W. Dabney, *Universal Education in the South,* 2 vols. (Chapel Hill, 1936).

Among the better studies of individual colleges are James H. Easterby, *A History of the College of Charleston* ([Charleston], 1935); Philip A. Bruce, *History of the University of Virginia, 1819–1919,* 5 vols. (New York, 1920–1922); George W. Paschal, *History of Wake Forest College,* 3 vols. (Wake Forest, N.C., 1935–1943); Nora C. Chaffin, "Trinity College, 1839–1892: The Beginnings of Duke University," in *Southern As-*

sociation Quarterly (Durham, 1937-), IX (1945), 312–25; and Kemp P. Battle, *History of the University of North Carolina,* 2 vols. (Raleigh, 1907–1912).

Titles of publications of the presses in the South tell much about intellectual interests of Southerners. Numerous checklists were prepared by the late Douglas C. McMurtrie. The best guide to these lists is Charles F. Heartman, *McMurtrie Imprints, A Bibliography of Separately Printed Writings by Douglas C. McMurtrie . . .* (Hattiesburg, Miss., 1942).

There is a distinct need for a history of Southern literature. At the present writing, the second volume of Vernon L. Parrington, *Main Currents in American Thought,* 3 vols. (New York, 1927–1930), is probably the best guide to the middle period of Southern literary history. The first two volumes of the *Cambridge History of American Literature,* 4 vols. (New York [1917–1921]), are valuable. Montrose J. Moses, *The Literature of the South* (New York, 1910), is stimulating, but its interpretations are too often marred by insufficient knowledge of Southern history. Some of the biographies, listed elsewhere, contain information about literary figures. It would be a waste of space to repeat here most of the titles and discussions of literary matters in Chapter XIII.

Walter Blair, *Native American Humor* (New York, 1937), is the best book on the subject. Constance M. Rourke, *American Humor: A Study of the National Character* (New York, 1931); and Jennette R. Tandy, *Crackerbox Philosophers in American Humor and Satire,* in Columbia University *Studies in English and Comparative Literature,* No. 84 (New York, 1925), are also helpful in understanding the evolution of the local-color humorous sketch.

Frank L. Mott, *A History of American Magazines,* 3 vols. (Cambridge, Mass., 1938), is the chief authority on this subject. Thomas Cary Johnson, Jr., *Scientific Interests in the Old South* (New York, 1936), amply proves that Southerners were interested in many fields of science.

The decline of Southern liberalism can be traced in Clement Eaton, *Freedom of Thought in the Old South* (Durham, 1940); Joseph C. Robert, *The Road from Monticello: A Study of the Virginia Slavery Debate of 1832* (Durham, 1941); William G. Bean, "Anti-Jeffersonianism in the Ante-Bellum South," in *North Carolina Historical Review,* XII (1935), 103–24; and Charles S. Sydnor, "The Southerner and the Laws," in *Journal of Southern History,* VI (1940), 3–23. Francis P. Gaines, *The Southern Plantation: A Study in the Development and the Accuracy of a Tradition* (New York, 1924), throws much light on the development of the romantic tradition about the Old South.

Little study has been given to attempts to improve the lot of those

Southerners who through physical infirmity or legal handicaps needed help. Gustave de Beaumont and Alexis de Tocqueville, *On the Penitentiary System in the United States, and Its Application in France . . . ,* trans. by Francis Lieber (Philadelphia, 1833), is an excellent account of American theory and practice, at the time of its publication, in dealing with criminals; but it contains little information about conditions in the slave states. General studies that throw light on conditions in the South are Blake McKelvey, *American Prisons: A Study in American Social History prior to 1915* (Chicago, 1936); and Helen E. Marshall, *Dorothea Dix: Forgotten Samaritan* (Chapel Hill, 1937). Special phases of the social reform movement in the South are treated in Eleanor M. Boatwright, "The Political and Civil Status of Women in Georgia, 1783–1860," in *Georgia Historical Quarterly,* XXV (1941), 301–24; E. Bruce Thompson, "Reforms in the Penal System of Tennessee, 1820–1850," in *Tennessee Historical Quarterly* (Nashville, 1942–), I (1942), 291–308; E. Bruce Thompson, "Reforms in the Penal System of Mississippi, 1820–1850," in *Journal of Mississippi History* (Jackson, 1939–), VII (1945), 51–74; and Charles P. White, "Early Experiments with Prison Labor in Tennessee," in East Tennessee Historical Society *Publications,* No. 12 (1940), 45–69.

INDEX

Abolition, of slavery in British colonies, 224; debated in Virginia, 227-29; literature burned at Charleston, 232; in District of Columbia, petitions for, 233; and the churches, 297-300

Abolition Intelligencer, The, 95

Abolition interpretation of the Mexican War, 328-29

Abolition movement, religious beginnings of, 229, 231; British connections, 224, 230, 240; goal, 231, 235, 237-38; early activities, 231-32; petitions and gag rule, 233-35; leadership shifts from New York to Washington, 236; begins to enter politics, 236-37, 242; Southern bitterness toward, 241-43, 248; *see also,* Antislavery periodicals; Antislavery sentiment in the North; Antislavery sentiment in the South

Academies, 58-59

Adams, John Quincy, 162, 239, 253 n.; on prospects of civil war, 132; political rebel, 160; his appraisal of Calhoun, 161-62; campaign in the South, 168; votes received in the South, 171-73; nationalistic program of, 179-80; state-rights conflict with Georgia, 183-84; in election of 1828, 191-94; on gag rule, 234-35

Affleck, Thomas, 266

Agricultural, reformers, 87, 264-67; societies, 87-88, 265-66; depression in South Atlantic states, 249-50, 252, 255; surveys, 88-89, 264-65; periodicals, 265-66; fairs, 266-67

Agriculture, per cent of Southerners en-

gaged in, 5; *see also,* Cotton; Hemp; Rice; Sugar; Tobacco

Aiken, S.C., 268 n.

Aimard, Gustave, 310

Alabama, 2, 204, 255, 258, 264, 292, 296, 320; Indian tribes in, 4-5; cotton in, 14; democratic local government in, 38-39; representation in legislature of, 46-47; no property qualifications for voting in, 48; illiteracy in, 59; canal construction in, 85; debtor laws in, 97; penitentiary in, 102; public-land debtors in, 105; state banks in, 107, 108; fiat money in, 115; asserts state sovereignty in Indian affairs, 184; election of 1828 in, 191, 193; conflict with national government, 218; opposition to nullification, 219; bank expansion in, 261-62; state agricultural society in, 265; railroads in, 273; railroad mileage in, 274 n.; democratic constitution of, 283-84; on the Harrisburg Convention, 188

Albemarle County, Va., agricultural society in, 88

Alexandria *Gazette,* 191 n.

Alexandria, Va., 19; depression in, 113

American Anti-Slavery Society, 230-34, 235

American Colonization Society, activities of, in South, 96, 97; Federal funds for, 185-86

American Farmer, 87

American Notes, 236

American Slavery as It Is, 236

American System, 203, 206, 317, 318, 319

Andrew, Bishop James O., 298